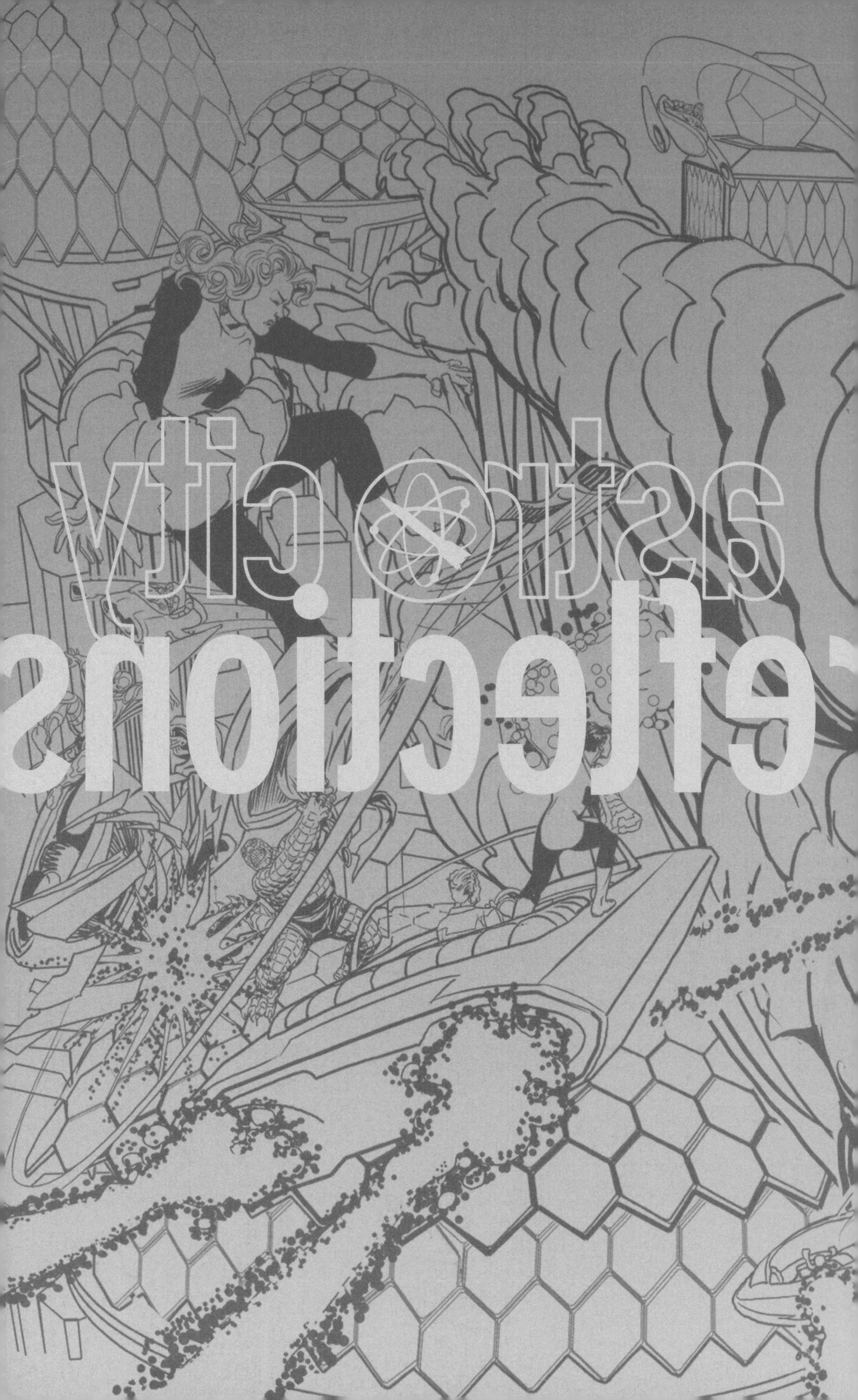
astro city
eflections

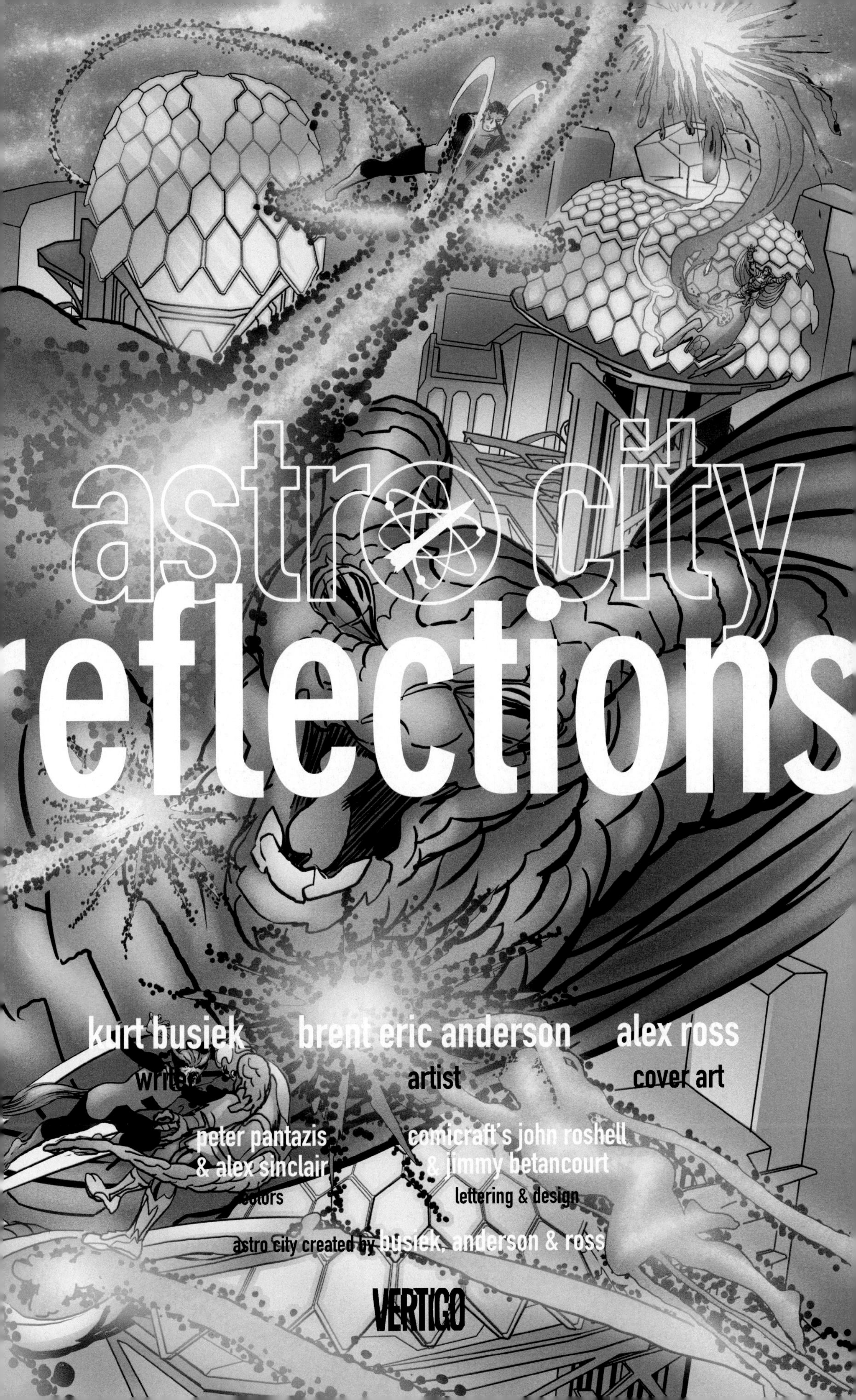

astro city
reflections

kurt busiek writer

brent eric anderson artist

alex ross cover art

peter pantazis & alex sinclair colors

comicraft's john roshell & jimmy betancourt lettering & design

astro city created by busiek, anderson & ross

VERTIGO

RICHARD STARKINGS
Art Director

VERTIGO

Molly Mahan
Kristy Quinn   Editors – Original Series
Jamie Rich   Group Editor – Vertigo Comics
Jeb Woodard   Group Editor – Collected Editions
Liz Erickson   Editor – Collected Edition
Steve Cook   Design Director – Books

Bob Harras   Senior VP – Editor-in-Chief, DC Comics
Mark Doyle   Executive Editor, Vertigo

Diane Nelson   President
Dan DiDio   Publisher
Jim Lee   Publisher
Geoff Johns   President & Chief Creative Officer
Amit Desai   Executive VP – Business & Marketing Strategy,
                    Direct to Consumer & Global Franchise Management
Sam Ades   Senior VP & General Manager, Digital Services
Bobbie Chase   VP & Executive Editor, Young Reader & Talent Development
Mark Chiarello   Senior VP – Art, Design & Collected Editions
John Cunningham   Senior VP – Sales & Trade Marketing
Anne DePies   Senior VP – Business Strategy, Finance & Administration
Don Falletti   VP – Manufacturing Operations
Lawrence Ganem   VP – Editorial Administration & Talent Relations
Alison Gill   Senior VP – Manufacturing & Operations
Hank Kanalz   Senior VP – Editorial Strategy & Administration
Jay Kogan   VP – Legal Affairs
Jack Mahan   VP – Business Affairs
Nick J. Napolitano VP – Manufacturing Administration
Eddie Scannell   VP – Consumer Marketing
Courtney Simmons   Senior VP – Publicity & Communications
Jim (Ski) Sokolowski VP – Comic Book Specialty Sales & Trade Marketing
Nancy Spears   VP – Mass, Book, Digital Sales & Trade Marketing
Michele R. Wells   VP – Content Strategy

ASTRO CITY VOL. 14: REFLECTIONS
Published by DC Comics. Compilation, cover and all new material
Copyright © 2017 Juke Box Productions. All Rights Reserved.

Originally published in single magazine form as ASTRO CITY 26, 29, 30, 32–34 ©
2015, 2016 Juke Box Productions. All Rights Reserved. Astro City, its logos, symbols,
prominent characters featured in this volume and the distinctive likenesses thereof
are trademarks of Juke Box Productions. VERTIGO is a trademark of DC Comics. The
stories, characters and incidents featured in this publication are entirely fictional. DC
Comics does not read or accept unsolicited submissions of ideas, stories or artwork.

DC Comics, 2900 West Alameda Ave., Burbank, CA 91505
Printed by LSC Communications, Kendallville, IN, USA. 11/17/17. First Printing.
ISBN: 978-1-4012-7492-4

Library of Congress Cataloging-in-Publication Data is available

contents

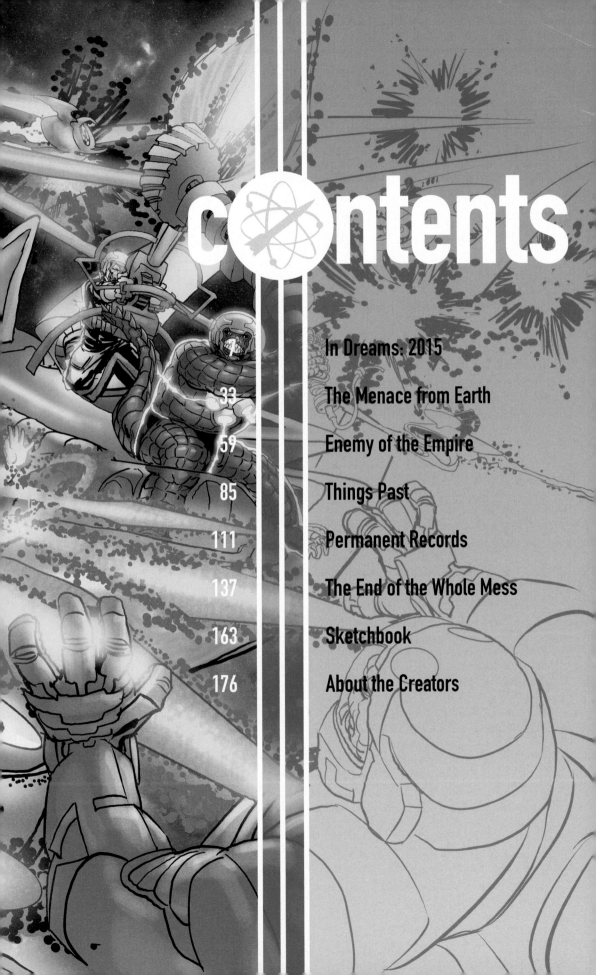

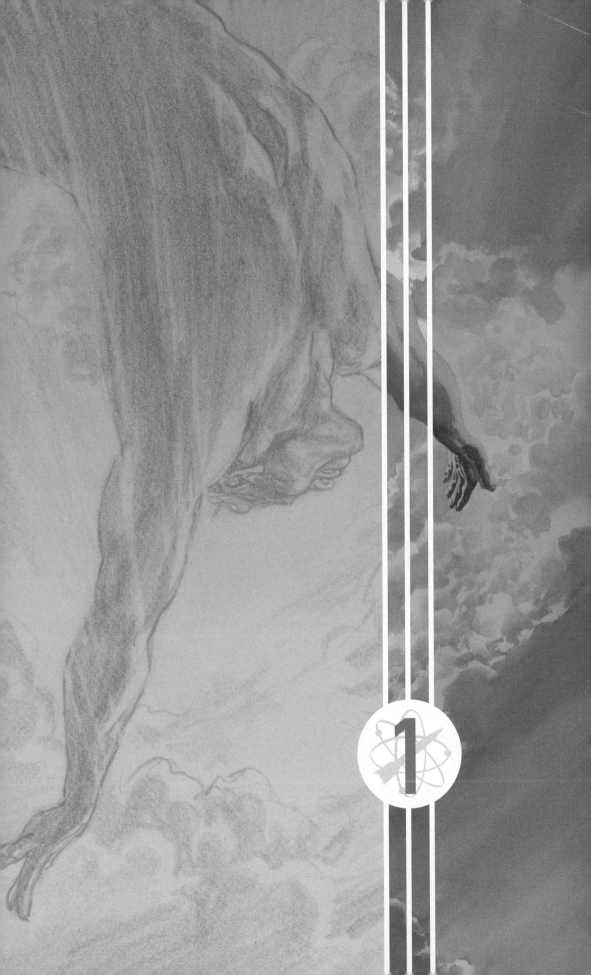

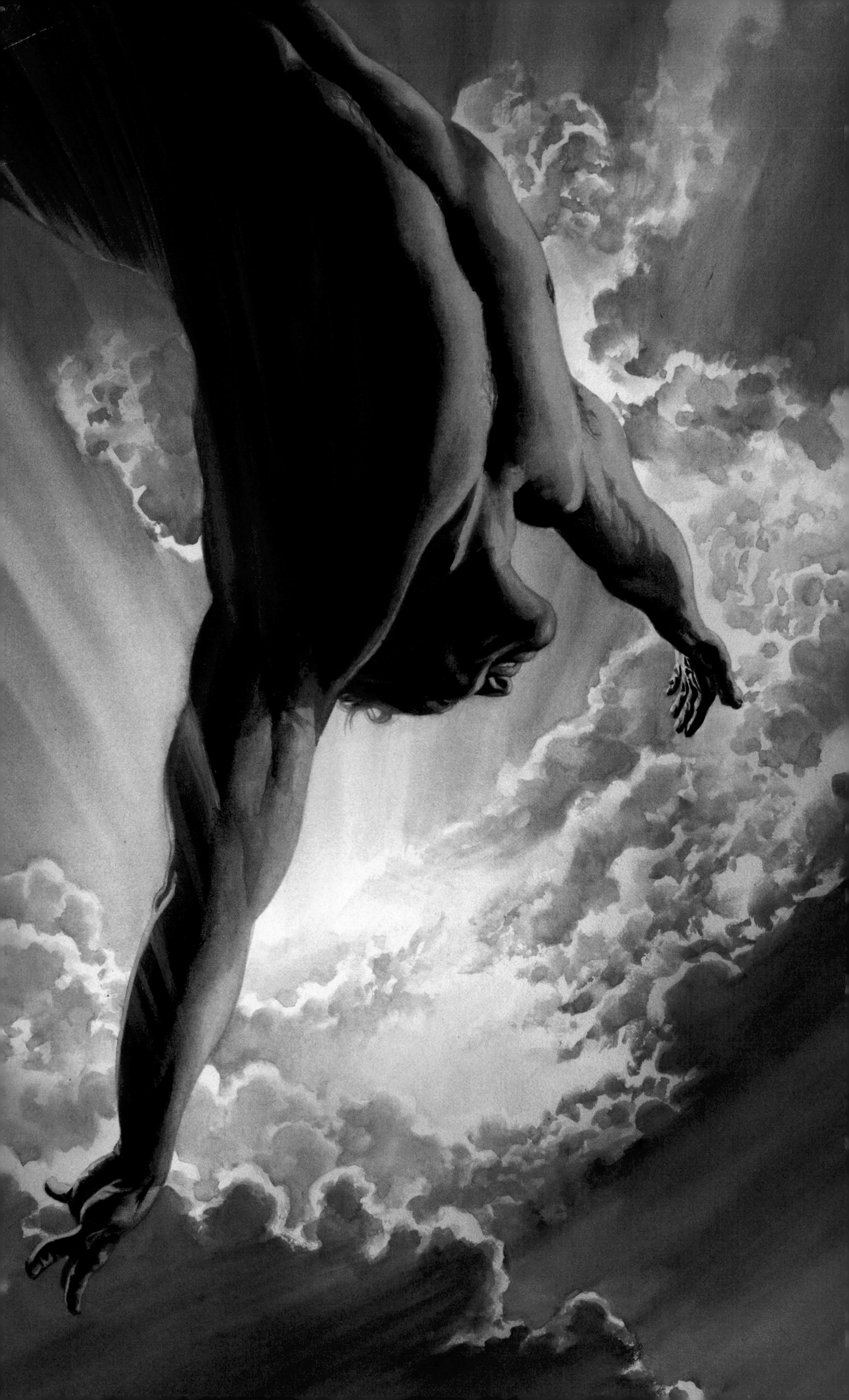

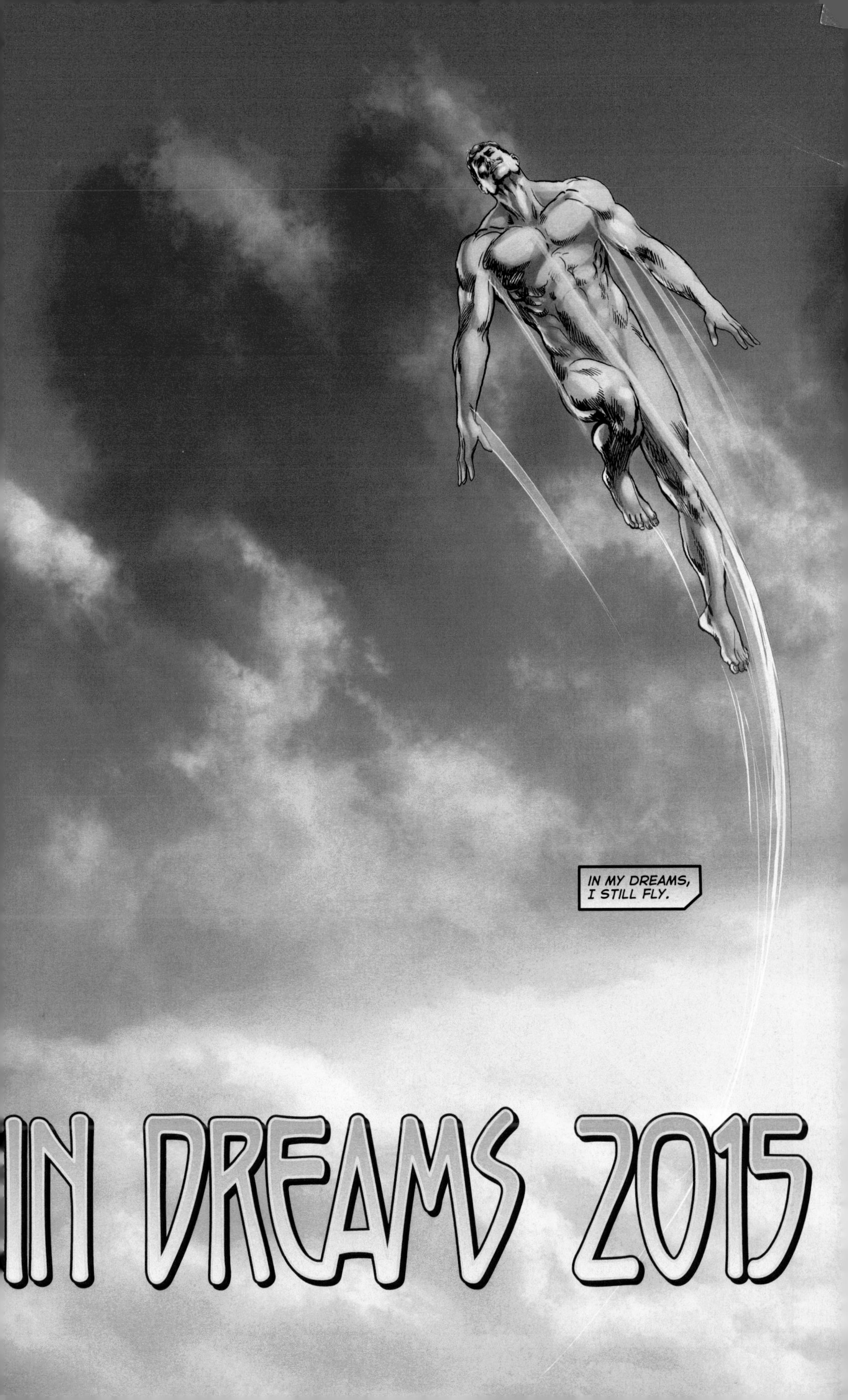
IN MY DREAMS,
I STILL FLY.
IN DREAMS 2015

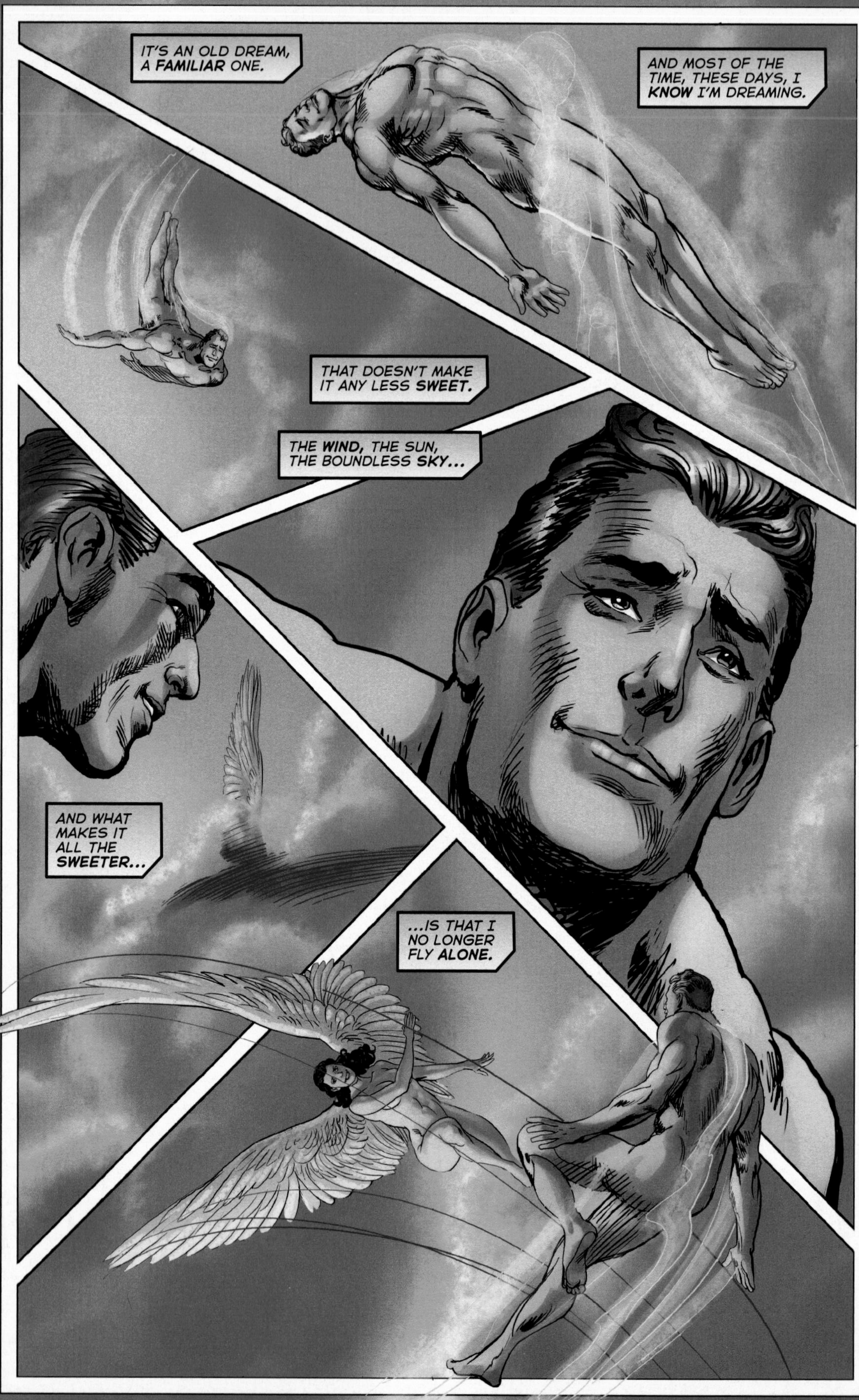
IT'S AN OLD DREAM, A FAMILIAR ONE.
AND MOST OF THE TIME, THESE DAYS, I KNOW I'M DREAMING.
THAT DOESN'T MAKE IT ANY LESS SWEET.
THE WIND, THE SUN, THE BOUNDLESS SKY...
AND WHAT MAKES IT ALL THE SWEETER...
...IS THAT I NO LONGER FLY ALONE.

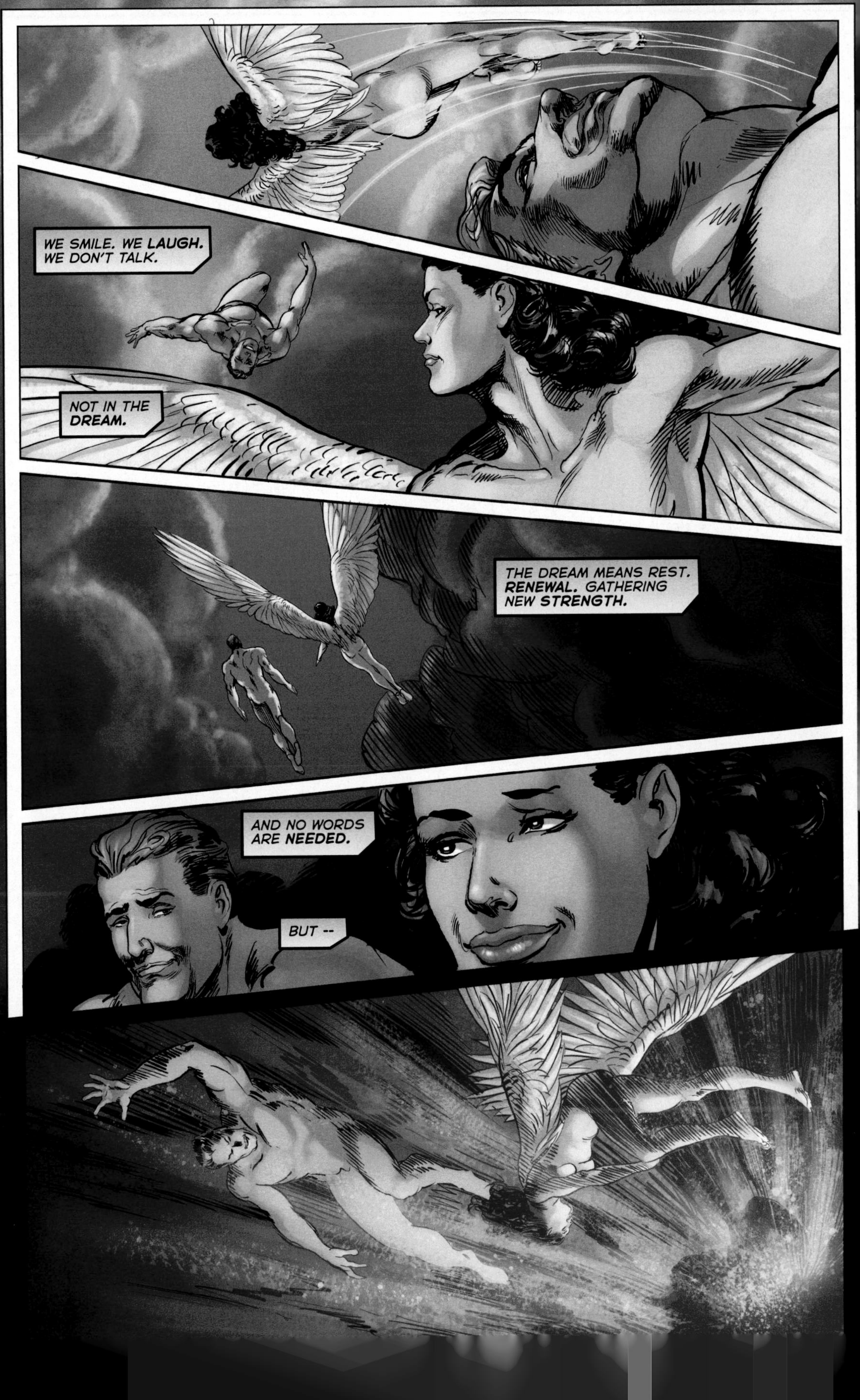
WE SMILE. WE LAUGH. WE DON'T TALK.
NOT IN THE DREAM.
THE DREAM MEANS REST. RENEWAL. GATHERING NEW STRENGTH.
AND NO WORDS ARE NEEDED.
BUT --

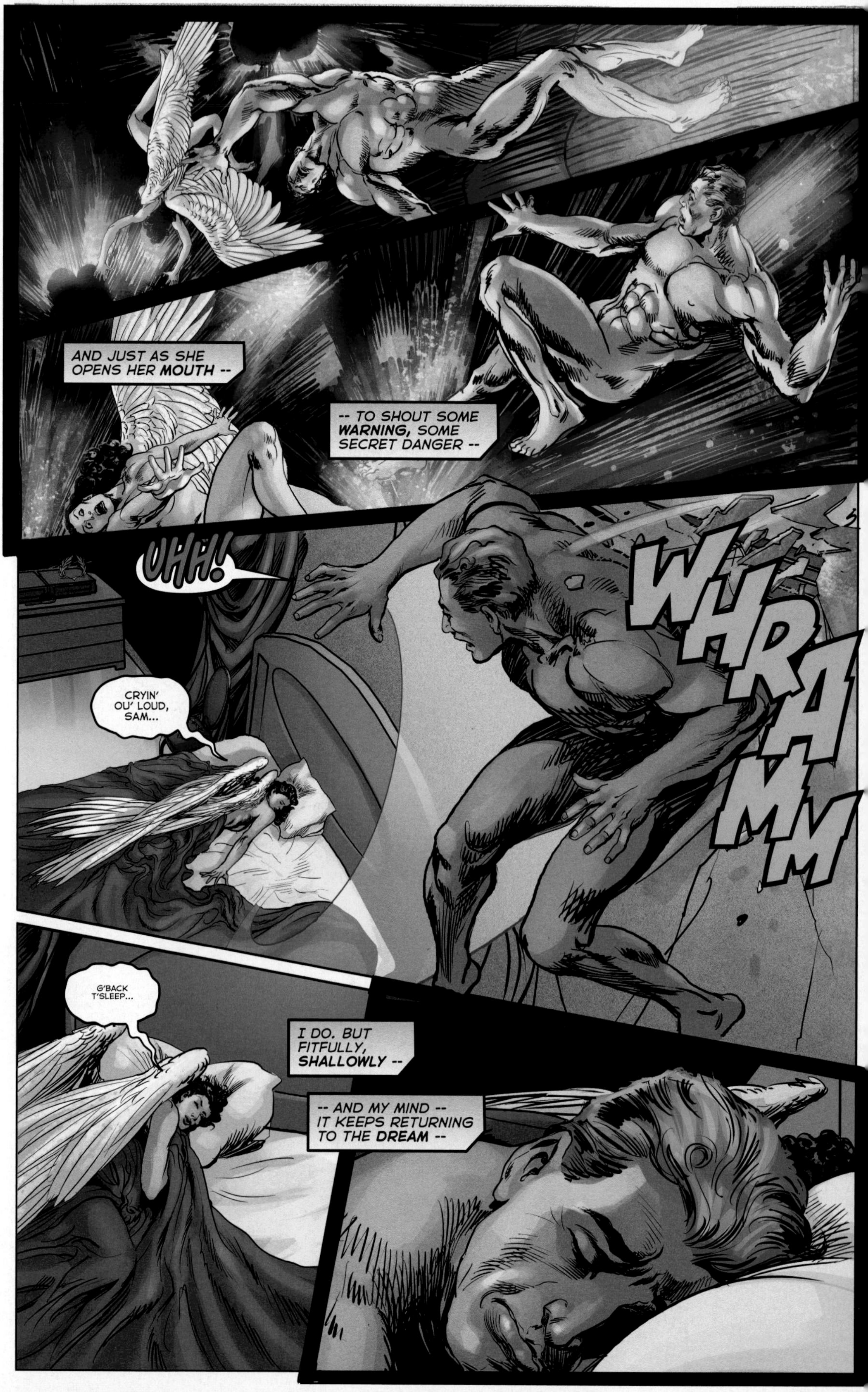
AND JUST AS SHE OPENS HER MOUTH --
-- TO SHOUT SOME WARNING, SOME SECRET DANGER --
UHH!
WHRAMMM
CRYIN' OU' LOUD, SAM...
G'BACK T'SLEEP...
I DO. BUT FITFULLY, SHALLOWLY --
-- AND MY MIND -- IT KEEPS RETURNING TO THE DREAM --

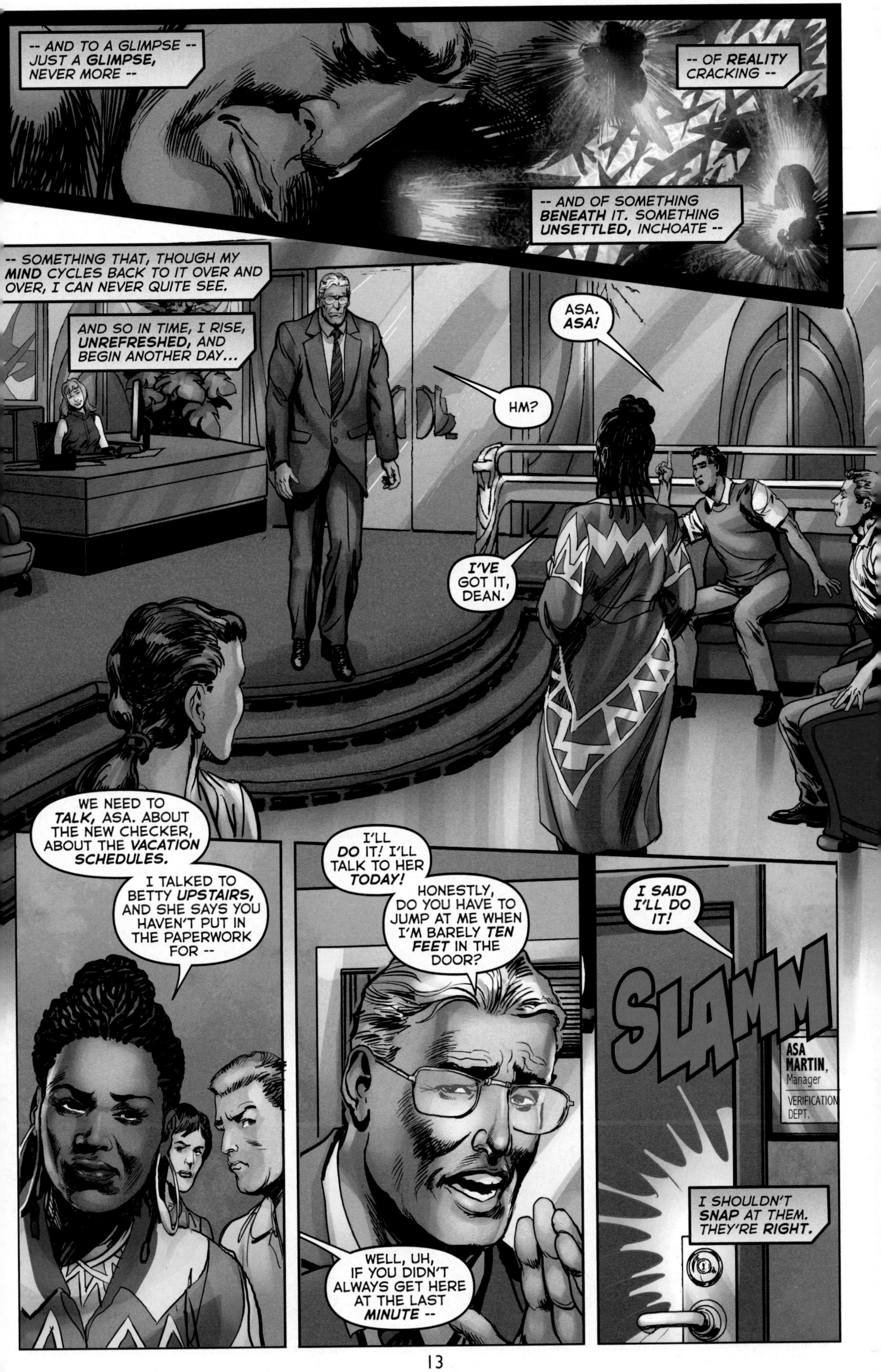
-- AND TO A GLIMPSE -- JUST A GLIMPSE, NEVER MORE --
-- OF REALITY CRACKING --
-- AND OF SOMETHING BENEATH IT. SOMETHING UNSETTLED, INCHOATE --
-- SOMETHING THAT, THOUGH MY MIND CYCLES BACK TO IT OVER AND OVER, I CAN NEVER QUITE SEE.
AND SO IN TIME, I RISE, UNREFRESHED, AND BEGIN ANOTHER DAY...
ASA. ASA!
HM?
I'VE GOT IT, DEAN.
WE NEED TO TALK, ASA. ABOUT THE NEW CHECKER, ABOUT THE VACATION SCHEDULES.
I TALKED TO BETTY UPSTAIRS, AND SHE SAYS YOU HAVEN'T PUT IN THE PAPERWORK FOR --
I'LL DO IT! I'LL TALK TO HER TODAY!
HONESTLY, DO YOU HAVE TO JUMP AT ME WHEN I'M BARELY TEN FEET IN THE DOOR?
WELL, UH, IF YOU DIDN'T ALWAYS GET HERE AT THE LAST MINUTE --
I SAID I'LL DO IT!
SLAMM
ASA MARTIN, Manager
VERIFICATION DEPT.
I SHOULDN'T SNAP AT THEM. THEY'RE RIGHT.

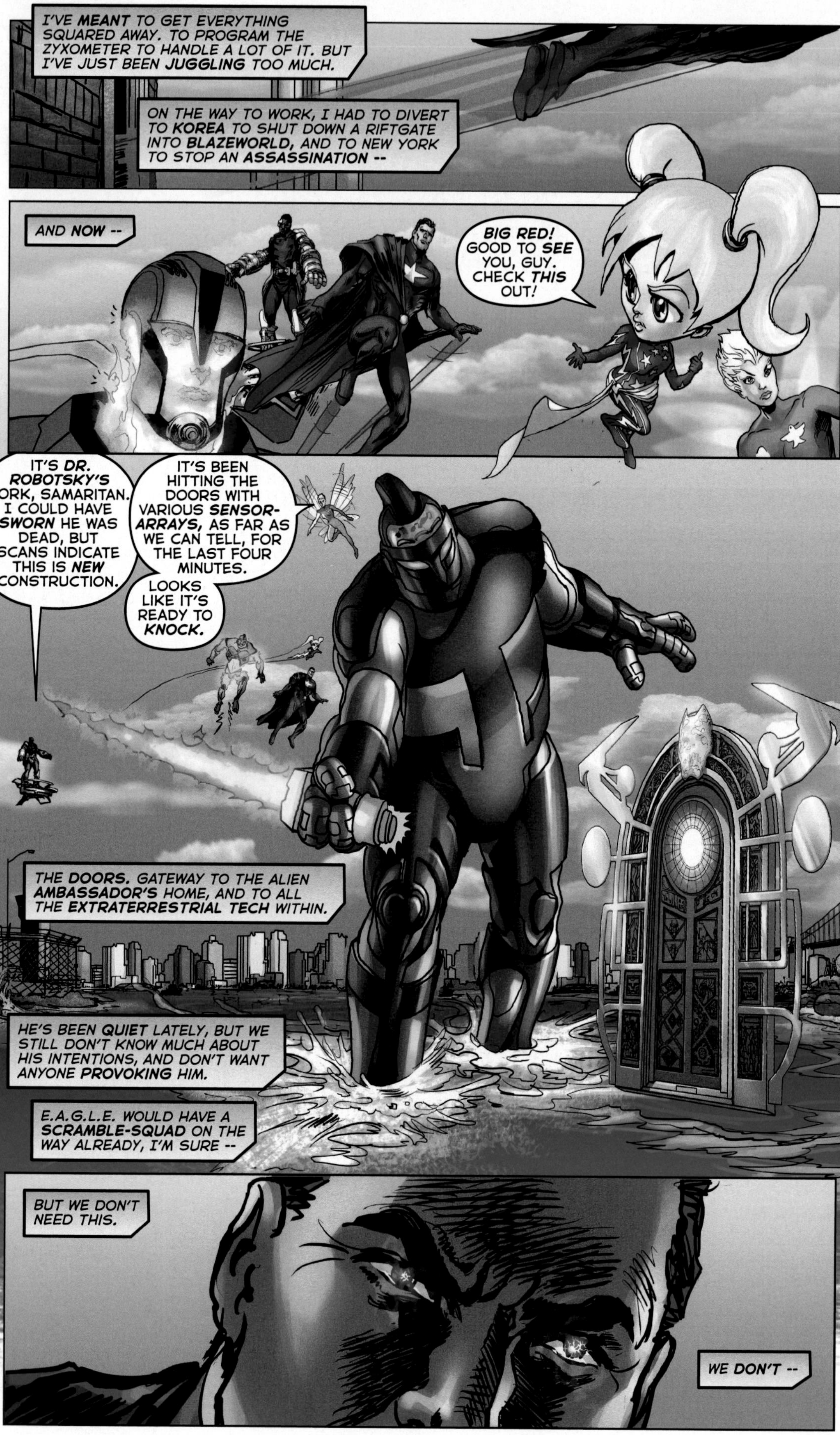
I'VE MEANT TO GET EVERYTHING SQUARED AWAY. TO PROGRAM THE ZYXOMETER TO HANDLE A LOT OF IT. BUT I'VE JUST BEEN JUGGLING TOO MUCH.
ON THE WAY TO WORK, I HAD TO DIVERT TO KOREA TO SHUT DOWN A RIFTGATE INTO BLAZEWORLD, AND TO NEW YORK TO STOP AN ASSASSINATION --
AND NOW --
BIG RED! GOOD TO SEE YOU, GUY. CHECK THIS OUT!
IT'S DR. ROBOTSKY'S WORK, SAMARITAN. I COULD HAVE SWORN HE WAS DEAD, BUT SCANS INDICATE THIS IS NEW CONSTRUCTION.
IT'S BEEN HITTING THE DOORS WITH VARIOUS SENSOR-ARRAYS, AS FAR AS WE CAN TELL, FOR THE LAST FOUR MINUTES.
LOOKS LIKE IT'S READY TO KNOCK.
THE DOORS. GATEWAY TO THE ALIEN AMBASSADOR'S HOME, AND TO ALL THE EXTRATERRESTRIAL TECH WITHIN.
HE'S BEEN QUIET LATELY, BUT WE STILL DON'T KNOW MUCH ABOUT HIS INTENTIONS, AND DON'T WANT ANYONE PROVOKING HIM.
E.A.G.L.E. WOULD HAVE A SCRAMBLE-SQUAD ON THE WAY ALREADY, I'M SURE --
BUT WE DON'T NEED THIS.
WE DON'T --

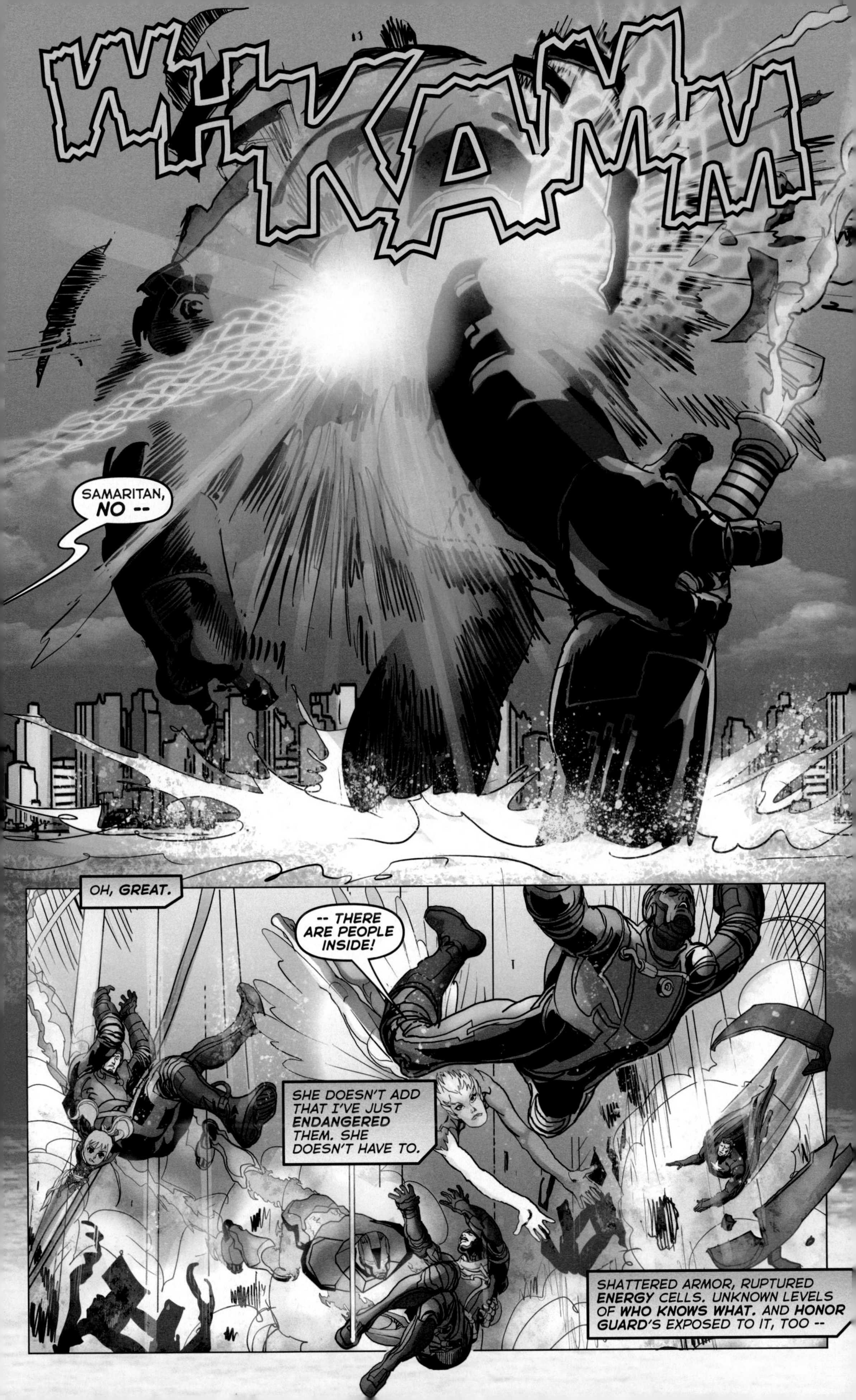
WHKAM
SAMARITAN, NO --
OH, GREAT.
-- THERE ARE PEOPLE INSIDE!
SHE DOESN'T ADD THAT I'VE JUST ENDANGERED THEM. SHE DOESN'T HAVE TO.
SHATTERED ARMOR, RUPTURED ENERGY CELLS. UNKNOWN LEVELS OF WHO KNOWS WHAT. AND HONOR GUARD'S EXPOSED TO IT, TOO --

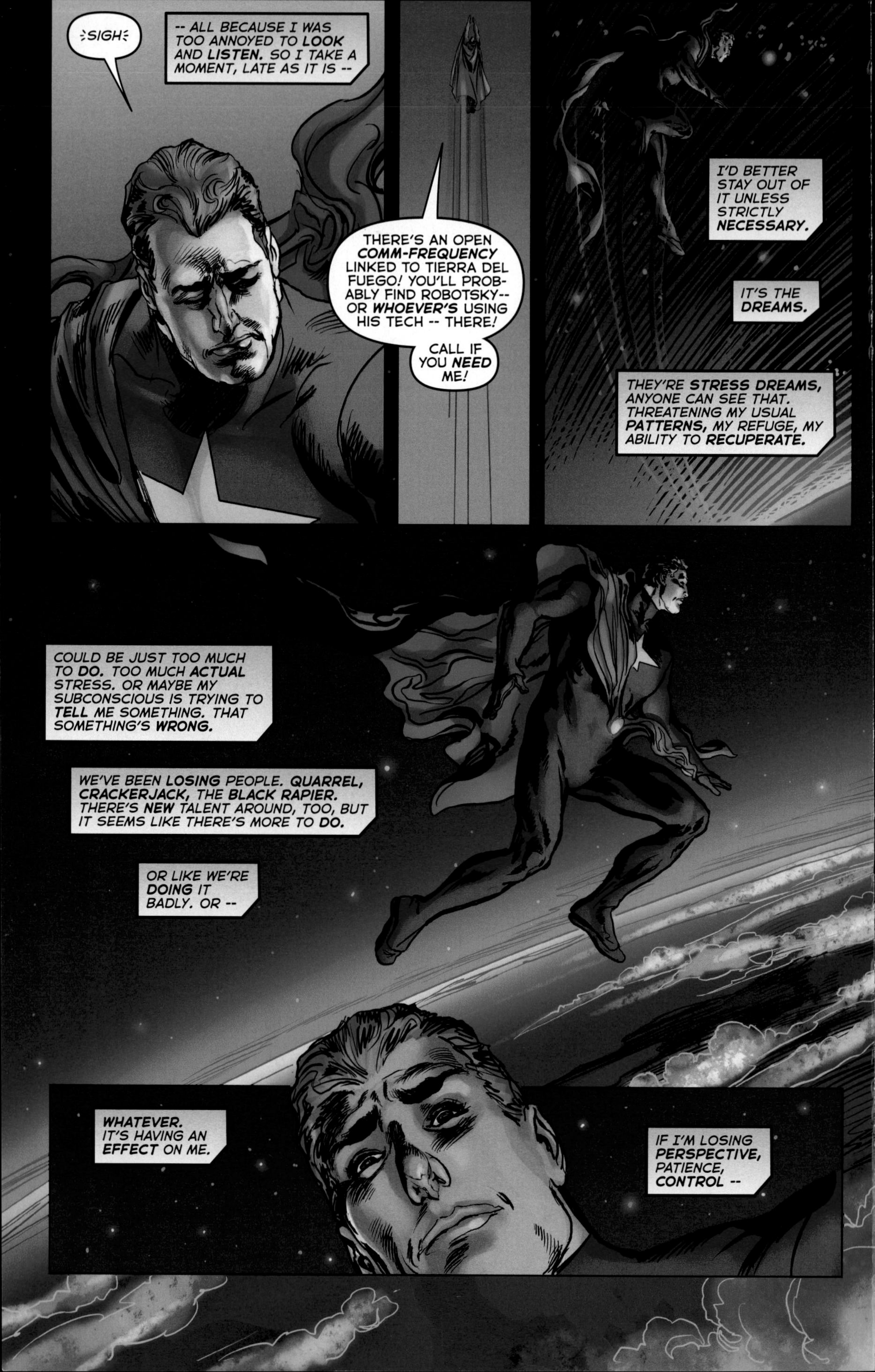

⁝SIGH⁝
-- ALL BECAUSE I WAS TOO ANNOYED TO LOOK AND LISTEN. SO I TAKE A MOMENT, LATE AS IT IS --
THERE'S AN OPEN COMM-FREQUENCY LINKED TO TIERRA DEL FUEGO! YOU'LL PROBABLY FIND ROBOTSKY-- OR WHOEVER'S USING HIS TECH -- THERE!
CALL IF YOU NEED ME!
I'D BETTER STAY OUT OF IT UNLESS STRICTLY NECESSARY.
IT'S THE DREAMS.
THEY'RE STRESS DREAMS, ANYONE CAN SEE THAT. THREATENING MY USUAL PATTERNS, MY REFUGE, MY ABILITY TO RECUPERATE.
COULD BE JUST TOO MUCH TO DO. TOO MUCH ACTUAL STRESS. OR MAYBE MY SUBCONSCIOUS IS TRYING TO TELL ME SOMETHING. THAT SOMETHING'S WRONG.
WE'VE BEEN LOSING PEOPLE. QUARREL, CRACKERJACK, THE BLACK RAPIER. THERE'S NEW TALENT AROUND, TOO, BUT IT SEEMS LIKE THERE'S MORE TO DO.
OR LIKE WE'RE DOING IT BADLY. OR --
WHATEVER. IT'S HAVING AN EFFECT ON ME.
IF I'M LOSING PERSPECTIVE, PATIENCE, CONTROL --

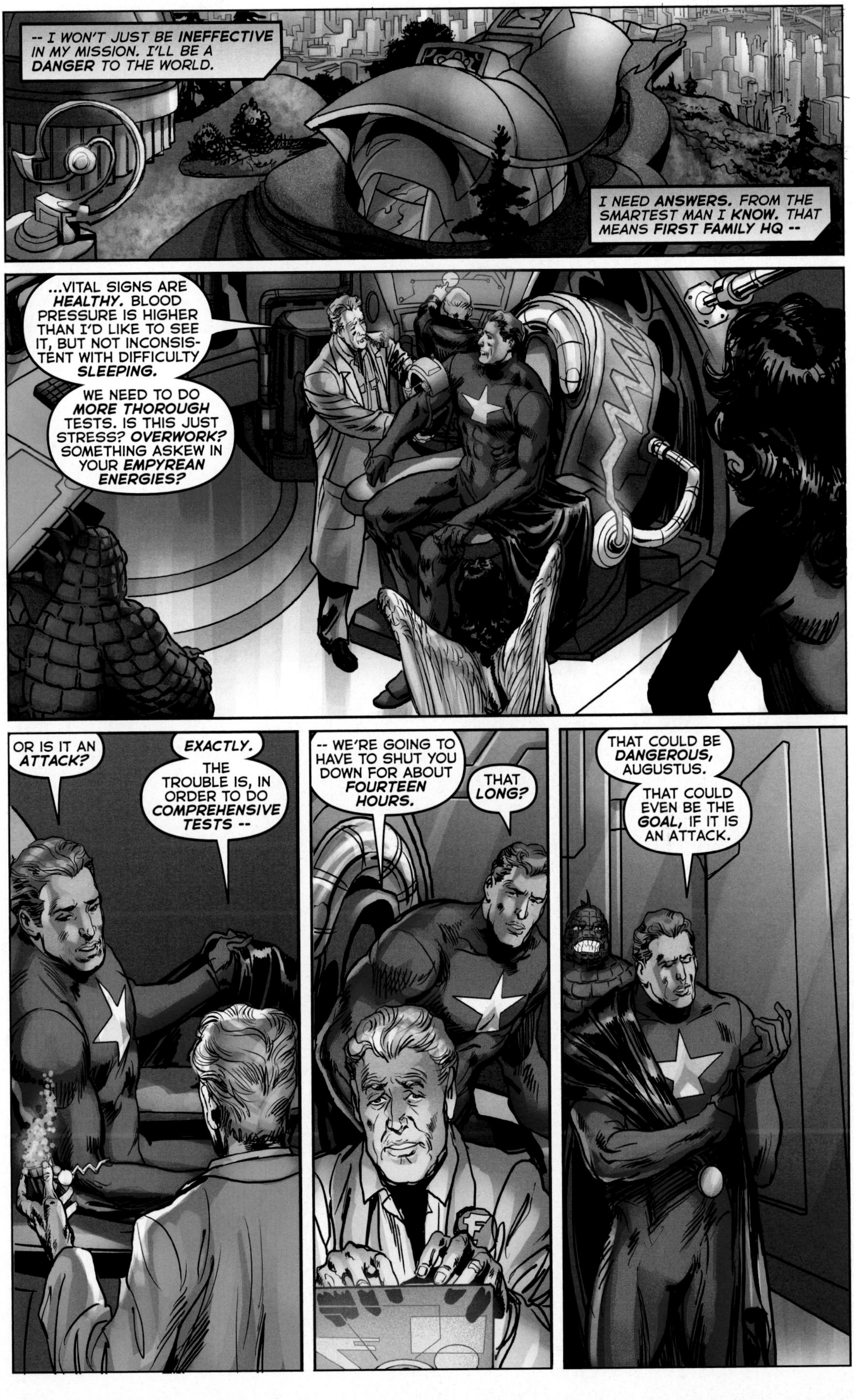
-- I WON'T JUST BE INEFFECTIVE IN MY MISSION. I'LL BE A DANGER TO THE WORLD.
I NEED ANSWERS. FROM THE SMARTEST MAN I KNOW. THAT MEANS FIRST FAMILY HQ --
...VITAL SIGNS ARE HEALTHY. BLOOD PRESSURE IS HIGHER THAN I'D LIKE TO SEE IT, BUT NOT INCONSISTENT WITH DIFFICULTY SLEEPING.
WE NEED TO DO MORE THOROUGH TESTS. IS THIS JUST STRESS? OVERWORK? SOMETHING ASKEW IN YOUR EMPYREAN ENERGIES?
OR IS IT AN ATTACK?
EXACTLY.
THE TROUBLE IS, IN ORDER TO DO COMPREHENSIVE TESTS --
-- WE'RE GOING TO HAVE TO SHUT YOU DOWN FOR ABOUT FOURTEEN HOURS.
THAT LONG?
THAT COULD BE DANGEROUS, AUGUSTUS.
THAT COULD EVEN BE THE GOAL, IF IT IS AN ATTACK.

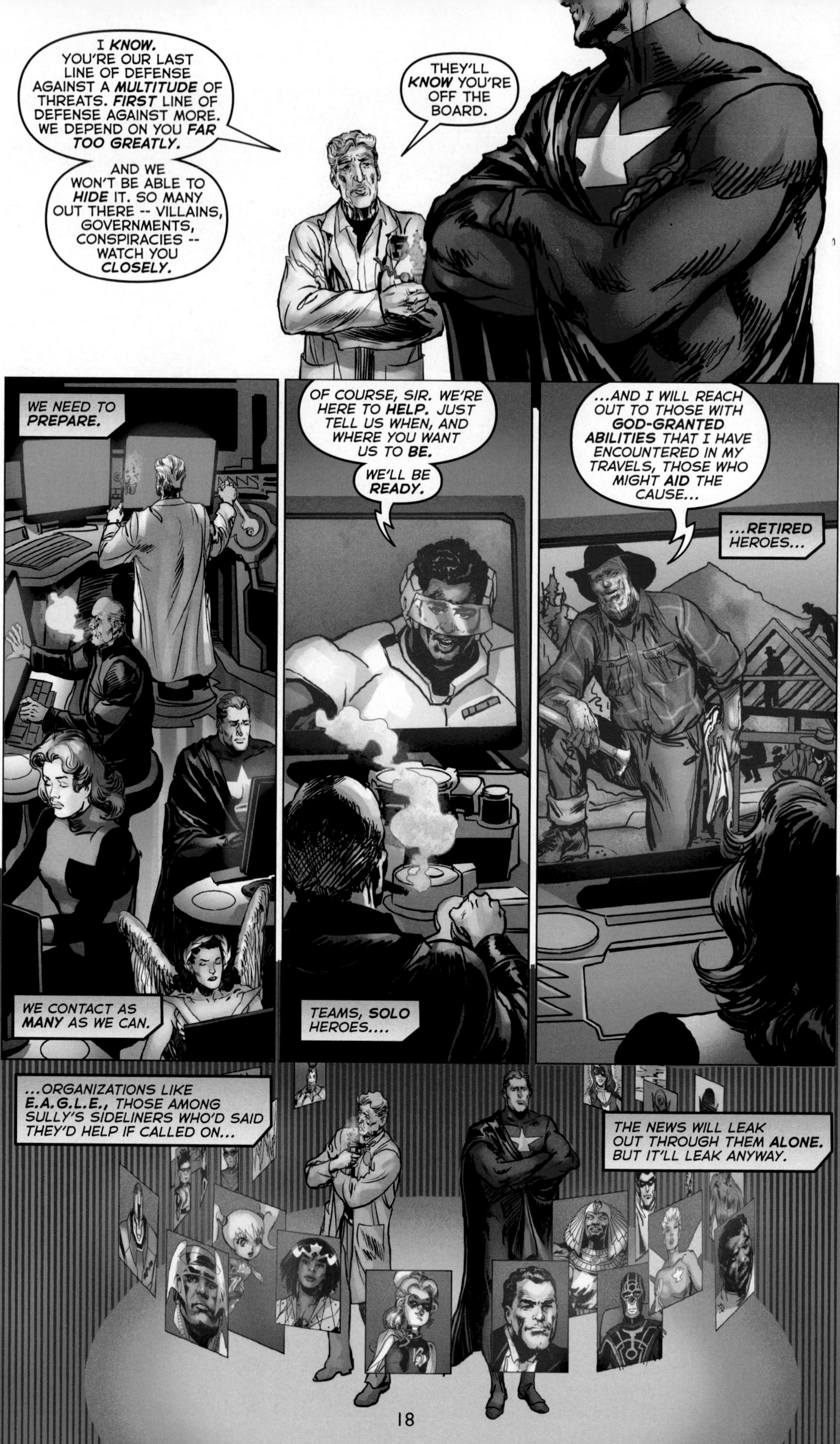
I KNOW. YOU'RE OUR LAST LINE OF DEFENSE AGAINST A MULTITUDE OF THREATS. FIRST LINE OF DEFENSE AGAINST MORE. WE DEPEND ON YOU FAR TOO GREATLY.
AND WE WON'T BE ABLE TO HIDE IT. SO MANY OUT THERE -- VILLAINS, GOVERNMENTS, CONSPIRACIES -- WATCH YOU CLOSELY.
THEY'LL KNOW YOU'RE OFF THE BOARD.
WE NEED TO PREPARE.
WE CONTACT AS MANY AS WE CAN.
OF COURSE, SIR. WE'RE HERE TO HELP. JUST TELL US WHEN, AND WHERE YOU WANT US TO BE.
WE'LL BE READY.
TEAMS, SOLO HEROES....
...AND I WILL REACH OUT TO THOSE WITH GOD-GRANTED ABILITIES THAT I HAVE ENCOUNTERED IN MY TRAVELS, THOSE WHO MIGHT AID THE CAUSE...
...RETIRED HEROES...
...ORGANIZATIONS LIKE E.A.G.L.E., THOSE AMONG SULLY'S SIDELINERS WHO'D SAID THEY'D HELP IF CALLED ON...
THE NEWS WILL LEAK OUT THROUGH THEM ALONE. BUT IT'LL LEAK ANYWAY.

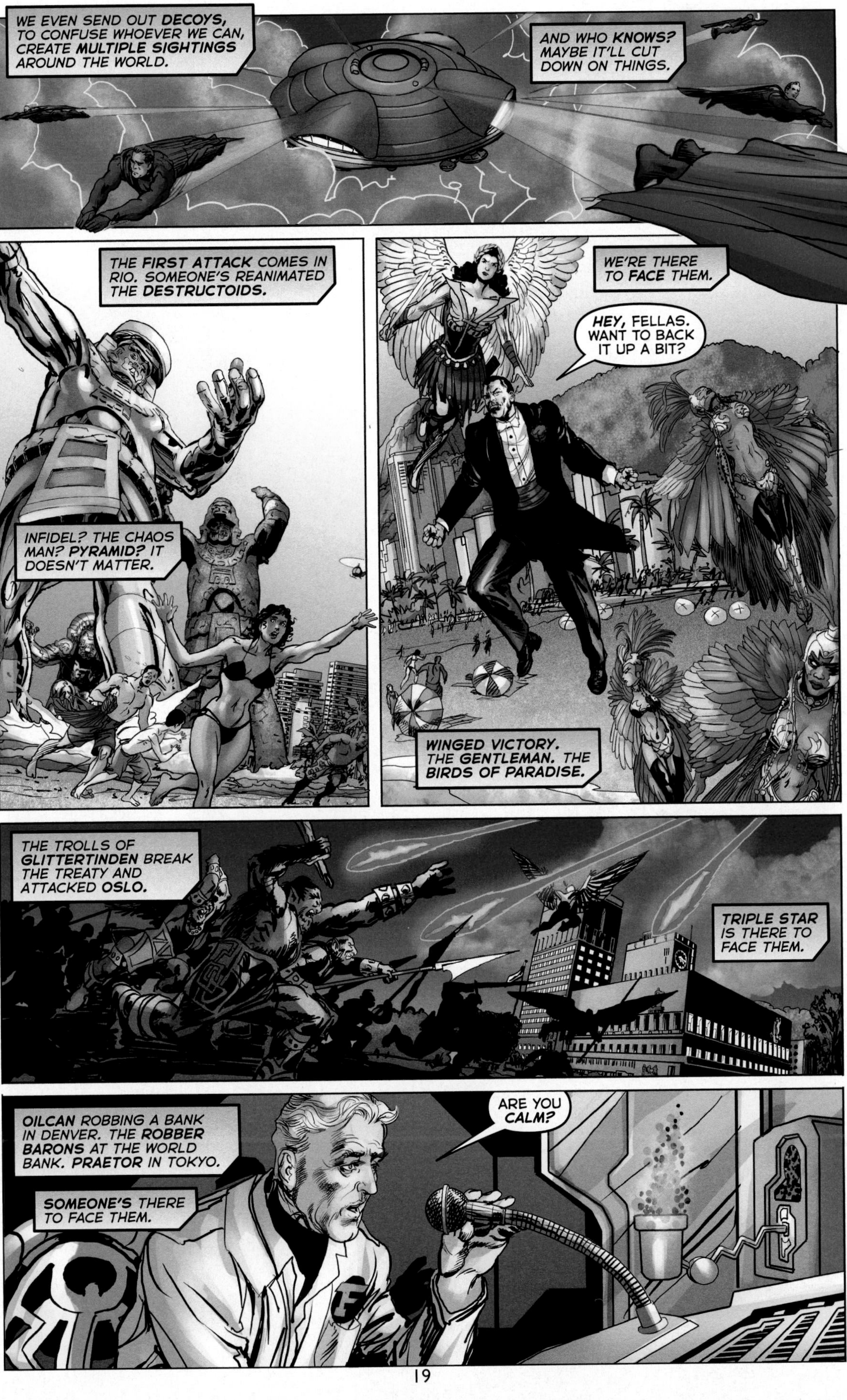

WE EVEN SEND OUT DECOYS, TO CONFUSE WHOEVER WE CAN, CREATE MULTIPLE SIGHTINGS AROUND THE WORLD.
AND WHO KNOWS? MAYBE IT'LL CUT DOWN ON THINGS.
THE FIRST ATTACK COMES IN RIO. SOMEONE'S REANIMATED THE DESTRUCTOIDS.
INFIDEL? THE CHAOS MAN? PYRAMID? IT DOESN'T MATTER.
WE'RE THERE TO FACE THEM.
HEY, FELLAS. WANT TO BACK IT UP A BIT?
WINGED VICTORY. THE GENTLEMAN. THE BIRDS OF PARADISE.
THE TROLLS OF GLITTERTINDEN BREAK THE TREATY AND ATTACKED OSLO.
TRIPLE STAR IS THERE TO FACE THEM.
OILCAN ROBBING A BANK IN DENVER. THE ROBBER BARONS AT THE WORLD BANK. PRAETOR IN TOKYO.
SOMEONE'S THERE TO FACE THEM.
ARE YOU CALM?

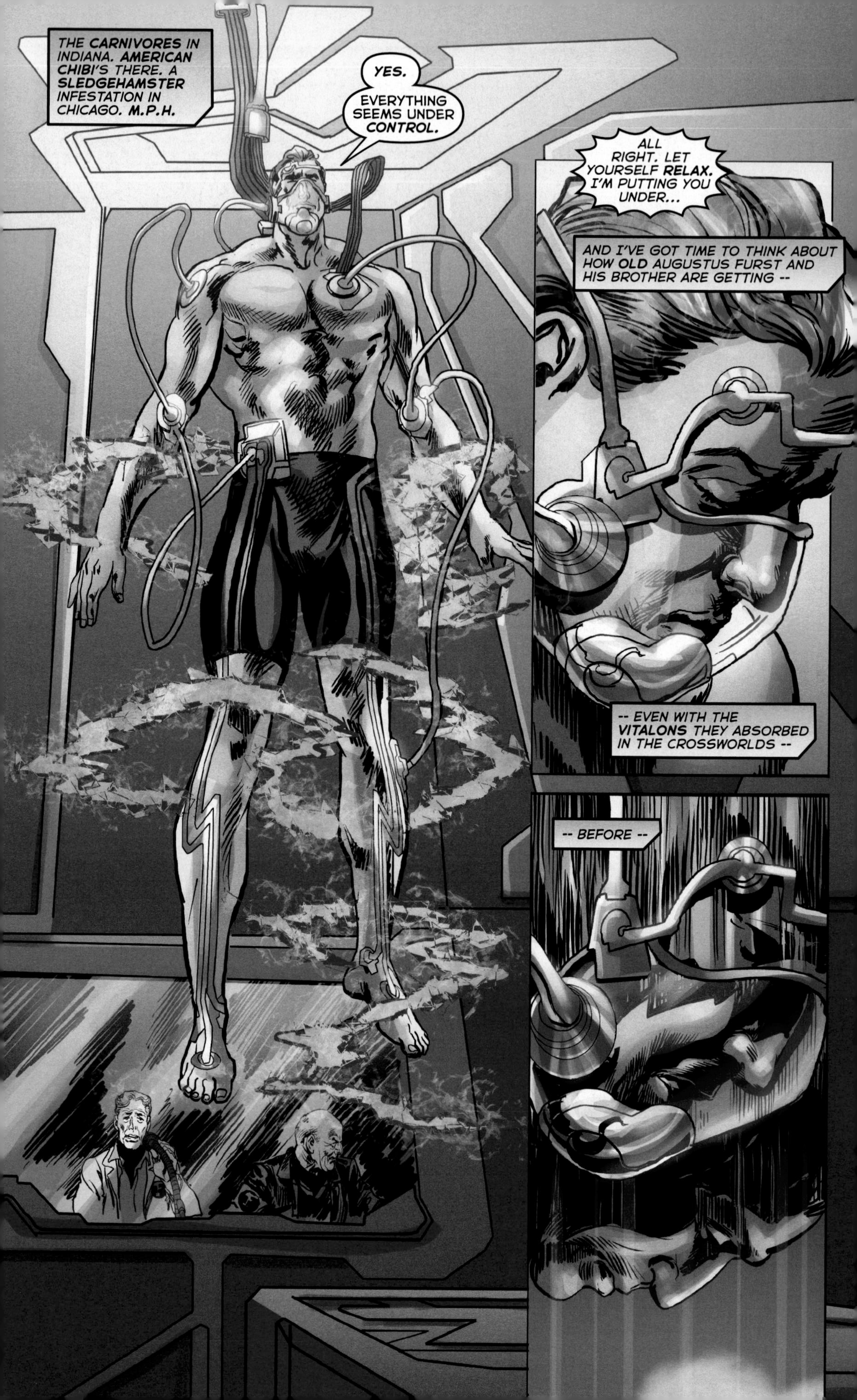
THE CARNIVORES IN INDIANA. AMERICAN CHIBI'S THERE. A SLEDGEHAMSTER INFESTATION IN CHICAGO. M.P.H.
YES.
EVERYTHING SEEMS UNDER CONTROL.
ALL RIGHT. LET YOURSELF RELAX. I'M PUTTING YOU UNDER...
AND I'VE GOT TIME TO THINK ABOUT HOW OLD AUGUSTUS FURST AND HIS BROTHER ARE GETTING --
-- EVEN WITH THE VITALONS THEY ABSORBED IN THE CROSSWORLDS --
-- BEFORE --

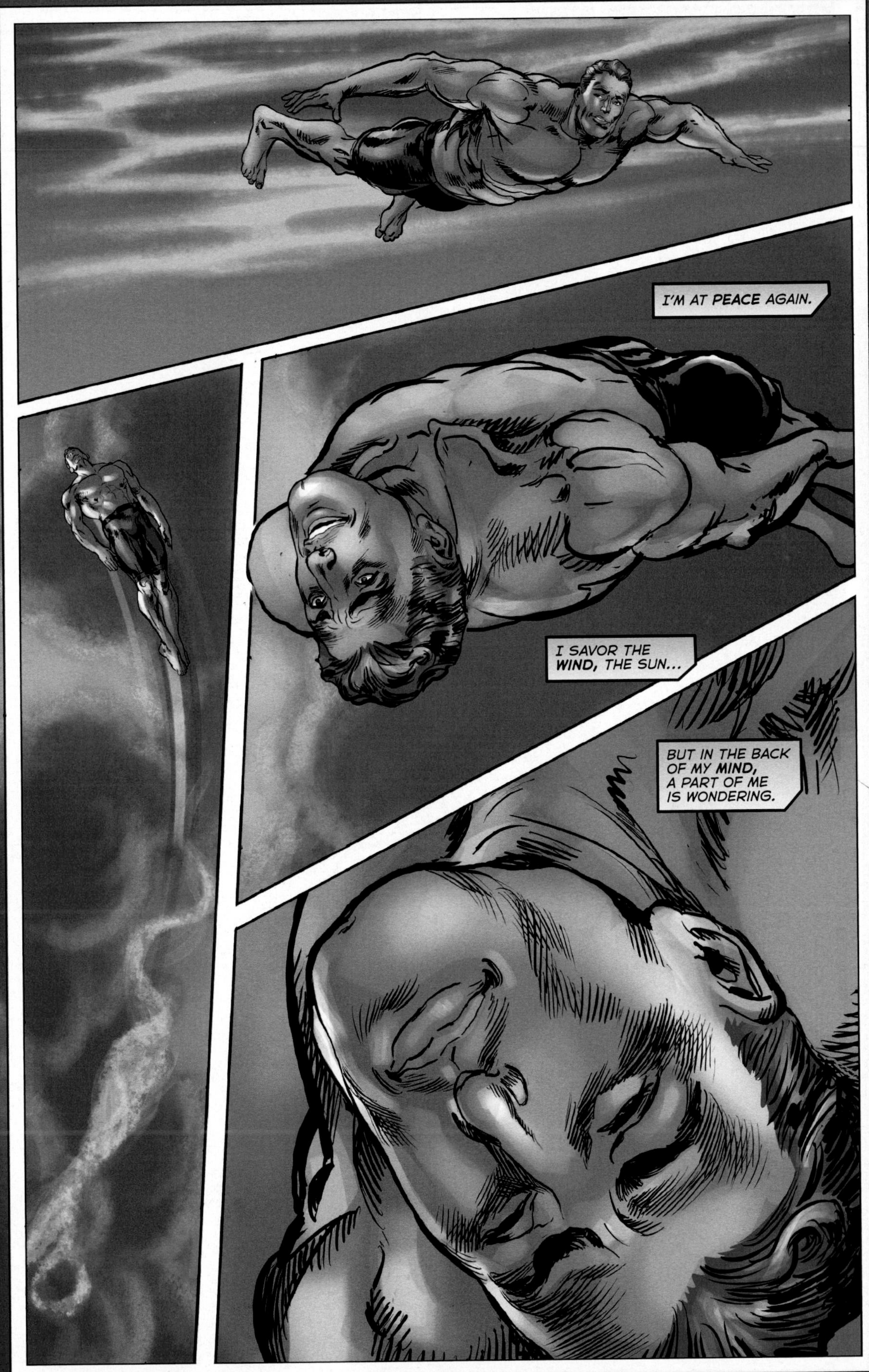
I'M AT PEACE AGAIN.
I SAVOR THE WIND, THE SUN...
BUT IN THE BACK OF MY MIND, A PART OF ME IS WONDERING.

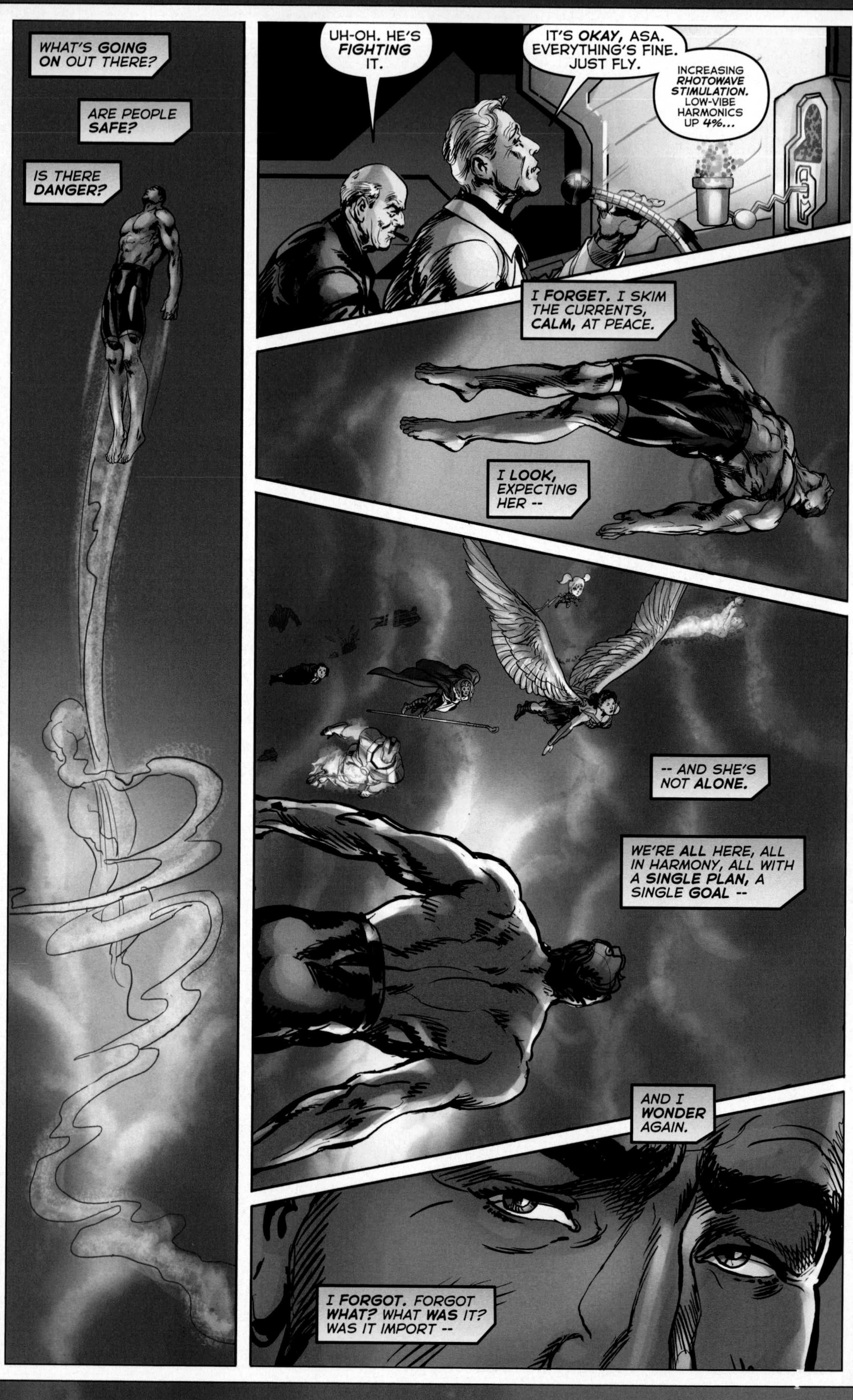

WHAT'S GOING ON OUT THERE?
ARE PEOPLE SAFE?
IS THERE DANGER?
UH-OH. HE'S FIGHTING IT.
IT'S OKAY, ASA. EVERYTHING'S FINE. JUST FLY.
INCREASING RHOTOWAVE STIMULATION. LOW-VIBE HARMONICS UP 4%...
I FORGET. I SKIM THE CURRENTS, CALM, AT PEACE.
I LOOK, EXPECTING HER --
-- AND SHE'S NOT ALONE.
WE'RE ALL HERE, ALL IN HARMONY, ALL WITH A SINGLE PLAN, A SINGLE GOAL --
AND I WONDER AGAIN.
I FORGOT. FORGOT WHAT? WHAT WAS IT? WAS IT IMPORT --

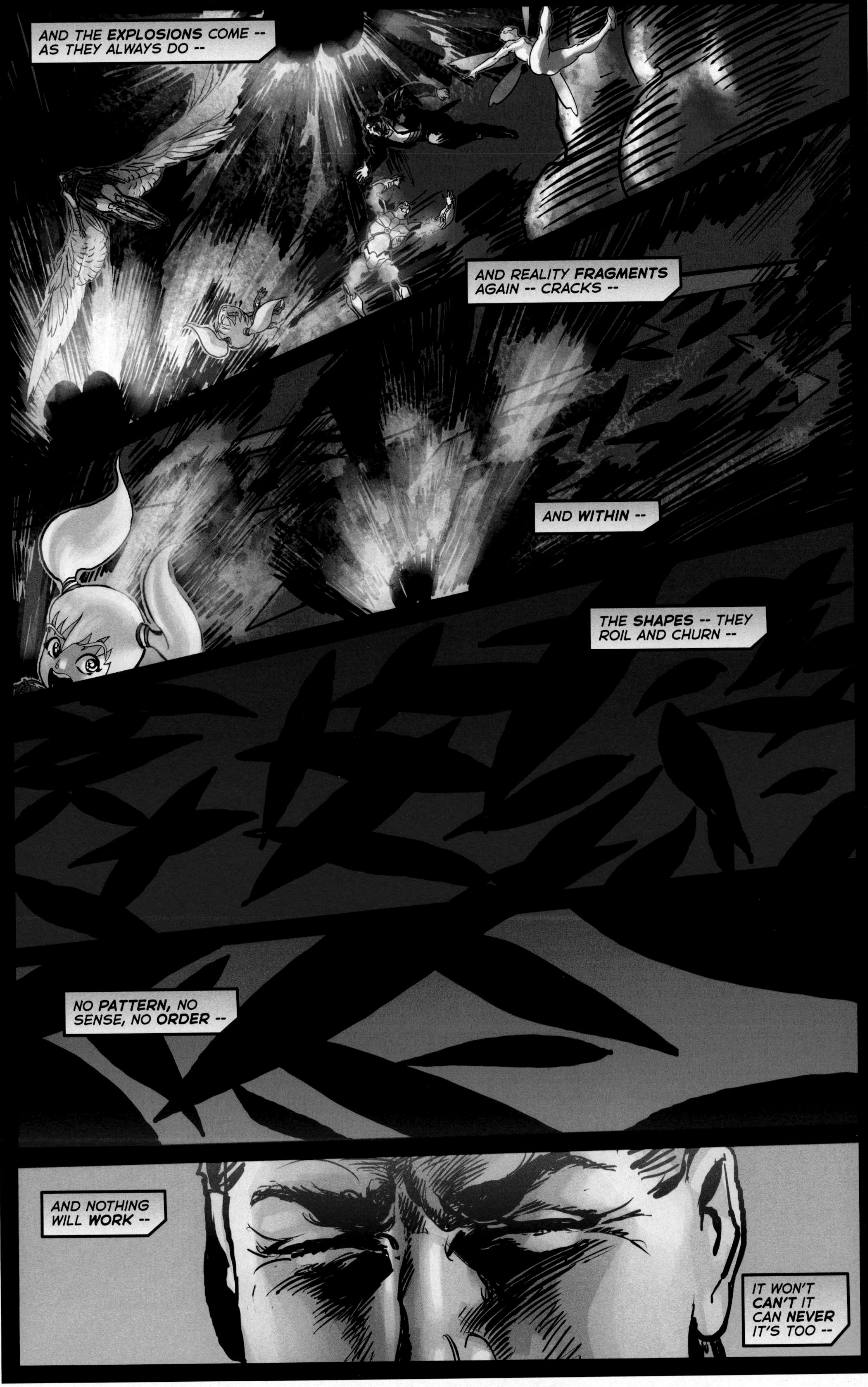
AND THE EXPLOSIONS COME -- AS THEY ALWAYS DO --
AND REALITY FRAGMENTS AGAIN -- CRACKS --
AND WITHIN --
THE SHAPES -- THEY ROIL AND CHURN --
NO PATTERN, NO SENSE, NO ORDER --
AND NOTHING WILL WORK --
IT WON'T CAN'T IT CAN NEVER IT'S TOO --

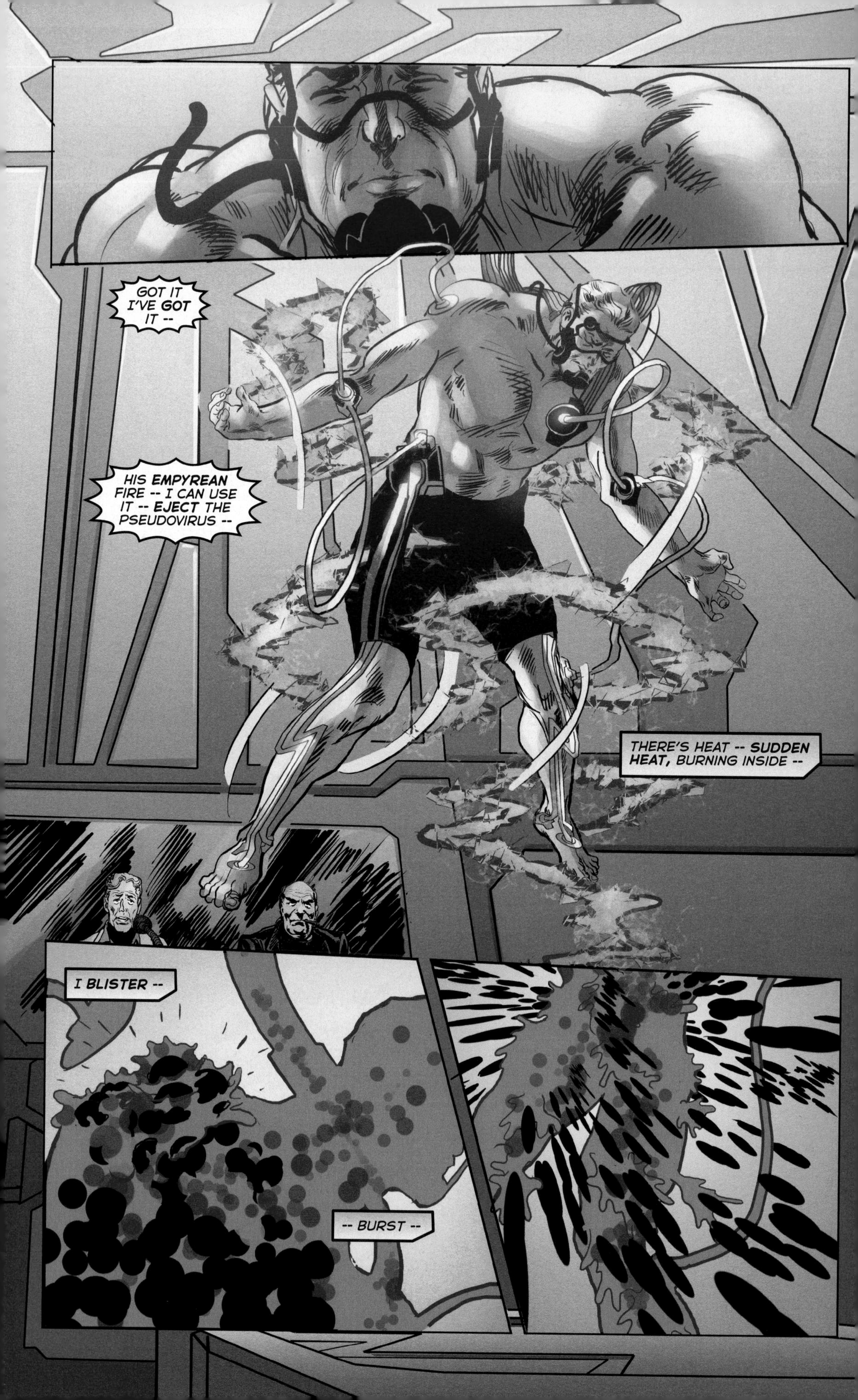
GOT IT I'VE GOT IT --
HIS EMPYREAN FIRE -- I CAN USE IT -- EJECT THE PSEUDOVIRUS --
THERE'S HEAT -- SUDDEN HEAT, BURNING INSIDE --
I BLISTER --
-- BURST --

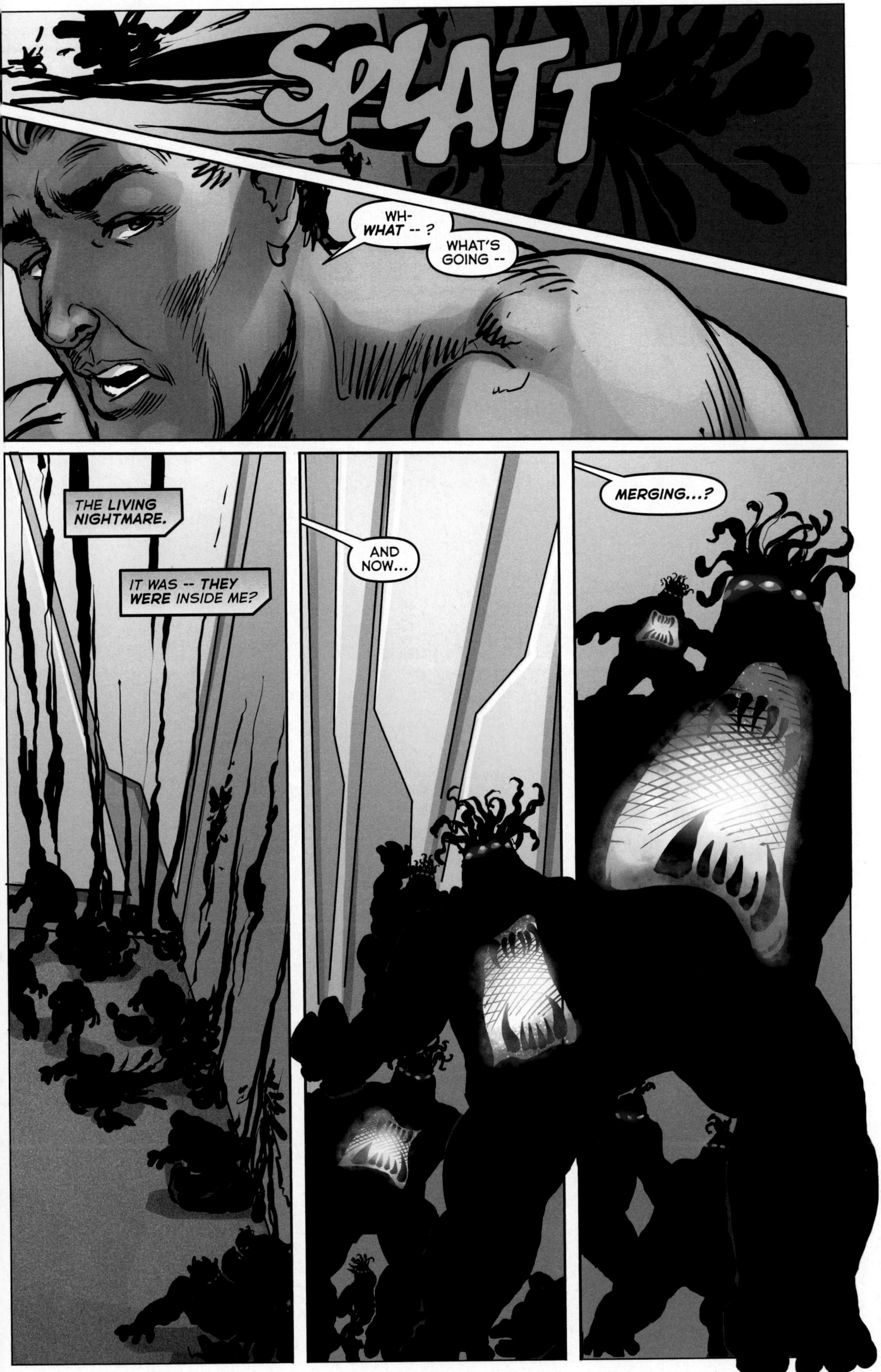
SPLATT
WH- WHAT -- ?
WHAT'S GOING --
THE LIVING NIGHTMARE.
IT WAS -- THEY WERE INSIDE ME?
AND NOW...
MERGING...?

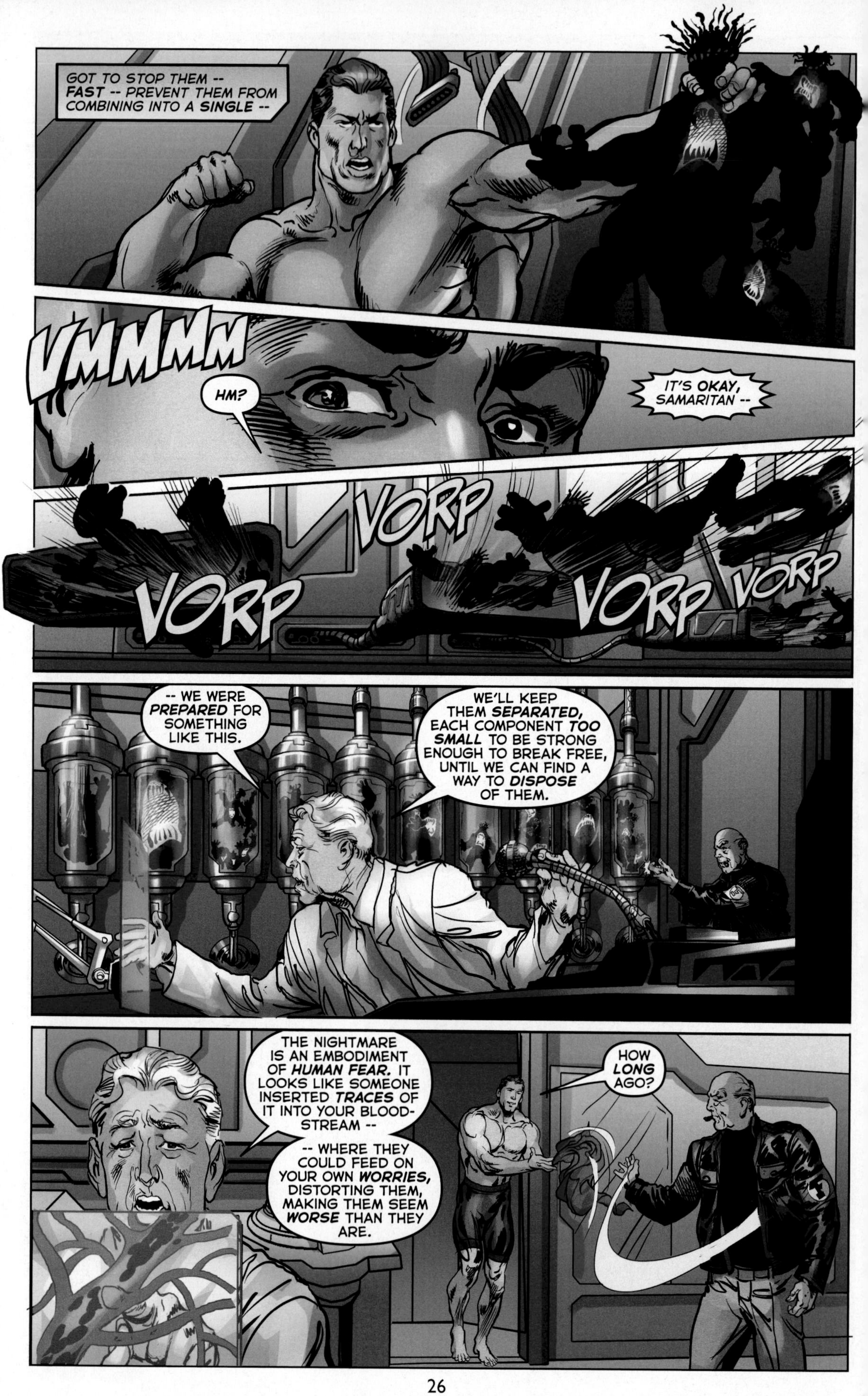
GOT TO STOP THEM -- FAST -- PREVENT THEM FROM COMBINING INTO A SINGLE --
UMMMM
HM?
IT'S OKAY, SAMARITAN --
VORP
VORP
VORP
VORP
-- WE WERE PREPARED FOR SOMETHING LIKE THIS.
WE'LL KEEP THEM SEPARATED, EACH COMPONENT TOO SMALL TO BE STRONG ENOUGH TO BREAK FREE, UNTIL WE CAN FIND A WAY TO DISPOSE OF THEM.
THE NIGHTMARE IS AN EMBODIMENT OF HUMAN FEAR. IT LOOKS LIKE SOMEONE INSERTED TRACES OF IT INTO YOUR BLOOD-STREAM --
-- WHERE THEY COULD FEED ON YOUR OWN WORRIES, DISTORTING THEM, MAKING THEM SEEM WORSE THAN THEY ARE.
HOW LONG AGO?

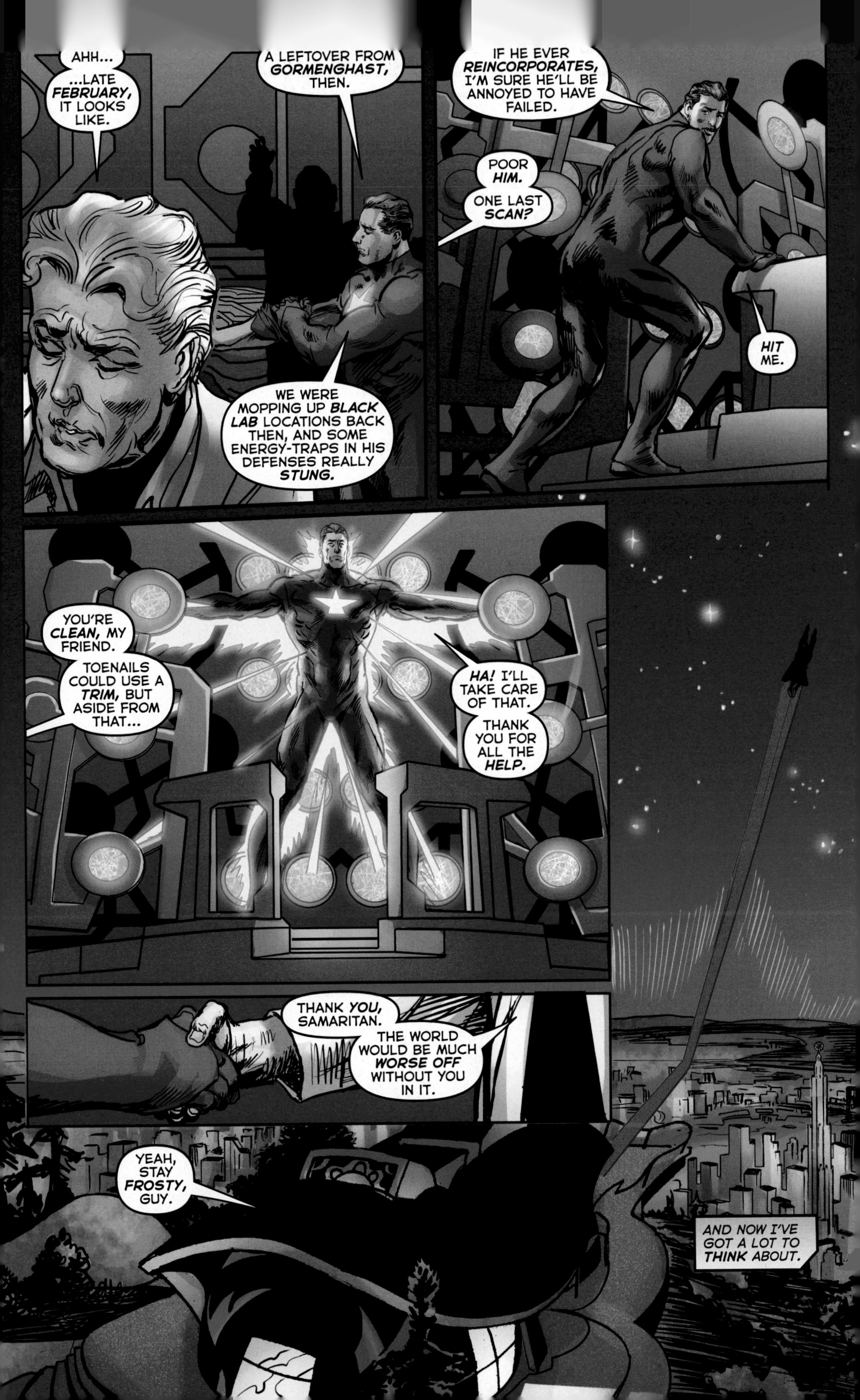
AHH...
...LATE FEBRUARY, IT LOOKS LIKE.
A LEFTOVER FROM GORMENGHAST, THEN.
WE WERE MOPPING UP BLACK LAB LOCATIONS BACK THEN, AND SOME ENERGY-TRAPS IN HIS DEFENSES REALLY STUNG.
IF HE EVER REINCORPORATES, I'M SURE HE'LL BE ANNOYED TO HAVE FAILED.
POOR HIM.
ONE LAST SCAN?
HIT ME.
YOU'RE CLEAN, MY FRIEND.
TOENAILS COULD USE A TRIM, BUT ASIDE FROM THAT...
HA! I'LL TAKE CARE OF THAT.
THANK YOU FOR ALL THE HELP.
THANK YOU, SAMARITAN.
THE WORLD WOULD BE MUCH WORSE OFF WITHOUT YOU IN IT.
YEAH, STAY FROSTY, GUY.
AND NOW I'VE GOT A LOT TO THINK ABOUT.

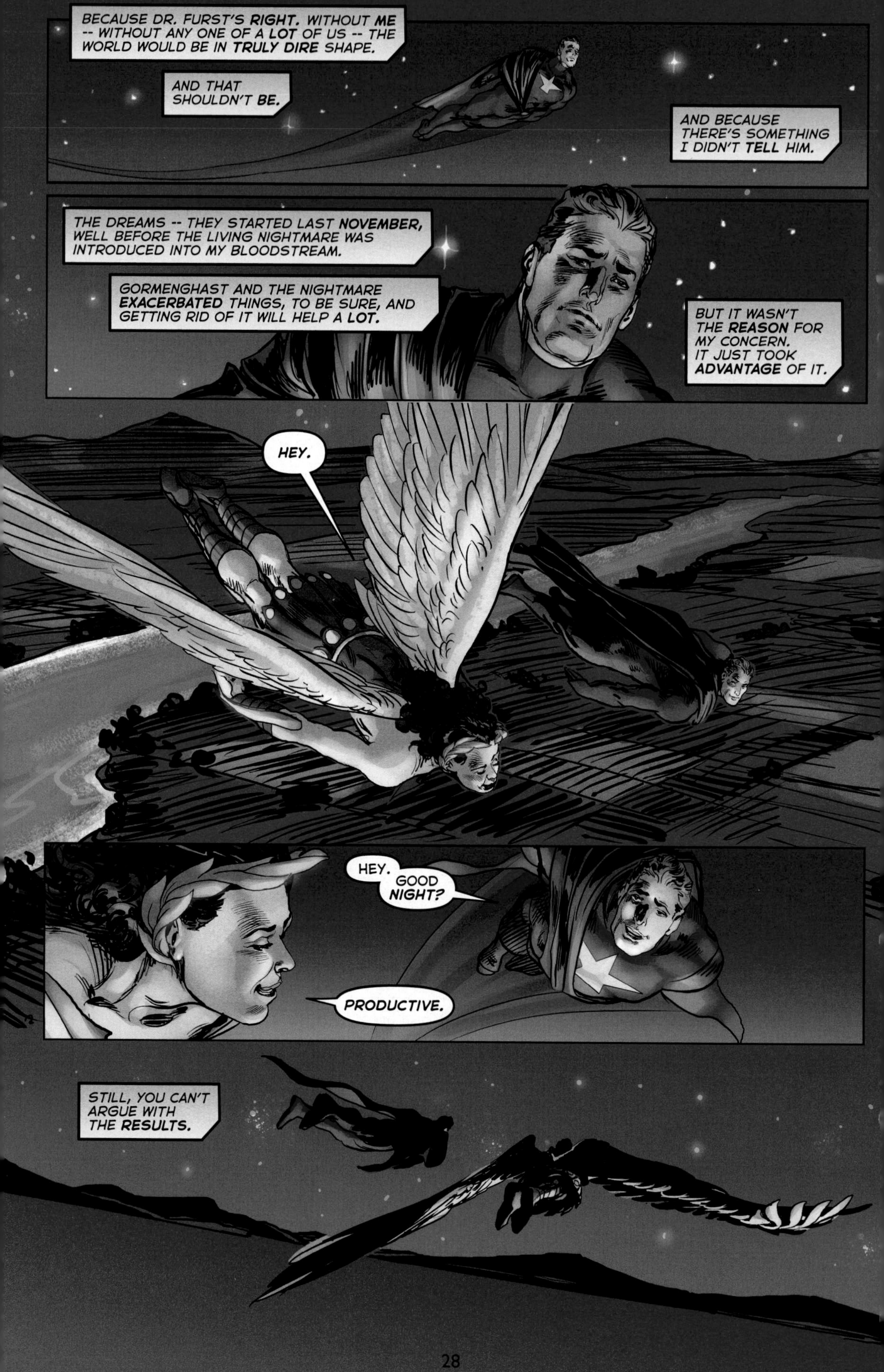
BECAUSE DR. FURST'S RIGHT. WITHOUT ME -- WITHOUT ANY ONE OF A LOT OF US -- THE WORLD WOULD BE IN TRULY DIRE SHAPE.
AND THAT SHOULDN'T BE.
AND BECAUSE THERE'S SOMETHING I DIDN'T TELL HIM.
THE DREAMS -- THEY STARTED LAST NOVEMBER, WELL BEFORE THE LIVING NIGHTMARE WAS INTRODUCED INTO MY BLOODSTREAM.
GORMENGHAST AND THE NIGHTMARE EXACERBATED THINGS, TO BE SURE, AND GETTING RID OF IT WILL HELP A LOT.
BUT IT WASN'T THE REASON FOR MY CONCERN. IT JUST TOOK ADVANTAGE OF IT.
HEY.
HEY. GOOD NIGHT?
PRODUCTIVE.
STILL, YOU CAN'T ARGUE WITH THE RESULTS.

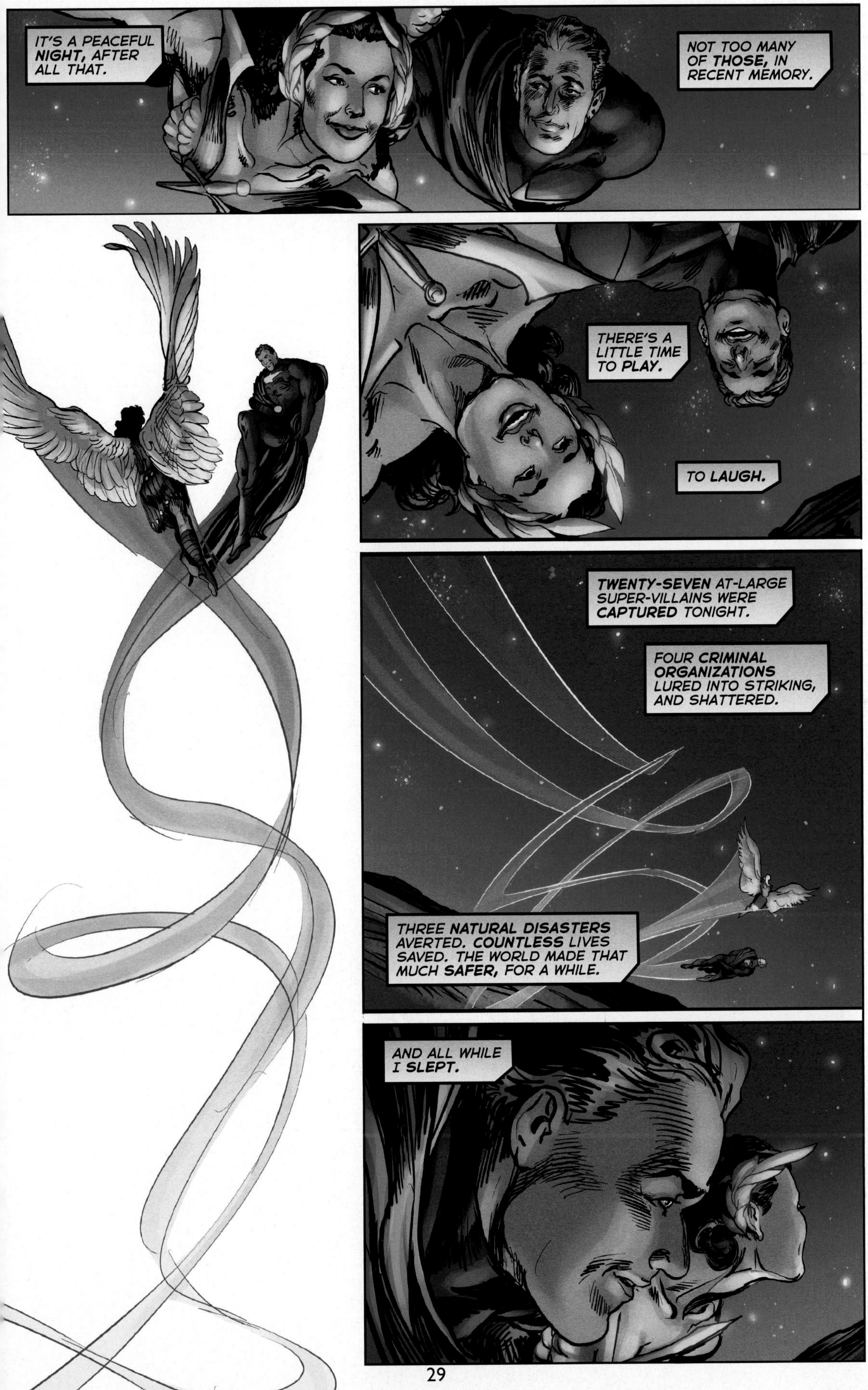
IT'S A PEACEFUL NIGHT, AFTER ALL THAT.
NOT TOO MANY OF THOSE, IN RECENT MEMORY.
THERE'S A LITTLE TIME TO PLAY.
TO LAUGH.
TWENTY-SEVEN AT-LARGE SUPER-VILLAINS WERE CAPTURED TONIGHT.
FOUR CRIMINAL ORGANIZATIONS LURED INTO STRIKING, AND SHATTERED.
THREE NATURAL DISASTERS AVERTED. COUNTLESS LIVES SAVED. THE WORLD MADE THAT MUCH SAFER, FOR A WHILE.
AND ALL WHILE I SLEPT.

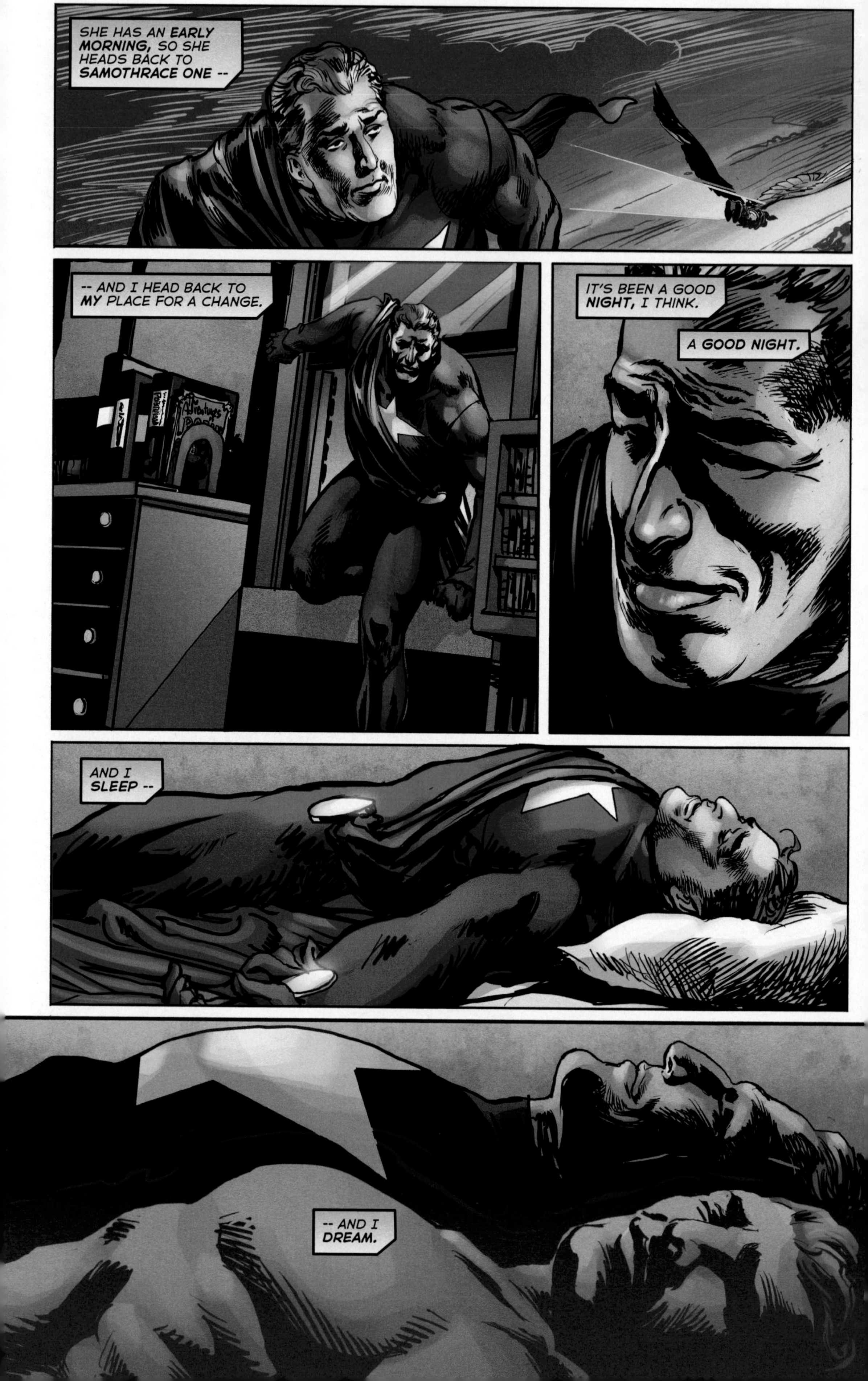
SHE HAS AN EARLY MORNING, SO SHE HEADS BACK TO SAMOTHRACE ONE --
-- AND I HEAD BACK TO MY PLACE FOR A CHANGE.
IT'S BEEN A GOOD NIGHT, I THINK.
A GOOD NIGHT.
AND I SLEEP --
-- AND I DREAM.

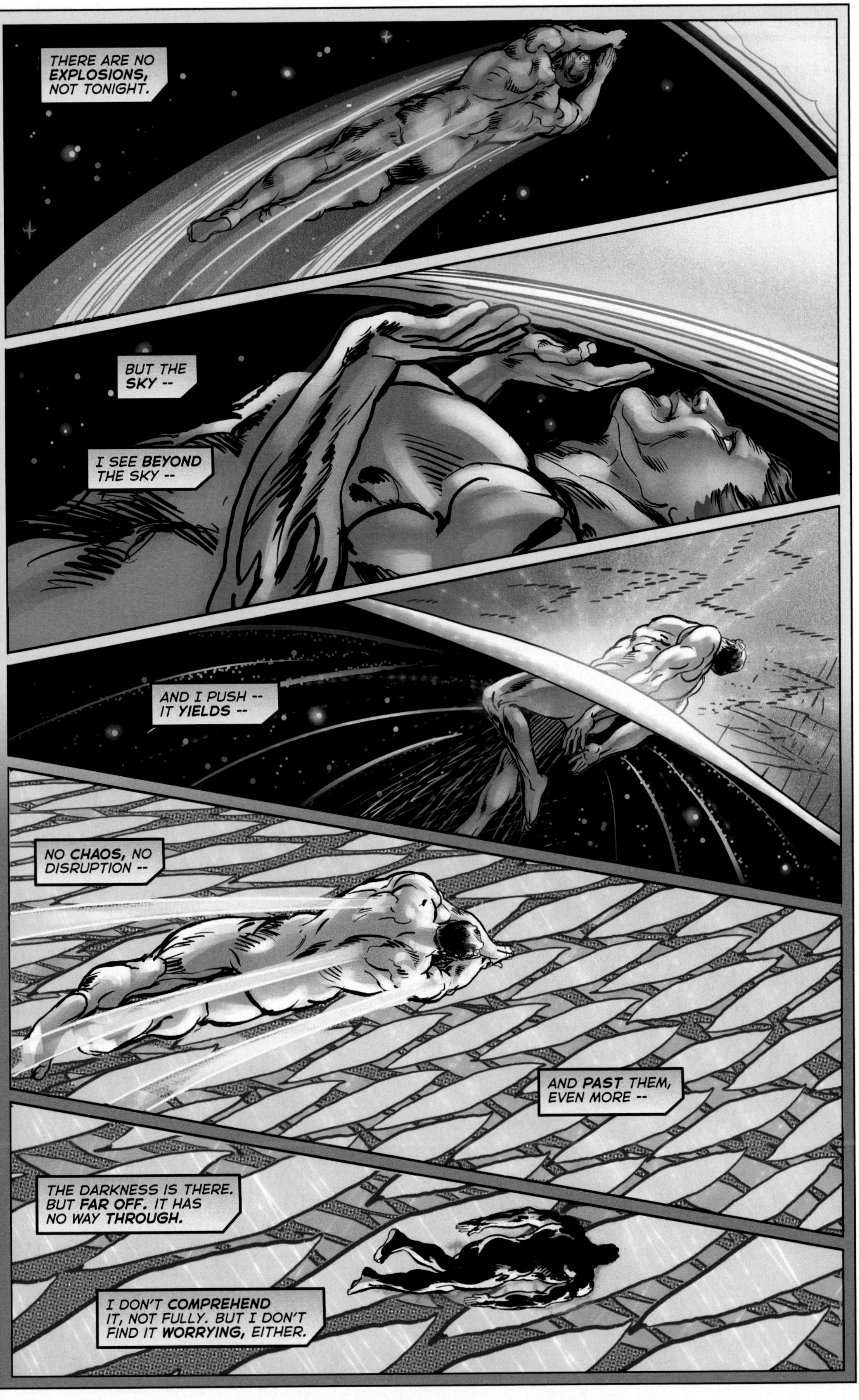
THERE ARE NO EXPLOSIONS, NOT TONIGHT.
BUT THE SKY --
I SEE BEYOND THE SKY --
AND I PUSH -- IT YIELDS --
NO CHAOS, NO DISRUPTION --
AND PAST THEM, EVEN MORE --
THE DARKNESS IS THERE. BUT FAR OFF. IT HAS NO WAY THROUGH.
I DON'T COMPREHEND IT, NOT FULLY. BUT I DON'T FIND IT WORRYING, EITHER.

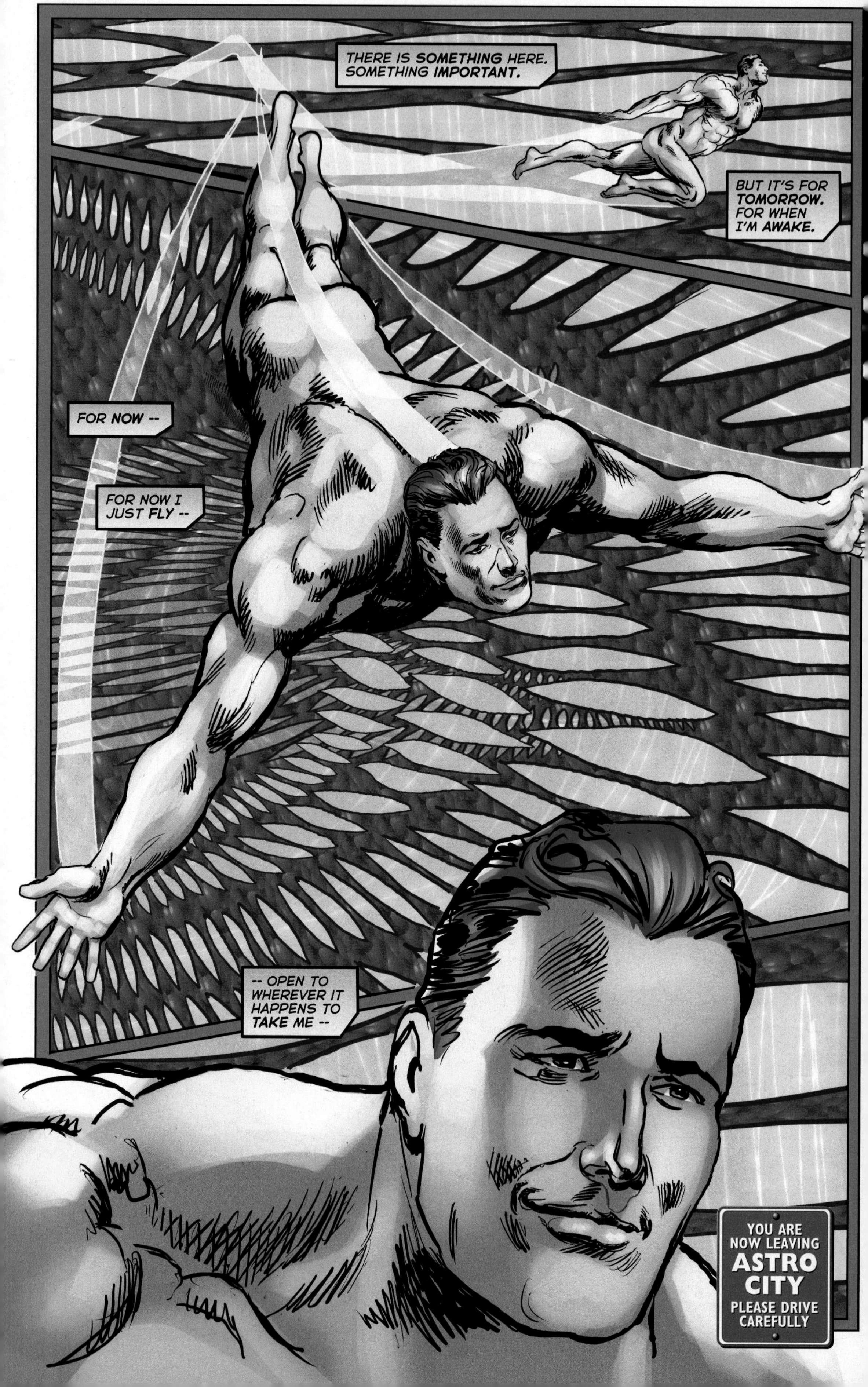
THERE IS SOMETHING HERE. SOMETHING IMPORTANT.
BUT IT'S FOR TOMORROW. FOR WHEN I'M AWAKE.
FOR NOW --
FOR NOW I JUST FLY --
-- OPEN TO WHEREVER IT HAPPENS TO TAKE ME --
YOU ARE NOW LEAVING ASTRO CITY PLEASE DRIVE CAREFULLY

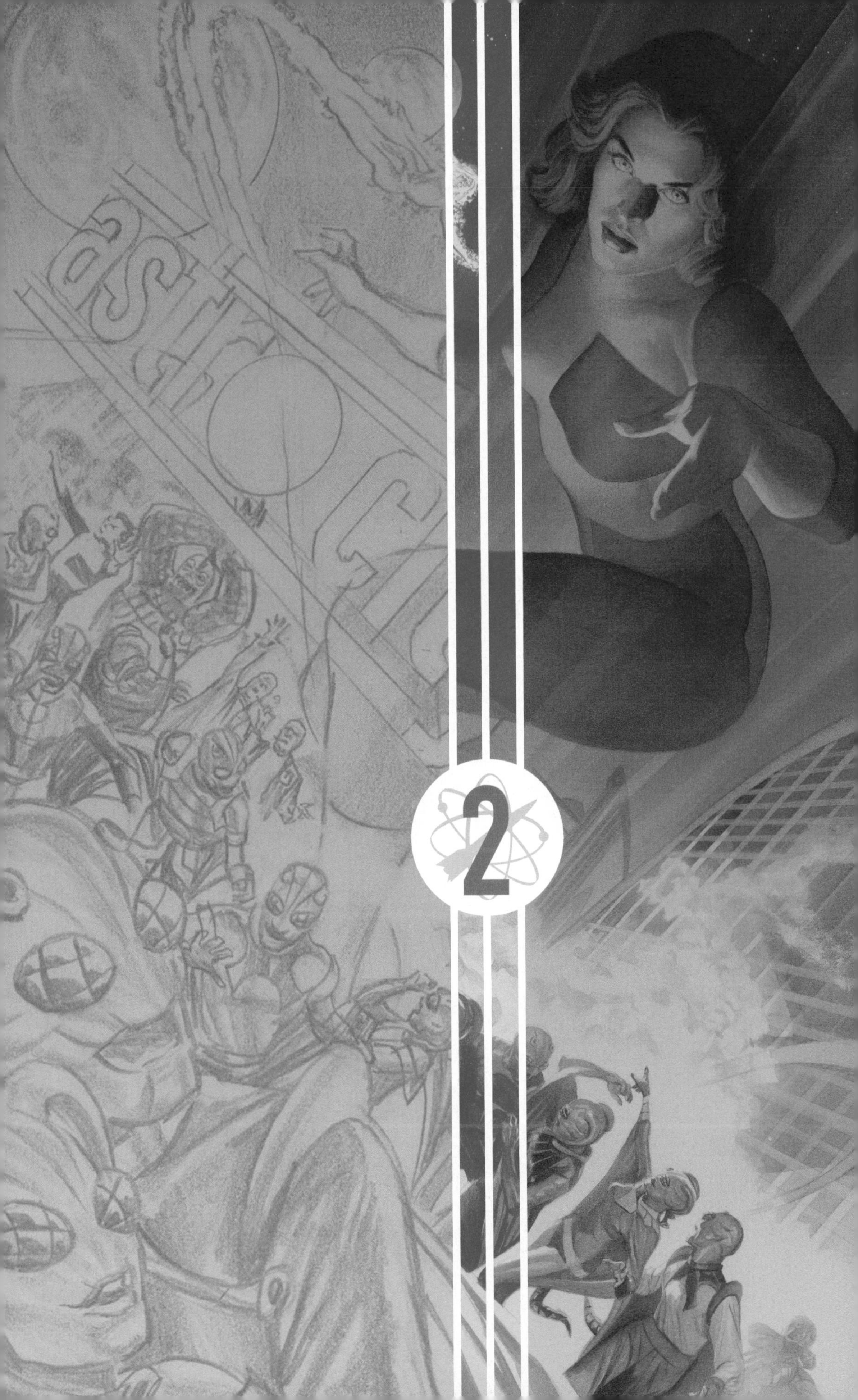
2

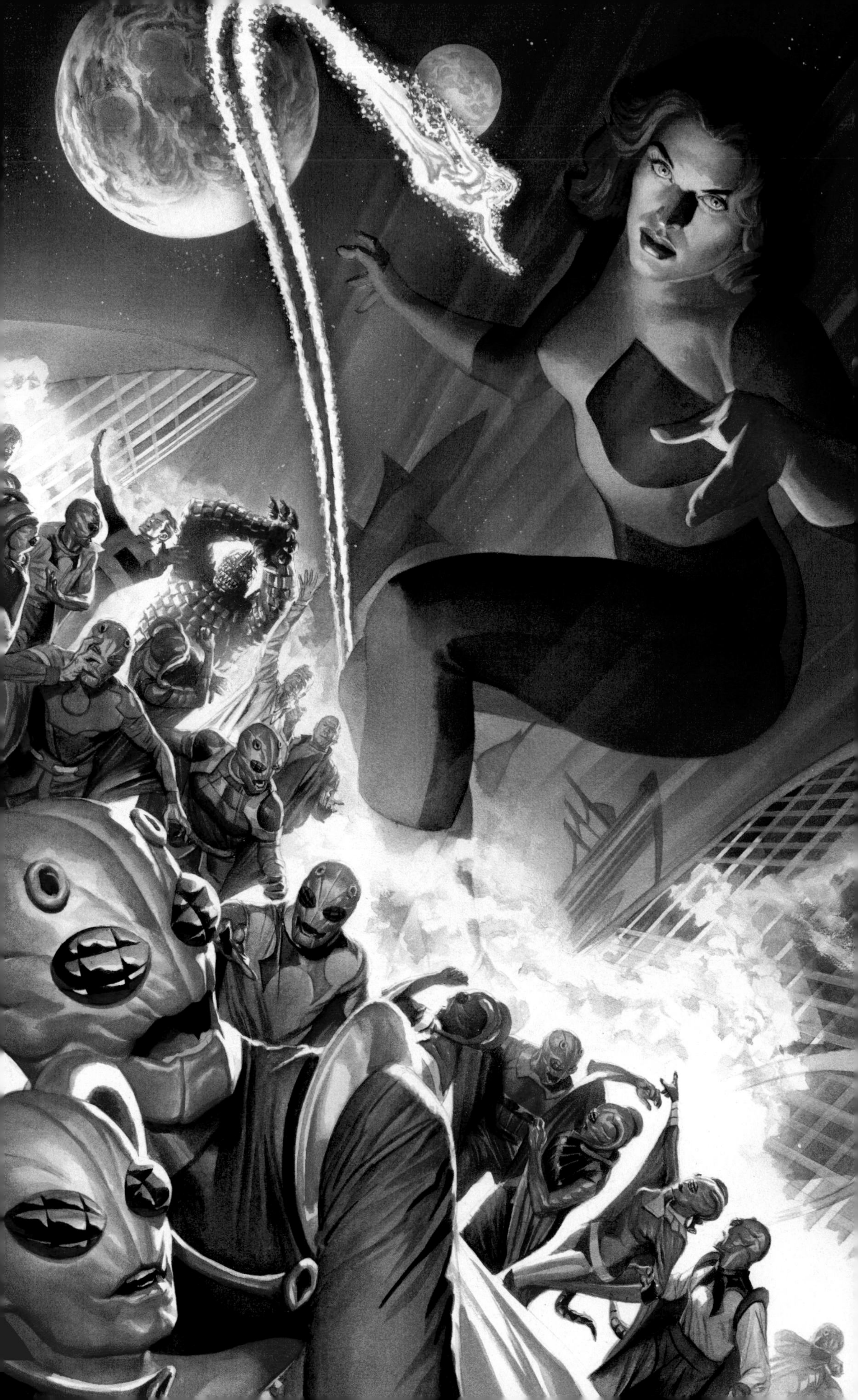

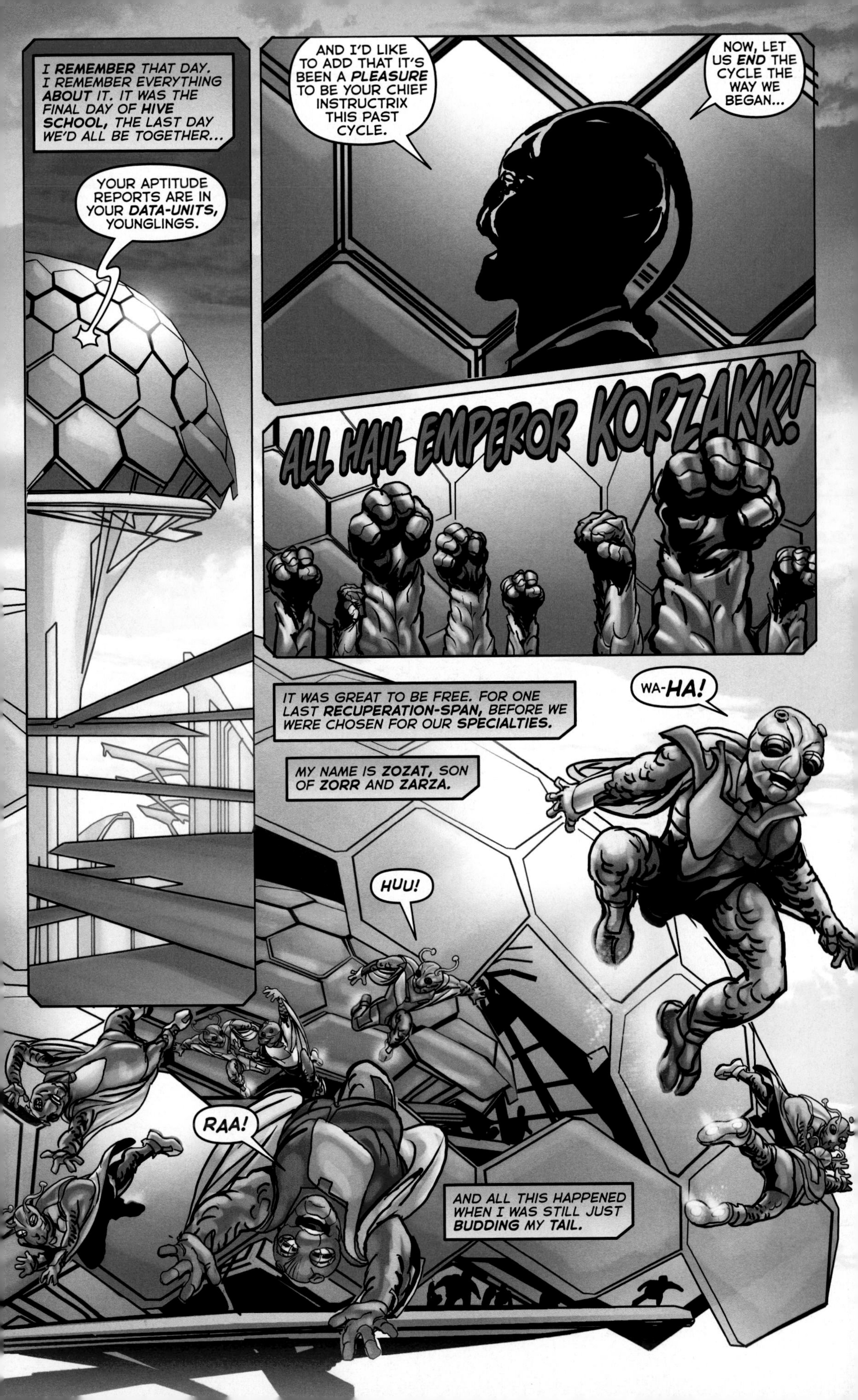

I REMEMBER THAT DAY. I REMEMBER EVERYTHING ABOUT IT. IT WAS THE FINAL DAY OF HIVE SCHOOL, THE LAST DAY WE'D ALL BE TOGETHER...
YOUR APTITUDE REPORTS ARE IN YOUR DATA-UNITS, YOUNGLINGS.
AND I'D LIKE TO ADD THAT IT'S BEEN A PLEASURE TO BE YOUR CHIEF INSTRUCTRIX THIS PAST CYCLE.
NOW, LET US END THE CYCLE THE WAY WE BEGAN...
ALL HAIL EMPEROR KORZAKK!
IT WAS GREAT TO BE FREE. FOR ONE LAST RECUPERATION-SPAN, BEFORE WE WERE CHOSEN FOR OUR SPECIALTIES.
WA-HA!
MY NAME IS ZOZAT, SON OF ZORR AND ZARZA.
HUU!
RAA!
AND ALL THIS HAPPENED WHEN I WAS STILL JUST BUDDING MY TAIL.

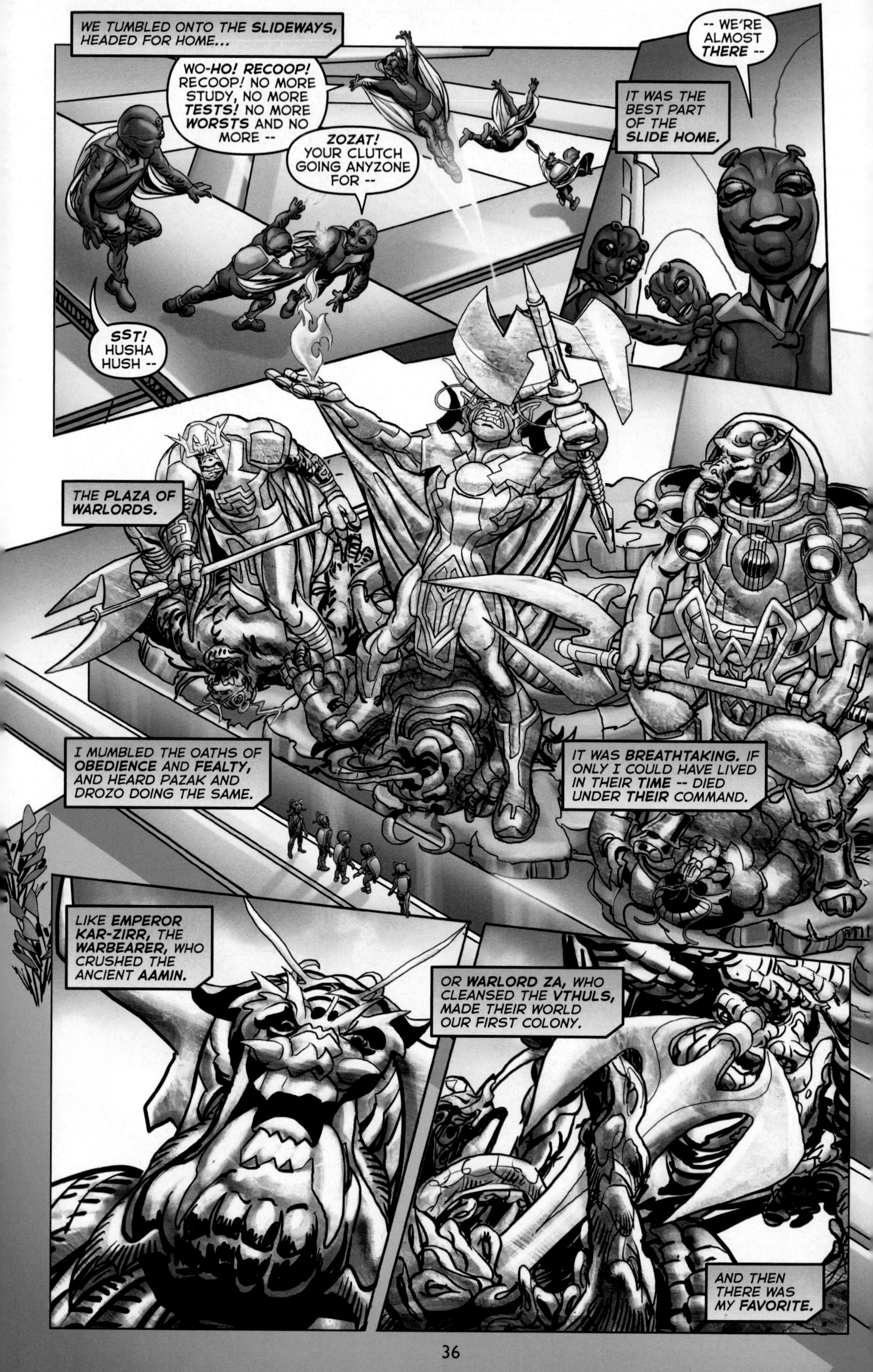
WE TUMBLED ONTO THE SLIDEWAYS, HEADED FOR HOME...
WO-HO! RECOOP! RECOOP! NO MORE STUDY, NO MORE TESTS! NO MORE WORSTS AND NO MORE --
ZOZAT! YOUR CLUTCH GOING ANYZONE FOR --
SST! HUSHA HUSH --
-- WE'RE ALMOST THERE --
IT WAS THE BEST PART OF THE SLIDE HOME.
THE PLAZA OF WARLORDS.
I MUMBLED THE OATHS OF OBEDIENCE AND FEALTY, AND HEARD PAZAK AND DROZO DOING THE SAME.
IT WAS BREATHTAKING. IF ONLY I COULD HAVE LIVED IN THEIR TIME -- DIED UNDER THEIR COMMAND.
LIKE EMPEROR KAR-ZIRR, THE WARBEARER, WHO CRUSHED THE ANCIENT AAMIN.
OR WARLORD ZA, WHO CLEANSED THE VTHULS, MADE THEIR WORLD OUR FIRST COLONY.
AND THEN THERE WAS MY FAVORITE.

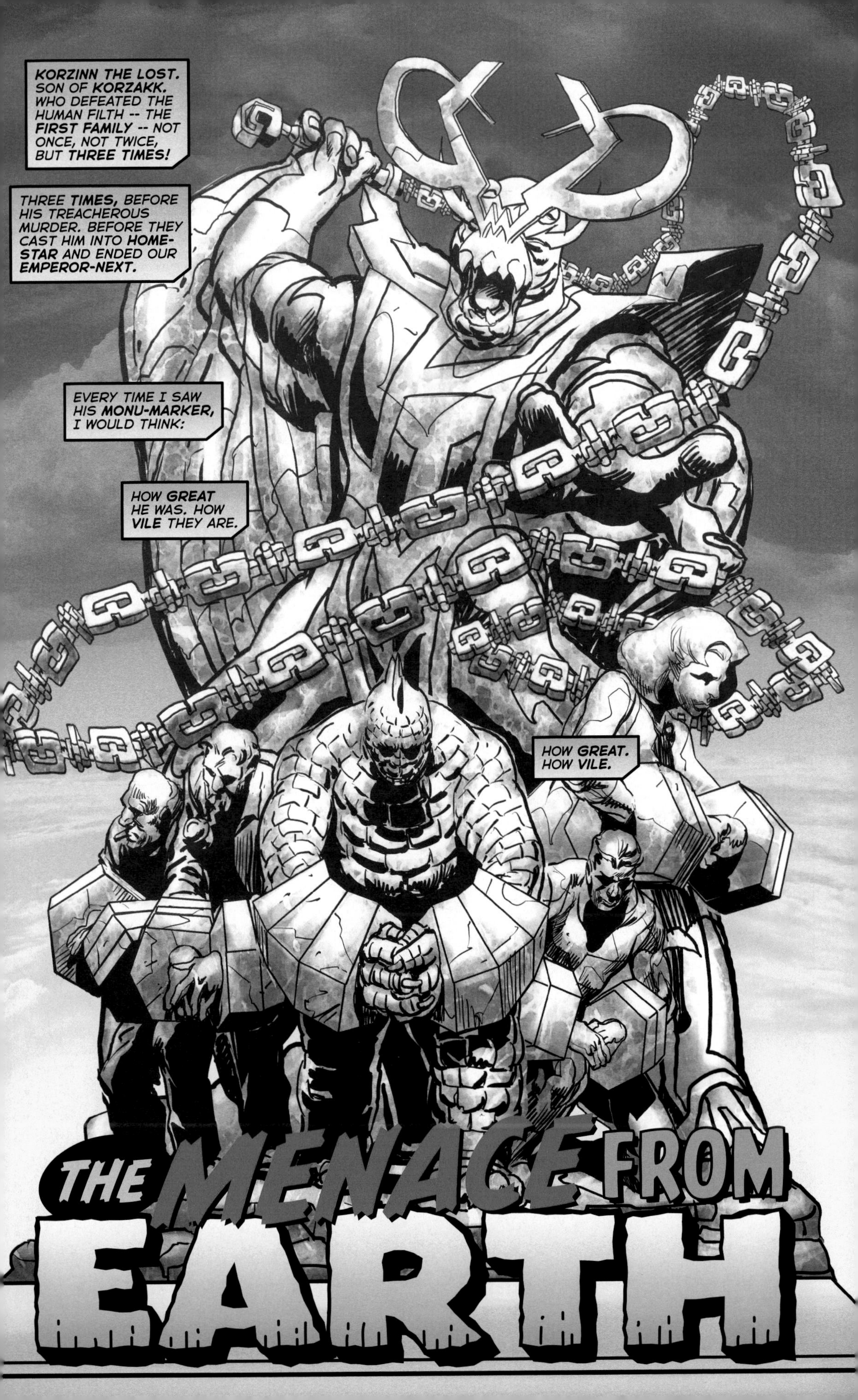
KORZINN THE LOST. SON OF KORZAKK. WHO DEFEATED THE HUMAN FILTH -- THE FIRST FAMILY -- NOT ONCE, NOT TWICE, BUT THREE TIMES!
THREE TIMES, BEFORE HIS TREACHEROUS MURDER. BEFORE THEY CAST HIM INTO HOME-STAR AND ENDED OUR EMPEROR-NEXT.
EVERY TIME I SAW HIS MONU-MARKER, I WOULD THINK:
HOW GREAT HE WAS. HOW VILE THEY ARE.
HOW GREAT. HOW VILE.
THE MENACE FROM EARTH

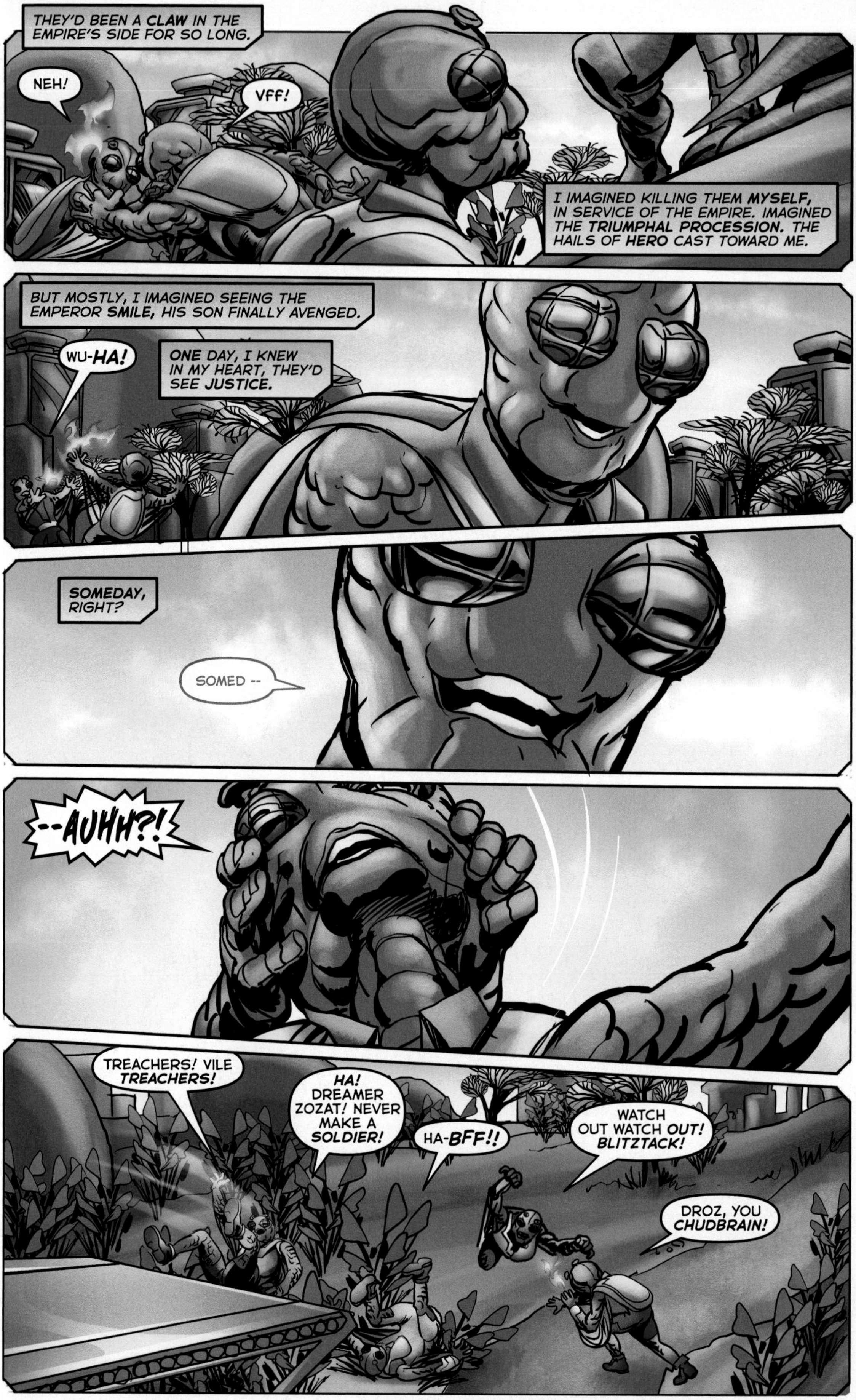
THEY'D BEEN A CLAW IN THE EMPIRE'S SIDE FOR SO LONG.
NEH!
VFF!
I IMAGINED KILLING THEM MYSELF, IN SERVICE OF THE EMPIRE. IMAGINED THE TRIUMPHAL PROCESSION. THE HAILS OF HERO CAST TOWARD ME.
BUT MOSTLY, I IMAGINED SEEING THE EMPEROR SMILE, HIS SON FINALLY AVENGED.
WU-HA!
ONE DAY, I KNEW IN MY HEART, THEY'D SEE JUSTICE.
SOMEDAY, RIGHT?
SOMED --
--AUHH?!
TREACHERS! VILE TREACHERS!
HA! DREAMER ZOZAT! NEVER MAKE A SOLDIER!
HA-BFF!!
WATCH OUT WATCH OUT! BLITZTACK!
DROZ, YOU CHUDBRAIN!

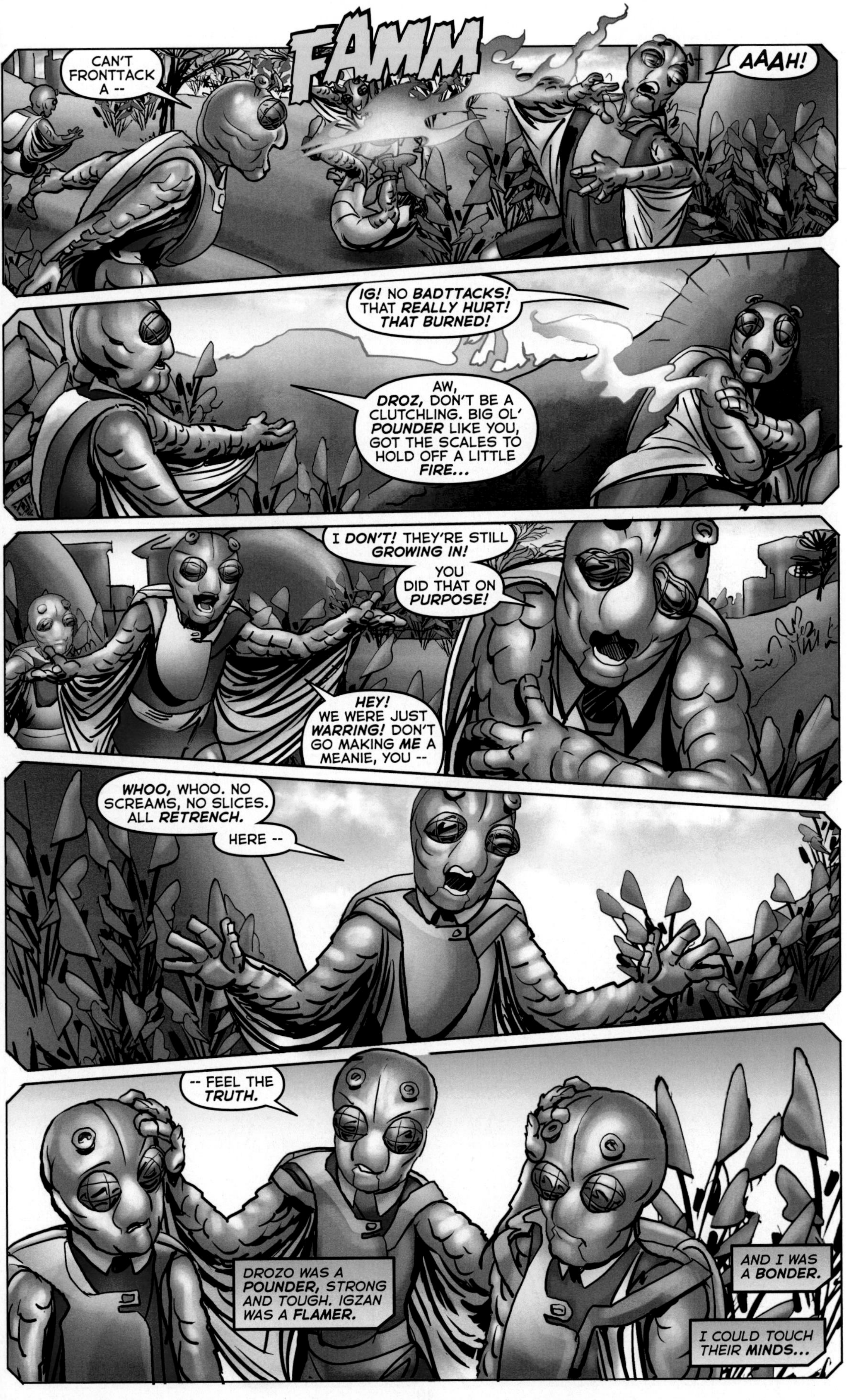
FAMM
CAN'T FRONTTACK A --
AAAH!
IG! NO BADTTACKS! THAT REALLY HURT! THAT BURNED!
AW, DROZ, DON'T BE A CLUTCHLING. BIG OL' POUNDER LIKE YOU, GOT THE SCALES TO HOLD OFF A LITTLE FIRE...
I DON'T! THEY'RE STILL GROWING IN!
YOU DID THAT ON PURPOSE!
HEY! WE WERE JUST WARRING! DON'T GO MAKING ME A MEANIE, YOU --
WHOO, WHOO. NO SCREAMS, NO SLICES. ALL RETRENCH.
HERE --
-- FEEL THE TRUTH.
DROZO WAS A POUNDER, STRONG AND TOUGH. IGZAN WAS A FLAMER.
AND I WAS A BONDER.
I COULD TOUCH THEIR MINDS...

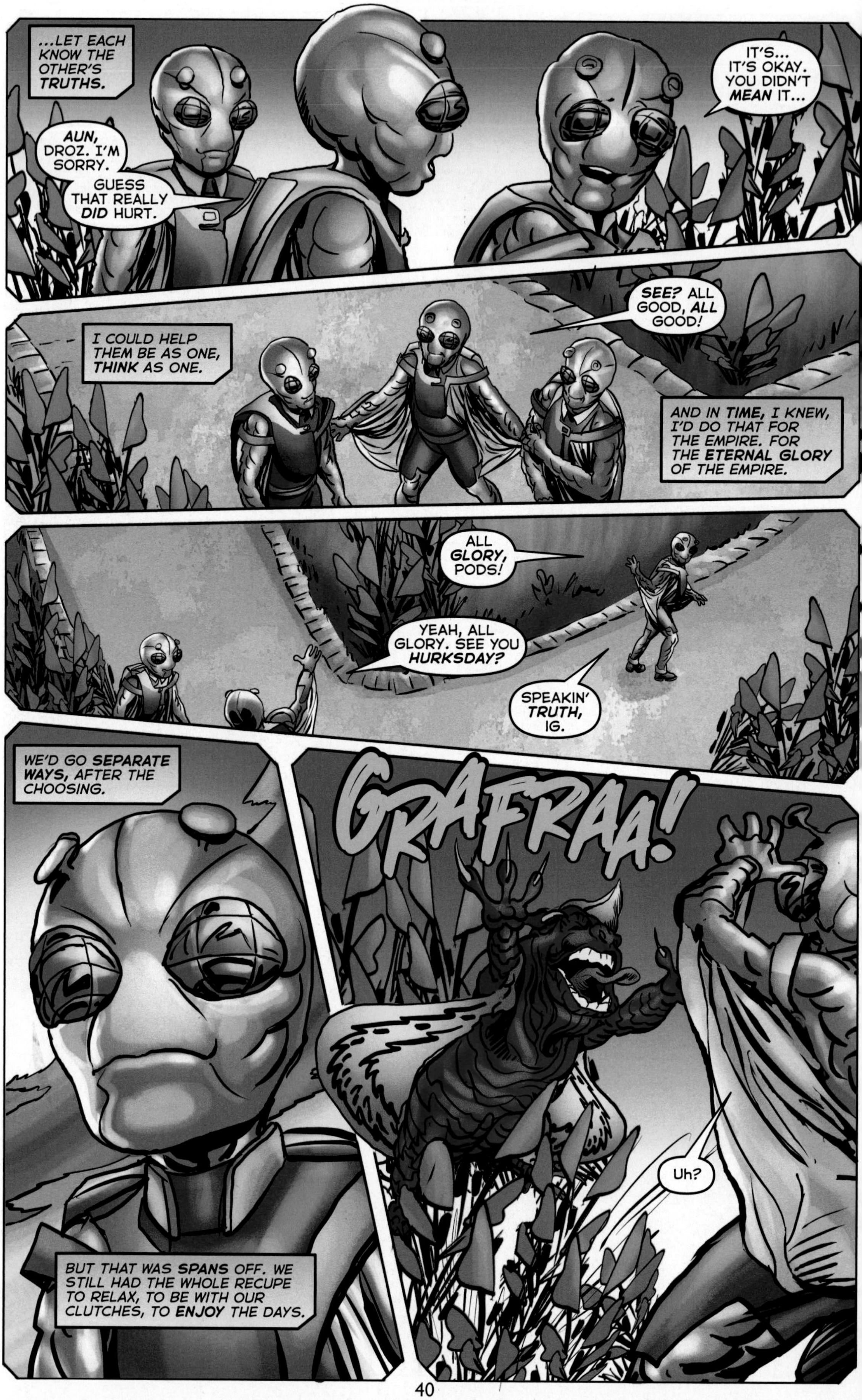
...LET EACH KNOW THE OTHER'S TRUTHS.
AUN, DROZ. I'M SORRY.
GUESS THAT REALLY DID HURT.
IT'S... IT'S OKAY. YOU DIDN'T MEAN IT...
I COULD HELP THEM BE AS ONE, THINK AS ONE.
SEE? ALL GOOD, ALL GOOD!
AND IN TIME, I KNEW, I'D DO THAT FOR THE EMPIRE. FOR THE ETERNAL GLORY OF THE EMPIRE.
ALL GLORY, PODS!
YEAH, ALL GLORY. SEE YOU HURKSDAY?
SPEAKIN' TRUTH, IG.
WE'D GO SEPARATE WAYS, AFTER THE CHOOSING.
BUT THAT WAS SPANS OFF. WE STILL HAD THE WHOLE RECUPE TO RELAX, TO BE WITH OUR CLUTCHES, TO ENJOY THE DAYS.
GRAFRAA!
Uh?

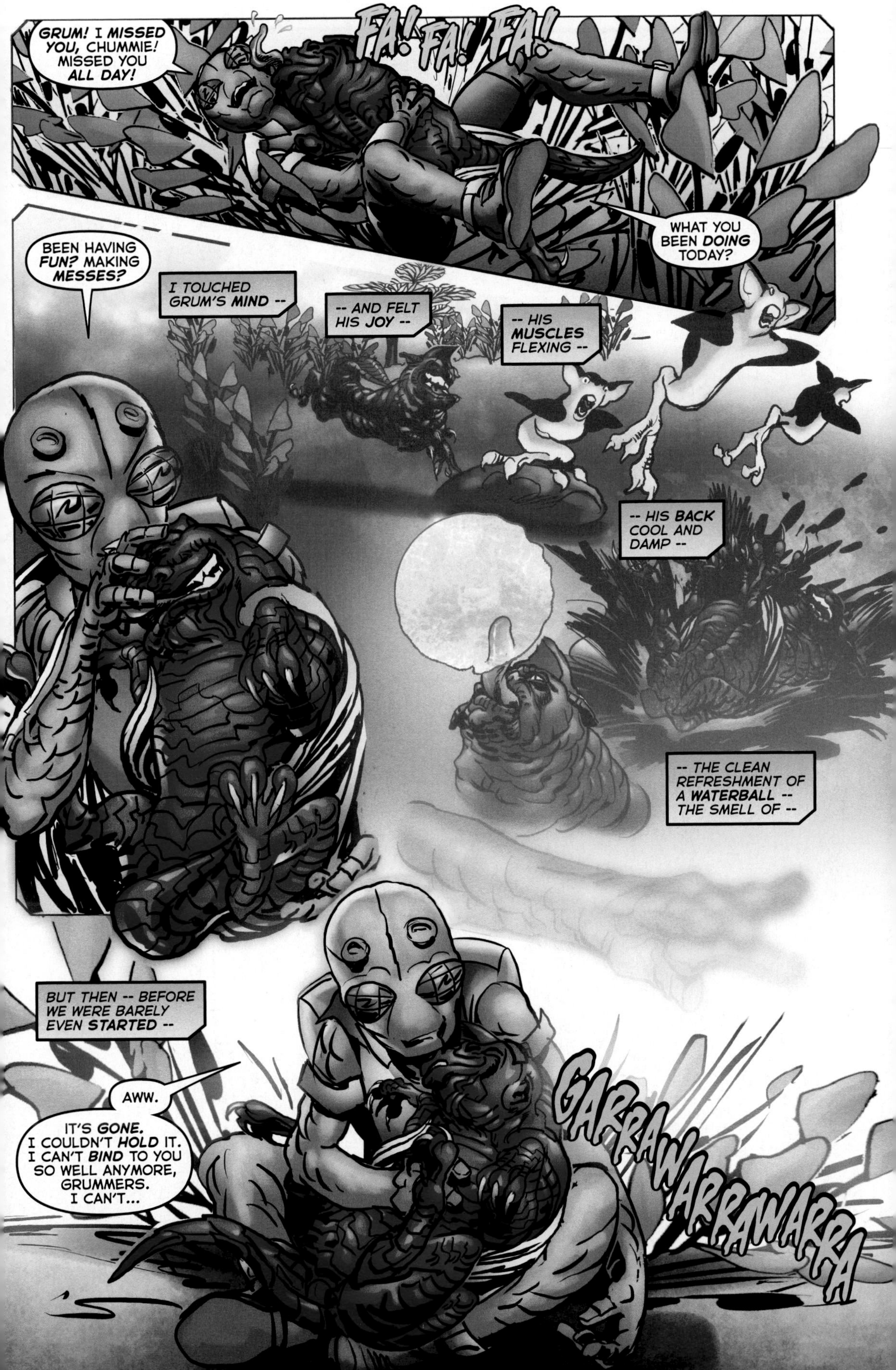
GRUM! I MISSED YOU, CHUMMIE! MISSED YOU ALL DAY!
FA! FA! FA!
WHAT YOU BEEN DOING TODAY?
BEEN HAVING FUN? MAKING MESSES?
I TOUCHED GRUM'S MIND --
-- AND FELT HIS JOY --
-- HIS MUSCLES FLEXING --
-- HIS BACK COOL AND DAMP --
-- THE CLEAN REFRESHMENT OF A WATERBALL -- THE SMELL OF --
BUT THEN -- BEFORE WE WERE BARELY EVEN STARTED --
AWW.
IT'S GONE. I COULDN'T HOLD IT. I CAN'T BIND TO YOU SO WELL ANYMORE, GRUMMERS. I CAN'T...
GARRAWARRAWARRA

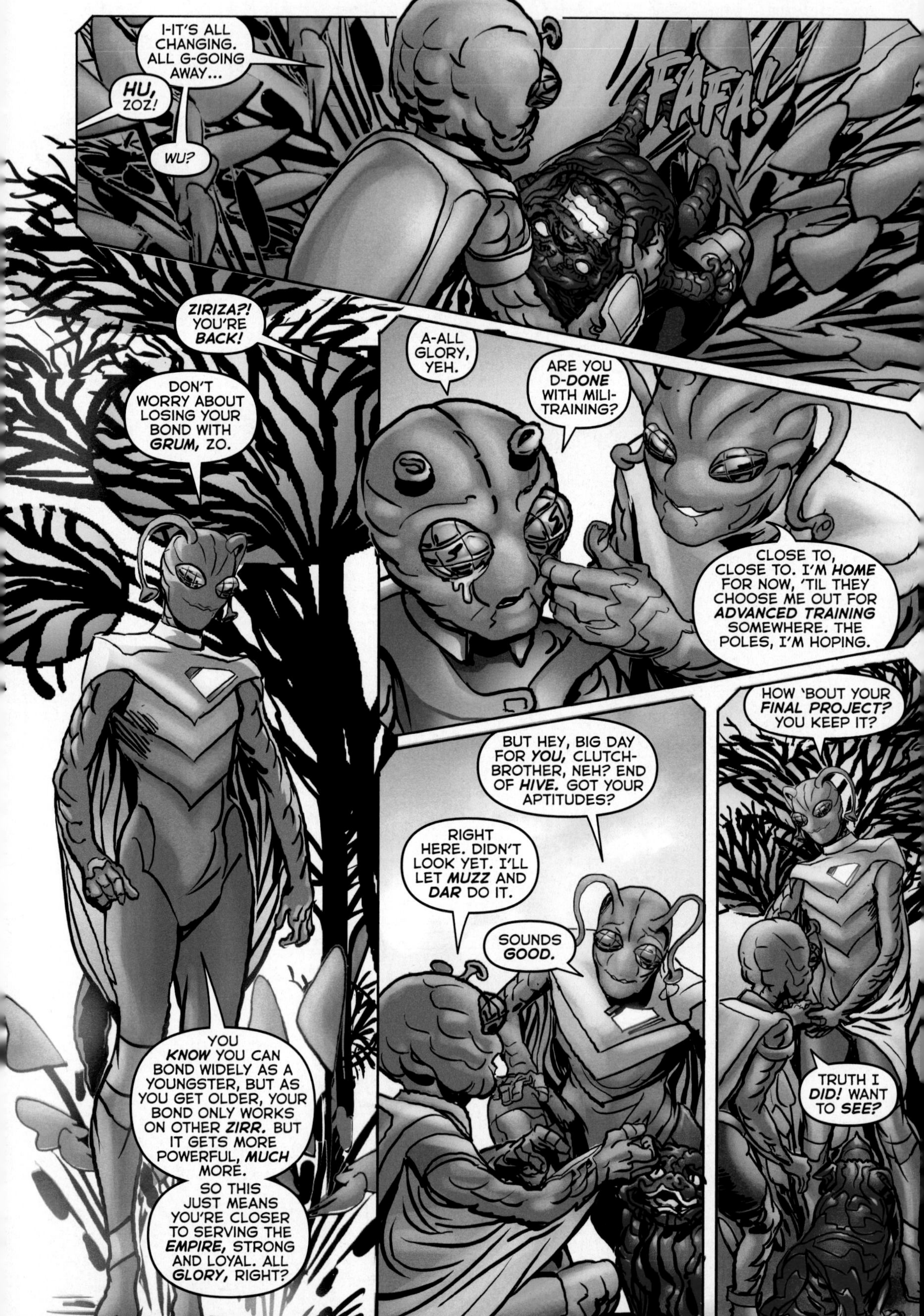
I-IT'S ALL CHANGING. ALL G-GOING AWAY...
HU, ZOZ!
WU?
FAFA!
ZIRIZA?! YOU'RE BACK!
A-ALL GLORY, YEH.
ARE YOU D-DONE WITH MILI-TRAINING?
CLOSE TO, CLOSE TO. I'M HOME FOR NOW, 'TIL THEY CHOOSE ME OUT FOR ADVANCED TRAINING SOMEWHERE. THE POLES, I'M HOPING.
DON'T WORRY ABOUT LOSING YOUR BOND WITH GRUM, ZO.
YOU KNOW YOU CAN BOND WIDELY AS A YOUNGSTER, BUT AS YOU GET OLDER, YOUR BOND ONLY WORKS ON OTHER ZIRR. BUT IT GETS MORE POWERFUL, MUCH MORE.
SO THIS JUST MEANS YOU'RE CLOSER TO SERVING THE EMPIRE, STRONG AND LOYAL. ALL GLORY, RIGHT?
BUT HEY, BIG DAY FOR YOU, CLUTCH-BROTHER, NEH? END OF HIVE. GOT YOUR APTITUDES?
RIGHT HERE. DIDN'T LOOK YET. I'LL LET MUZZ AND DAR DO IT.
SOUNDS GOOD.
HOW 'BOUT YOUR FINAL PROJECT? YOU KEEP IT?
TRUTH I DID! WANT TO SEE?

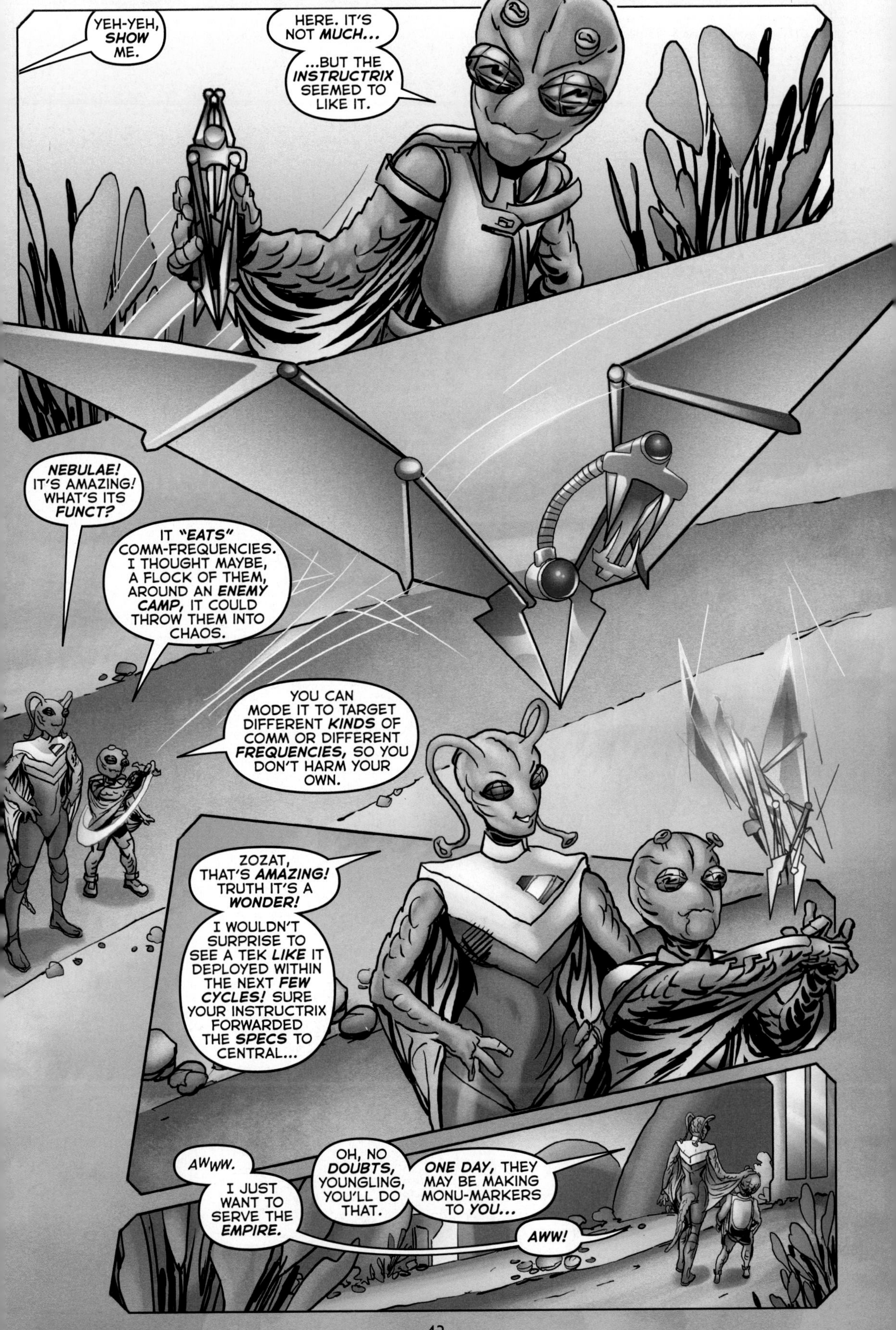
YEH-YEH, SHOW ME.
HERE. IT'S NOT MUCH...
...BUT THE INSTRUCTRIX SEEMED TO LIKE IT.
NEBULAE! IT'S AMAZING! WHAT'S ITS FUNCT?
IT "EATS" COMM-FREQUENCIES. I THOUGHT MAYBE, A FLOCK OF THEM, AROUND AN ENEMY CAMP, IT COULD THROW THEM INTO CHAOS.
YOU CAN MODE IT TO TARGET DIFFERENT KINDS OF COMM OR DIFFERENT FREQUENCIES, SO YOU DON'T HARM YOUR OWN.
ZOZAT, THAT'S AMAZING! TRUTH IT'S A WONDER!
I WOULDN'T SURPRISE TO SEE A TEK LIKE IT DEPLOYED WITHIN THE NEXT FEW CYCLES! SURE YOUR INSTRUCTRIX FORWARDED THE SPECS TO CENTRAL...
AWWW.
I JUST WANT TO SERVE THE EMPIRE.
OH, NO DOUBTS, YOUNGLING, YOU'LL DO THAT.
ONE DAY, THEY MAY BE MAKING MONU-MARKERS TO YOU...
AWW!

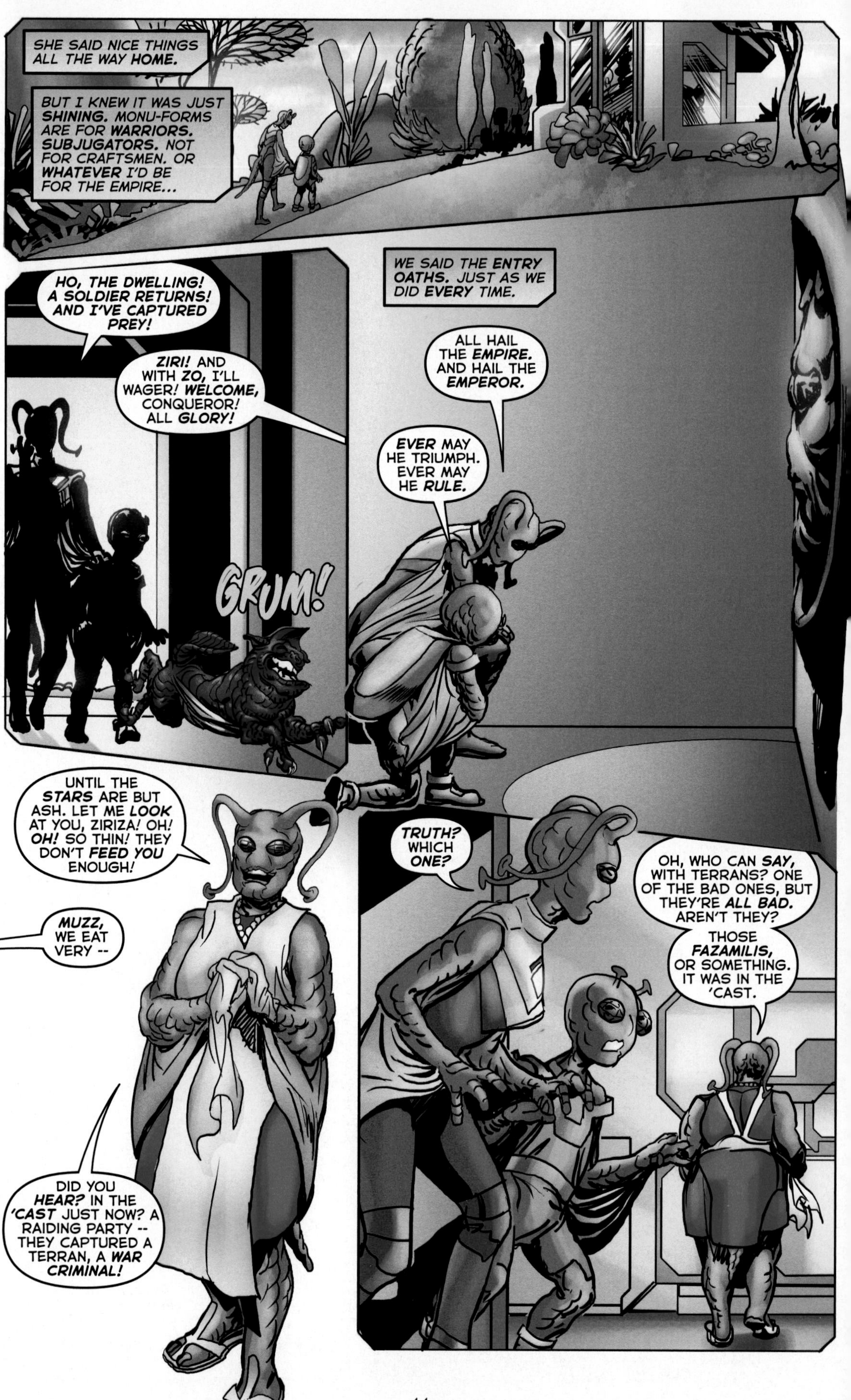

SHE SAID NICE THINGS ALL THE WAY HOME.
BUT I KNEW IT WAS JUST SHINING. MONU-FORMS ARE FOR WARRIORS. SUBJUGATORS. NOT FOR CRAFTSMEN. OR WHATEVER I'D BE FOR THE EMPIRE...
HO, THE DWELLING! A SOLDIER RETURNS! AND I'VE CAPTURED PREY!
ZIRI! AND WITH ZO, I'LL WAGER! WELCOME, CONQUEROR! ALL GLORY!
GRUM!
WE SAID THE ENTRY OATHS. JUST AS WE DID EVERY TIME.
ALL HAIL THE EMPIRE. AND HAIL THE EMPEROR.
EVER MAY HE TRIUMPH. EVER MAY HE RULE.
UNTIL THE STARS ARE BUT ASH. LET ME LOOK AT YOU, ZIRIZA! OH! OH! SO THIN! THEY DON'T FEED YOU ENOUGH!
MUZZ, WE EAT VERY --
DID YOU HEAR? IN THE 'CAST JUST NOW? A RAIDING PARTY -- THEY CAPTURED A TERRAN, A WAR CRIMINAL!
TRUTH? WHICH ONE?
OH, WHO CAN SAY, WITH TERRANS? ONE OF THE BAD ONES, BUT THEY'RE ALL BAD. AREN'T THEY?
THOSE FAZAMILIS, OR SOMETHING. IT WAS IN THE 'CAST.

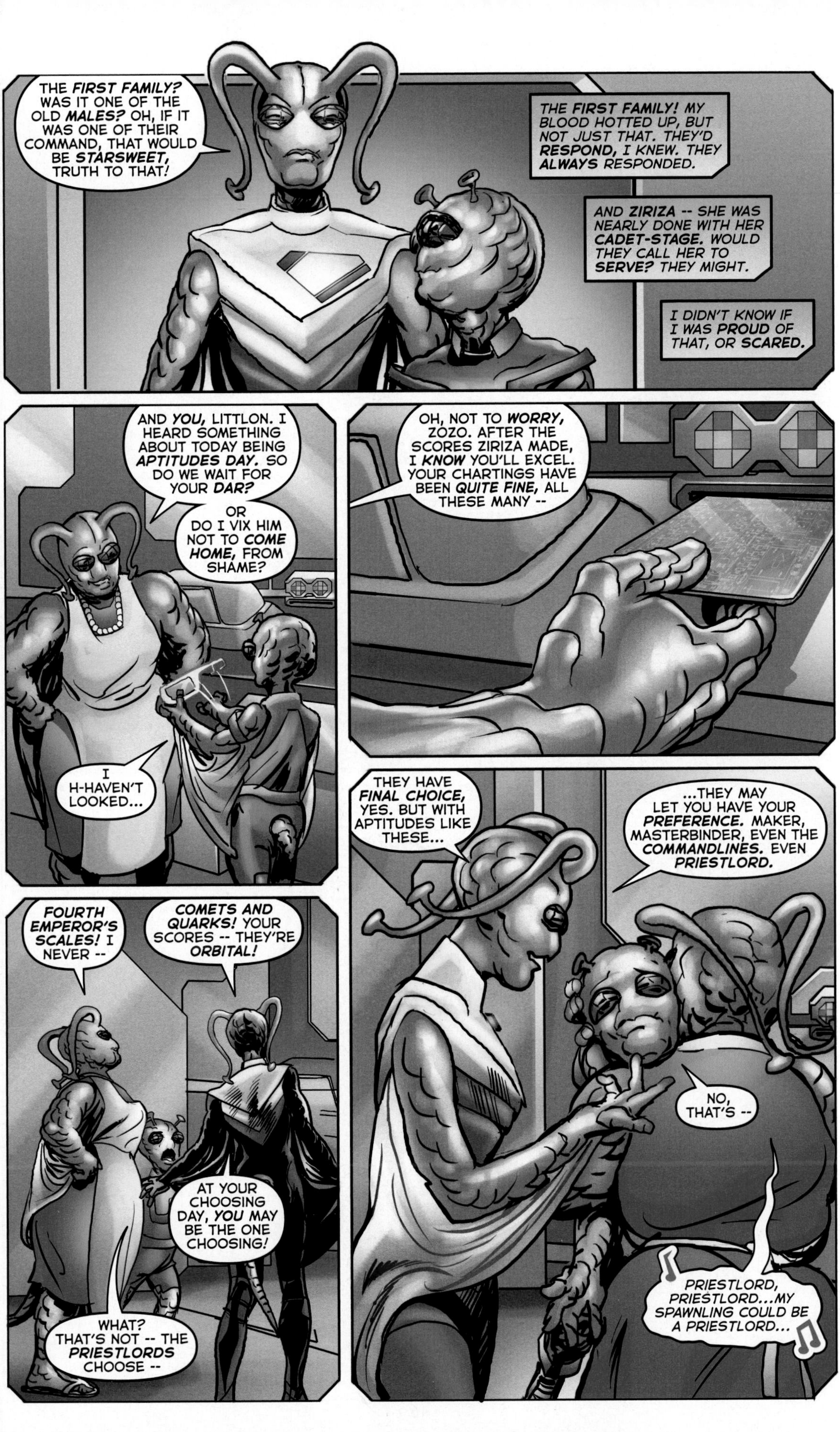
THE FIRST FAMILY? WAS IT ONE OF THE OLD MALES? OH, IF IT WAS ONE OF THEIR COMMAND, THAT WOULD BE STARSWEET, TRUTH TO THAT!
THE FIRST FAMILY! MY BLOOD HOTTED UP, BUT NOT JUST THAT. THEY'D RESPOND, I KNEW. THEY ALWAYS RESPONDED.
AND ZIRIZA -- SHE WAS NEARLY DONE WITH HER CADET-STAGE. WOULD THEY CALL HER TO SERVE? THEY MIGHT.
I DIDN'T KNOW IF I WAS PROUD OF THAT, OR SCARED.
AND YOU, LITTLON. I HEARD SOMETHING ABOUT TODAY BEING APTITUDES DAY. SO DO WE WAIT FOR YOUR DAR?
OR DO I VIX HIM NOT TO COME HOME, FROM SHAME?
I H-HAVEN'T LOOKED...
OH, NOT TO WORRY, ZOZO. AFTER THE SCORES ZIRIZA MADE, I KNOW YOU'LL EXCEL. YOUR CHARTINGS HAVE BEEN QUITE FINE, ALL THESE MANY --
FOURTH EMPEROR'S SCALES! I NEVER --
COMETS AND QUARKS! YOUR SCORES -- THEY'RE ORBITAL!
AT YOUR CHOOSING DAY, YOU MAY BE THE ONE CHOOSING!
WHAT? THAT'S NOT -- THE PRIESTLORDS CHOOSE --
THEY HAVE FINAL CHOICE, YES. BUT WITH APTITUDES LIKE THESE...
...THEY MAY LET YOU HAVE YOUR PREFERENCE. MAKER, MASTERBINDER, EVEN THE COMMANDLINES. EVEN PRIESTLORD.
NO, THAT'S --
PRIESTLORD, PRIESTLORD...MY SPAWNLING COULD BE A PRIESTLORD...

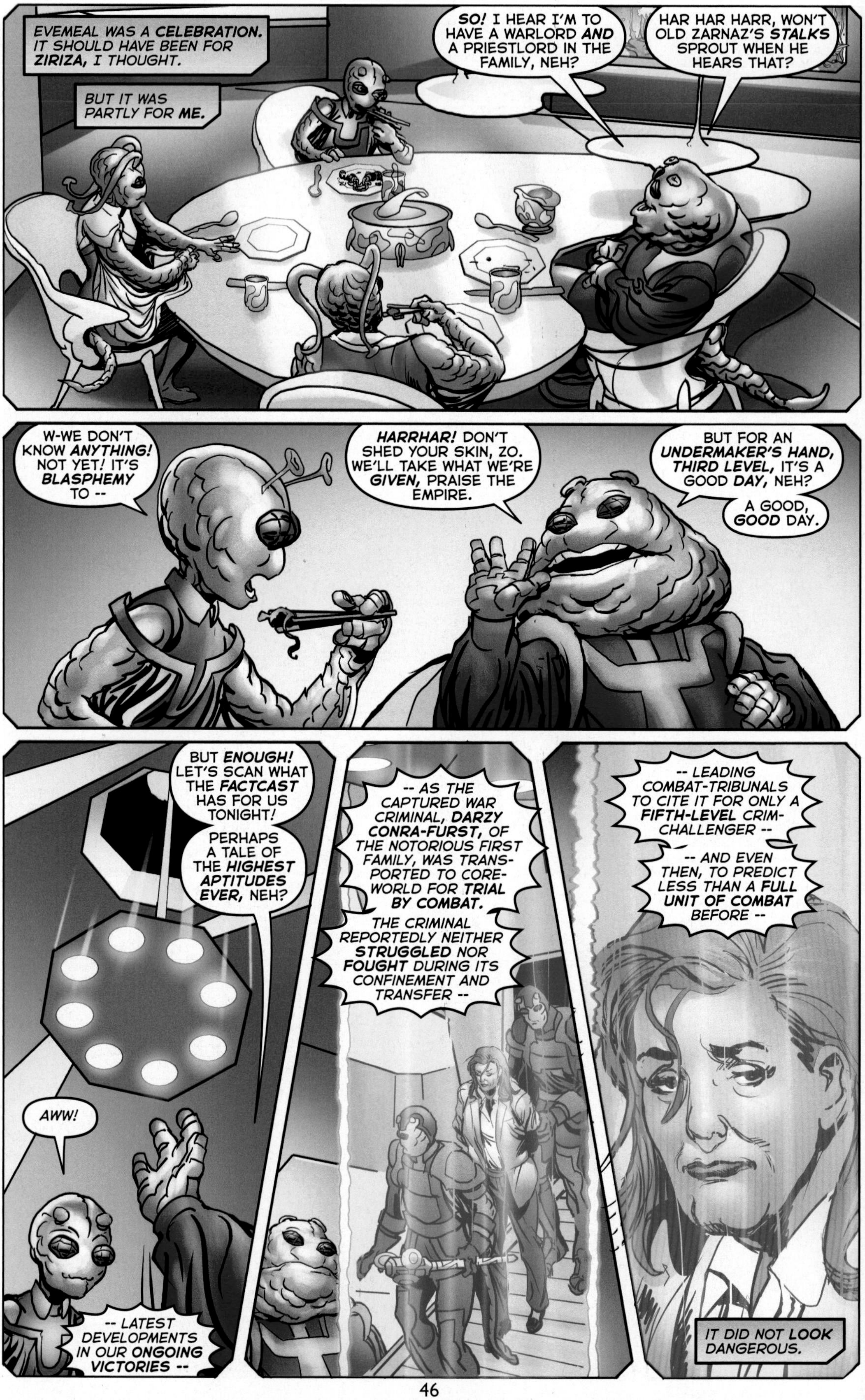

EVEMEAL WAS A CELEBRATION. IT SHOULD HAVE BEEN FOR ZIRIZA, I THOUGHT.
BUT IT WAS PARTLY FOR ME.
SO! I HEAR I'M TO HAVE A WARLORD AND A PRIESTLORD IN THE FAMILY, NEH?
HAR HAR HARR, WON'T OLD ZARNAZ'S STALKS SPROUT WHEN HE HEARS THAT?
W-WE DON'T KNOW ANYTHING! NOT YET! IT'S BLASPHEMY TO --
HARRHAR! DON'T SHED YOUR SKIN, ZO. WE'LL TAKE WHAT WE'RE GIVEN, PRAISE THE EMPIRE.
BUT FOR AN UNDERMAKER'S HAND, THIRD LEVEL, IT'S A GOOD DAY, NEH?
A GOOD, GOOD DAY.
BUT ENOUGH! LET'S SCAN WHAT THE FACTCAST HAS FOR US TONIGHT!
PERHAPS A TALE OF THE HIGHEST APTITUDES EVER, NEH?
AWW!
-- LATEST DEVELOPMENTS IN OUR ONGOING VICTORIES --
-- AS THE CAPTURED WAR CRIMINAL, DARZY CONRA-FURST, OF THE NOTORIOUS FIRST FAMILY, WAS TRANSPORTED TO CORE-WORLD FOR TRIAL BY COMBAT.
THE CRIMINAL REPORTEDLY NEITHER STRUGGLED NOR FOUGHT DURING ITS CONFINEMENT AND TRANSFER --
-- LEADING COMBAT-TRIBUNALS TO CITE IT FOR ONLY A FIFTH-LEVEL CRIM-CHALLENGER --
-- AND EVEN THEN, TO PREDICT LESS THAN A FULL UNIT OF COMBAT BEFORE --
IT DID NOT LOOK DANGEROUS.

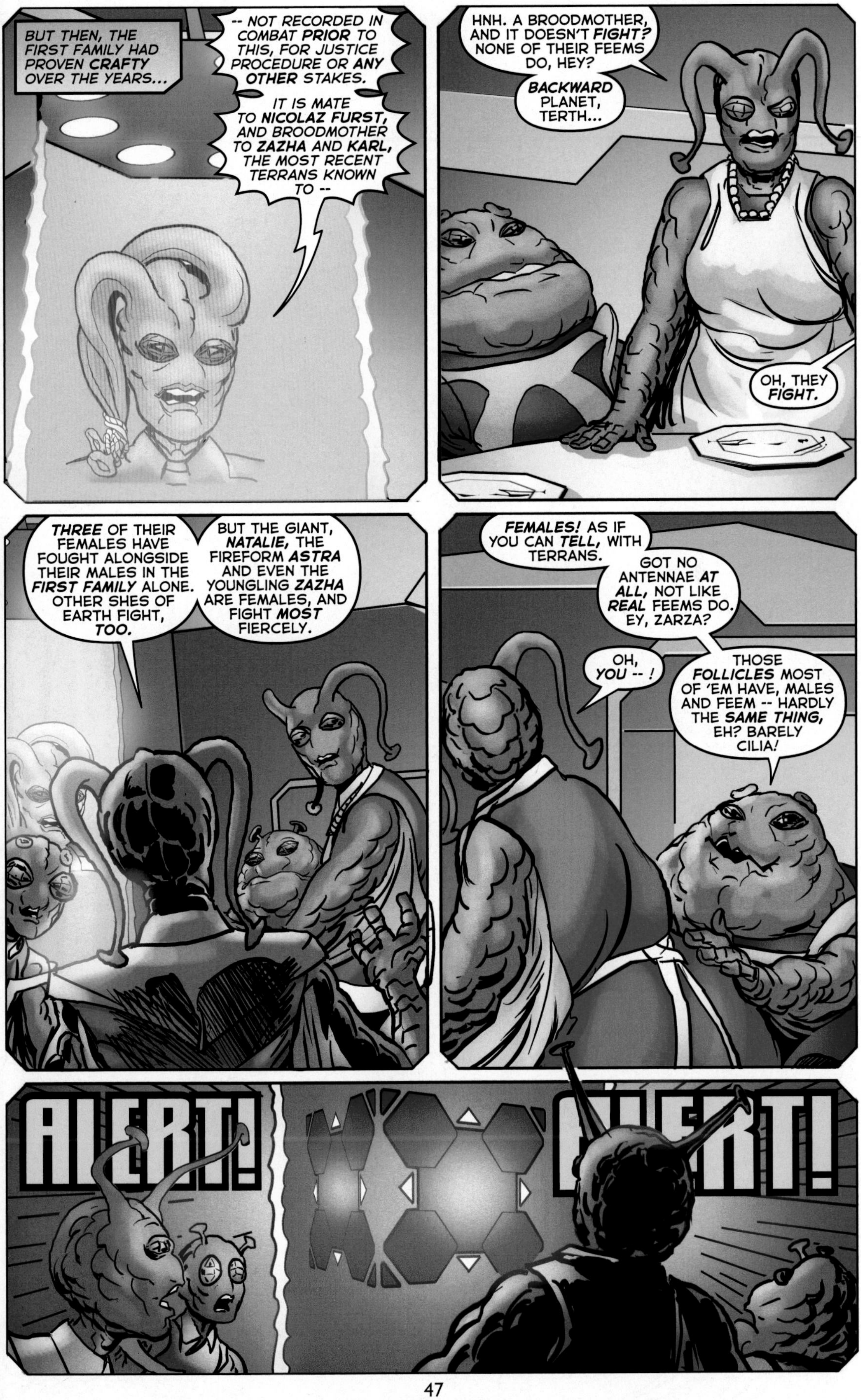
BUT THEN, THE FIRST FAMILY HAD PROVEN CRAFTY OVER THE YEARS...
-- NOT RECORDED IN COMBAT PRIOR TO THIS, FOR JUSTICE PROCEDURE OR ANY OTHER STAKES.
IT IS MATE TO NICOLAZ FURST, AND BROODMOTHER TO ZAZHA AND KARL, THE MOST RECENT TERRANS KNOWN TO --
HNH. A BROODMOTHER, AND IT DOESN'T FIGHT? NONE OF THEIR FEEMS DO, HEY?
BACKWARD PLANET, TERTH...
OH, THEY FIGHT.
THREE OF THEIR FEMALES HAVE FOUGHT ALONGSIDE THEIR MALES IN THE FIRST FAMILY ALONE. OTHER SHES OF EARTH FIGHT, TOO.
BUT THE GIANT, NATALIE, THE FIREFORM ASTRA AND EVEN THE YOUNGLING ZAZHA ARE FEMALES, AND FIGHT MOST FIERCELY.
FEMALES! AS IF YOU CAN TELL, WITH TERRANS.
GOT NO ANTENNAE AT ALL, NOT LIKE REAL FEEMS DO. EY, ZARZA?
OH, YOU -- !
THOSE FOLLICLES MOST OF 'EM HAVE, MALES AND FEEM -- HARDLY THE SAME THING, EH? BARELY CILIA!
ALERT!
ALERT!

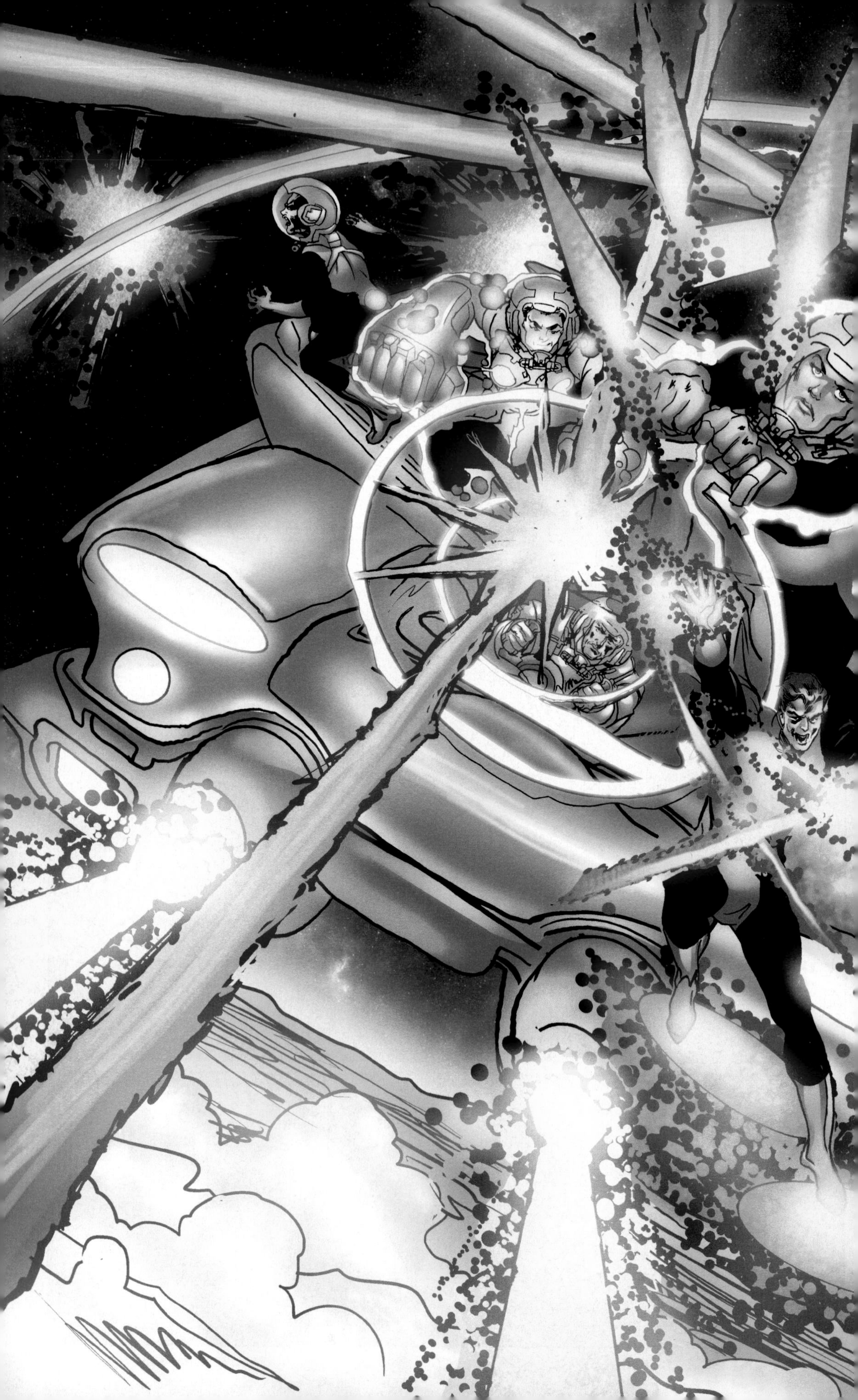

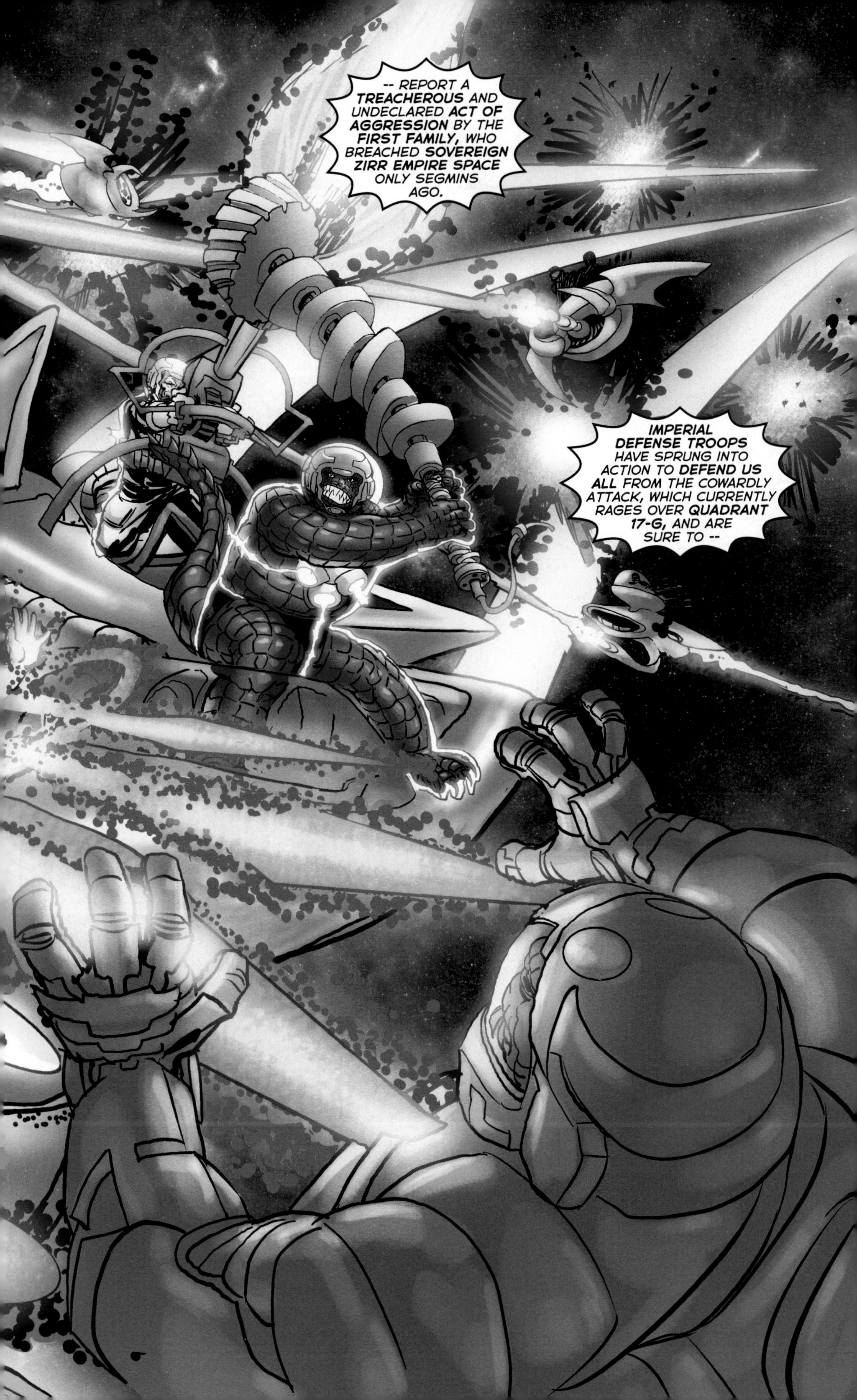
-- REPORT A TREACHEROUS AND UNDECLARED ACT OF AGGRESSION BY THE FIRST FAMILY, WHO BREACHED SOVEREIGN ZIRR EMPIRE SPACE ONLY SEGMINS AGO.
IMPERIAL DEFENSE TROOPS HAVE SPRUNG INTO ACTION TO DEFEND US ALL FROM THE COWARDLY ATTACK, WHICH CURRENTLY RAGES OVER QUADRANT 17-G, AND ARE SURE TO --

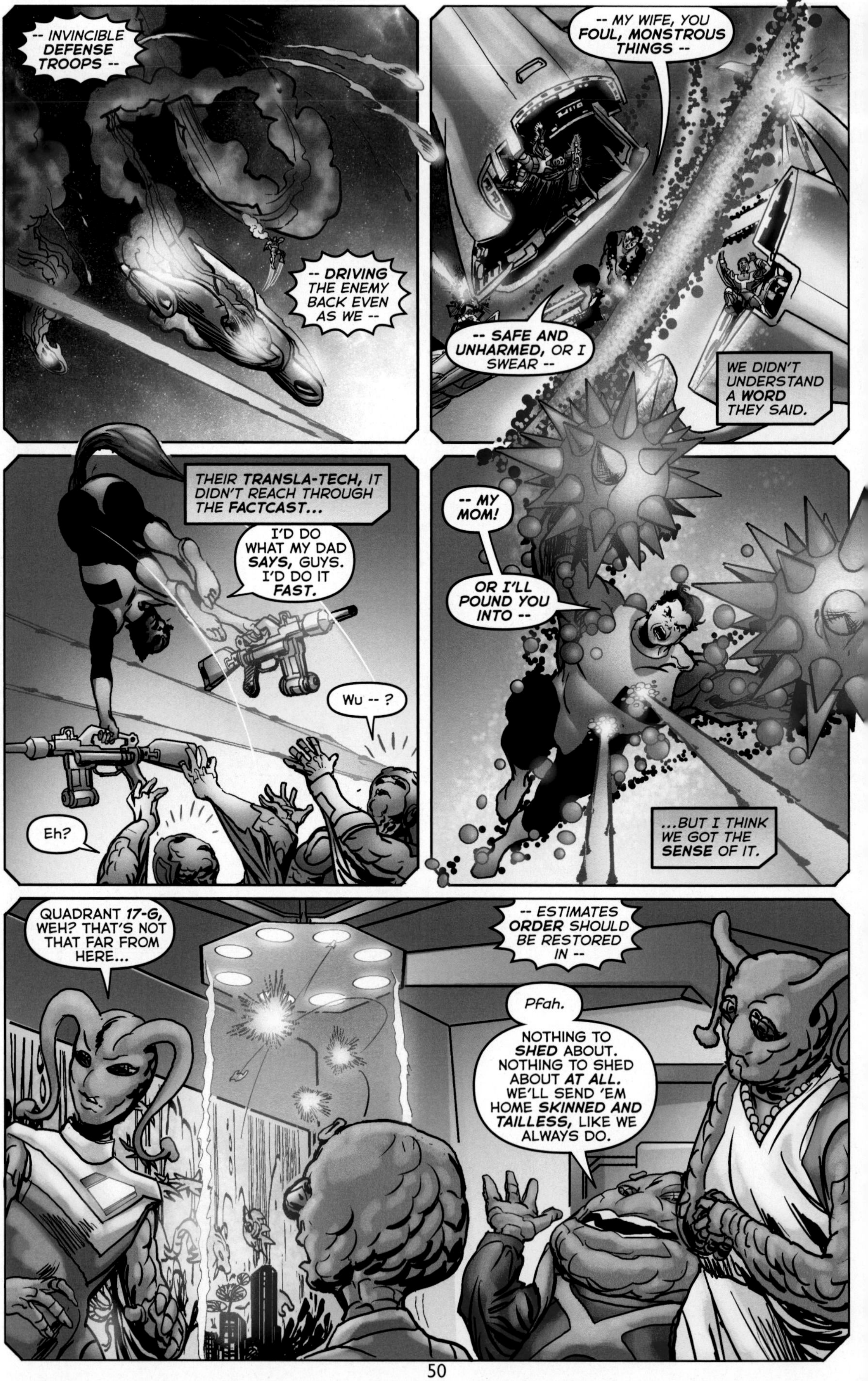
-- INVINCIBLE DEFENSE TROOPS --
-- DRIVING THE ENEMY BACK EVEN AS WE --
-- MY WIFE, YOU FOUL, MONSTROUS THINGS --
-- SAFE AND UNHARMED, OR I SWEAR --
WE DIDN'T UNDERSTAND A WORD THEY SAID.
THEIR TRANSLA-TECH, IT DIDN'T REACH THROUGH THE FACTCAST...
I'D DO WHAT MY DAD SAYS, GUYS. I'D DO IT FAST.
Wu -- ?
Eh?
-- MY MOM!
OR I'LL POUND YOU INTO --
...BUT I THINK WE GOT THE SENSE OF IT.
QUADRANT 17-G, WEH? THAT'S NOT THAT FAR FROM HERE...
-- ESTIMATES ORDER SHOULD BE RESTORED IN --
Pfah.
NOTHING TO SHED ABOUT. NOTHING TO SHED ABOUT AT ALL. WE'LL SEND 'EM HOME SKINNED AND TAILLESS, LIKE WE ALWAYS DO.

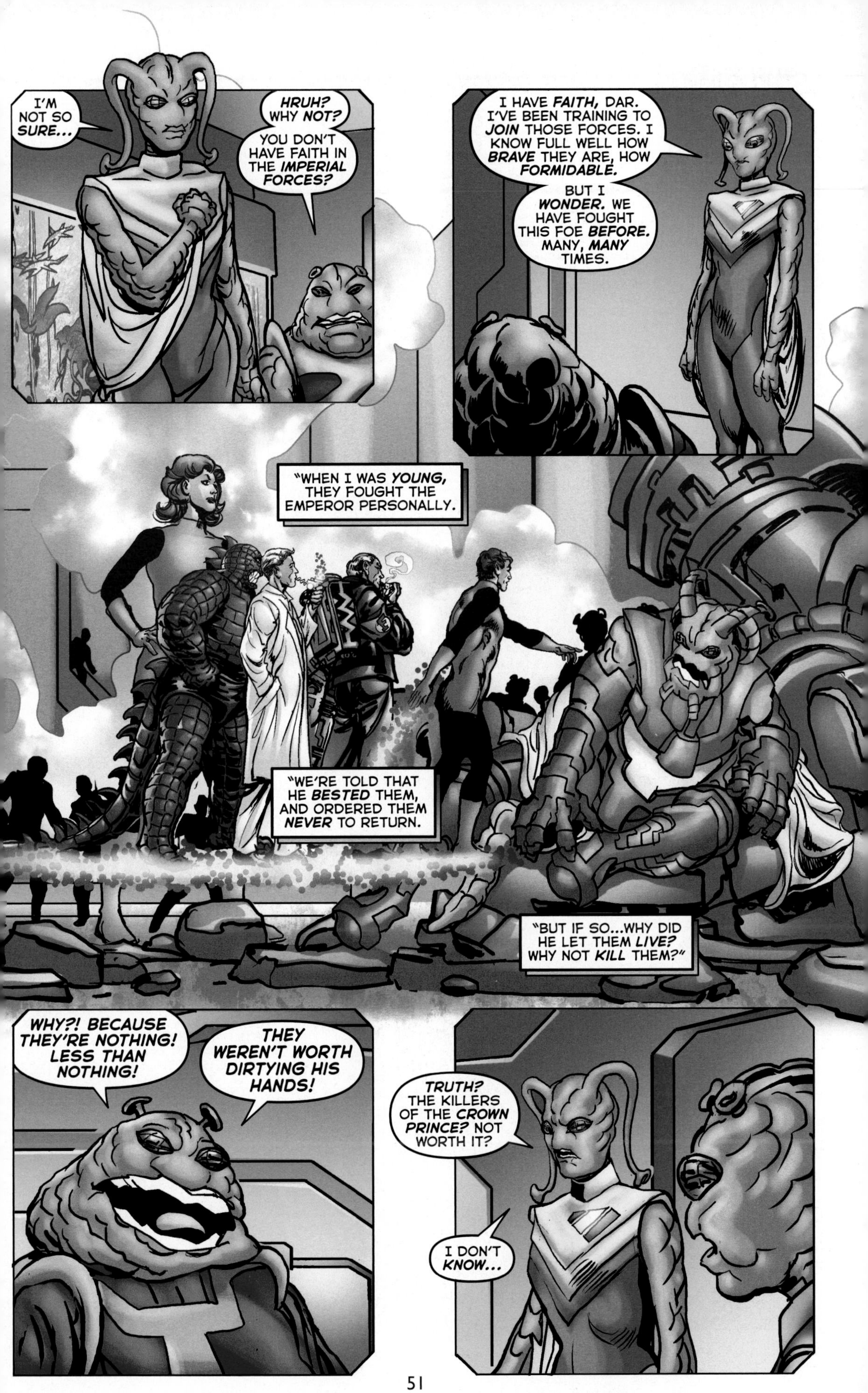
I'M NOT SO SURE...
HRUH? WHY NOT?
YOU DON'T HAVE FAITH IN THE IMPERIAL FORCES?
I HAVE FAITH, DAR. I'VE BEEN TRAINING TO JOIN THOSE FORCES. I KNOW FULL WELL HOW BRAVE THEY ARE, HOW FORMIDABLE.
BUT I WONDER. WE HAVE FOUGHT THIS FOE BEFORE. MANY, MANY TIMES.
"WHEN I WAS YOUNG, THEY FOUGHT THE EMPEROR PERSONALLY.
"WE'RE TOLD THAT HE BESTED THEM, AND ORDERED THEM NEVER TO RETURN.
"BUT IF SO...WHY DID HE LET THEM LIVE? WHY NOT KILL THEM?"
WHY?! BECAUSE THEY'RE NOTHING! LESS THAN NOTHING!
THEY WEREN'T WORTH DIRTYING HIS HANDS!
TRUTH? THE KILLERS OF THE CROWN PRINCE? NOT WORTH IT?
I DON'T KNOW...

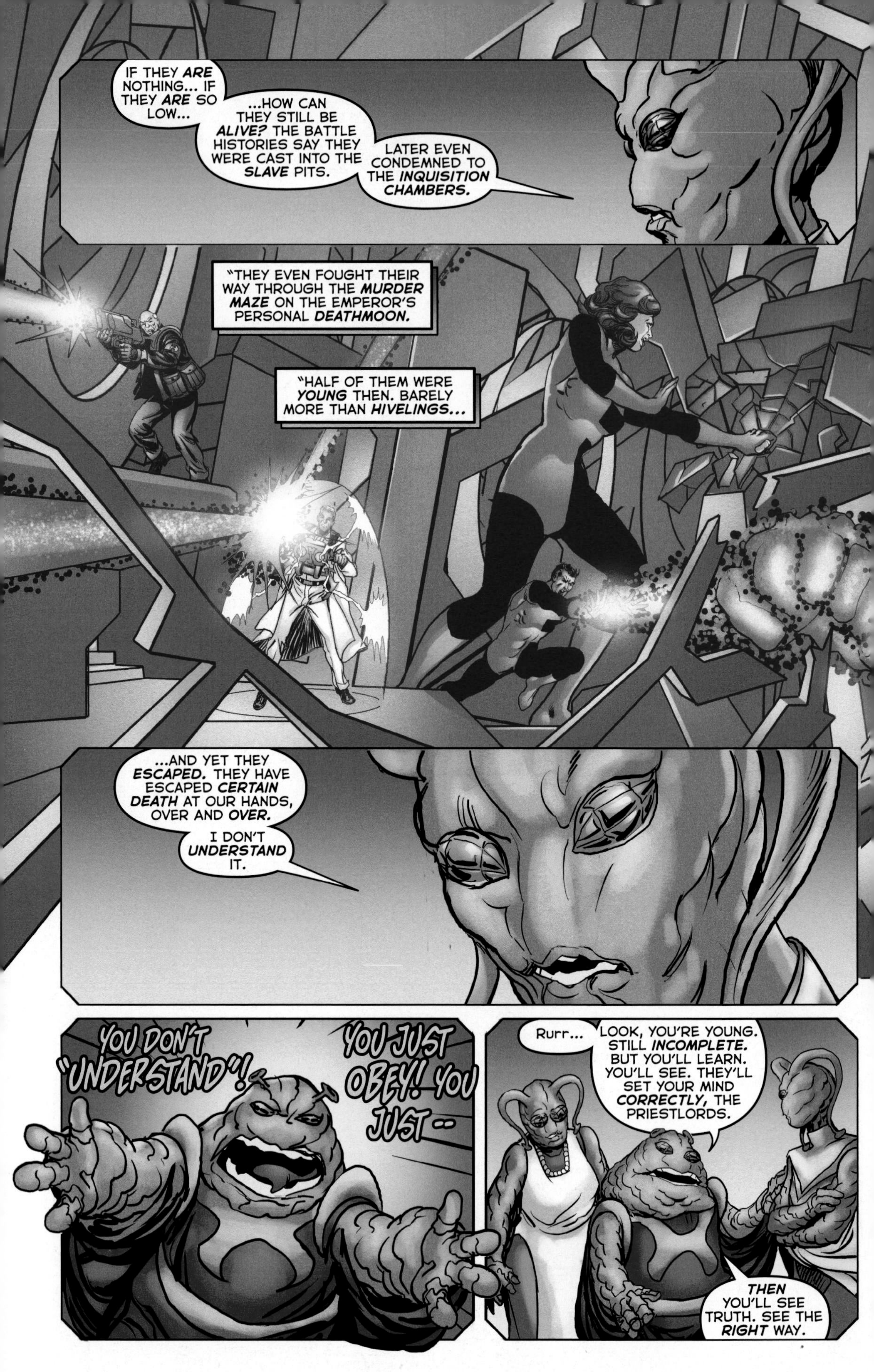
IF THEY ARE NOTHING... IF THEY ARE SO LOW...
...HOW CAN THEY STILL BE ALIVE? THE BATTLE HISTORIES SAY THEY WERE CAST INTO THE SLAVE PITS.
LATER EVEN CONDEMNED TO THE INQUISITION CHAMBERS.
"THEY EVEN FOUGHT THEIR WAY THROUGH THE MURDER MAZE ON THE EMPEROR'S PERSONAL DEATHMOON.
"HALF OF THEM WERE YOUNG THEN. BARELY MORE THAN HIVELINGS...
...AND YET THEY ESCAPED. THEY HAVE ESCAPED CERTAIN DEATH AT OUR HANDS, OVER AND OVER.
I DON'T UNDERSTAND IT.
YOU DON'T "UNDERSTAND"!
YOU JUST OBEY! YOU JUST --
Rurr...
LOOK, YOU'RE YOUNG. STILL INCOMPLETE. BUT YOU'LL LEARN. YOU'LL SEE. THEY'LL SET YOUR MIND CORRECTLY, THE PRIESTLORDS.
THEN YOU'LL SEE TRUTH. SEE THE RIGHT WAY.

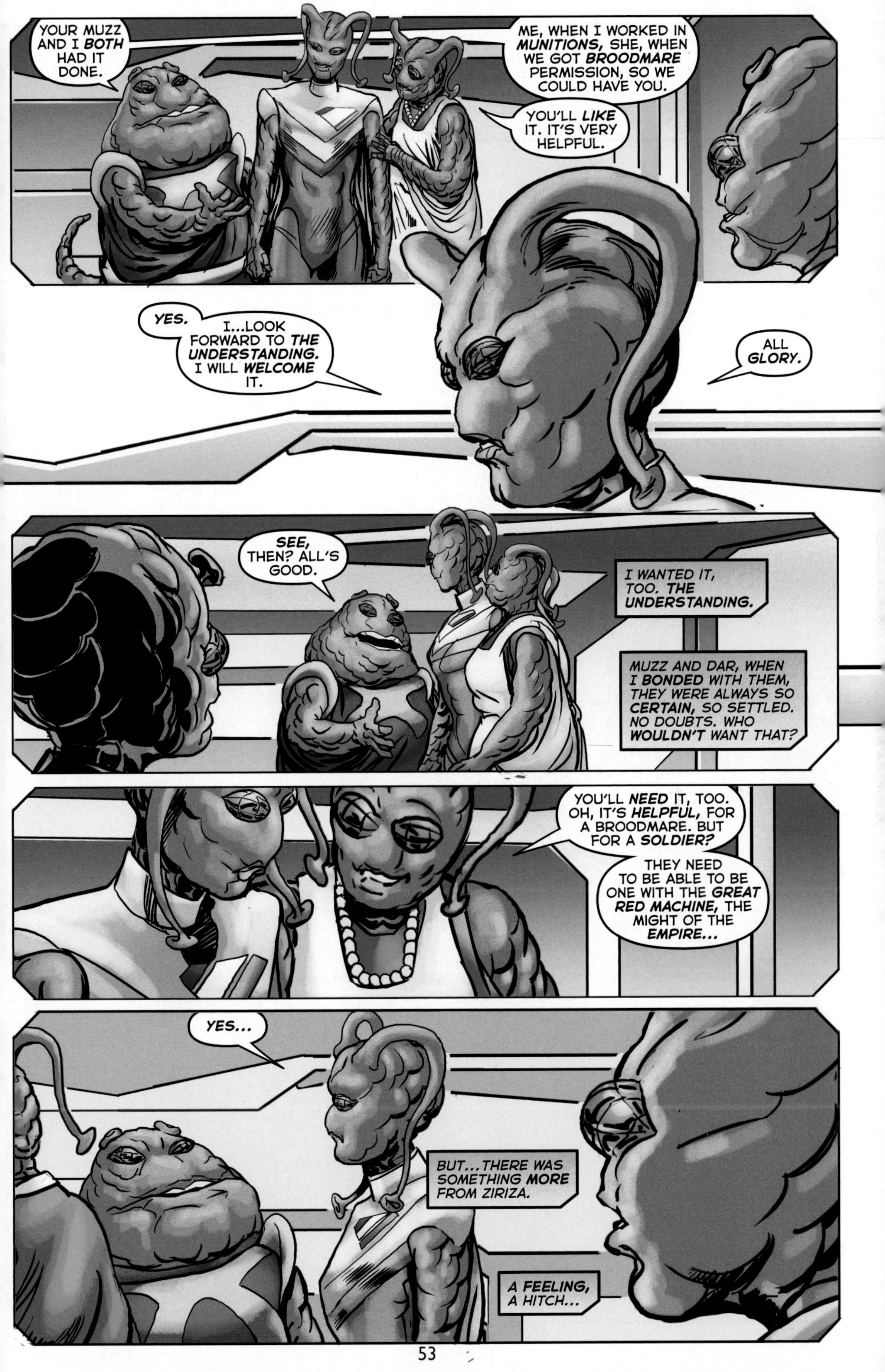
YOUR MUZZ AND I *BOTH* HAD IT DONE.
ME, WHEN I WORKED IN *MUNITIONS,* SHE, WHEN WE GOT *BROODMARE* PERMISSION, SO WE COULD HAVE YOU.
YOU'LL *LIKE* IT. IT'S VERY HELPFUL.
YES.
I...LOOK FORWARD TO *THE UNDERSTANDING.* I WILL *WELCOME* IT.
ALL *GLORY.*
SEE, THEN? ALL'S GOOD.
I WANTED IT, TOO. THE UNDERSTANDING.
MUZZ AND DAR, WHEN I BONDED WITH THEM, THEY WERE ALWAYS SO CERTAIN, SO SETTLED. NO DOUBTS. WHO WOULDN'T WANT THAT?
YOU'LL *NEED* IT, TOO. OH, IT'S *HELPFUL,* FOR A BROODMARE. BUT FOR A *SOLDIER?*
THEY NEED TO BE ABLE TO BE ONE WITH THE *GREAT RED MACHINE,* THE MIGHT OF THE *EMPIRE...*
YES...
BUT...THERE WAS SOMETHING MORE FROM ZIRIZA.
A FEELING, A HITCH...

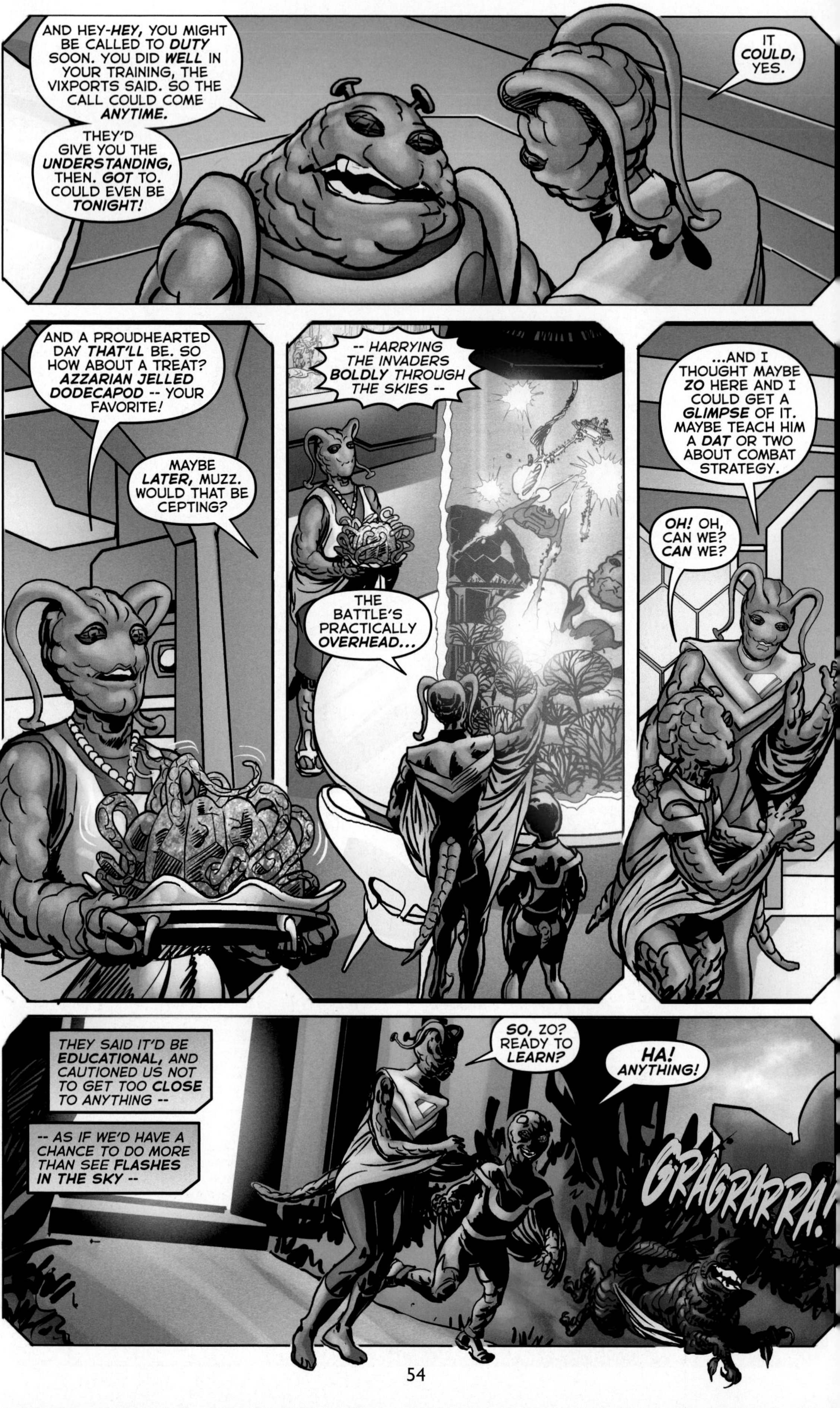

AND HEY-HEY, YOU MIGHT BE CALLED TO DUTY SOON. YOU DID WELL IN YOUR TRAINING, THE VIXPORTS SAID. SO THE CALL COULD COME ANYTIME.
THEY'D GIVE YOU THE UNDERSTANDING, THEN. GOT TO. COULD EVEN BE TONIGHT!
IT COULD, YES.
AND A PROUDHEARTED DAY THAT'LL BE. SO HOW ABOUT A TREAT? AZZARIAN JELLED DODECAPOD -- YOUR FAVORITE!
MAYBE LATER, MUZZ. WOULD THAT BE CEPTING?
-- HARRYING THE INVADERS BOLDLY THROUGH THE SKIES --
THE BATTLE'S PRACTICALLY OVERHEAD...
...AND I THOUGHT MAYBE ZO HERE AND I COULD GET A GLIMPSE OF IT. MAYBE TEACH HIM A DAT OR TWO ABOUT COMBAT STRATEGY.
OH! OH, CAN WE? CAN WE?
THEY SAID IT'D BE EDUCATIONAL, AND CAUTIONED US NOT TO GET TOO CLOSE TO ANYTHING --
-- AS IF WE'D HAVE A CHANCE TO DO MORE THAN SEE FLASHES IN THE SKY --
SO, ZO? READY TO LEARN?
HA! ANYTHING!
GRAGRARRA!

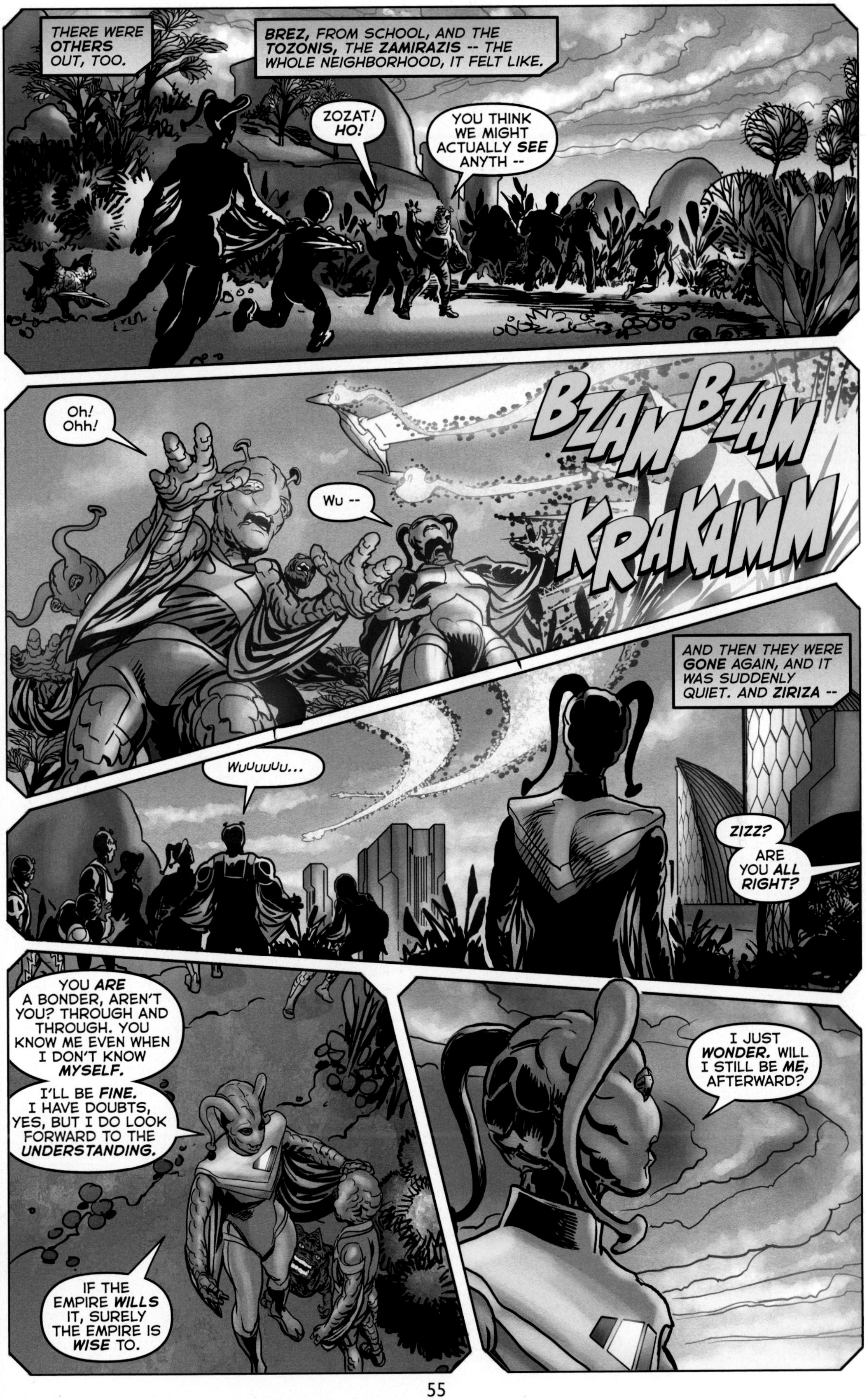

THERE WERE OTHERS OUT, TOO.
BREZ, FROM SCHOOL, AND THE TOZONIS, THE ZAMIRAZIS -- THE WHOLE NEIGHBORHOOD, IT FELT LIKE.
ZOZAT! HO!
YOU THINK WE MIGHT ACTUALLY SEE ANYTH --
Oh! Ohh!
Wu --
BZAM BZAM
KRAKAMM
AND THEN THEY WERE GONE AGAIN, AND IT WAS SUDDENLY QUIET. AND ZIRIZA --
WUUUUUU...
ZIZZ?
ARE YOU ALL RIGHT?
YOU ARE A BONDER, AREN'T YOU? THROUGH AND THROUGH. YOU KNOW ME EVEN WHEN I DON'T KNOW MYSELF.
I'LL BE FINE. I HAVE DOUBTS, YES, BUT I DO LOOK FORWARD TO THE UNDERSTANDING.
IF THE EMPIRE WILLS IT, SURELY THE EMPIRE IS WISE TO.
I JUST WONDER. WILL I STILL BE ME, AFTERWARD?

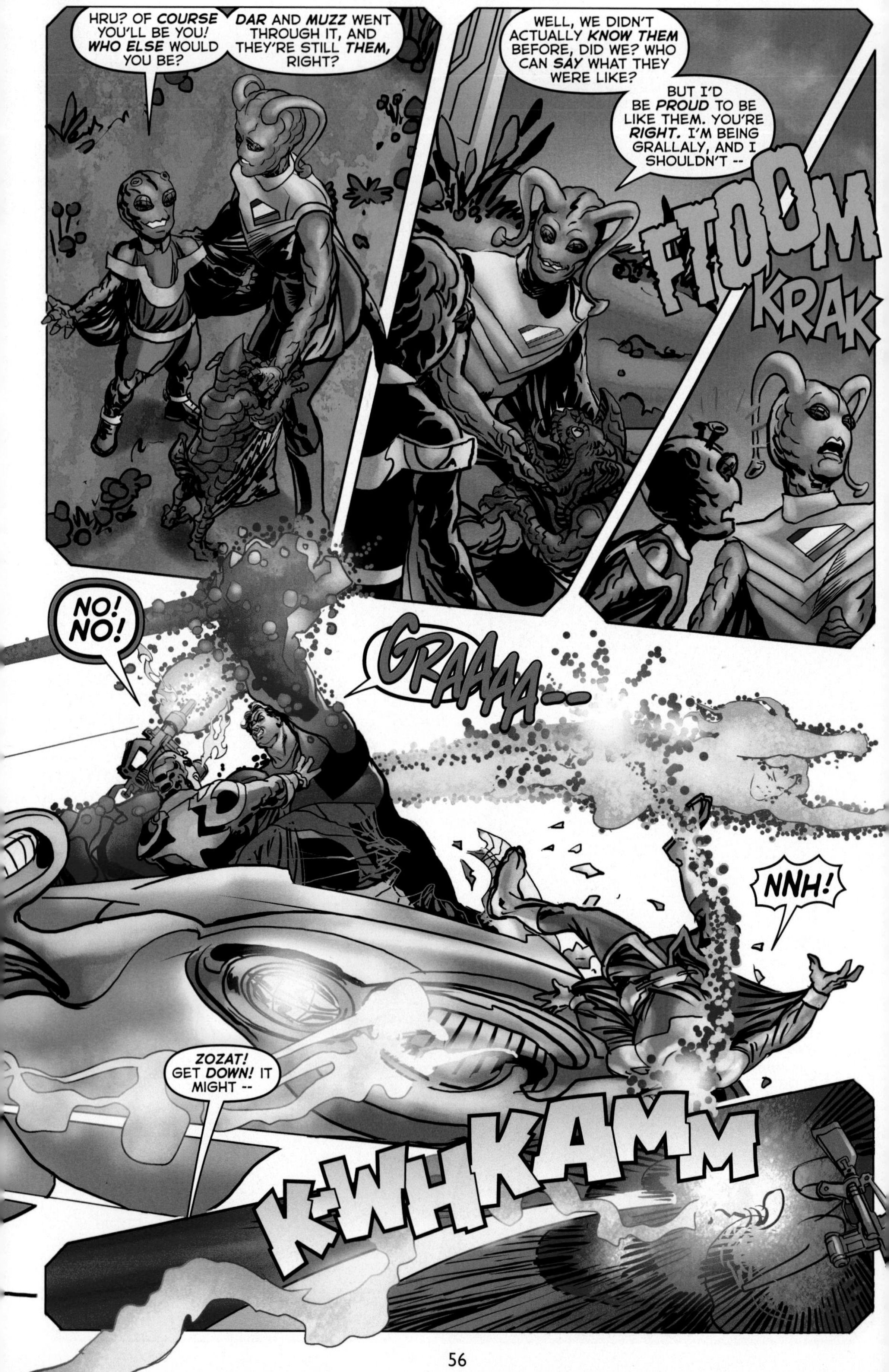
HRU? OF COURSE YOU'LL BE YOU! WHO ELSE WOULD YOU BE?
DAR AND MUZZ WENT THROUGH IT, AND THEY'RE STILL THEM, RIGHT?
WELL, WE DIDN'T ACTUALLY KNOW THEM BEFORE, DID WE? WHO CAN SAY WHAT THEY WERE LIKE?
BUT I'D BE PROUD TO BE LIKE THEM. YOU'RE RIGHT. I'M BEING GRALLALY, AND I SHOULDN'T --
FTOOM
KRAK
NO! NO!
GRAAAAA--
NNH!
ZOZAT! GET DOWN! IT MIGHT --
K-WHKAMM

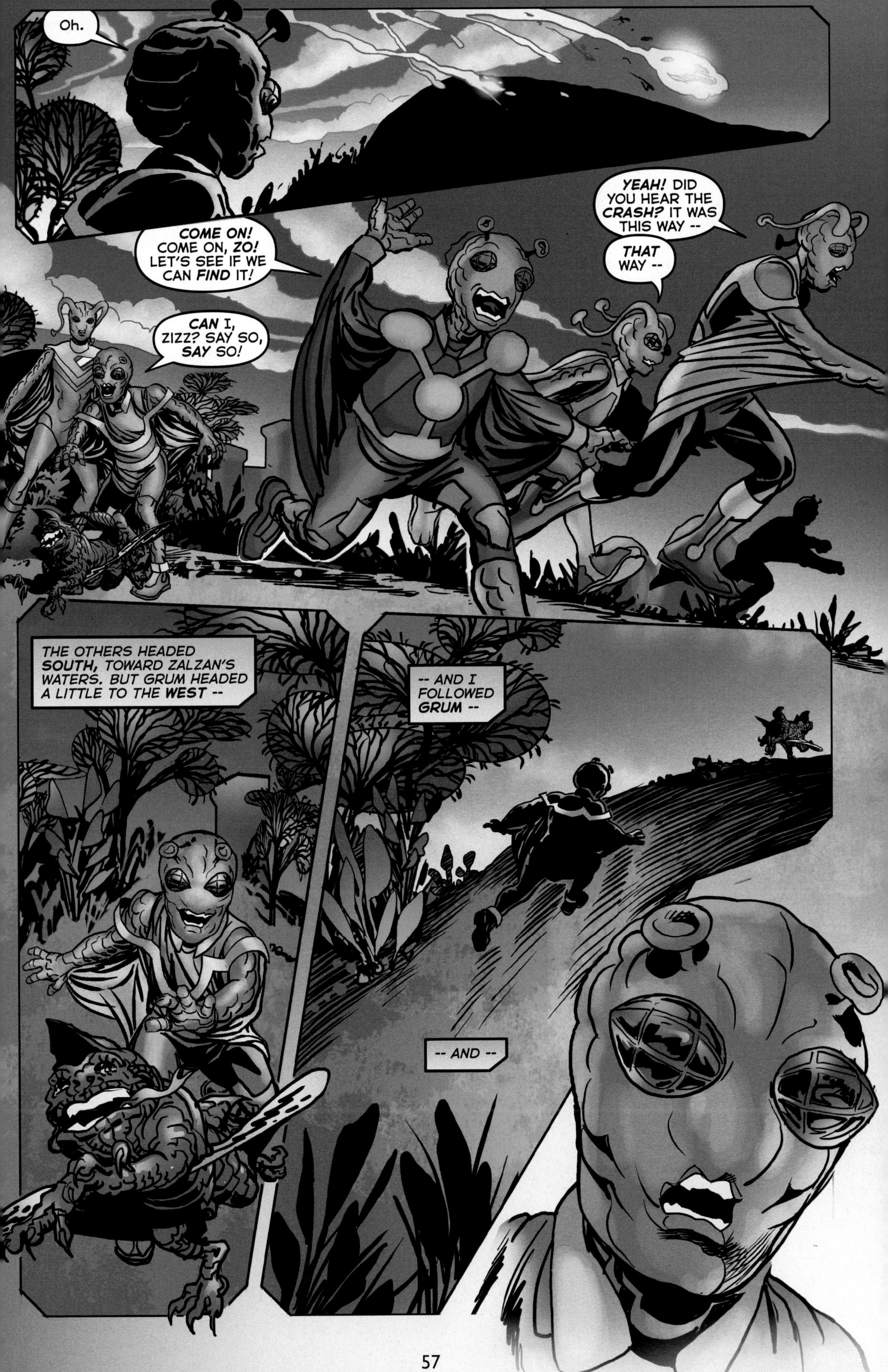

Oh.
COME ON! COME ON, ZO! LET'S SEE IF WE CAN FIND IT!
CAN I, ZIZZ? SAY SO, SAY SO!
YEAH! DID YOU HEAR THE CRASH? IT WAS THIS WAY --
THAT WAY --
THE OTHERS HEADED SOUTH, TOWARD ZALZAN'S WATERS. BUT GRUM HEADED A LITTLE TO THE WEST --
-- AND I FOLLOWED GRUM --
-- AND --

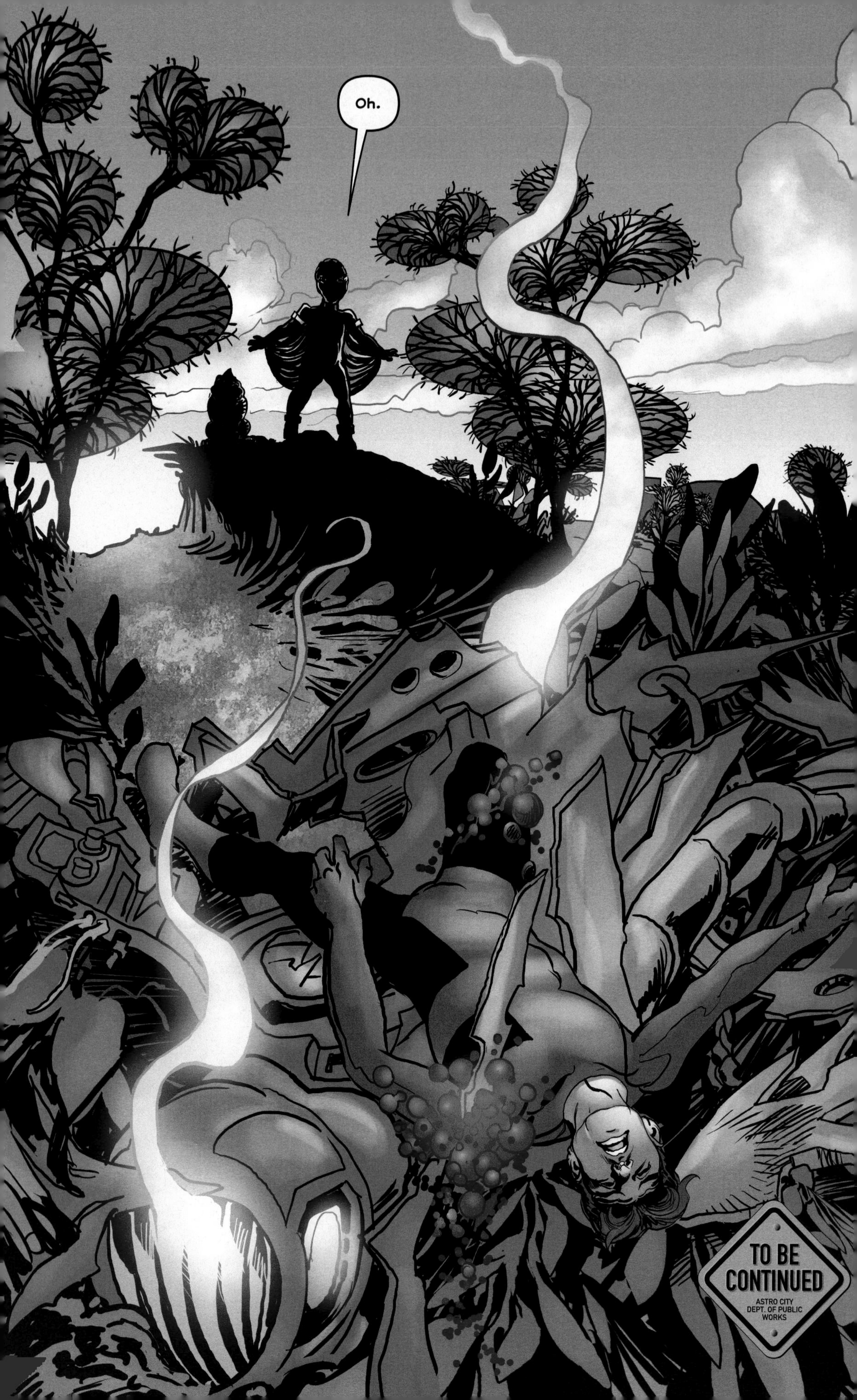
Oh.
TO BE CONTINUED
ASTRO CITY DEPT. OF PUBLIC WORKS

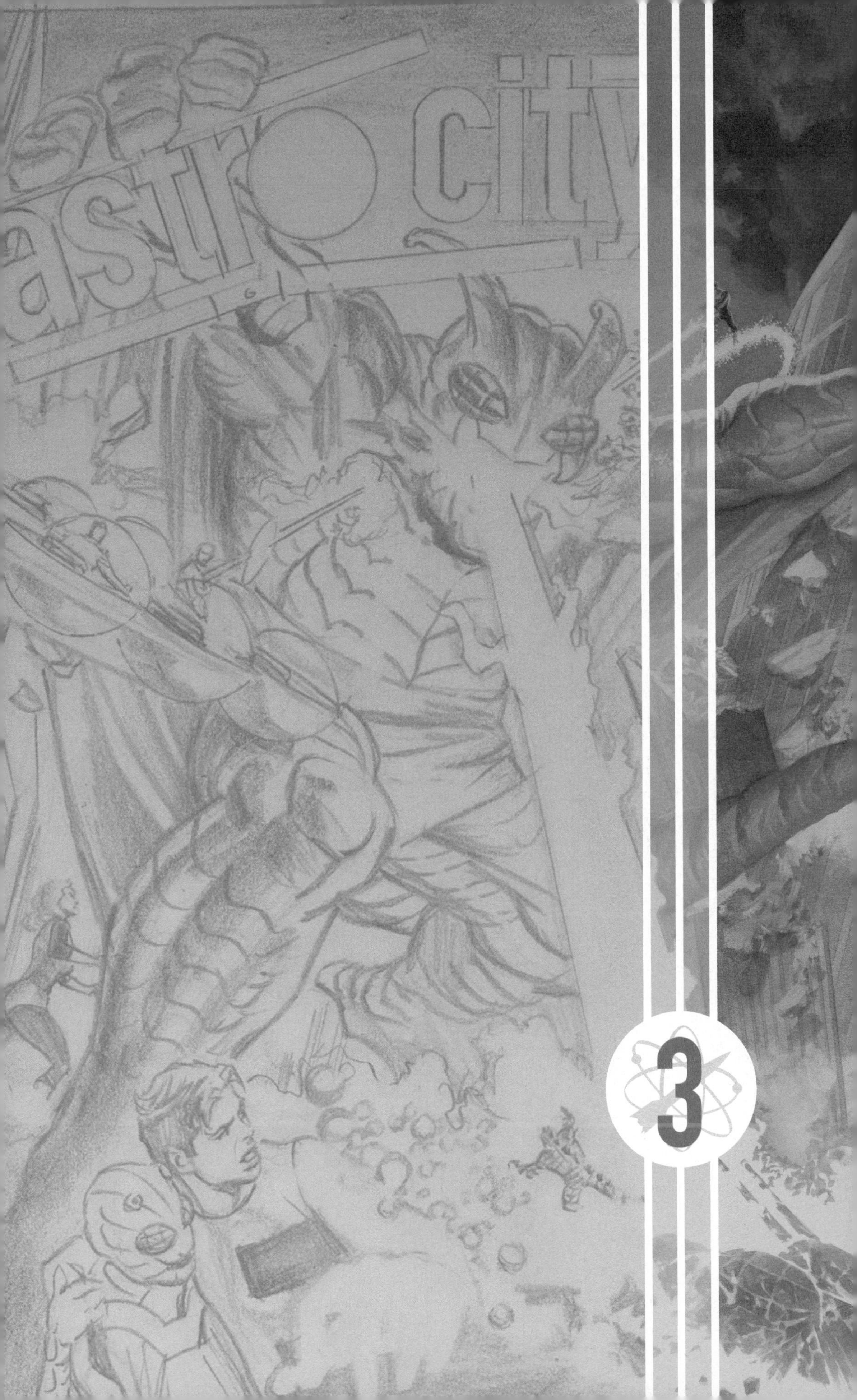
astro city
3

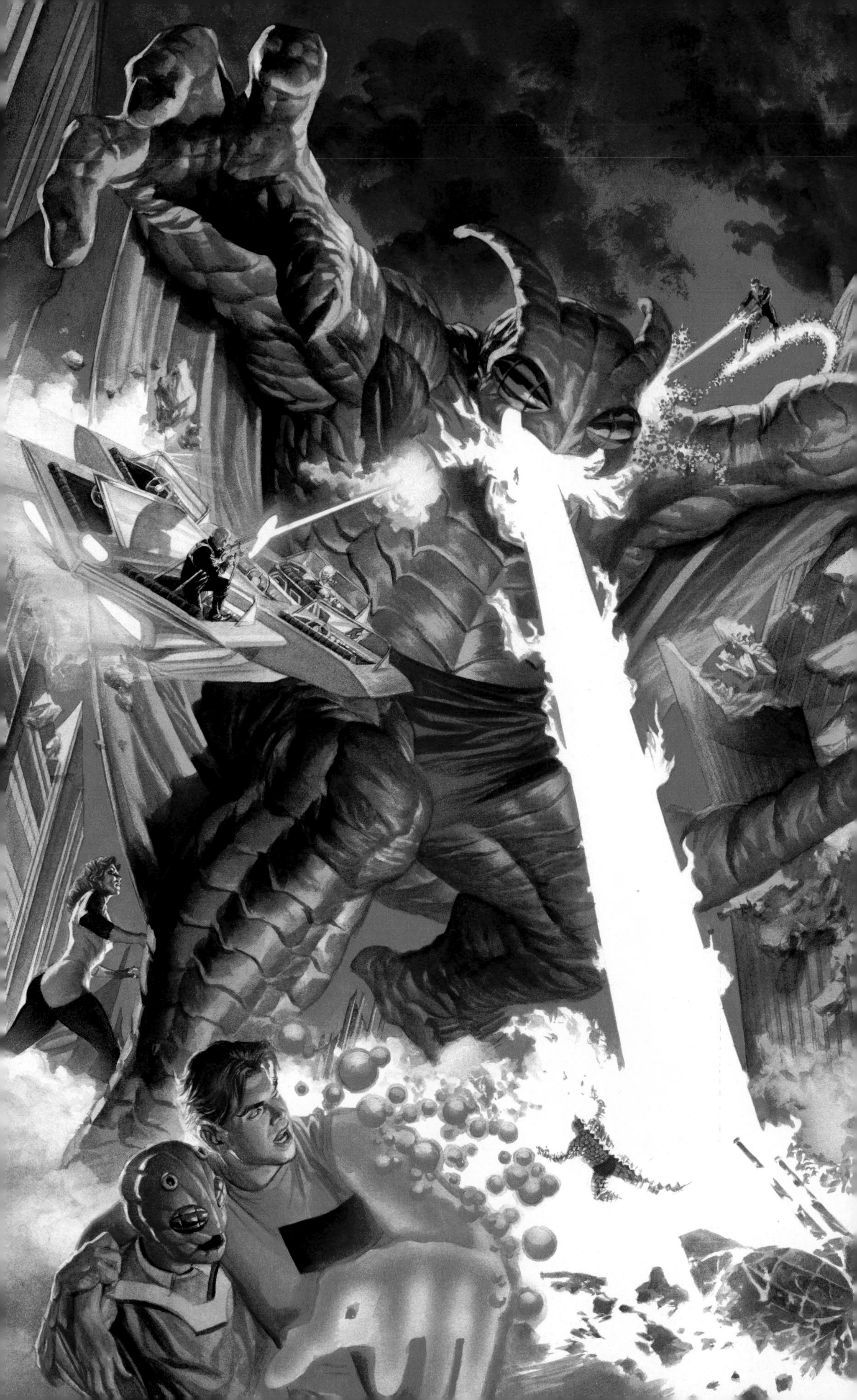

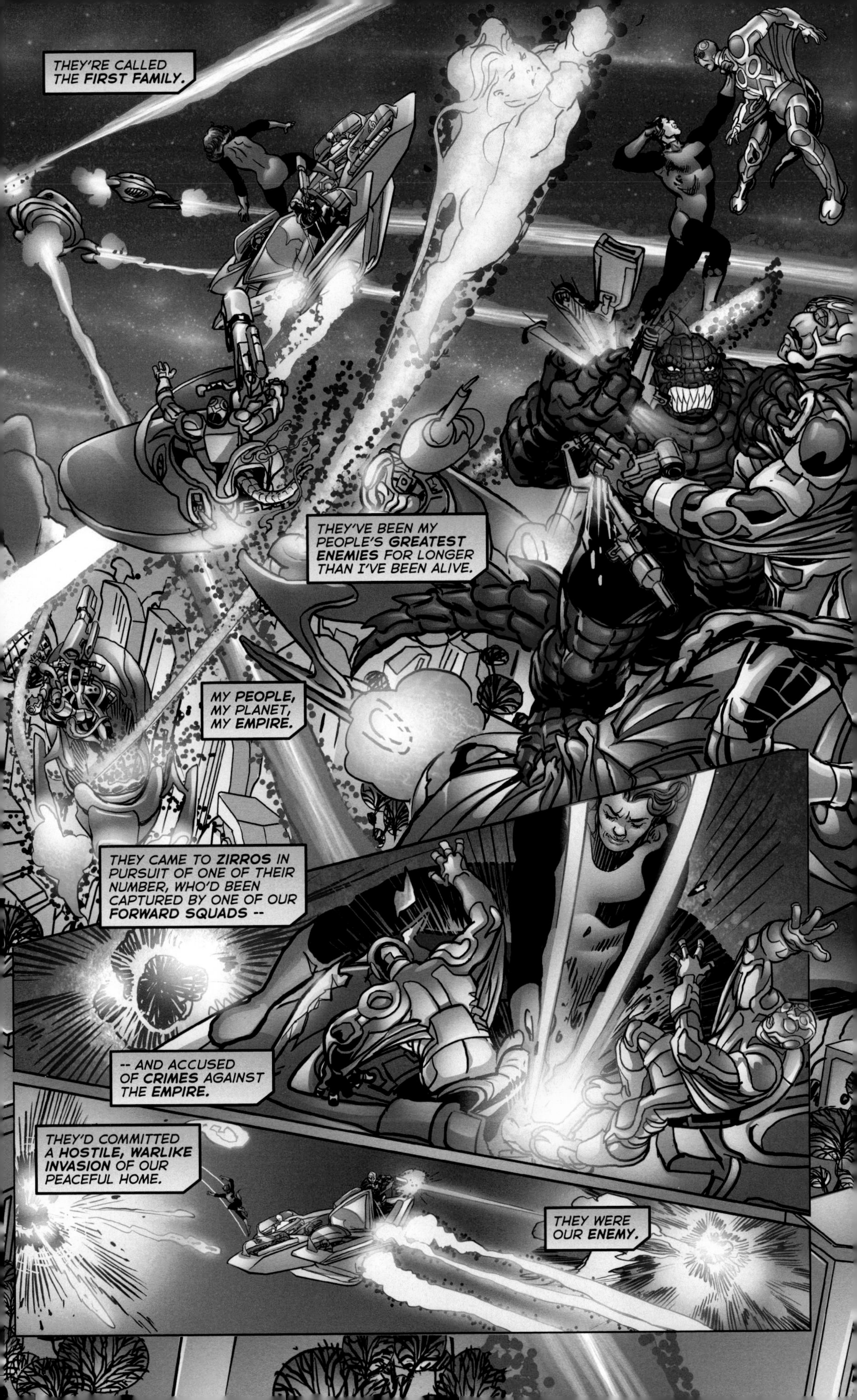

THEY'RE CALLED THE **FIRST FAMILY.**
THEY'VE BEEN MY PEOPLE'S **GREATEST ENEMIES** FOR LONGER THAN I'VE BEEN ALIVE.
MY **PEOPLE,** MY **PLANET,** MY **EMPIRE.**
THEY CAME TO **ZIRROS** IN PURSUIT OF ONE OF THEIR NUMBER, WHO'D BEEN CAPTURED BY ONE OF OUR **FORWARD SQUADS --**
-- AND ACCUSED OF **CRIMES** AGAINST THE **EMPIRE.**
THEY'D COMMITTED **A HOSTILE, WARLIKE INVASION** OF OUR PEACEFUL HOME.
THEY WERE OUR **ENEMY.**

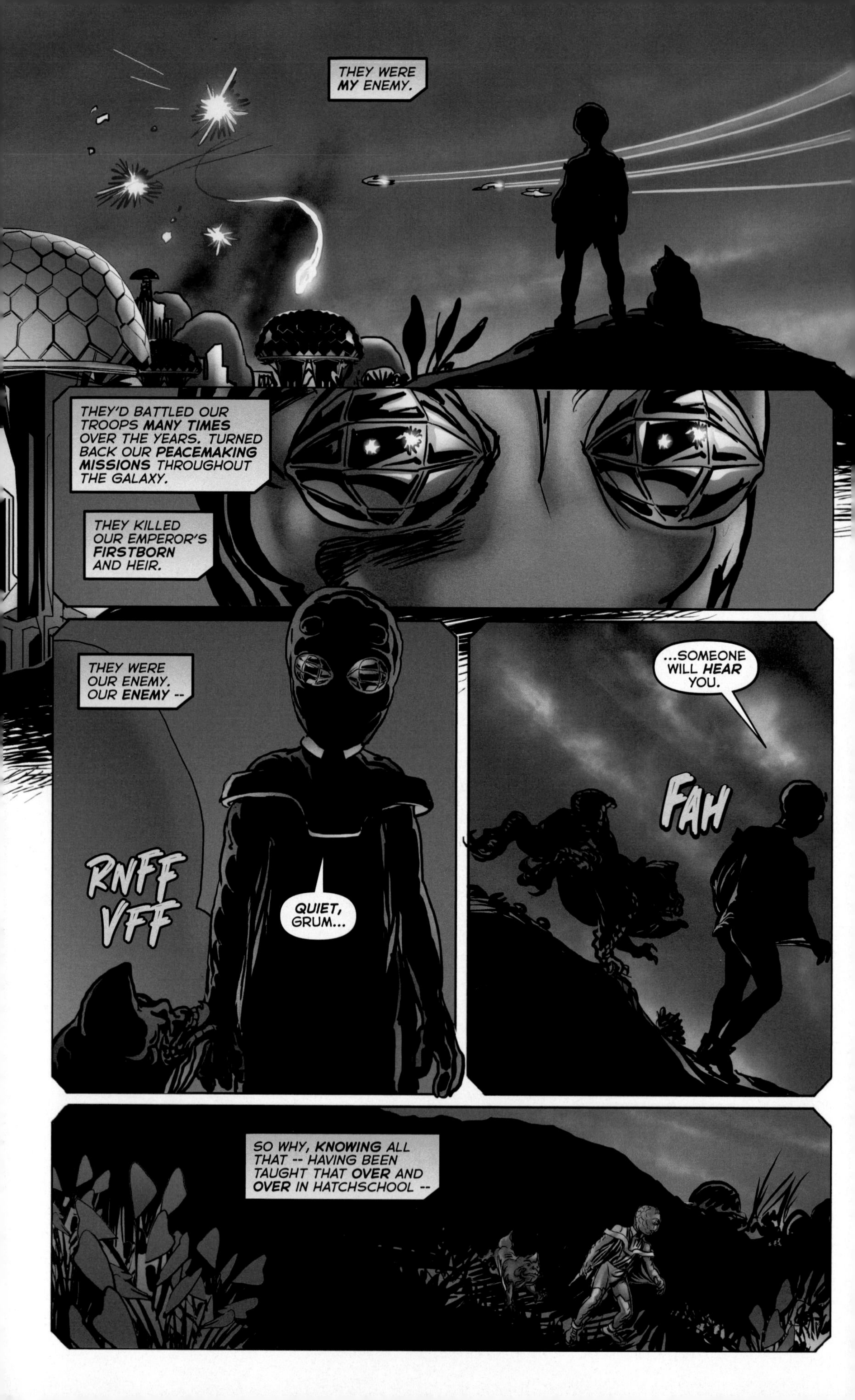
THEY WERE MY ENEMY.
THEY'D BATTLED OUR TROOPS MANY TIMES OVER THE YEARS. TURNED BACK OUR PEACEMAKING MISSIONS THROUGHOUT THE GALAXY.
THEY KILLED OUR EMPEROR'S FIRSTBORN AND HEIR.
THEY WERE OUR ENEMY. OUR ENEMY --
RNFF VFF
QUIET, GRUM...
...SOMEONE WILL HEAR YOU.
FAH
SO WHY, KNOWING ALL THAT -- HAVING BEEN TAUGHT THAT OVER AND OVER IN HATCHSCHOOL --

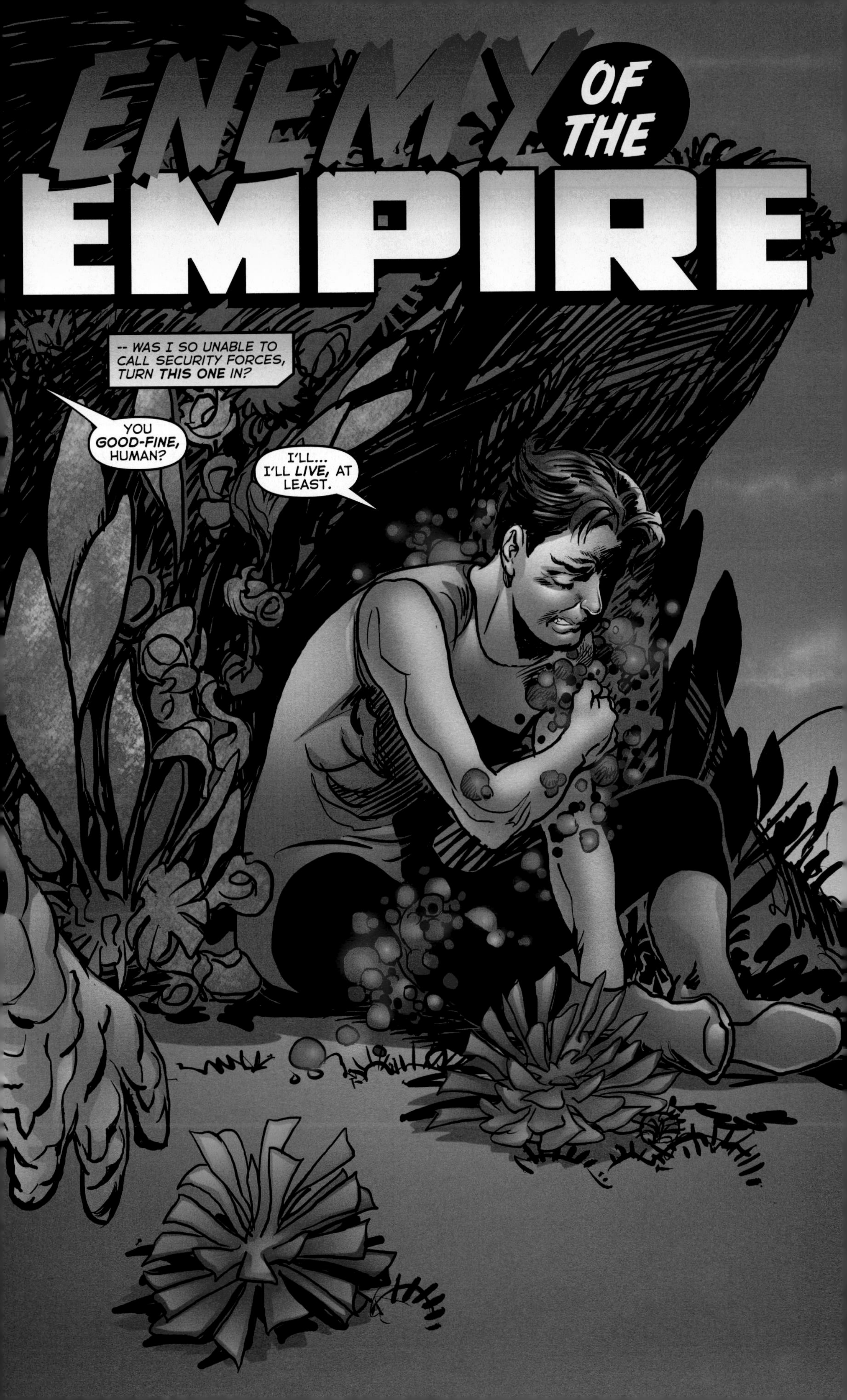
ENEMY OF THE EMPIRE
-- WAS I SO UNABLE TO CALL SECURITY FORCES, TURN THIS ONE IN?
YOU GOOD-FINE, HUMAN?
I'LL... I'LL LIVE, AT LEAST.

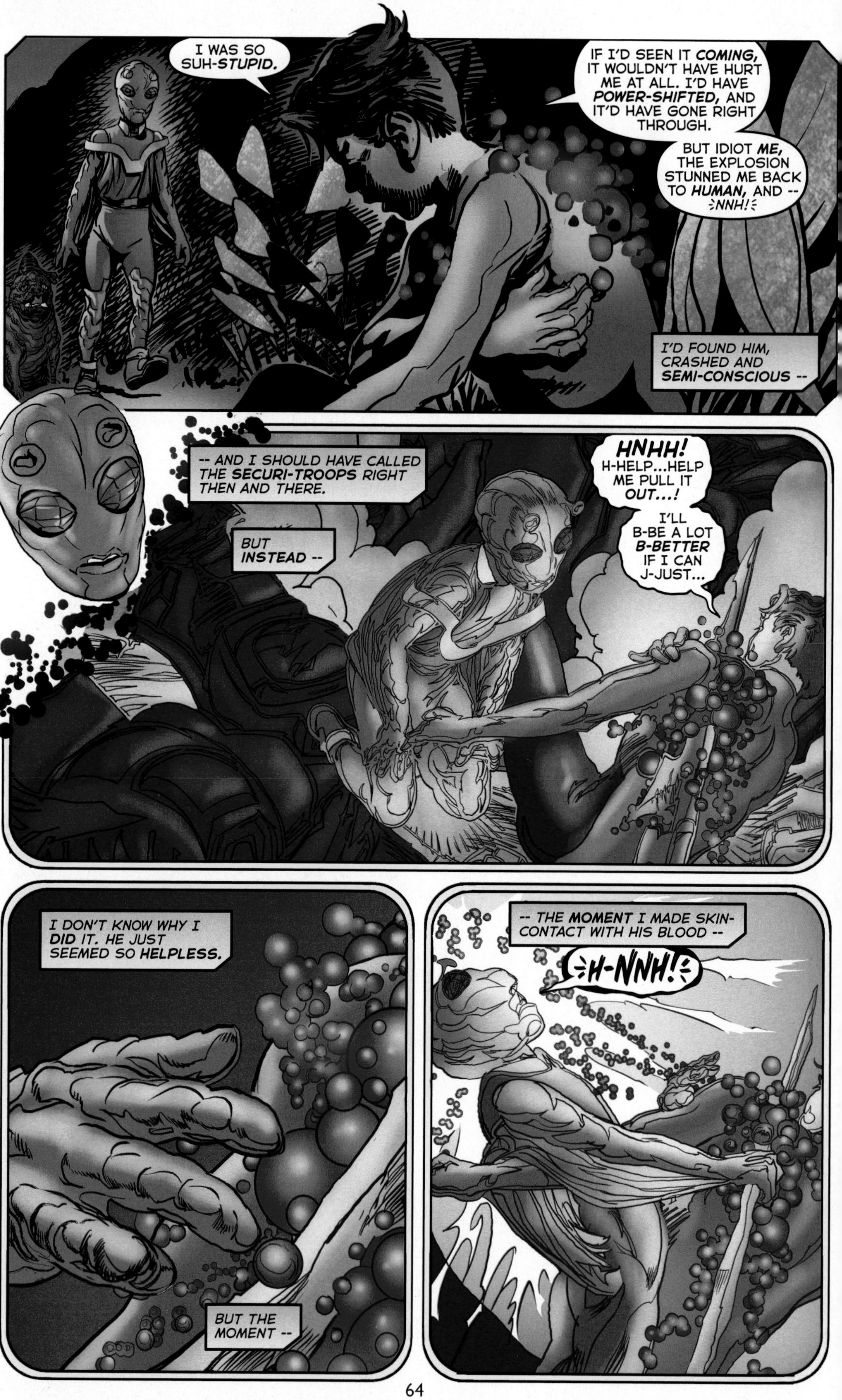
I WAS SO SUH-STUPID.
IF I'D SEEN IT COMING, IT WOULDN'T HAVE HURT ME AT ALL. I'D HAVE POWER-SHIFTED, AND IT'D HAVE GONE RIGHT THROUGH.
BUT IDIOT ME, THE EXPLOSION STUNNED ME BACK TO HUMAN, AND -- NNH!
I'D FOUND HIM, CRASHED AND SEMI-CONSCIOUS --
-- AND I SHOULD HAVE CALLED THE SECURI-TROOPS RIGHT THEN AND THERE.
BUT INSTEAD --
HNHH! H-HELP...HELP ME PULL IT OUT...!
I'LL B-BE A LOT B-BETTER IF I CAN J-JUST...
I DON'T KNOW WHY I DID IT. HE JUST SEEMED SO HELPLESS.
BUT THE MOMENT --
-- THE MOMENT I MADE SKIN-CONTACT WITH HIS BLOOD --
H-NNH!

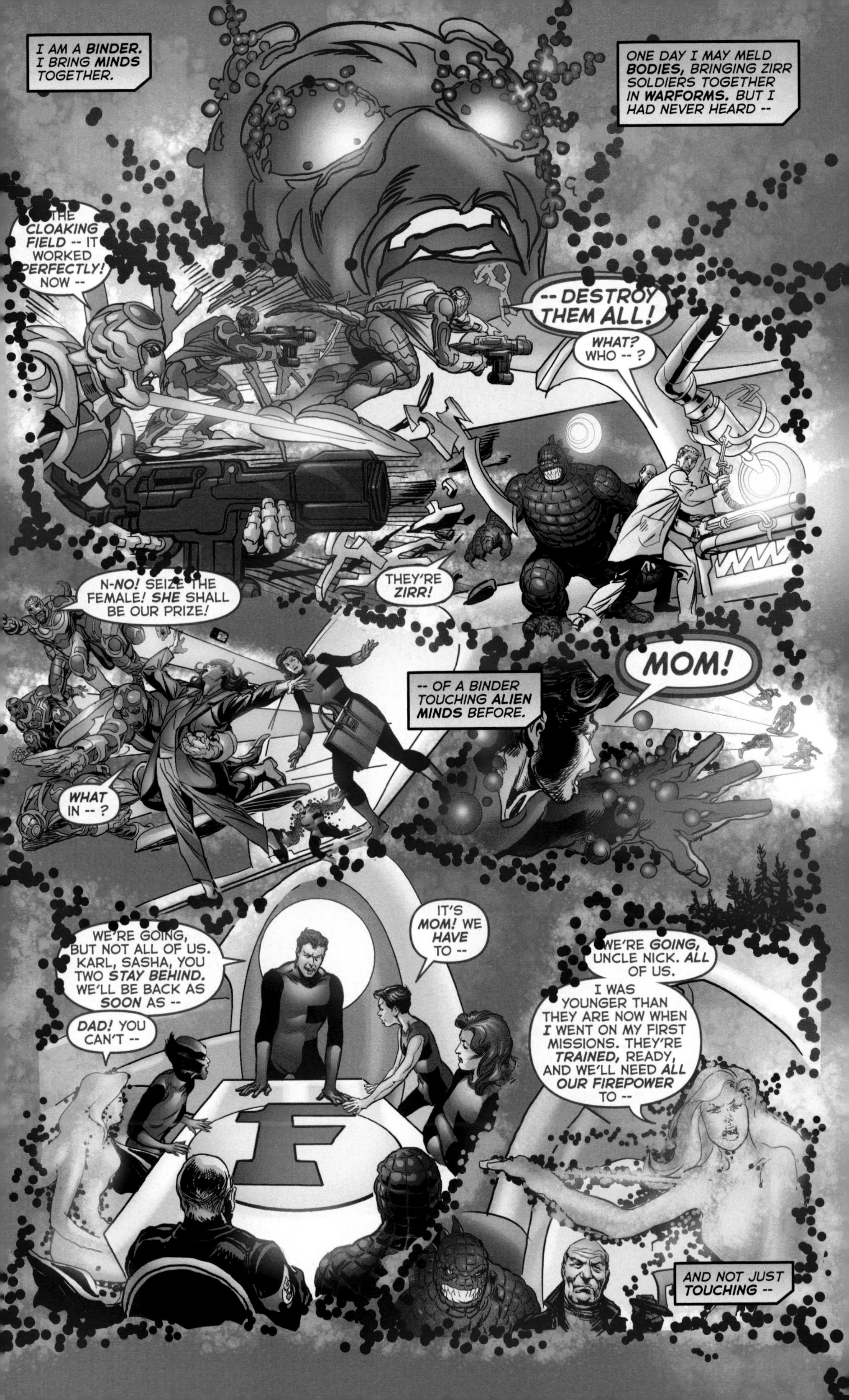

I AM A BINDER. I BRING MINDS TOGETHER.
ONE DAY I MAY MELD BODIES, BRINGING ZIRR SOLDIERS TOGETHER IN WARFORMS. BUT I HAD NEVER HEARD --
-- THE CLOAKING FIELD -- IT WORKED PERFECTLY! NOW --
-- DESTROY THEM ALL!
WHAT? WHO -- ?
N-NO! SEIZE THE FEMALE! SHE SHALL BE OUR PRIZE!
THEY'RE ZIRR!
-- OF A BINDER TOUCHING ALIEN MINDS BEFORE.
MOM!
WHAT IN -- ?
WE'RE GOING, BUT NOT ALL OF US. KARL, SASHA, YOU TWO STAY BEHIND. WE'LL BE BACK AS SOON AS --
IT'S MOM! WE HAVE TO --
DAD! YOU CAN'T --
WE'RE GOING, UNCLE NICK. ALL OF US.
I WAS YOUNGER THAN THEY ARE NOW WHEN I WENT ON MY FIRST MISSIONS. THEY'RE TRAINED, READY, AND WE'LL NEED ALL OUR FIREPOWER TO --
AND NOT JUST TOUCHING --

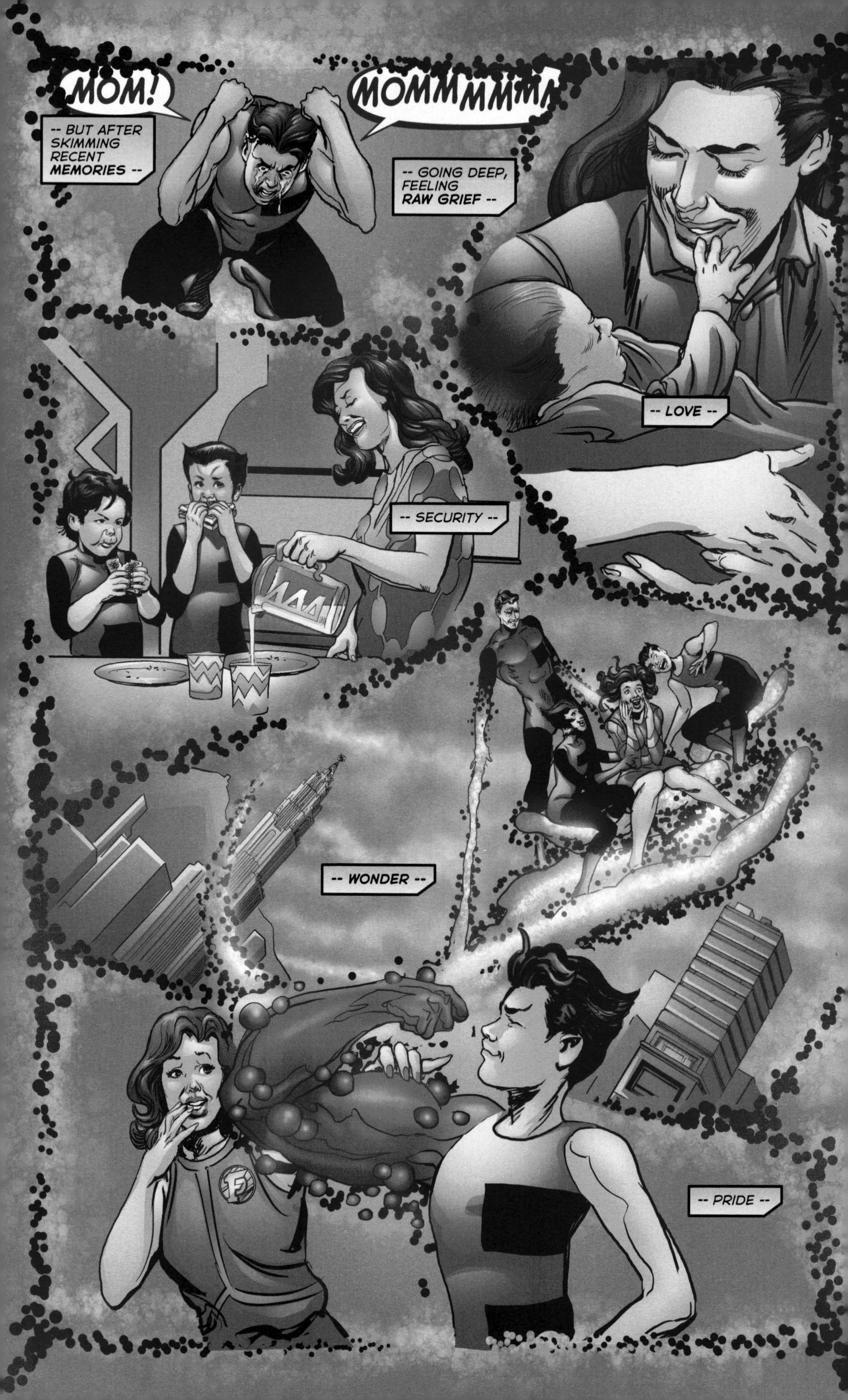
MOM!
-- BUT AFTER SKIMMING RECENT MEMORIES --
MOMMMMM!
-- GOING DEEP, FEELING RAW GRIEF --
-- LOVE --
-- SECURITY --
-- WONDER --
-- PRIDE --

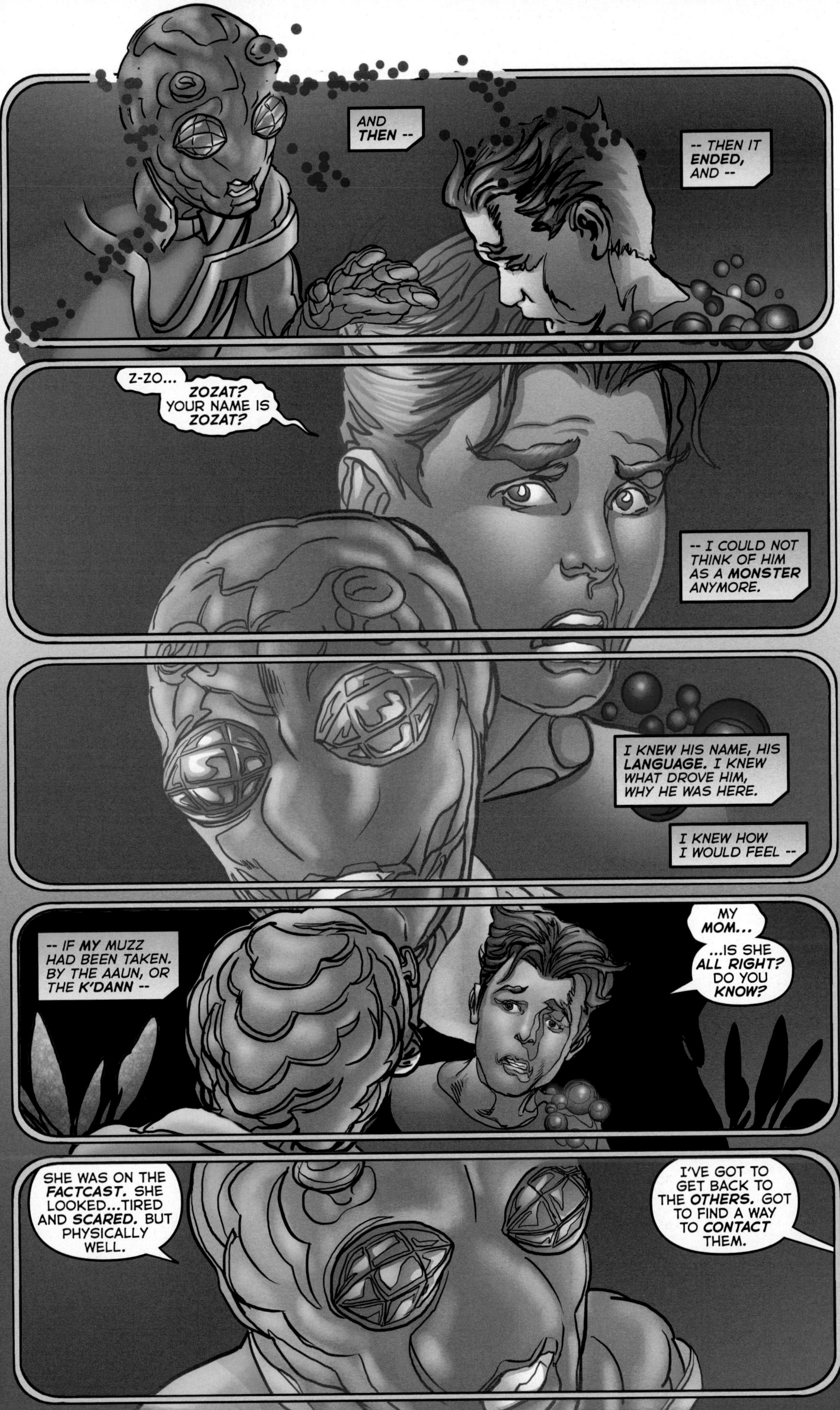
AND THEN --
-- THEN IT ENDED, AND --
Z-ZO... ZOZAT? YOUR NAME IS ZOZAT?
-- I COULD NOT THINK OF HIM AS A MONSTER ANYMORE.
I KNEW HIS NAME, HIS LANGUAGE. I KNEW WHAT DROVE HIM, WHY HE WAS HERE.
I KNEW HOW I WOULD FEEL --
-- IF MY MUZZ HAD BEEN TAKEN. BY THE AAUN, OR THE K'DANN --
MY MOM... ...IS SHE ALL RIGHT? DO YOU KNOW?
SHE WAS ON THE FACTCAST. SHE LOOKED...TIRED AND SCARED. BUT PHYSICALLY WELL.
I'VE GOT TO GET BACK TO THE OTHERS. GOT TO FIND A WAY TO CONTACT THEM.

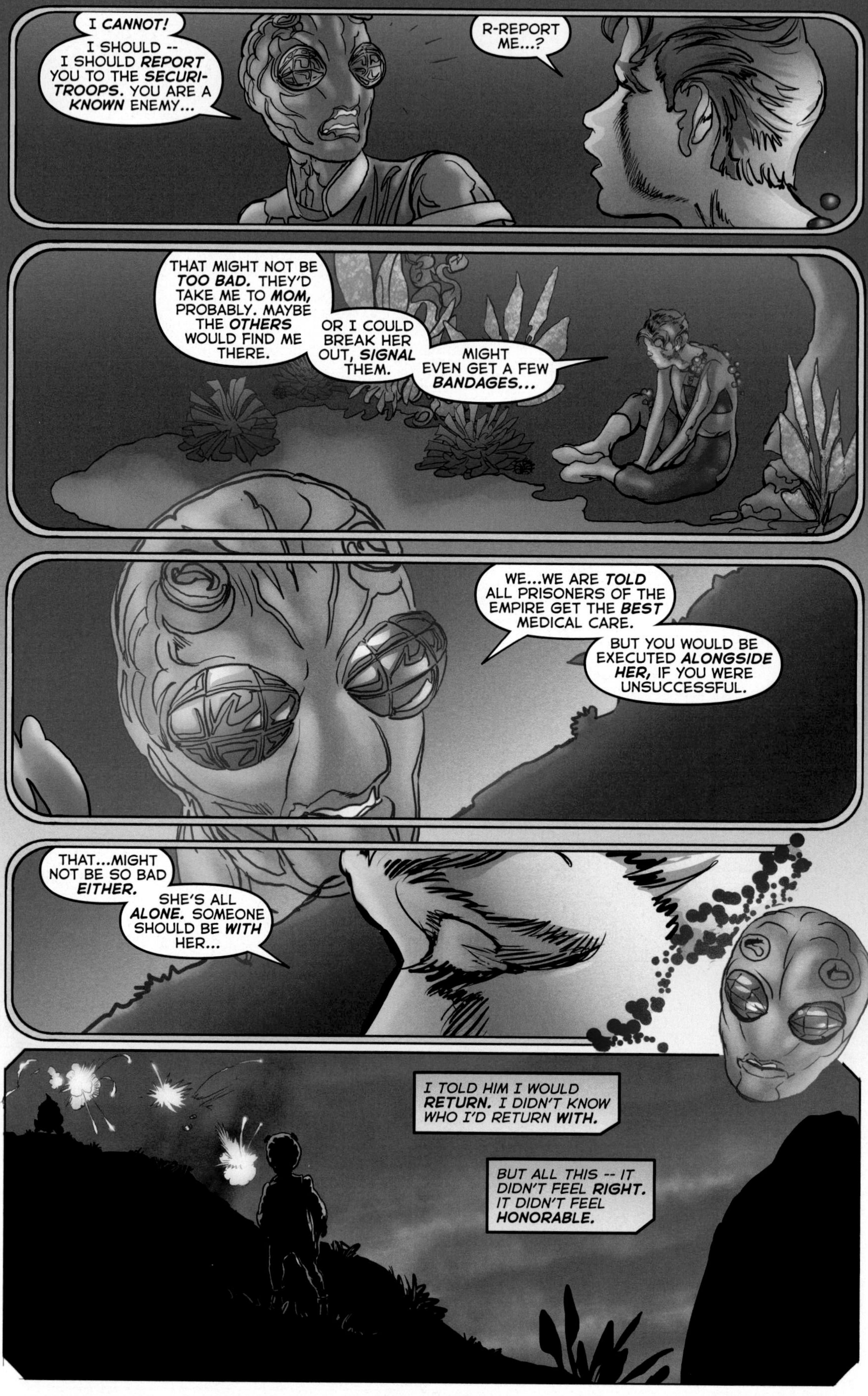

I CANNOT!
I SHOULD -- I SHOULD REPORT YOU TO THE SECURI-TROOPS. YOU ARE A KNOWN ENEMY...
R-REPORT ME...?
THAT MIGHT NOT BE TOO BAD. THEY'D TAKE ME TO MOM, PROBABLY. MAYBE THE OTHERS WOULD FIND ME THERE.
OR I COULD BREAK HER OUT, SIGNAL THEM.
MIGHT EVEN GET A FEW BANDAGES...
WE...WE ARE TOLD ALL PRISONERS OF THE EMPIRE GET THE BEST MEDICAL CARE.
BUT YOU WOULD BE EXECUTED ALONGSIDE HER, IF YOU WERE UNSUCCESSFUL.
THAT...MIGHT NOT BE SO BAD EITHER.
SHE'S ALL ALONE. SOMEONE SHOULD BE WITH HER...
I TOLD HIM I WOULD RETURN. I DIDN'T KNOW WHO I'D RETURN WITH.
BUT ALL THIS -- IT DIDN'T FEEL RIGHT. IT DIDN'T FEEL HONORABLE.

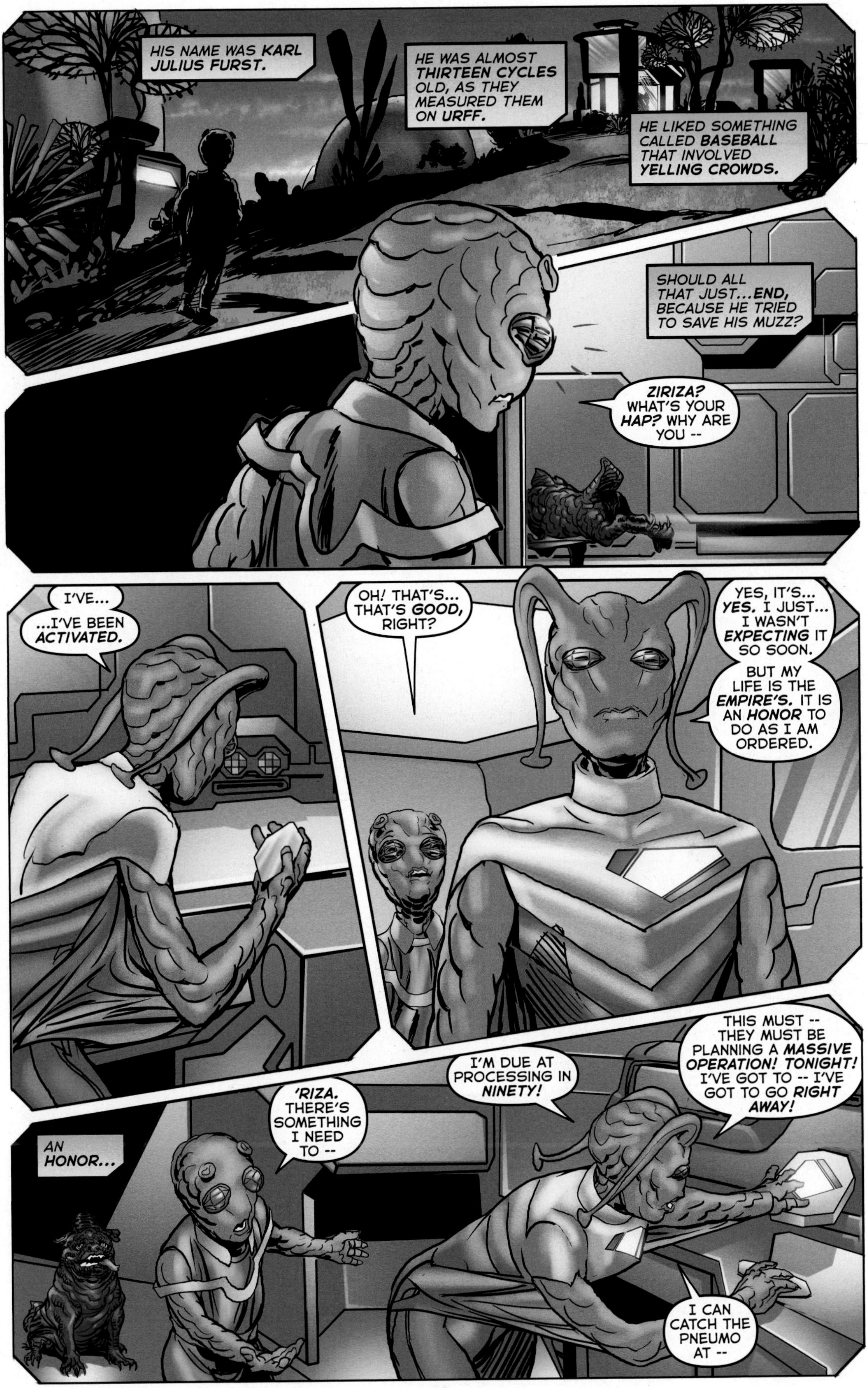
HIS NAME WAS KARL JULIUS FURST.
HE WAS ALMOST THIRTEEN CYCLES OLD, AS THEY MEASURED THEM ON URFF.
HE LIKED SOMETHING CALLED BASEBALL THAT INVOLVED YELLING CROWDS.
SHOULD ALL THAT JUST...END, BECAUSE HE TRIED TO SAVE HIS MUZZ?
ZIRIZA? WHAT'S YOUR HAP? WHY ARE YOU --
I'VE... ...I'VE BEEN ACTIVATED.
OH! THAT'S... THAT'S GOOD, RIGHT?
YES, IT'S... YES. I JUST... I WASN'T EXPECTING IT SO SOON.
BUT MY LIFE IS THE EMPIRE'S. IT IS AN HONOR TO DO AS I AM ORDERED.
AN HONOR...
'RIZA. THERE'S SOMETHING I NEED TO --
I'M DUE AT PROCESSING IN NINETY!
THIS MUST -- THEY MUST BE PLANNING A MASSIVE OPERATION! TONIGHT! I'VE GOT TO -- I'VE GOT TO GO RIGHT AWAY!
I CAN CATCH THE PNEUMO AT --

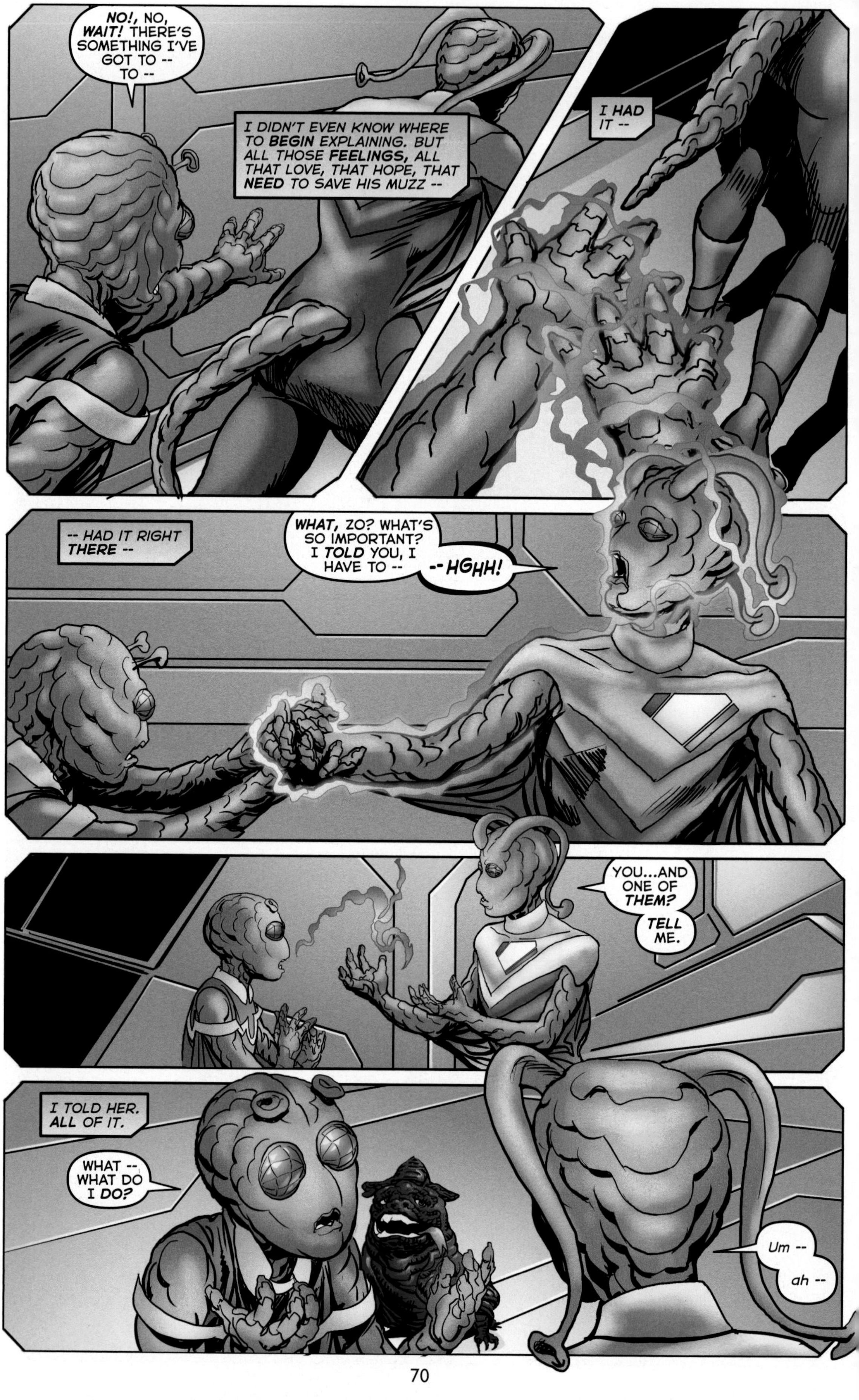
NO!, NO, WAIT! THERE'S SOMETHING I'VE GOT TO -- TO --
I DIDN'T EVEN KNOW WHERE TO BEGIN EXPLAINING. BUT ALL THOSE FEELINGS, ALL THAT LOVE, THAT HOPE, THAT NEED TO SAVE HIS MUZZ --
I HAD IT --
-- HAD IT RIGHT THERE --
WHAT, ZO? WHAT'S SO IMPORTANT? I TOLD YOU, I HAVE TO --
-- HGHH!
YOU...AND ONE OF THEM? TELL ME.
I TOLD HER. ALL OF IT.
WHAT -- WHAT DO I DO?
Um --
ah --

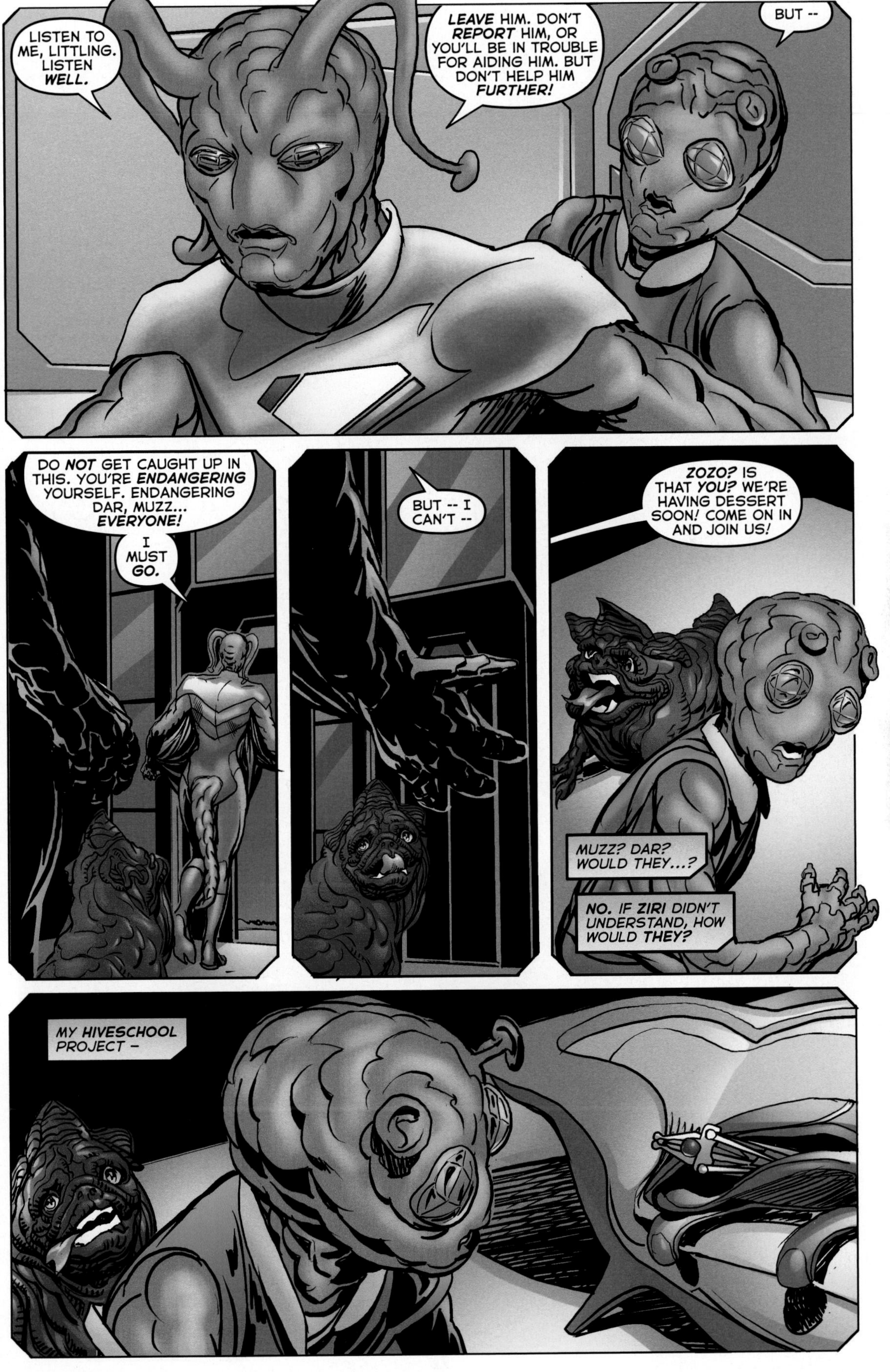
LISTEN TO ME, LITTLING. LISTEN WELL.
LEAVE HIM. DON'T REPORT HIM, OR YOU'LL BE IN TROUBLE FOR AIDING HIM. BUT DON'T HELP HIM FURTHER!
BUT --
DO NOT GET CAUGHT UP IN THIS. YOU'RE ENDANGERING YOURSELF. ENDANGERING DAR, MUZZ... EVERYONE!
I MUST GO.
BUT -- I CAN'T --
ZOZO? IS THAT YOU? WE'RE HAVING DESSERT SOON! COME ON IN AND JOIN US!
MUZZ? DAR? WOULD THEY...?
NO. IF ZIRI DIDN'T UNDERSTAND, HOW WOULD THEY?
MY HIVESCHOOL PROJECT –

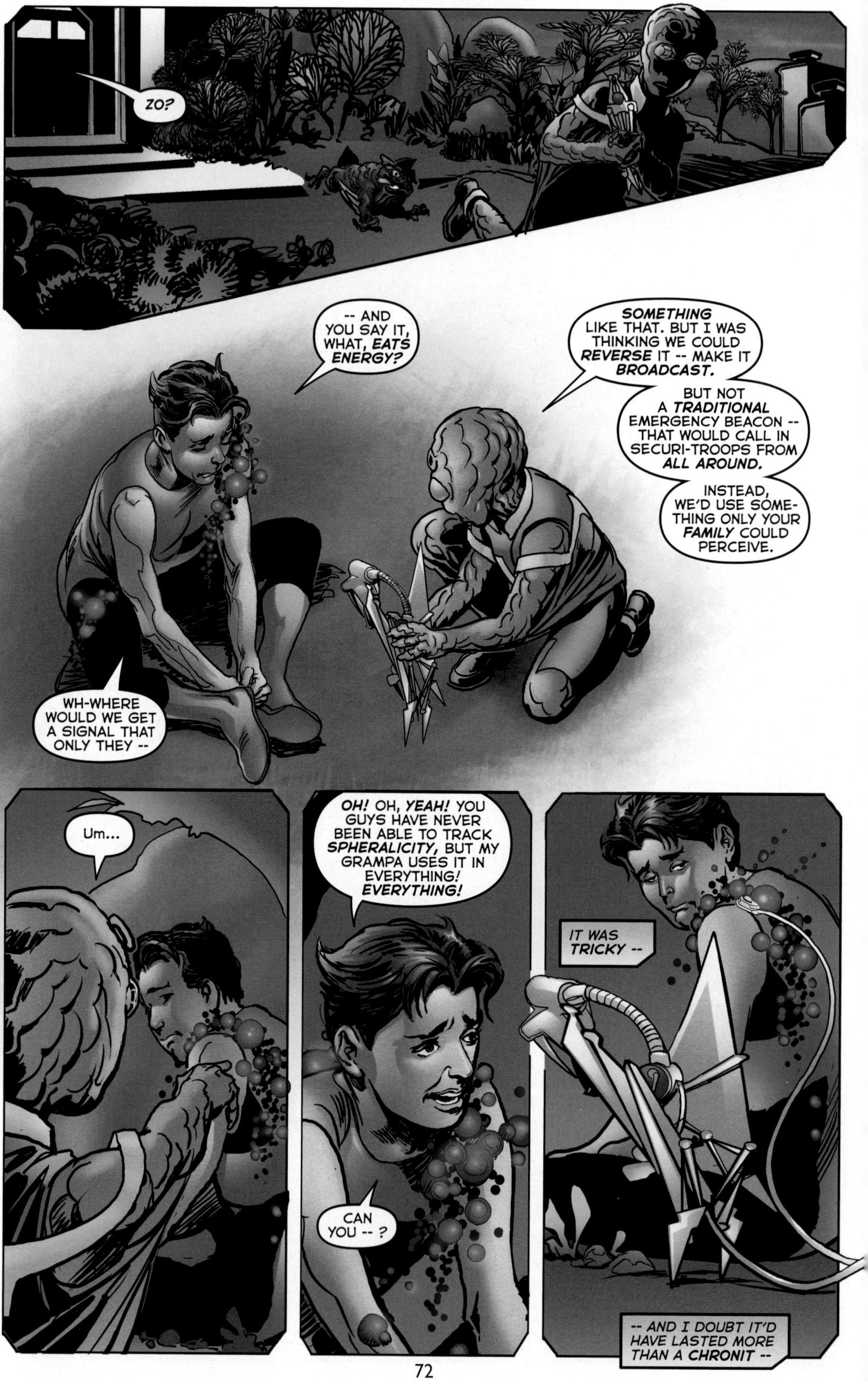
ZO?
-- AND YOU SAY IT, WHAT, EATS ENERGY?
SOMETHING LIKE THAT. BUT I WAS THINKING WE COULD REVERSE IT -- MAKE IT BROADCAST.
BUT NOT A TRADITIONAL EMERGENCY BEACON -- THAT WOULD CALL IN SECURI-TROOPS FROM ALL AROUND.
INSTEAD, WE'D USE SOME-THING ONLY YOUR FAMILY COULD PERCEIVE.
WH-WHERE WOULD WE GET A SIGNAL THAT ONLY THEY --
Um...
OH! OH, YEAH! YOU GUYS HAVE NEVER BEEN ABLE TO TRACK SPHERALICITY, BUT MY GRAMPA USES IT IN EVERYTHING! EVERYTHING!
CAN YOU -- ?
IT WAS TRICKY --
-- AND I DOUBT IT'D HAVE LASTED MORE THAN A CHRONIT --

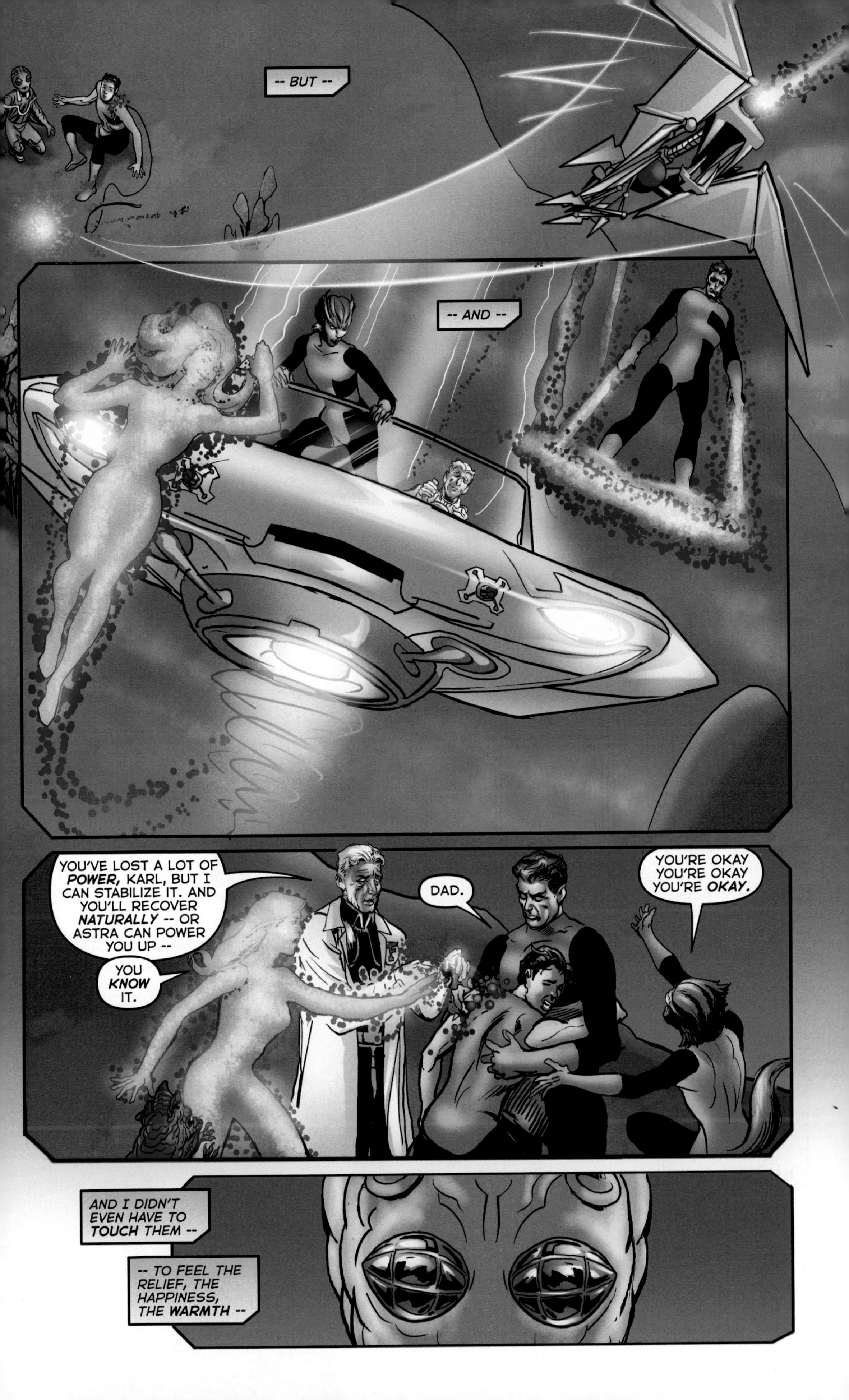
-- BUT --
-- AND --
YOU'VE LOST A LOT OF POWER, KARL, BUT I CAN STABILIZE IT. AND YOU'LL RECOVER NATURALLY -- OR ASTRA CAN POWER YOU UP --
YOU KNOW IT.
DAD.
YOU'RE OKAY YOU'RE OKAY YOU'RE OKAY.
AND I DIDN'T EVEN HAVE TO TOUCH THEM --
-- TO FEEL THE RELIEF, THE HAPPINESS, THE WARMTH --

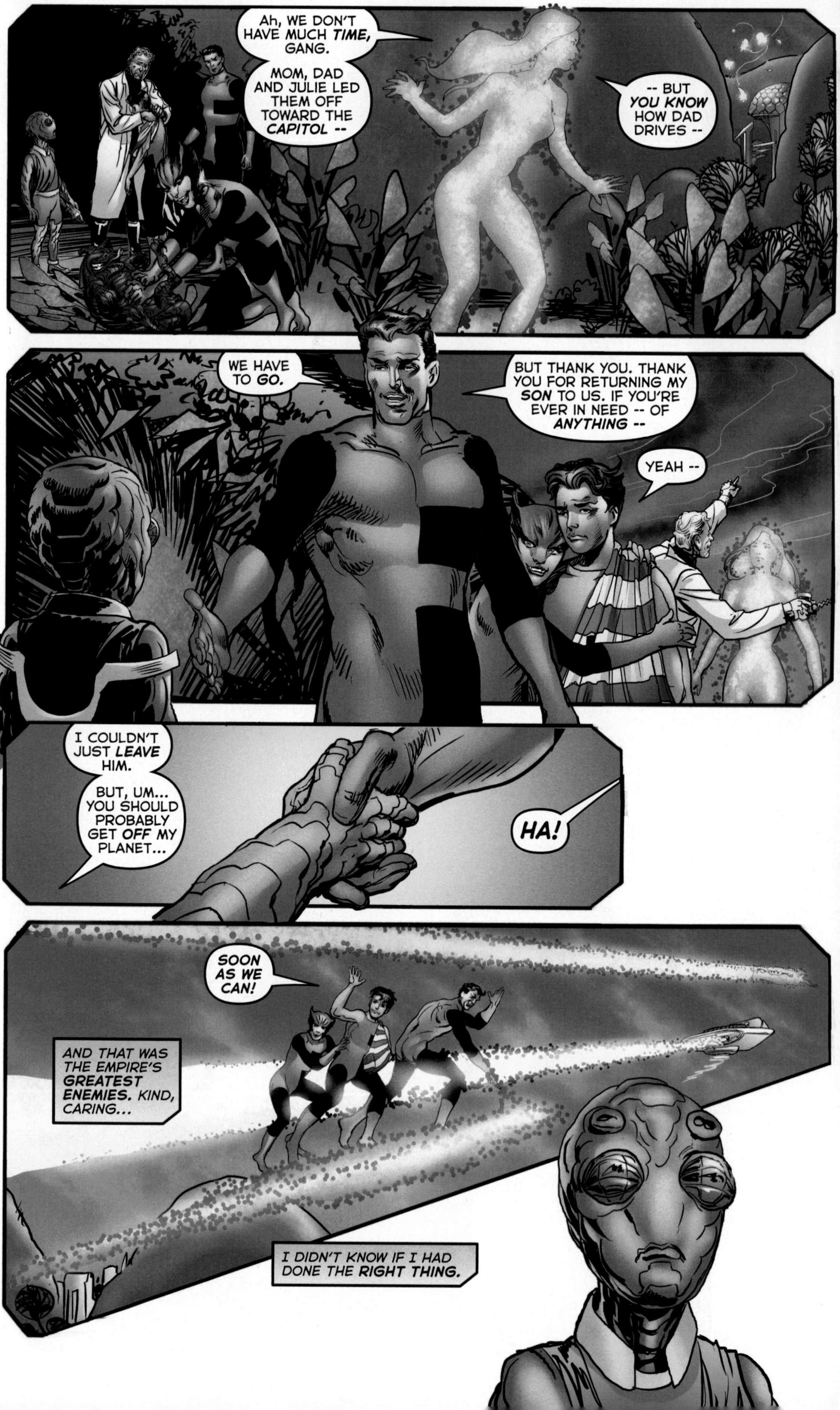
Ah, WE DON'T HAVE MUCH TIME, GANG.
MOM, DAD AND JULIE LED THEM OFF TOWARD THE CAPITOL --
-- BUT YOU KNOW HOW DAD DRIVES --
WE HAVE TO GO.
BUT THANK YOU. THANK YOU FOR RETURNING MY SON TO US. IF YOU'RE EVER IN NEED -- OF ANYTHING --
YEAH --
I COULDN'T JUST LEAVE HIM.
BUT, UM... YOU SHOULD PROBABLY GET OFF MY PLANET...
HA!
SOON AS WE CAN!
AND THAT WAS THE EMPIRE'S GREATEST ENEMIES. KIND, CARING...
I DIDN'T KNOW IF I HAD DONE THE RIGHT THING.

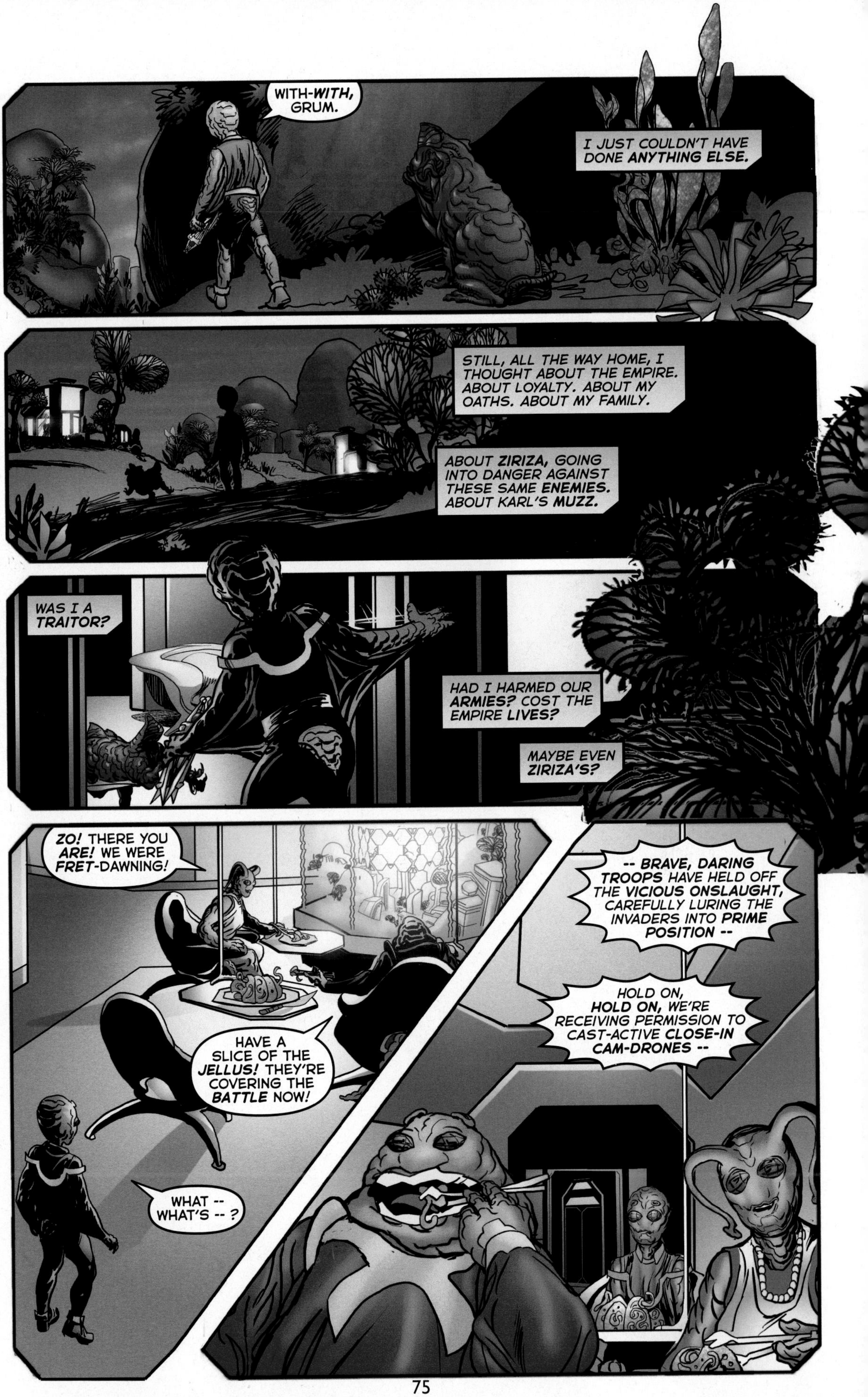
WITH-*WITH*, GRUM.
I JUST COULDN'T HAVE DONE **ANYTHING ELSE.**
STILL, ALL THE WAY HOME, I THOUGHT ABOUT THE EMPIRE. ABOUT LOYALTY. ABOUT MY OATHS. ABOUT MY FAMILY.
ABOUT **ZIRIZA**, GOING INTO DANGER AGAINST THESE SAME **ENEMIES.** ABOUT KARL'S **MUZZ.**
WAS I A **TRAITOR?**
HAD I HARMED OUR **ARMIES?** COST THE EMPIRE **LIVES?**
MAYBE EVEN **ZIRIZA'S?**
ZO! THERE YOU ***ARE!*** WE WERE ***FRET***-DAWNING!
HAVE A SLICE OF THE ***JELLUS!*** THEY'RE COVERING THE ***BATTLE*** NOW!
WHAT -- WHAT'S -- ?
-- **BRAVE, DARING TROOPS** HAVE HELD OFF THE **VICIOUS ONSLAUGHT,** CAREFULLY LURING THE INVADERS INTO **PRIME POSITION --**
HOLD ON, **HOLD ON,** WE'RE RECEIVING PERMISSION TO CAST-ACTIVE **CLOSE-IN CAM-DRONES --**

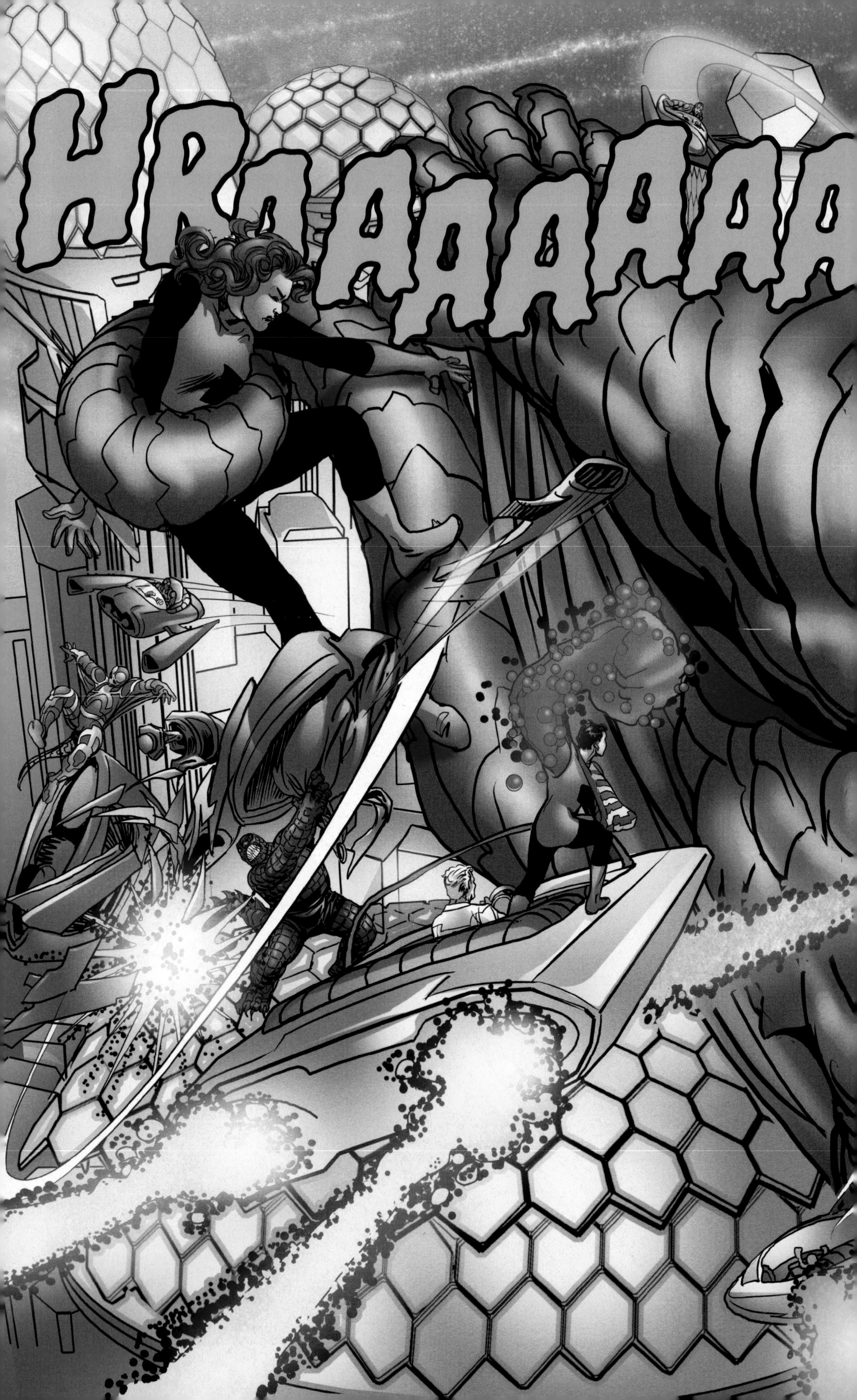
HRAAAAAAA

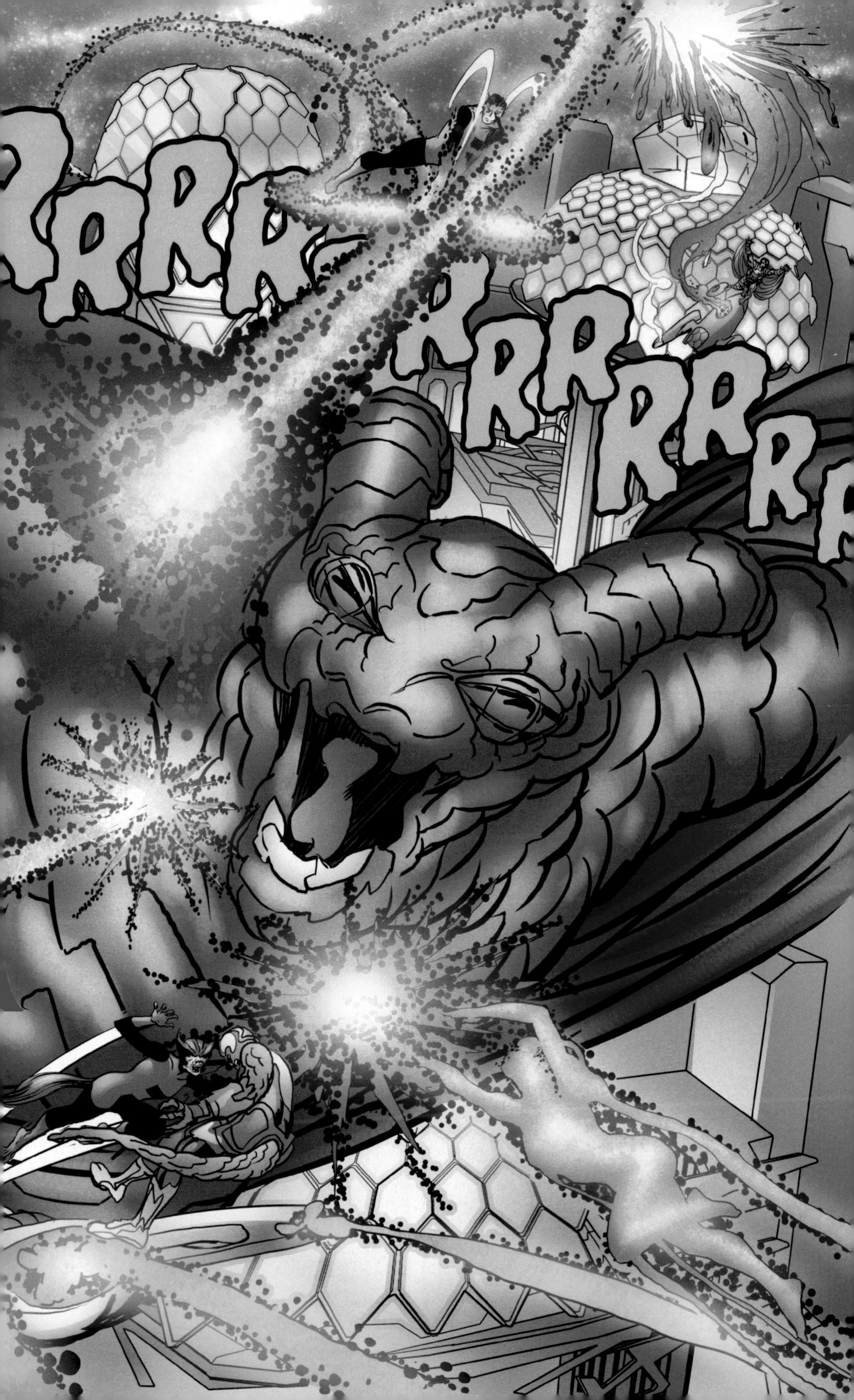
RRRR
RRRRRR

IT WAS THE UBERSAURUS.

THE EMPIRE'S -- MY EMPIRE'S -- NEWEST AND GREATEST WEAPON.

OVER 10,000 ZIRRI WARRIORS --

-- THE ELITE OF EACH SPECIALTY: FLIERS, RIPPERS, BURNERS, POUNDERS --

-- FUSED INTO ONE BY A CORE OF BINDERS.

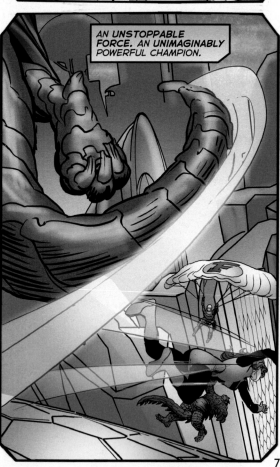

AN UNSTOPPABLE FORCE. AN UNIMAGINABLY POWERFUL CHAMPION.

BUT EVEN SO --

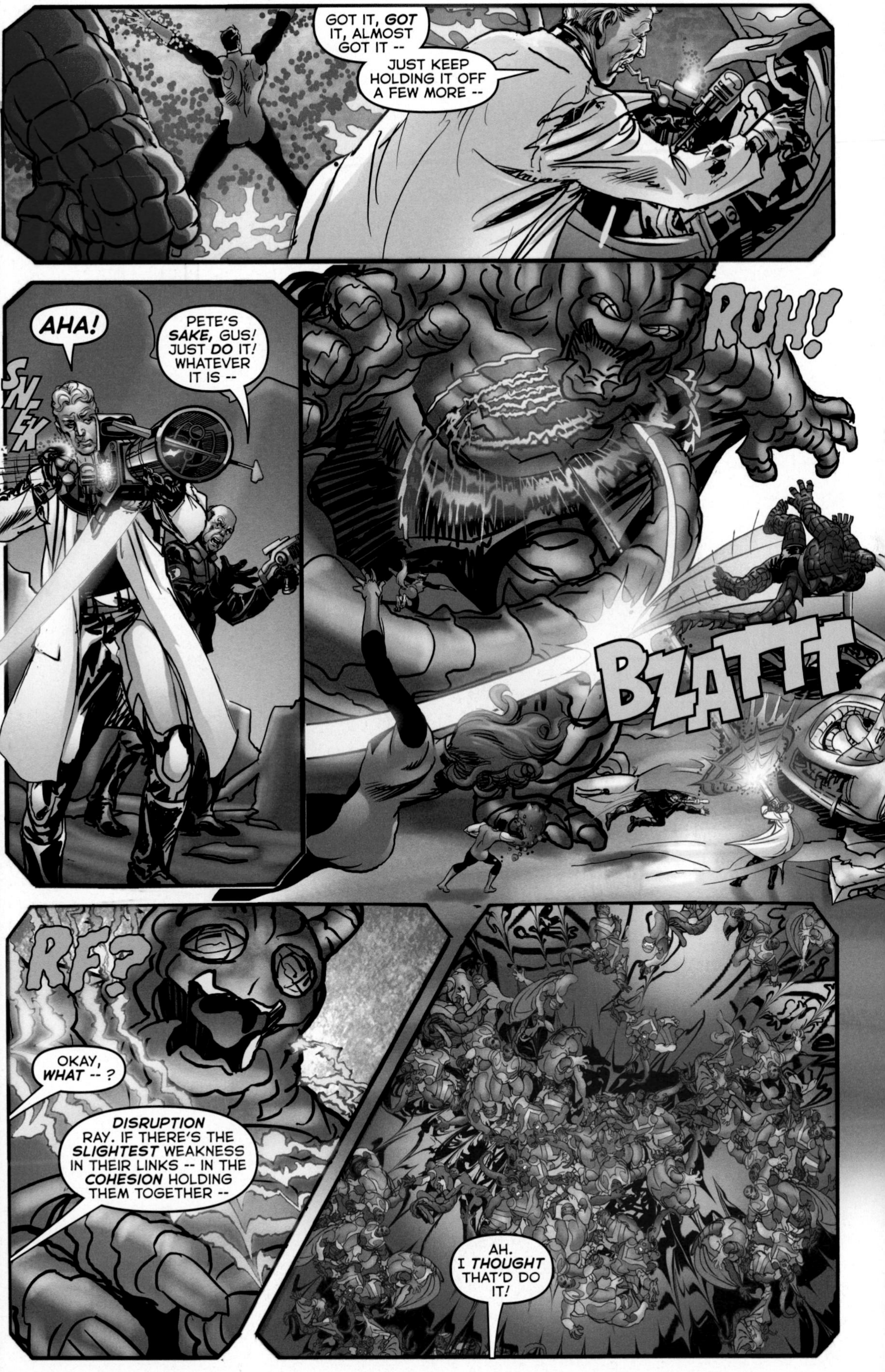

GOT IT, GOT IT, ALMOST GOT IT --
JUST KEEP HOLDING IT OFF A FEW MORE --
AHA!
SNEK
PETE'S SAKE, GUS! JUST DO IT! WHATEVER IT IS --
RUH!
BZATTT
RF?
OKAY, WHAT -- ?
DISRUPTION RAY. IF THERE'S THE SLIGHTEST WEAKNESS IN THEIR LINKS -- IN THE COHESION HOLDING THEM TOGETHER --
AH. I THOUGHT THAT'D DO IT!

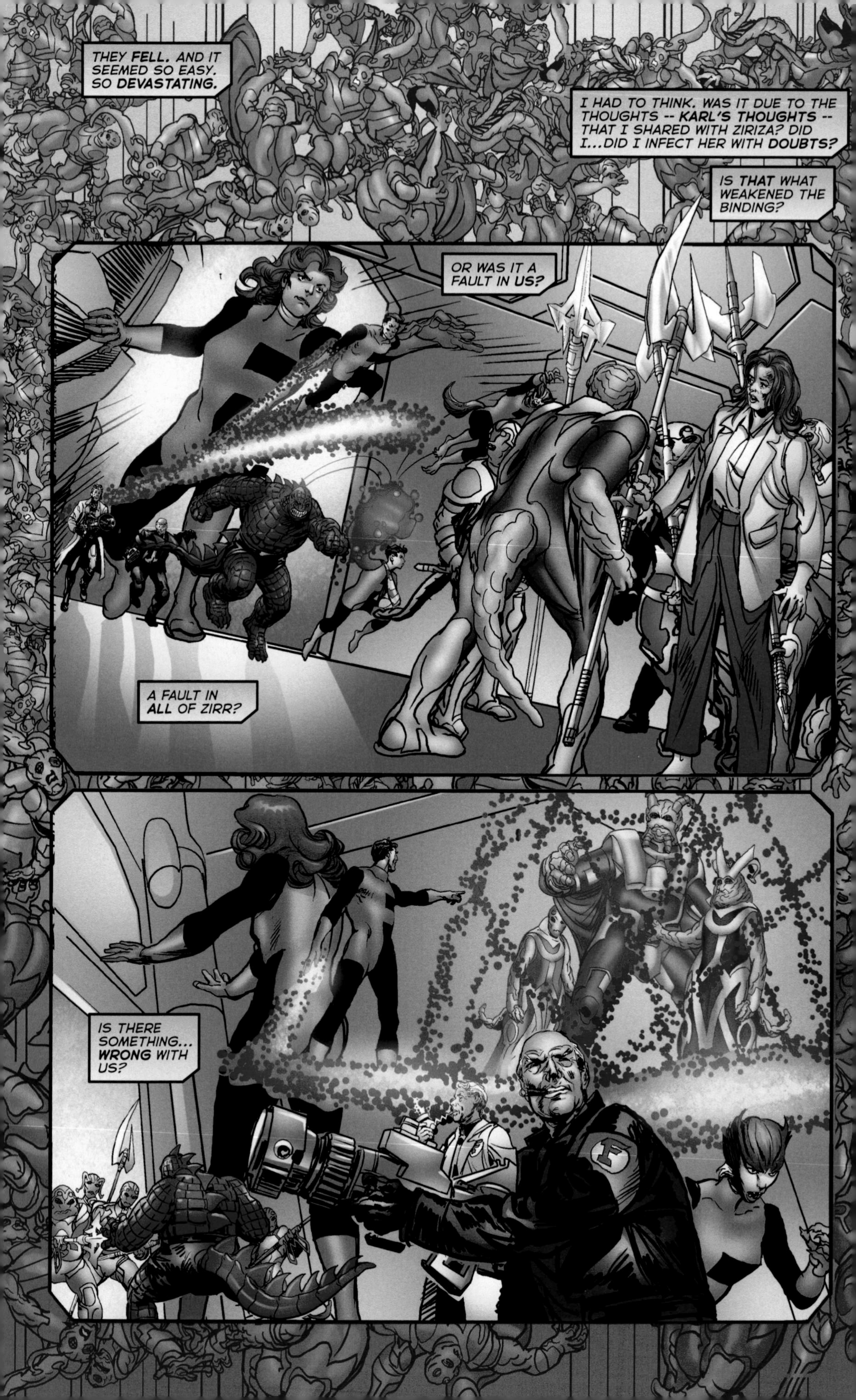
THEY FELL. AND IT SEEMED SO EASY. SO DEVASTATING.
I HAD TO THINK. WAS IT DUE TO THE THOUGHTS -- KARL'S THOUGHTS -- THAT I SHARED WITH ZIRIZA? DID I...DID I INFECT HER WITH DOUBTS?
IS THAT WHAT WEAKENED THE BINDING?
OR WAS IT A FAULT IN US?
A FAULT IN ALL OF ZIRR?
IS THERE SOMETHING... WRONG WITH US?

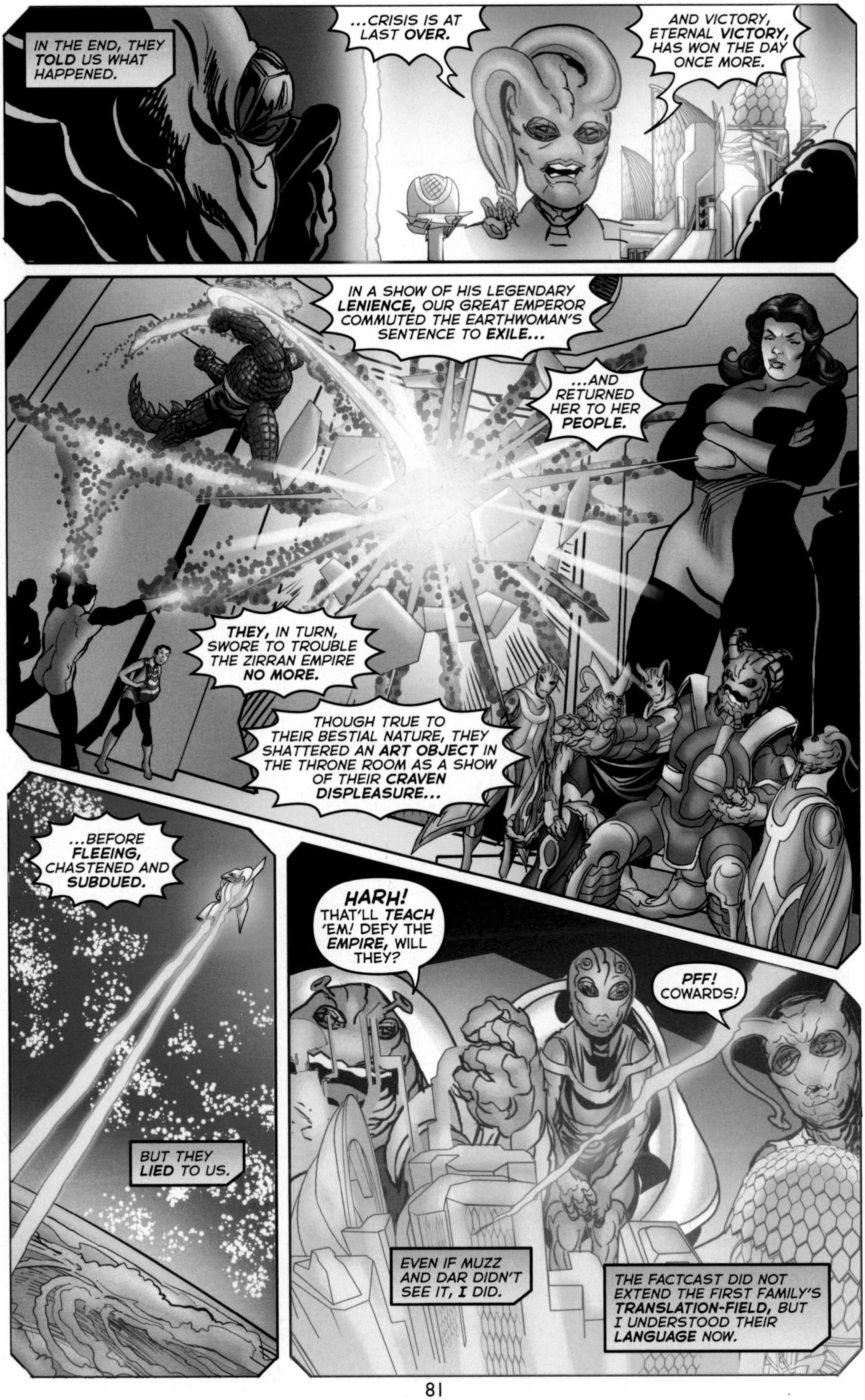
IN THE END, THEY TOLD US WHAT HAPPENED.
...CRISIS IS AT LAST OVER.
AND VICTORY, ETERNAL VICTORY, HAS WON THE DAY ONCE MORE.
IN A SHOW OF HIS LEGENDARY LENIENCE, OUR GREAT EMPEROR COMMUTED THE EARTHWOMAN'S SENTENCE TO EXILE...
...AND RETURNED HER TO HER PEOPLE.
THEY, IN TURN, SWORE TO TROUBLE THE ZIRRAN EMPIRE NO MORE.
THOUGH TRUE TO THEIR BESTIAL NATURE, THEY SHATTERED AN ART OBJECT IN THE THRONE ROOM AS A SHOW OF THEIR CRAVEN DISPLEASURE...
...BEFORE FLEEING, CHASTENED AND SUBDUED.
BUT THEY LIED TO US.
HARH! THAT'LL TEACH 'EM! DEFY THE EMPIRE, WILL THEY?
PFF! COWARDS!
EVEN IF MUZZ AND DAR DIDN'T SEE IT, I DID.
THE FACTCAST DID NOT EXTEND THE FIRST FAMILY'S TRANSLATION-FIELD, BUT I UNDERSTOOD THEIR LANGUAGE NOW.

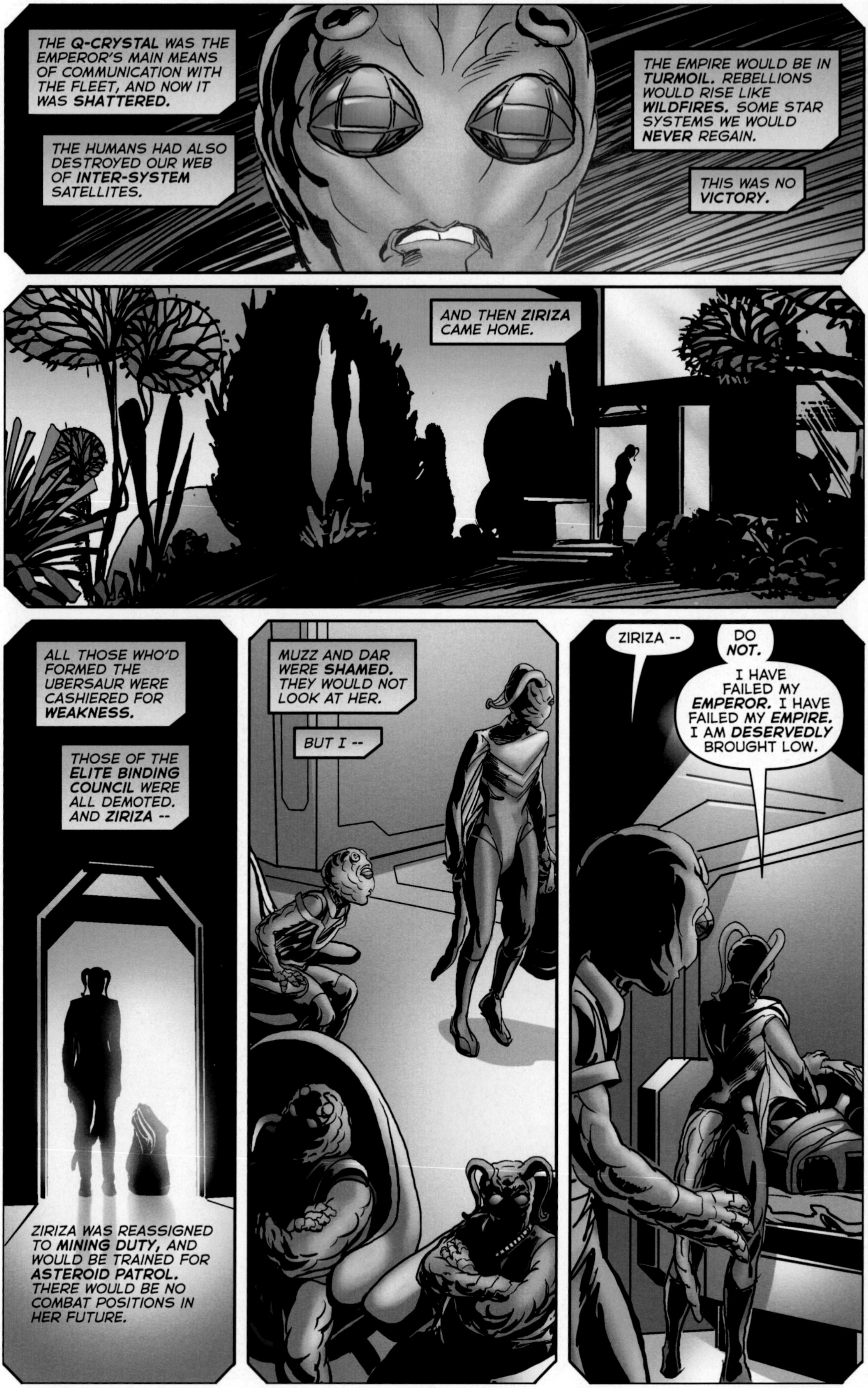
THE Q-CRYSTAL WAS THE EMPEROR'S MAIN MEANS OF COMMUNICATION WITH THE FLEET, AND NOW IT WAS SHATTERED.
THE HUMANS HAD ALSO DESTROYED OUR WEB OF INTER-SYSTEM SATELLITES.
THE EMPIRE WOULD BE IN TURMOIL. REBELLIONS WOULD RISE LIKE WILDFIRES. SOME STAR SYSTEMS WE WOULD NEVER REGAIN.
THIS WAS NO VICTORY.
AND THEN ZIRIZA CAME HOME.
ALL THOSE WHO'D FORMED THE UBERSAUR WERE CASHIERED FOR WEAKNESS.
THOSE OF THE ELITE BINDING COUNCIL WERE ALL DEMOTED. AND ZIRIZA --
ZIRIZA WAS REASSIGNED TO MINING DUTY, AND WOULD BE TRAINED FOR ASTEROID PATROL. THERE WOULD BE NO COMBAT POSITIONS IN HER FUTURE.
MUZZ AND DAR WERE SHAMED. THEY WOULD NOT LOOK AT HER.
BUT I --
ZIRIZA --
DO NOT.
I HAVE FAILED MY EMPEROR. I HAVE FAILED MY EMPIRE. I AM DESERVEDLY BROUGHT LOW.

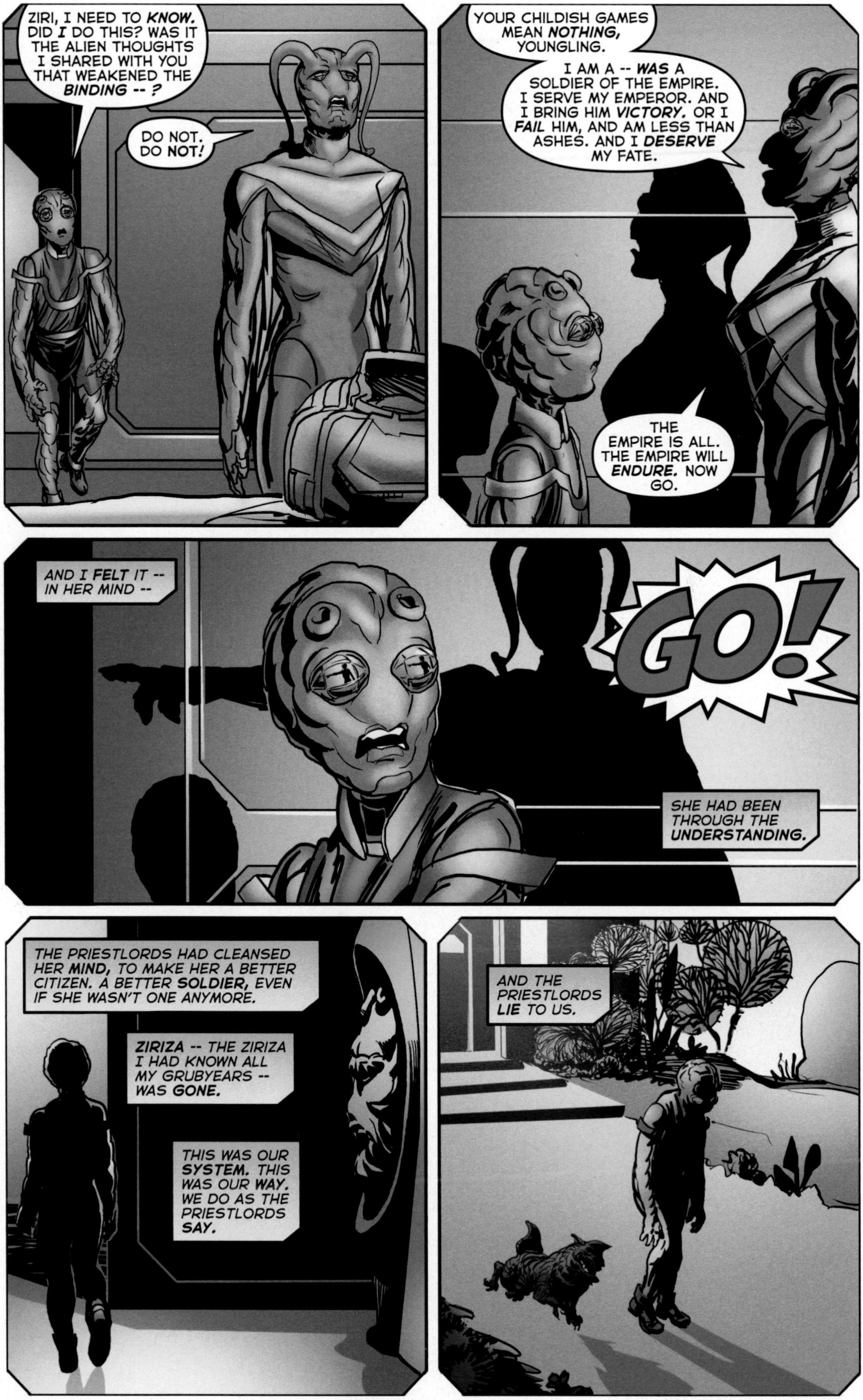
ZIRI, I NEED TO KNOW. DID I DO THIS? WAS IT THE ALIEN THOUGHTS I SHARED WITH YOU THAT WEAKENED THE BINDING -- ?
DO NOT. DO NOT!
YOUR CHILDISH GAMES MEAN NOTHING, YOUNGLING.
I AM A -- WAS A SOLDIER OF THE EMPIRE. I SERVE MY EMPEROR. AND I BRING HIM VICTORY. OR I FAIL HIM, AND AM LESS THAN ASHES. AND I DESERVE MY FATE.
THE EMPIRE IS ALL. THE EMPIRE WILL ENDURE. NOW GO.
AND I FELT IT -- IN HER MIND --
GO!
SHE HAD BEEN THROUGH THE UNDERSTANDING.
THE PRIESTLORDS HAD CLEANSED HER MIND, TO MAKE HER A BETTER CITIZEN. A BETTER SOLDIER, EVEN IF SHE WASN'T ONE ANYMORE.
ZIRIZA -- THE ZIRIZA I HAD KNOWN ALL MY GRUBYEARS -- WAS GONE.
THIS WAS OUR SYSTEM. THIS WAS OUR WAY. WE DO AS THE PRIESTLORDS SAY.
AND THE PRIESTLORDS LIE TO US.

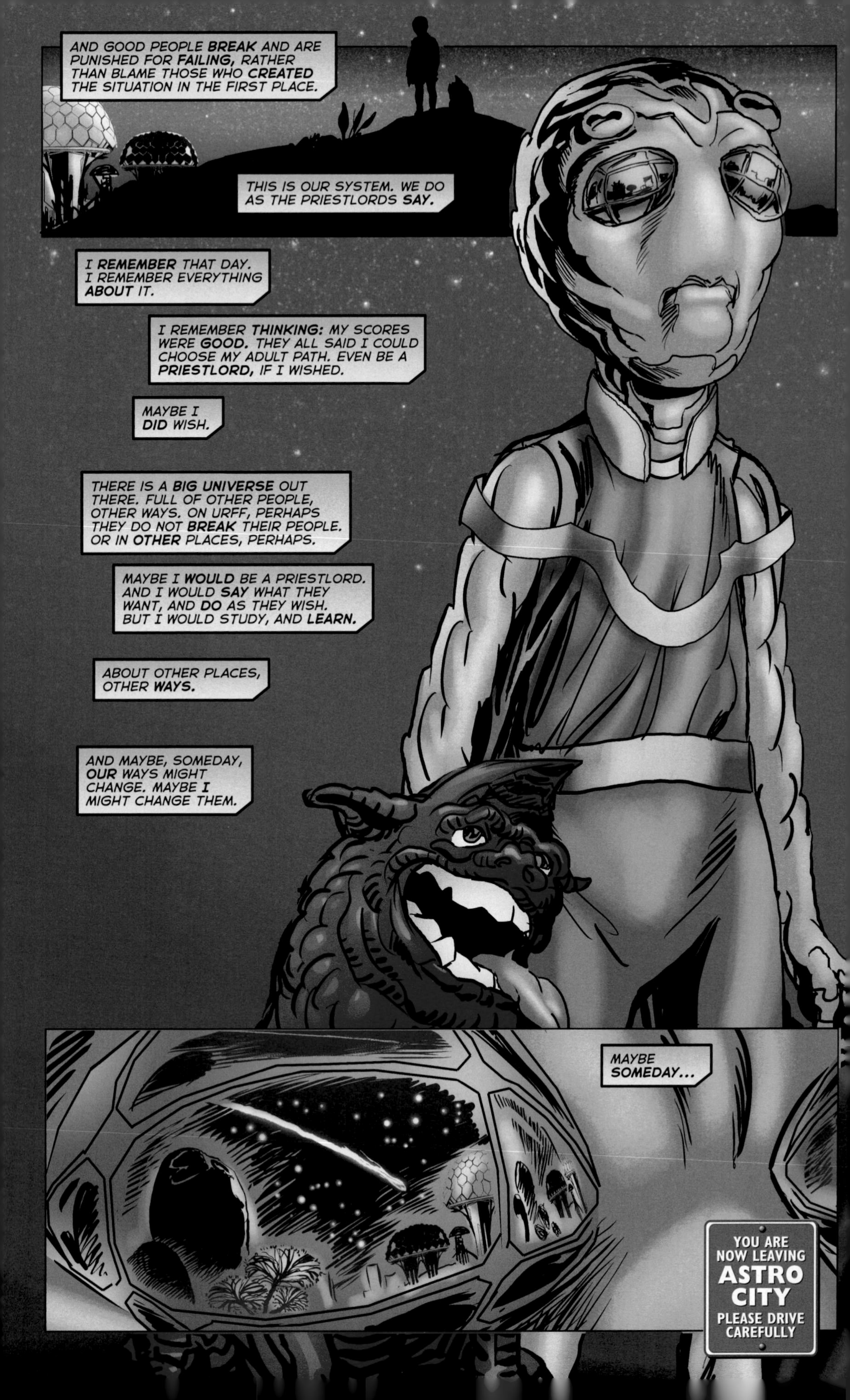
AND GOOD PEOPLE BREAK AND ARE PUNISHED FOR FAILING, RATHER THAN BLAME THOSE WHO CREATED THE SITUATION IN THE FIRST PLACE.
THIS IS OUR SYSTEM. WE DO AS THE PRIESTLORDS SAY.
I REMEMBER THAT DAY. I REMEMBER EVERYTHING ABOUT IT.
I REMEMBER THINKING: MY SCORES WERE GOOD. THEY ALL SAID I COULD CHOOSE MY ADULT PATH. EVEN BE A PRIESTLORD, IF I WISHED.
MAYBE I DID WISH.
THERE IS A BIG UNIVERSE OUT THERE. FULL OF OTHER PEOPLE, OTHER WAYS. ON URFF, PERHAPS THEY DO NOT BREAK THEIR PEOPLE. OR IN OTHER PLACES, PERHAPS.
MAYBE I WOULD BE A PRIESTLORD. AND I WOULD SAY WHAT THEY WANT, AND DO AS THEY WISH. BUT I WOULD STUDY, AND LEARN.
ABOUT OTHER PLACES, OTHER WAYS.
AND MAYBE, SOMEDAY, OUR WAYS MIGHT CHANGE. MAYBE I MIGHT CHANGE THEM.
MAYBE SOMEDAY...
YOU ARE NOW LEAVING ASTRO CITY PLEASE DRIVE CAREFULLY

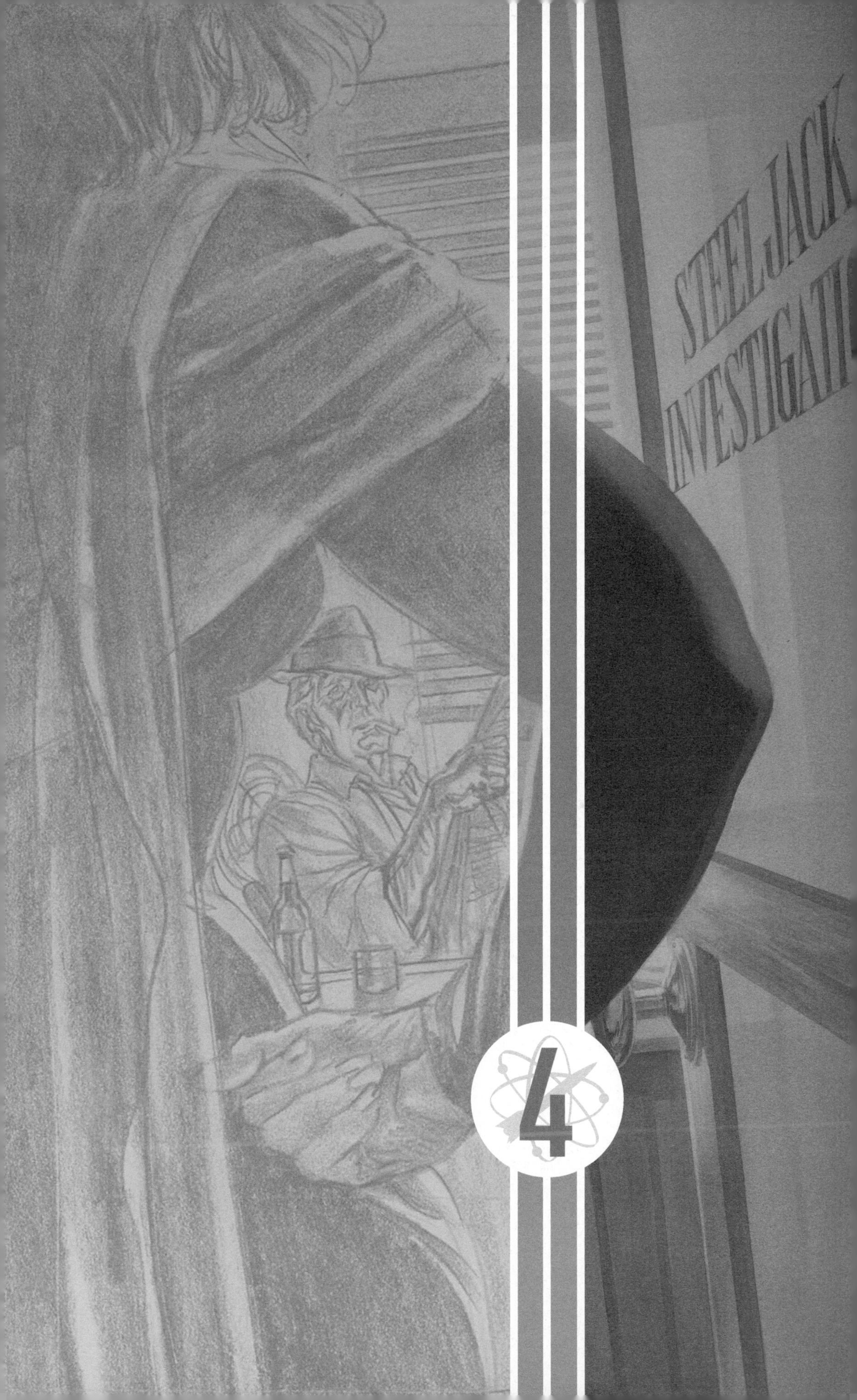
STEEL JACK
INVESTIGATI
4

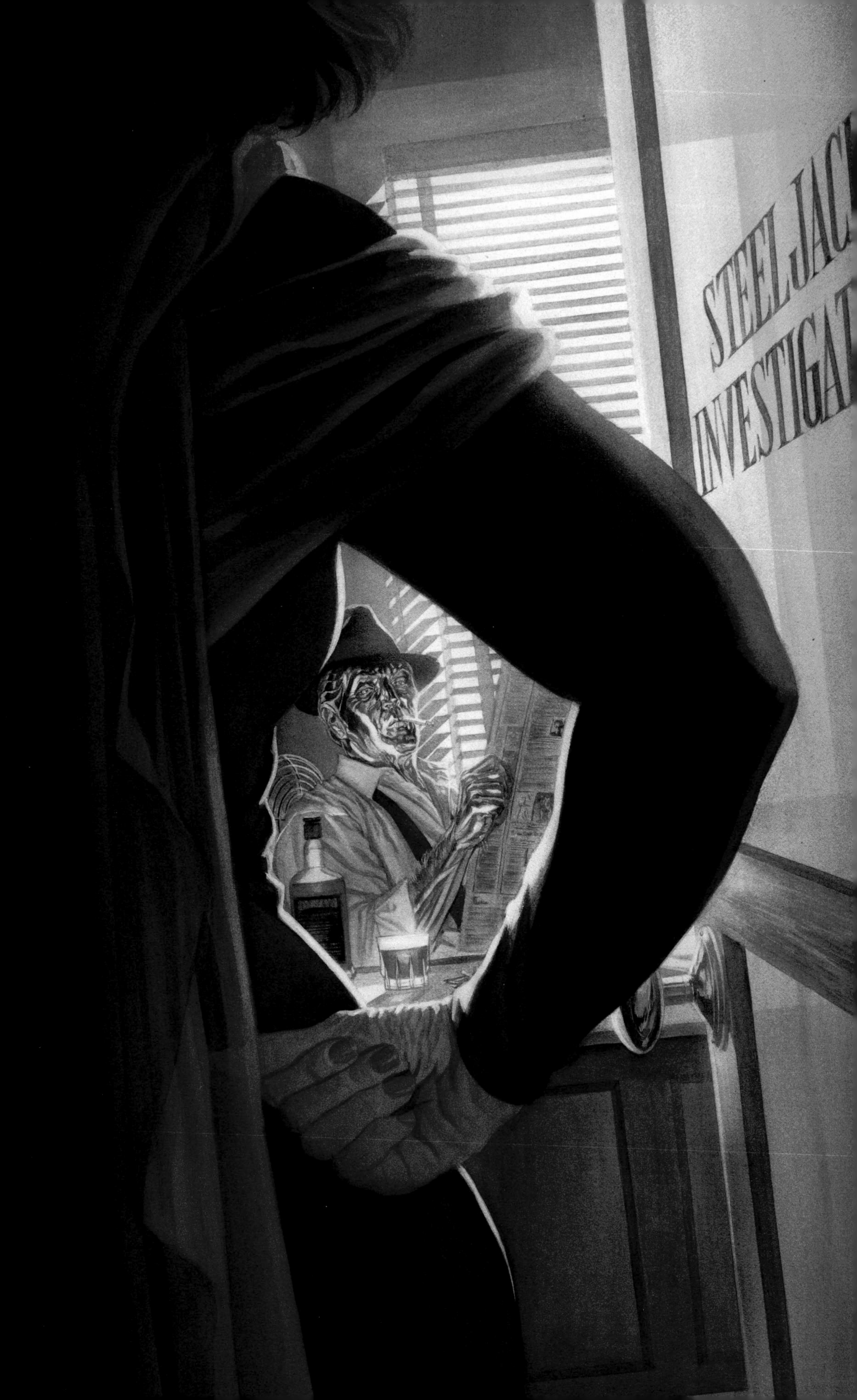
STEEL JAC
INVESTIGAT

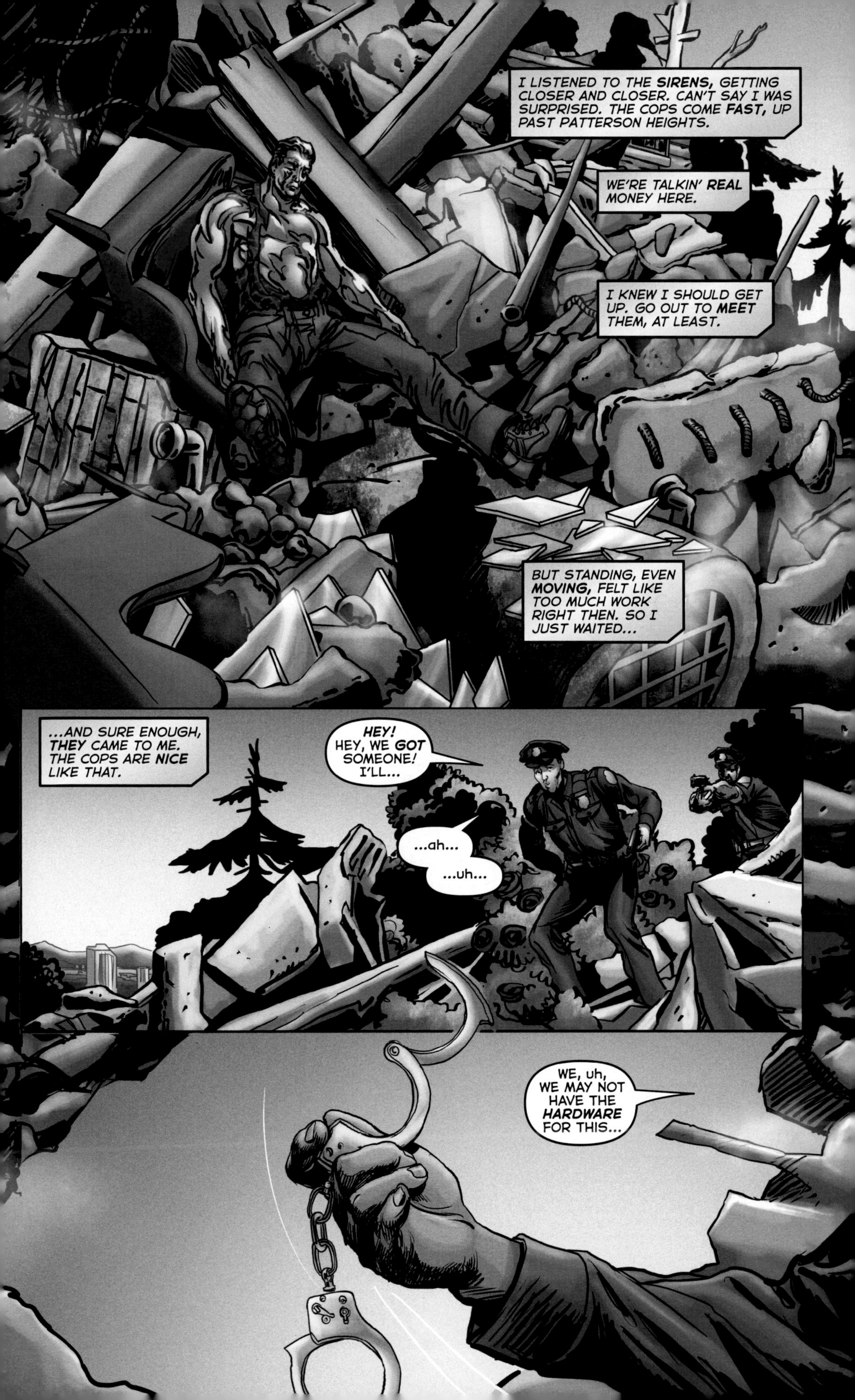
I LISTENED TO THE SIRENS, GETTING CLOSER AND CLOSER. CAN'T SAY I WAS SURPRISED. THE COPS COME FAST, UP PAST PATTERSON HEIGHTS.
WE'RE TALKIN' REAL MONEY HERE.
I KNEW I SHOULD GET UP. GO OUT TO MEET THEM, AT LEAST.
BUT STANDING, EVEN MOVING, FELT LIKE TOO MUCH WORK RIGHT THEN. SO I JUST WAITED...
...AND SURE ENOUGH, THEY CAME TO ME. THE COPS ARE NICE LIKE THAT.
HEY! HEY, WE GOT SOMEONE! I'LL...
...ah...
...uh...
WE, uh, WE MAY NOT HAVE THE HARDWARE FOR THIS...

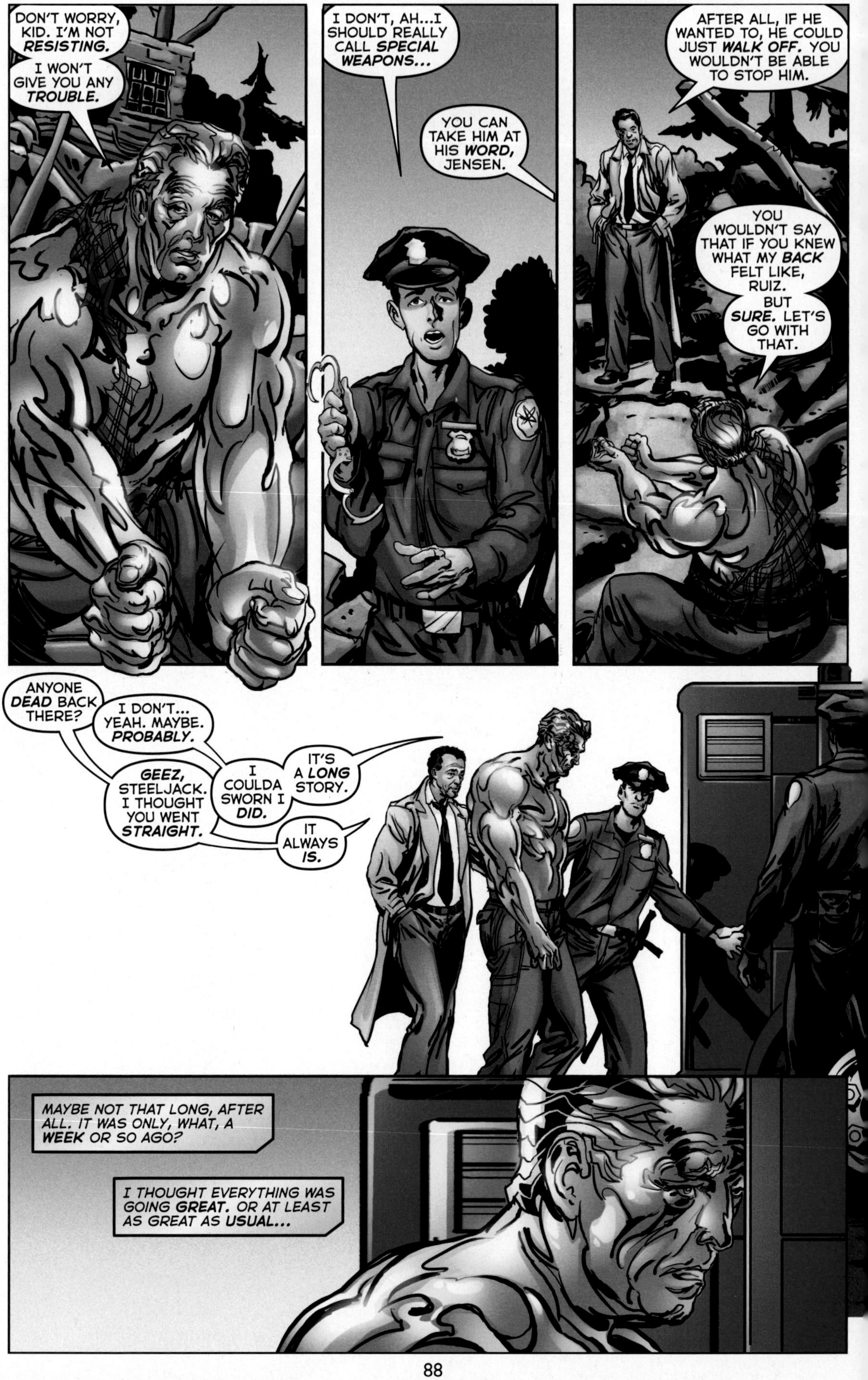
DON'T WORRY, KID. I'M NOT RESISTING.
I WON'T GIVE YOU ANY TROUBLE.
I DON'T, AH...I SHOULD REALLY CALL SPECIAL WEAPONS...
YOU CAN TAKE HIM AT HIS WORD, JENSEN.
AFTER ALL, IF HE WANTED TO, HE COULD JUST WALK OFF. YOU WOULDN'T BE ABLE TO STOP HIM.
YOU WOULDN'T SAY THAT IF YOU KNEW WHAT MY BACK FELT LIKE, RUIZ.
BUT SURE. LET'S GO WITH THAT.
ANYONE DEAD BACK THERE?
I DON'T... YEAH. MAYBE. PROBABLY.
GEEZ, STEELJACK. I THOUGHT YOU WENT STRAIGHT.
I COULDA SWORN I DID.
IT'S A LONG STORY.
IT ALWAYS IS.
MAYBE NOT THAT LONG, AFTER ALL. IT WAS ONLY, WHAT, A WEEK OR SO AGO?
I THOUGHT EVERYTHING WAS GOING GREAT. OR AT LEAST AS GREAT AS USUAL...

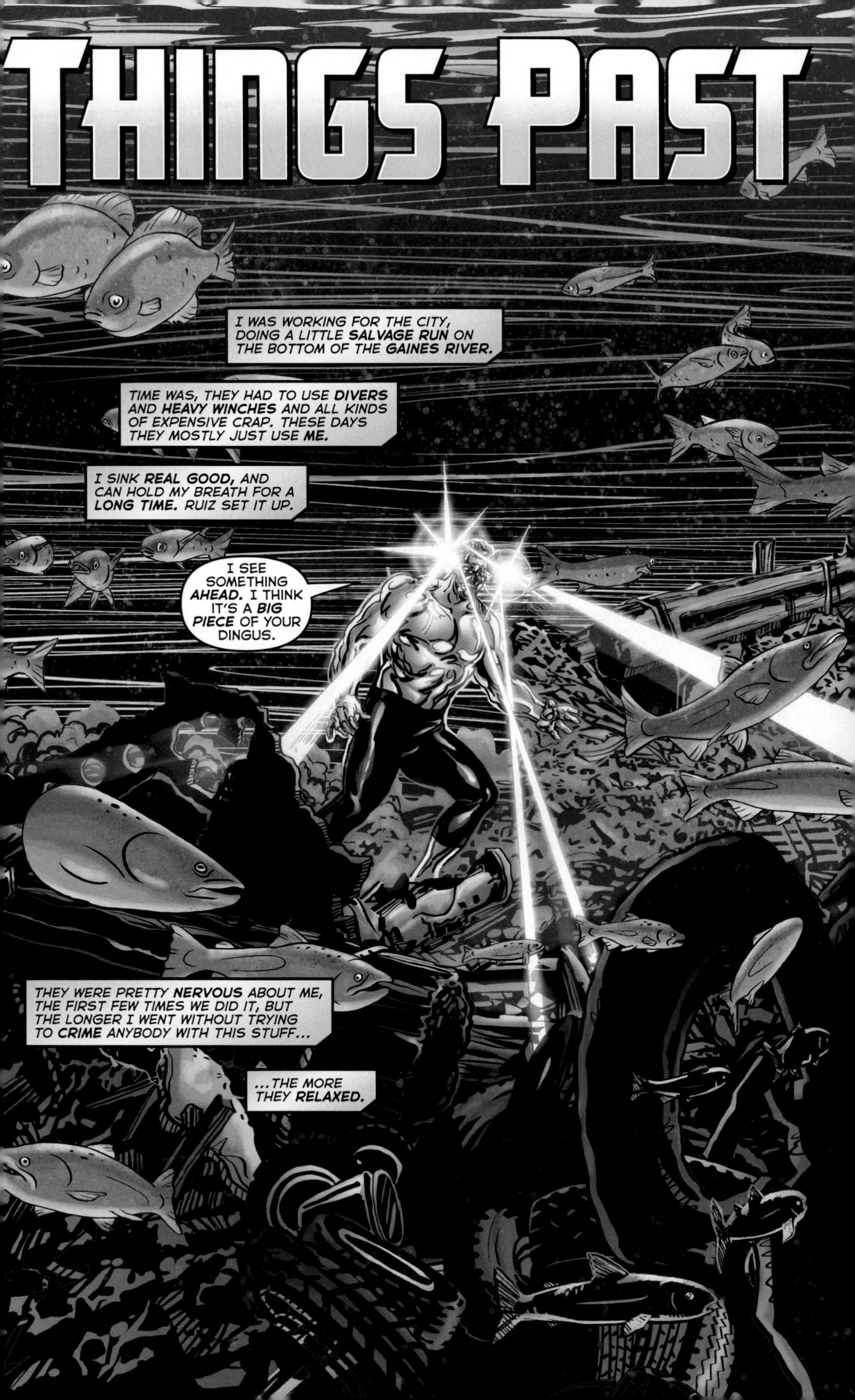
THINGS PAST
I WAS WORKING FOR THE CITY, DOING A LITTLE SALVAGE RUN ON THE BOTTOM OF THE GAINES RIVER.
TIME WAS, THEY HAD TO USE DIVERS AND HEAVY WINCHES AND ALL KINDS OF EXPENSIVE CRAP. THESE DAYS THEY MOSTLY JUST USE ME.
I SINK REAL GOOD, AND CAN HOLD MY BREATH FOR A LONG TIME. RUIZ SET IT UP.
I SEE SOMETHING AHEAD. I THINK IT'S A BIG PIECE OF YOUR DINGUS.
THEY WERE PRETTY NERVOUS ABOUT ME, THE FIRST FEW TIMES WE DID IT, BUT THE LONGER I WENT WITHOUT TRYING TO CRIME ANYBODY WITH THIS STUFF...
...THE MORE THEY RELAXED.

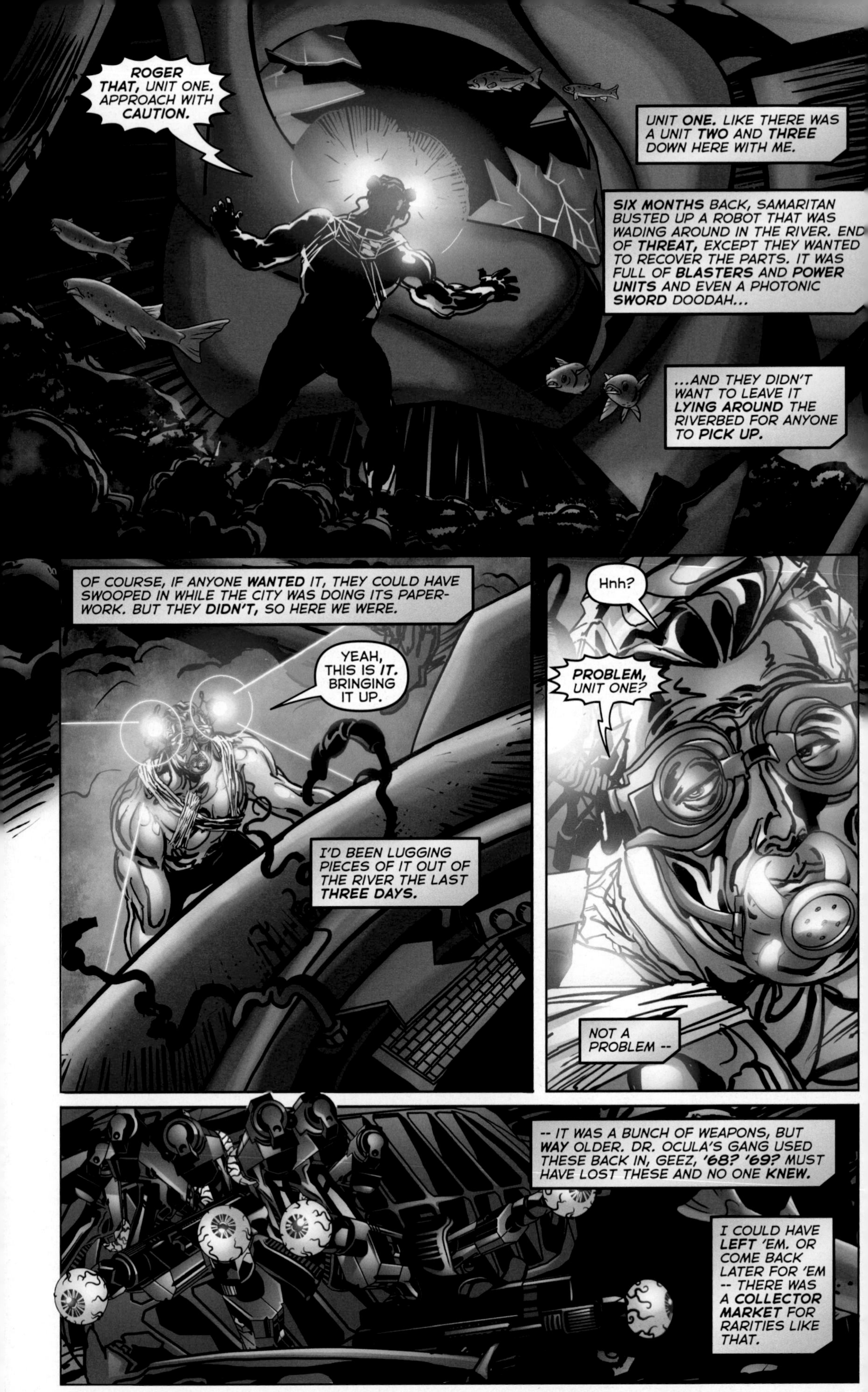
ROGER THAT, UNIT ONE. APPROACH WITH CAUTION.
UNIT ONE. LIKE THERE WAS A UNIT TWO AND THREE DOWN HERE WITH ME.
SIX MONTHS BACK, SAMARITAN BUSTED UP A ROBOT THAT WAS WADING AROUND IN THE RIVER. END OF THREAT, EXCEPT THEY WANTED TO RECOVER THE PARTS. IT WAS FULL OF BLASTERS AND POWER UNITS AND EVEN A PHOTONIC SWORD DOODAH...
...AND THEY DIDN'T WANT TO LEAVE IT LYING AROUND THE RIVERBED FOR ANYONE TO PICK UP.
OF COURSE, IF ANYONE WANTED IT, THEY COULD HAVE SWOOPED IN WHILE THE CITY WAS DOING ITS PAPER-WORK. BUT THEY DIDN'T, SO HERE WE WERE.
YEAH, THIS IS IT. BRINGING IT UP.
I'D BEEN LUGGING PIECES OF IT OUT OF THE RIVER THE LAST THREE DAYS.
Hnh?
PROBLEM, UNIT ONE?
NOT A PROBLEM --
-- IT WAS A BUNCH OF WEAPONS, BUT WAY OLDER. DR. OCULA'S GANG USED THESE BACK IN, GEEZ, '68? '69? MUST HAVE LOST THESE AND NO ONE KNEW.
I COULD HAVE LEFT 'EM. OR COME BACK LATER FOR 'EM -- THERE WAS A COLLECTOR MARKET FOR RARITIES LIKE THAT.

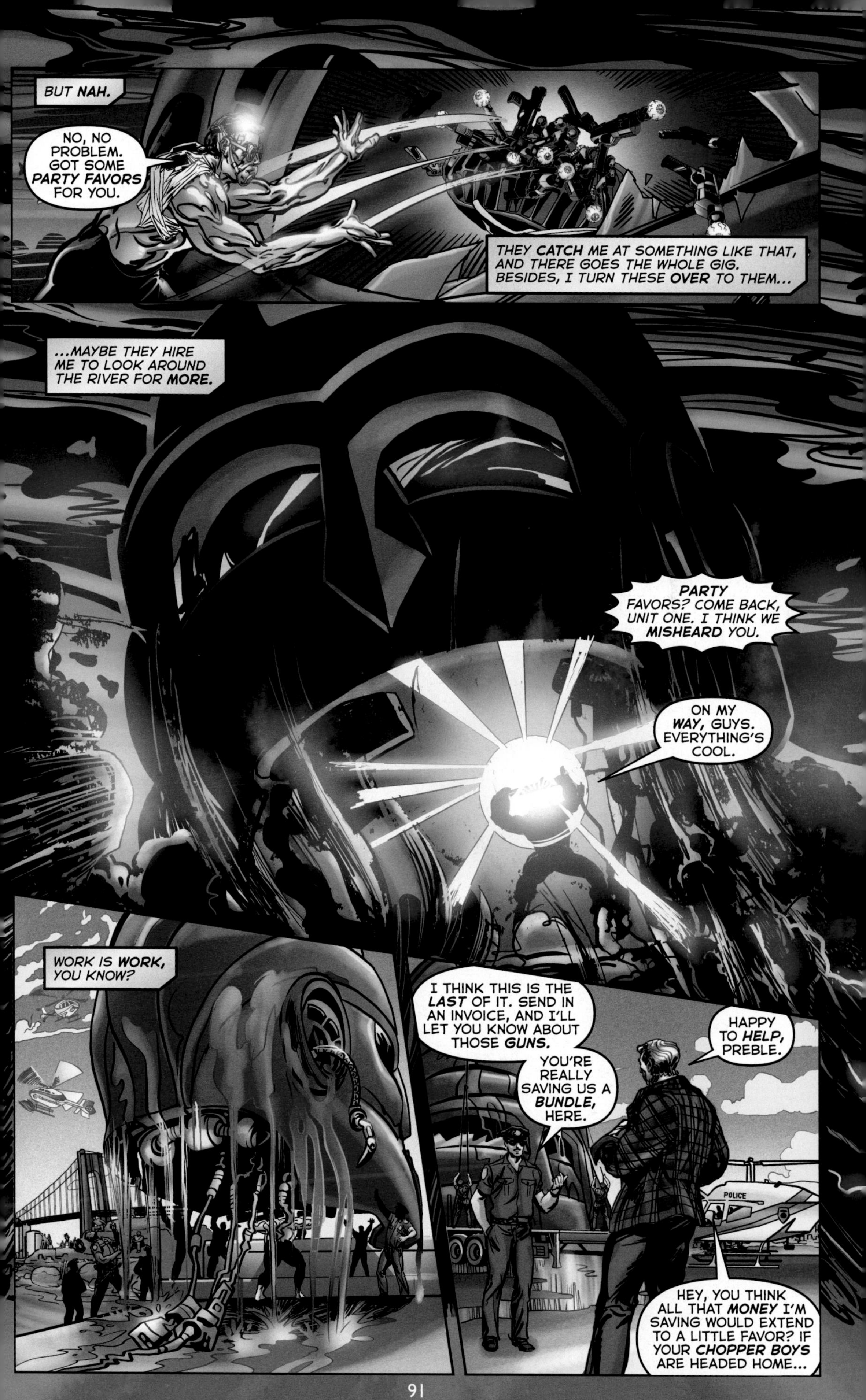
BUT NAH.
NO, NO PROBLEM. GOT SOME PARTY FAVORS FOR YOU.
THEY CATCH ME AT SOMETHING LIKE THAT, AND THERE GOES THE WHOLE GIG. BESIDES, I TURN THESE OVER TO THEM...
...MAYBE THEY HIRE ME TO LOOK AROUND THE RIVER FOR MORE.
PARTY FAVORS? COME BACK, UNIT ONE. I THINK WE MISHEARD YOU.
ON MY WAY, GUYS. EVERYTHING'S COOL.
WORK IS WORK, YOU KNOW?
I THINK THIS IS THE LAST OF IT. SEND IN AN INVOICE, AND I'LL LET YOU KNOW ABOUT THOSE GUNS.
YOU'RE REALLY SAVING US A BUNDLE, HERE.
HAPPY TO HELP, PREBLE.
POLICE
HEY, YOU THINK ALL THAT MONEY I'M SAVING WOULD EXTEND TO A LITTLE FAVOR? IF YOUR CHOPPER BOYS ARE HEADED HOME...

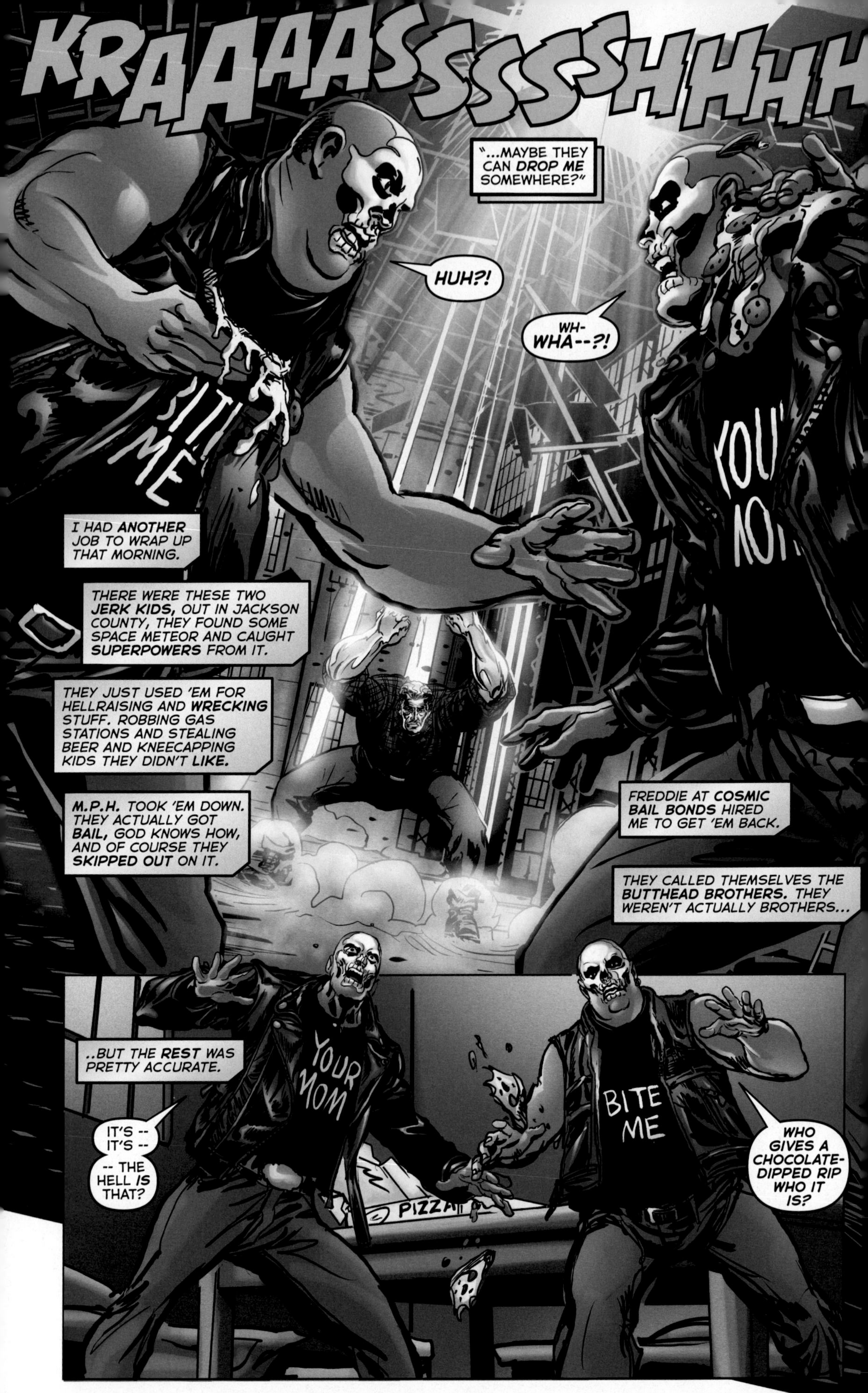
KRAAAASSSSSHHHH
"...MAYBE THEY CAN DROP ME SOMEWHERE?"
HUH?!
WH- WHA--?!
BITE ME
YOUR MOM
I HAD ANOTHER JOB TO WRAP UP THAT MORNING.
THERE WERE THESE TWO JERK KIDS, OUT IN JACKSON COUNTY, THEY FOUND SOME SPACE METEOR AND CAUGHT SUPERPOWERS FROM IT.
THEY JUST USED 'EM FOR HELLRAISING AND WRECKING STUFF. ROBBING GAS STATIONS AND STEALING BEER AND KNEECAPPING KIDS THEY DIDN'T LIKE.
M.P.H. TOOK 'EM DOWN. THEY ACTUALLY GOT BAIL, GOD KNOWS HOW, AND OF COURSE THEY SKIPPED OUT ON IT.
FREDDIE AT COSMIC BAIL BONDS HIRED ME TO GET 'EM BACK.
THEY CALLED THEMSELVES THE BUTTHEAD BROTHERS. THEY WEREN'T ACTUALLY BROTHERS...
..BUT THE REST WAS PRETTY ACCURATE.
YOUR MOM
BITE ME
IT'S -- IT'S --
-- THE HELL IS THAT?
PIZZA
WHO GIVES A CHOCOLATE-DIPPED RIP WHO IT IS?

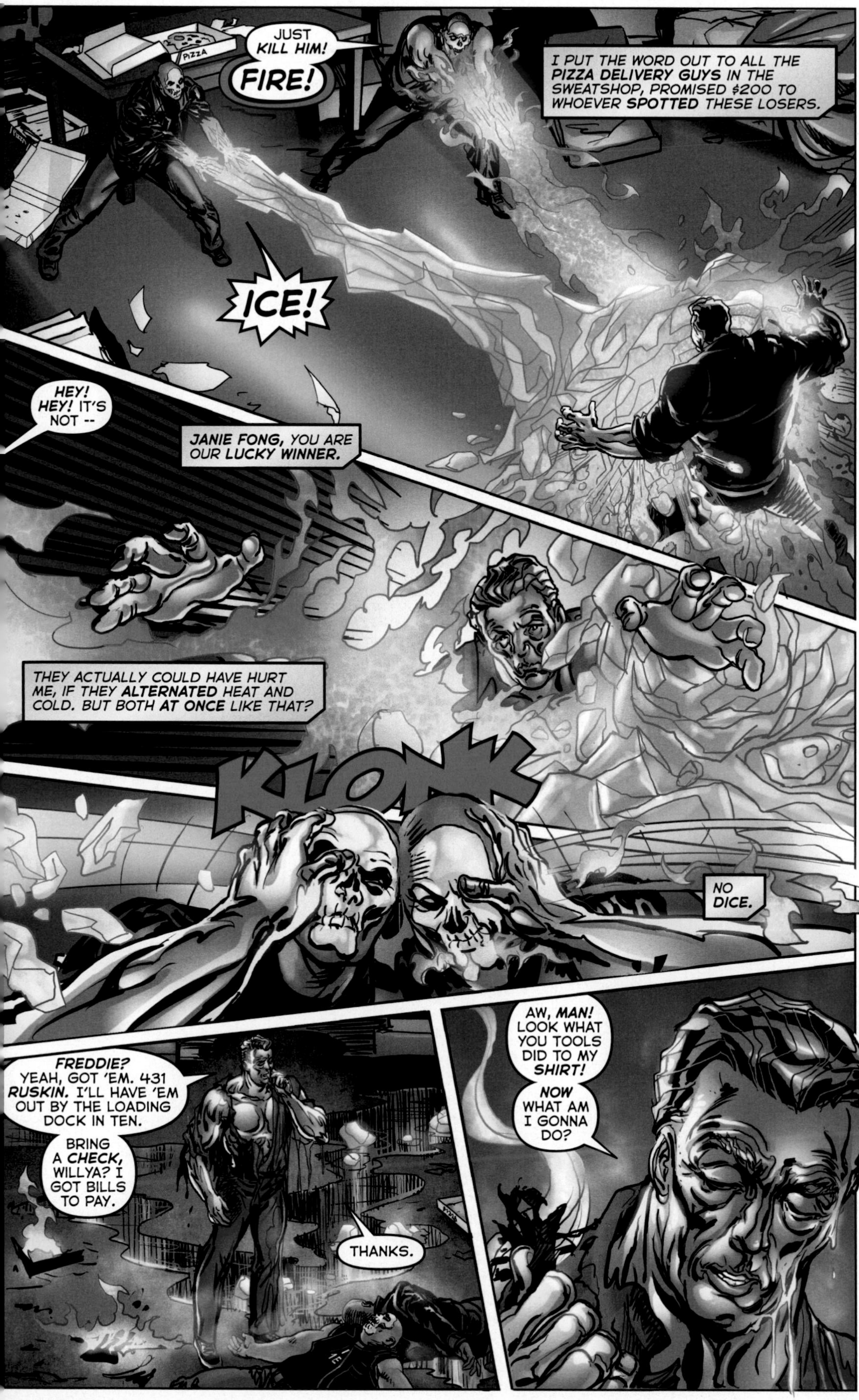
JUST KILL HIM!
FIRE!
I PUT THE WORD OUT TO ALL THE PIZZA DELIVERY GUYS IN THE SWEATSHOP, PROMISED $200 TO WHOEVER SPOTTED THESE LOSERS.
ICE!
HEY! HEY! IT'S NOT --
JANIE FONG, YOU ARE OUR LUCKY WINNER.
THEY ACTUALLY COULD HAVE HURT ME, IF THEY ALTERNATED HEAT AND COLD. BUT BOTH AT ONCE LIKE THAT?
KLONK
NO DICE.
FREDDIE? YEAH, GOT 'EM. 431 RUSKIN. I'LL HAVE 'EM OUT BY THE LOADING DOCK IN TEN.
BRING A CHECK, WILLYA? I GOT BILLS TO PAY.
THANKS.
AW, MAN! LOOK WHAT YOU TOOLS DID TO MY SHIRT!
NOW WHAT AM I GONNA DO?

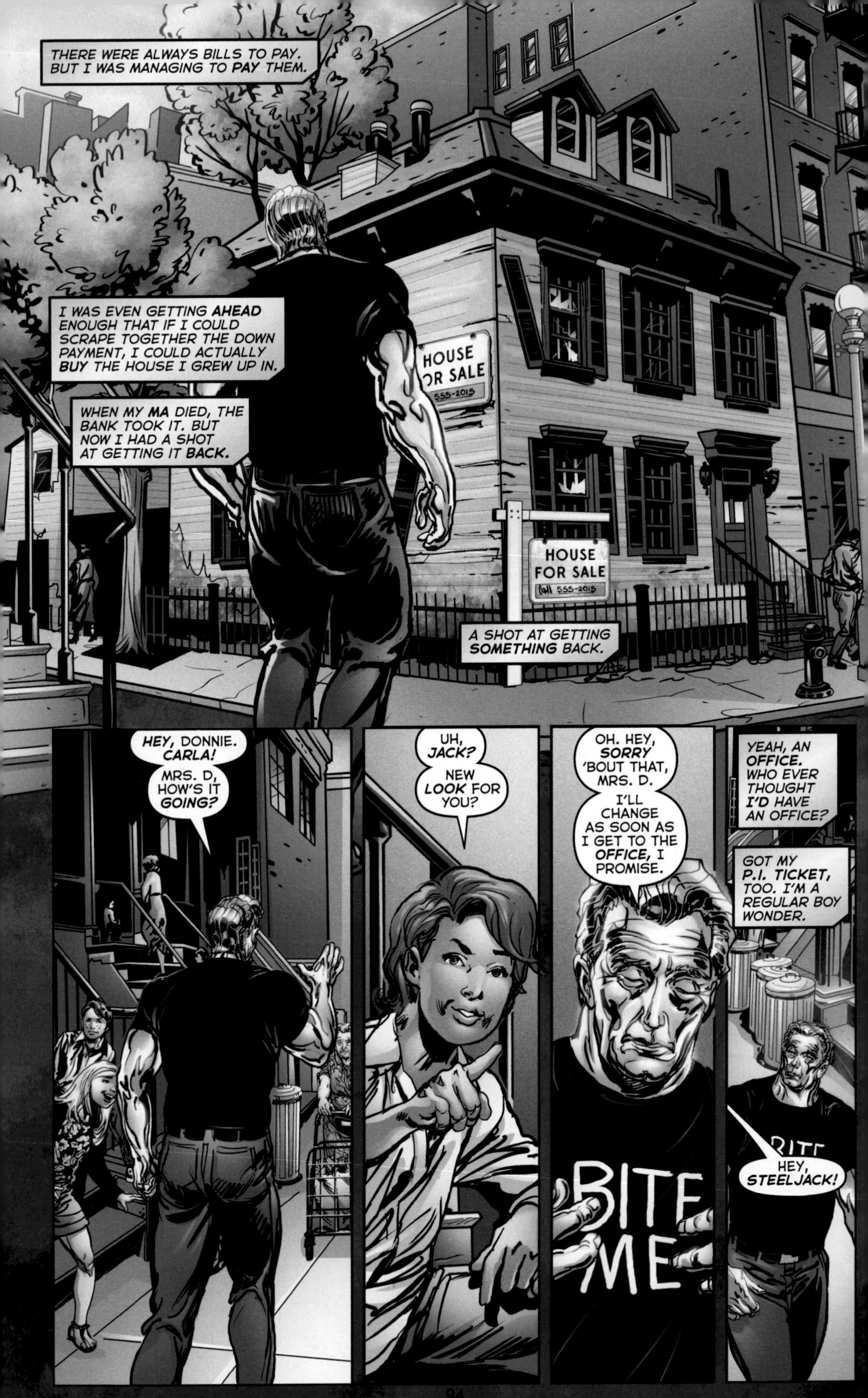
THERE WERE ALWAYS BILLS TO PAY. BUT I WAS MANAGING TO PAY THEM.
I WAS EVEN GETTING AHEAD ENOUGH THAT IF I COULD SCRAPE TOGETHER THE DOWN PAYMENT, I COULD ACTUALLY BUY THE HOUSE I GREW UP IN.
WHEN MY MA DIED, THE BANK TOOK IT. BUT NOW I HAD A SHOT AT GETTING IT BACK.
HOUSE FOR SALE 555-2015
HOUSE FOR SALE Call 555-2015
A SHOT AT GETTING SOMETHING BACK.
HEY, DONNIE. CARLA!
MRS. D, HOW'S IT GOING?
UH, JACK?
NEW LOOK FOR YOU?
OH. HEY, SORRY 'BOUT THAT, MRS. D.
I'LL CHANGE AS SOON AS I GET TO THE OFFICE, I PROMISE.
BITE ME
YEAH, AN OFFICE. WHO EVER THOUGHT I'D HAVE AN OFFICE?
GOT MY P.I. TICKET, TOO. I'M A REGULAR BOY WONDER.
HEY, STEELJACK!

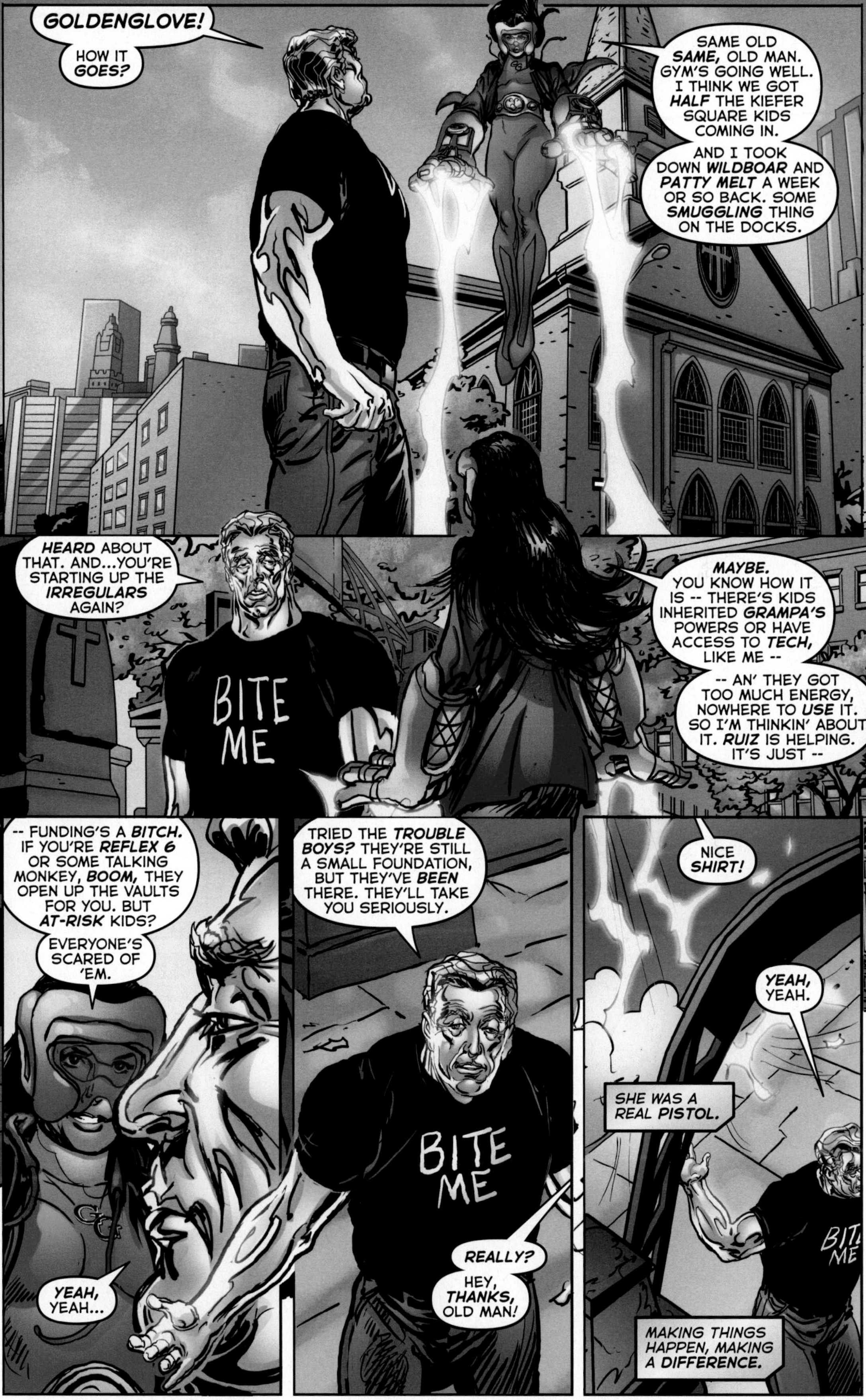
GOLDENGLOVE!
HOW IT GOES?
SAME OLD SAME, OLD MAN. GYM'S GOING WELL. I THINK WE GOT HALF THE KIEFER SQUARE KIDS COMING IN.
AND I TOOK DOWN WILDBOAR AND PATTY MELT A WEEK OR SO BACK. SOME SMUGGLING THING ON THE DOCKS.
HEARD ABOUT THAT. AND...YOU'RE STARTING UP THE IRREGULARS AGAIN?
MAYBE. YOU KNOW HOW IT IS -- THERE'S KIDS INHERITED GRAMPA'S POWERS OR HAVE ACCESS TO TECH, LIKE ME --
-- AN' THEY GOT TOO MUCH ENERGY, NOWHERE TO USE IT. SO I'M THINKIN' ABOUT IT. RUIZ IS HELPING. IT'S JUST --
BITE ME
-- FUNDING'S A BITCH. IF YOU'RE REFLEX 6 OR SOME TALKING MONKEY, BOOM, THEY OPEN UP THE VAULTS FOR YOU. BUT AT-RISK KIDS?
EVERYONE'S SCARED OF 'EM.
YEAH, YEAH...
TRIED THE TROUBLE BOYS? THEY'RE STILL A SMALL FOUNDATION, BUT THEY'VE BEEN THERE. THEY'LL TAKE YOU SERIOUSLY.
BITE ME
REALLY?
HEY, THANKS, OLD MAN!
NICE SHIRT!
YEAH, YEAH.
SHE WAS A REAL PISTOL.
MAKING THINGS HAPPEN, MAKING A DIFFERENCE.

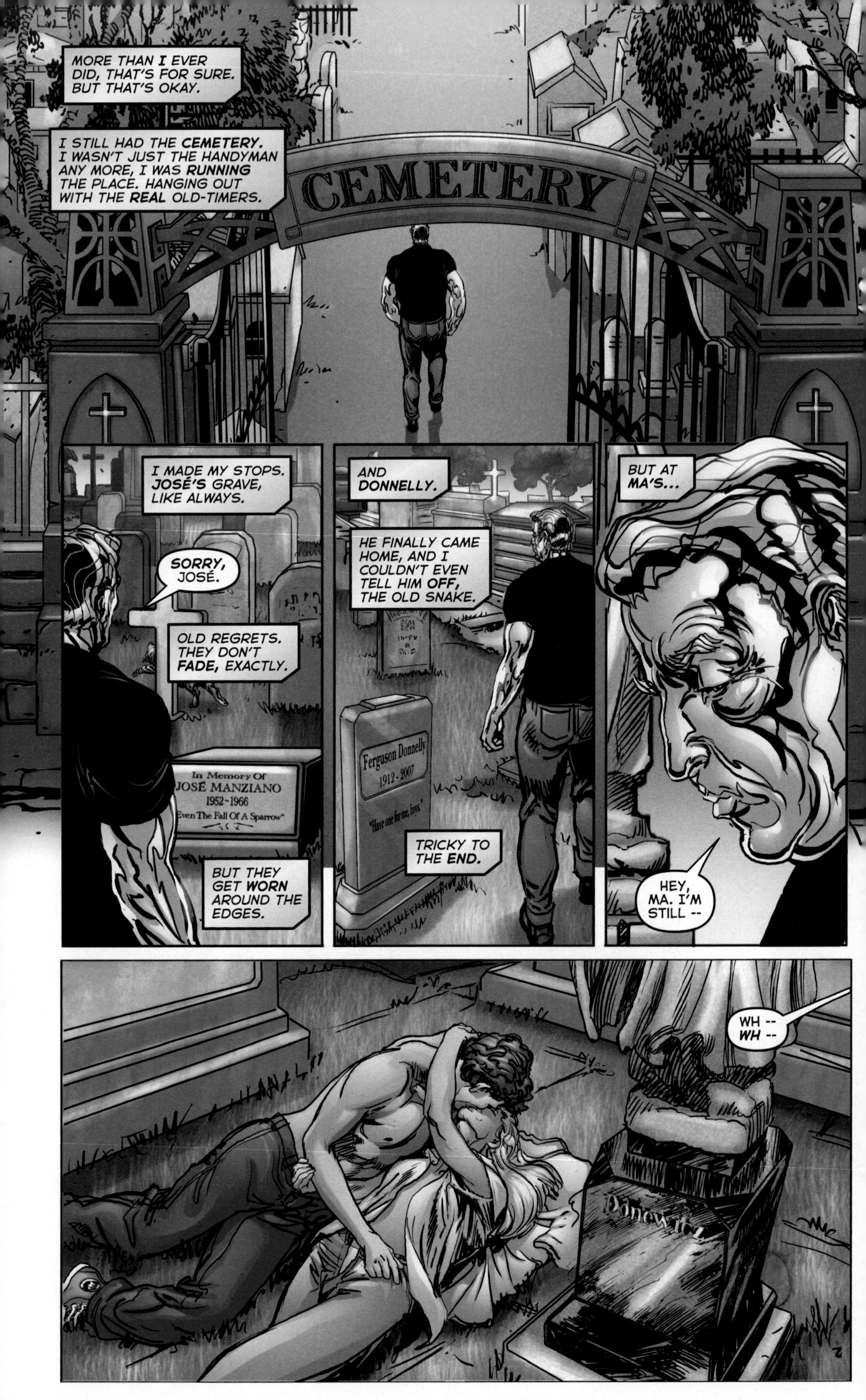
MORE THAN I EVER DID, THAT'S FOR SURE. BUT THAT'S OKAY.
I STILL HAD THE CEMETERY. I WASN'T JUST THE HANDYMAN ANY MORE, I WAS RUNNING THE PLACE. HANGING OUT WITH THE REAL OLD-TIMERS.
CEMETERY
I MADE MY STOPS. JOSÉ'S GRAVE, LIKE ALWAYS.
SORRY, JOSÉ.
OLD REGRETS. THEY DON'T FADE, EXACTLY.
In Memory Of JOSÉ MANZIANO 1952-1966 "Even The Fall Of A Sparrow"
BUT THEY GET WORN AROUND THE EDGES.
AND DONNELLY.
HE FINALLY CAME HOME, AND I COULDN'T EVEN TELL HIM OFF, THE OLD SNAKE.
Ferguson Donnelly 1912-2007 "Have one for me, boys."
TRICKY TO THE END.
BUT AT MA'S...
HEY, MA. I'M STILL --
WH -- WH --

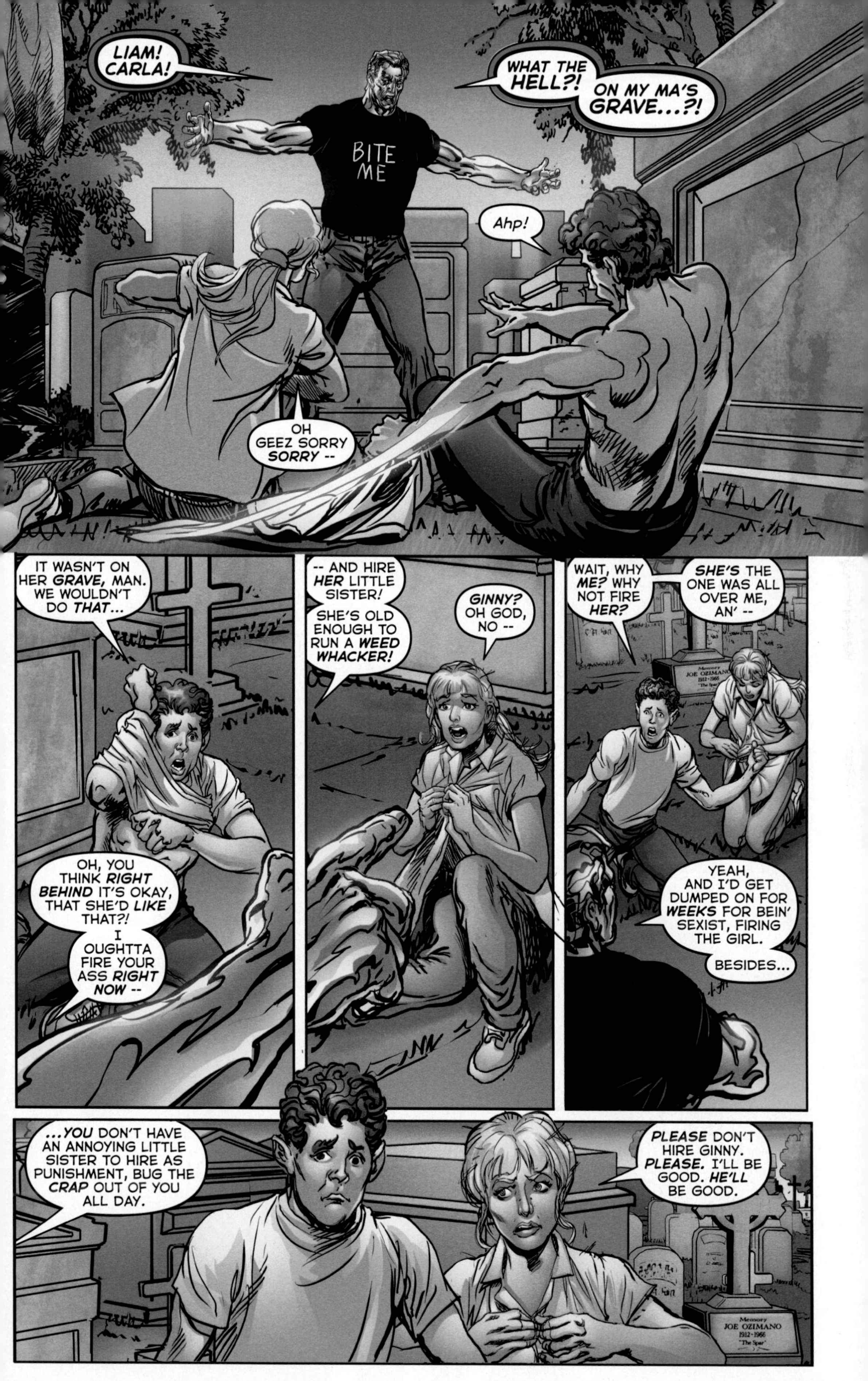
LIAM! CARLA!
WHAT THE HELL?!
ON MY MA'S GRAVE...?!
Ahp!
OH GEEZ SORRY SORRY --
IT WASN'T ON HER GRAVE, MAN. WE WOULDN'T DO THAT...
OH, YOU THINK RIGHT BEHIND IT'S OKAY, THAT SHE'D LIKE THAT?!
I OUGHTTA FIRE YOUR ASS RIGHT NOW --
-- AND HIRE HER LITTLE SISTER!
SHE'S OLD ENOUGH TO RUN A WEED WHACKER!
GINNY? OH GOD, NO --
WAIT, WHY ME? WHY NOT FIRE HER?
SHE'S THE ONE WAS ALL OVER ME, AN' --
YEAH, AND I'D GET DUMPED ON FOR WEEKS FOR BEIN' SEXIST, FIRING THE GIRL.
BESIDES...
...YOU DON'T HAVE AN ANNOYING LITTLE SISTER TO HIRE AS PUNISHMENT, BUG THE CRAP OUT OF YOU ALL DAY.
PLEASE DON'T HIRE GINNY. PLEASE. I'LL BE GOOD. HE'LL BE GOOD.

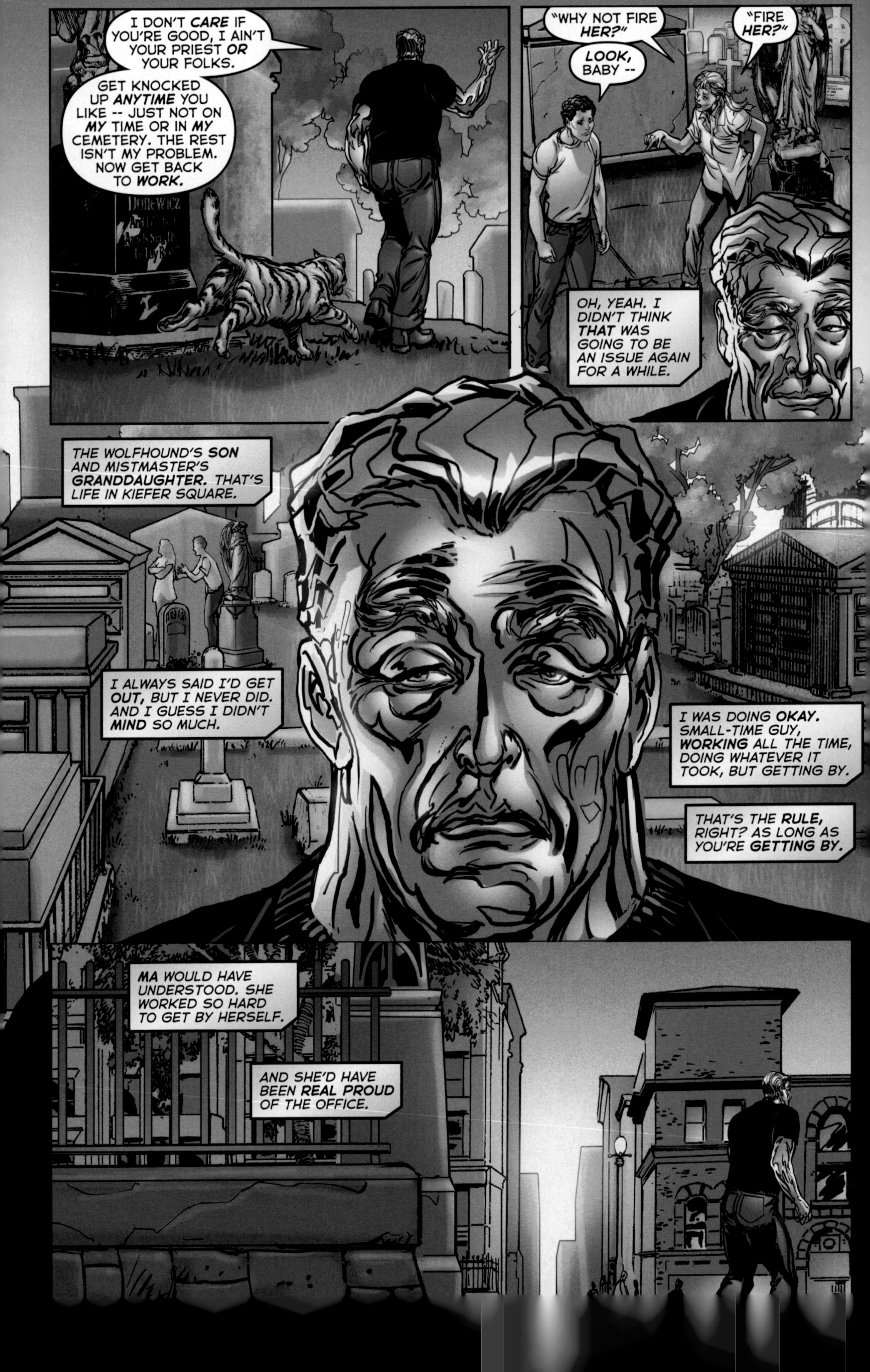
I DON'T CARE IF YOU'RE GOOD, I AIN'T YOUR PRIEST OR YOUR FOLKS.
GET KNOCKED UP ANYTIME YOU LIKE -- JUST NOT ON MY TIME OR IN MY CEMETERY. THE REST ISN'T MY PROBLEM. NOW GET BACK TO WORK.
"WHY NOT FIRE HER?"
LOOK, BABY --
"FIRE HER?"
OH, YEAH. I DIDN'T THINK THAT WAS GOING TO BE AN ISSUE AGAIN FOR A WHILE.
THE WOLFHOUND'S SON AND MISTMASTER'S GRANDDAUGHTER. THAT'S LIFE IN KIEFER SQUARE.
I ALWAYS SAID I'D GET OUT, BUT I NEVER DID. AND I GUESS I DIDN'T MIND SO MUCH.
I WAS DOING OKAY. SMALL-TIME GUY, WORKING ALL THE TIME, DOING WHATEVER IT TOOK, BUT GETTING BY.
THAT'S THE RULE, RIGHT? AS LONG AS YOU'RE GETTING BY.
MA WOULD HAVE UNDERSTOOD. SHE WORKED SO HARD TO GET BY HERSELF.
AND SHE'D HAVE BEEN REAL PROUD OF THE OFFICE.

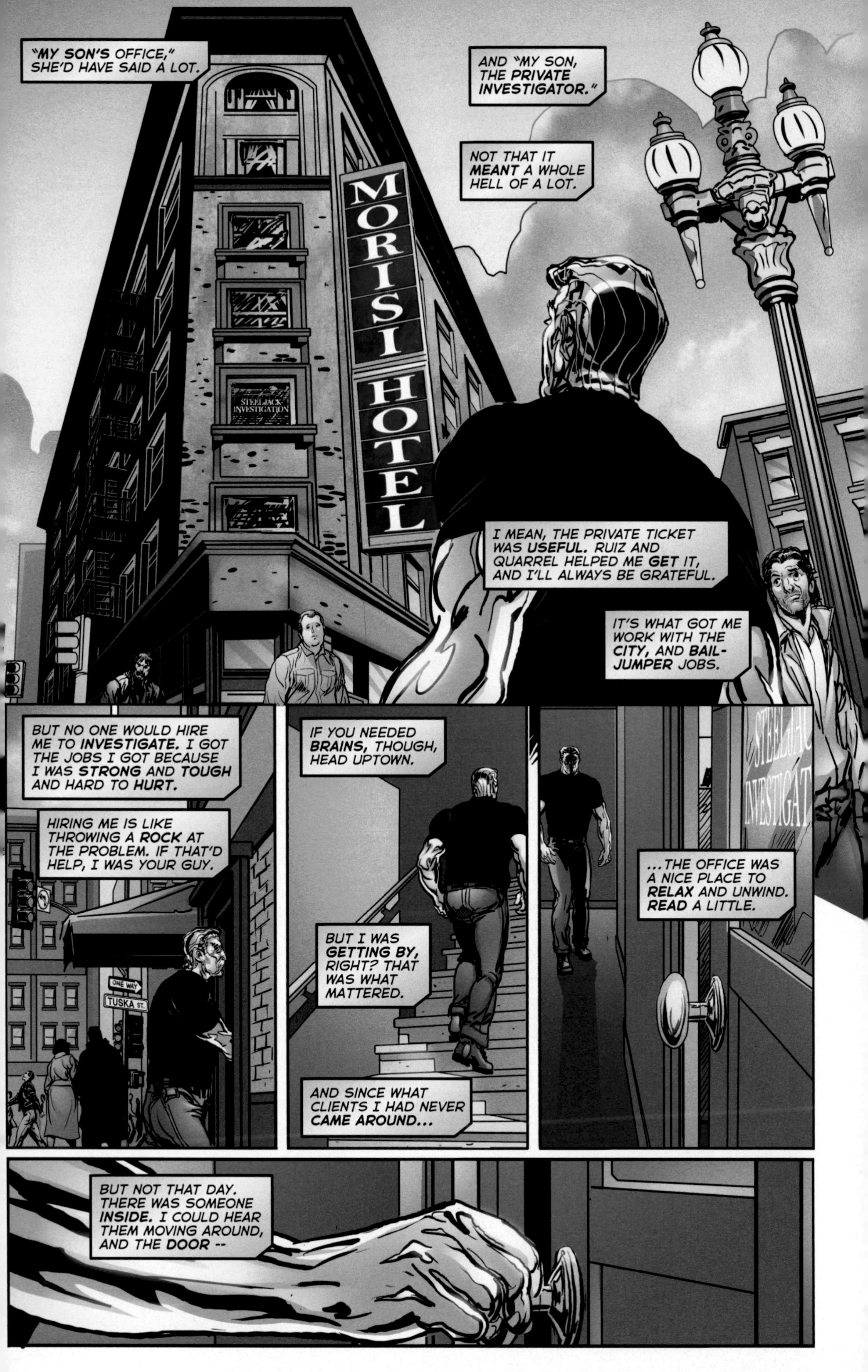

"MY SON'S OFFICE," SHE'D HAVE SAID A LOT.
AND "MY SON, THE PRIVATE INVESTIGATOR."
NOT THAT IT MEANT A WHOLE HELL OF A LOT.
MORISI HOTEL
STEELJACK INVESTIGATION
I MEAN, THE PRIVATE TICKET WAS USEFUL. RUIZ AND QUARREL HELPED ME GET IT, AND I'LL ALWAYS BE GRATEFUL.
IT'S WHAT GOT ME WORK WITH THE CITY, AND BAIL-JUMPER JOBS.
BUT NO ONE WOULD HIRE ME TO INVESTIGATE. I GOT THE JOBS I GOT BECAUSE I WAS STRONG AND TOUGH AND HARD TO HURT.
HIRING ME IS LIKE THROWING A ROCK AT THE PROBLEM. IF THAT'D HELP, I WAS YOUR GUY.
ONE WAY
TUSKA ST.
IF YOU NEEDED BRAINS, THOUGH, HEAD UPTOWN.
BUT I WAS GETTING BY, RIGHT? THAT WAS WHAT MATTERED.
AND SINCE WHAT CLIENTS I HAD NEVER CAME AROUND...
...THE OFFICE WAS A NICE PLACE TO RELAX AND UNWIND. READ A LITTLE.
BUT NOT THAT DAY. THERE WAS SOMEONE INSIDE. I COULD HEAR THEM MOVING AROUND, AND THE DOOR --

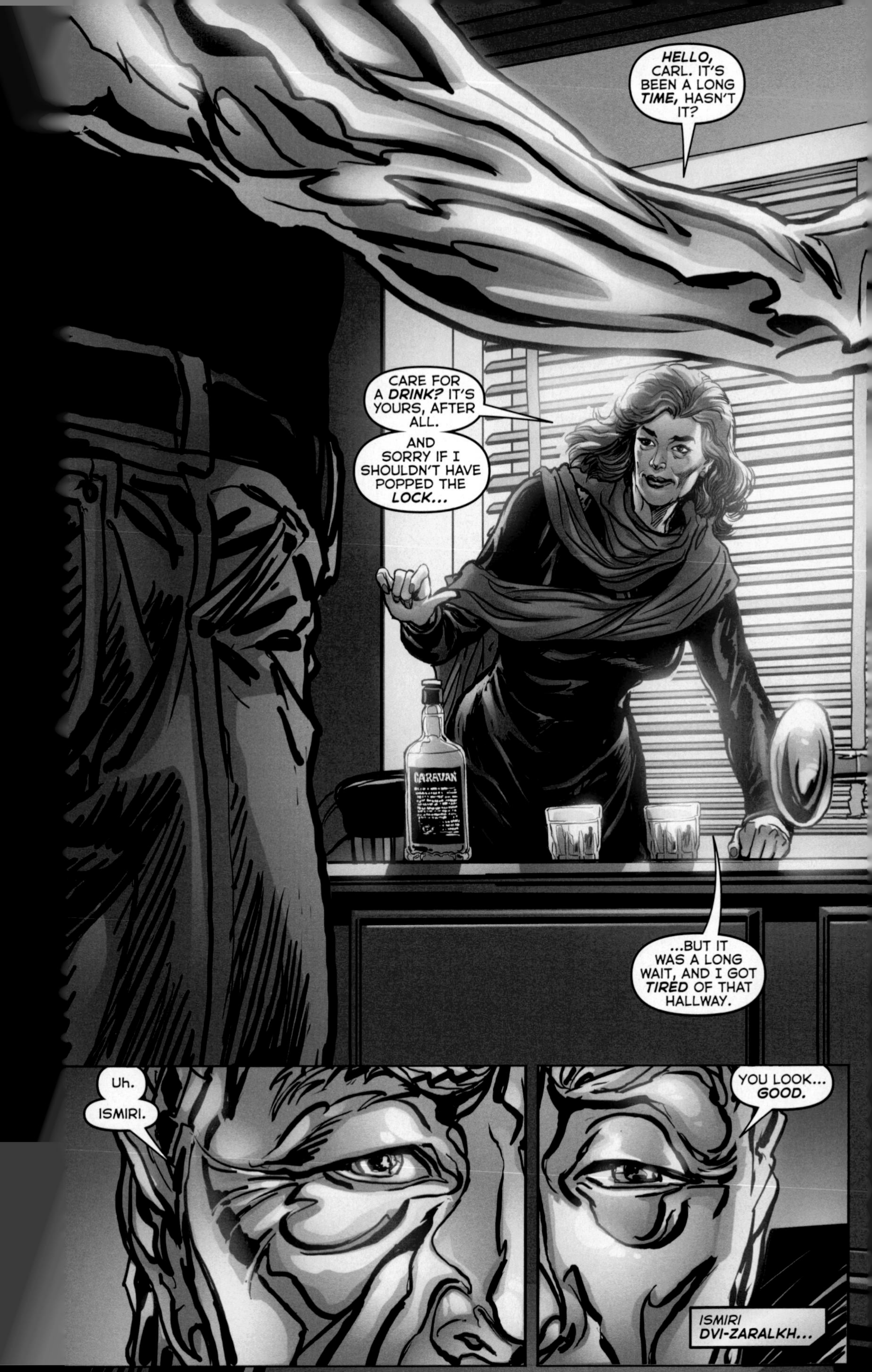
HELLO, CARL. IT'S BEEN A LONG TIME, HASN'T IT?
CARE FOR A DRINK? IT'S YOURS, AFTER ALL.
AND SORRY IF I SHOULDN'T HAVE POPPED THE LOCK...
CARAVAN
...BUT IT WAS A LONG WAIT, AND I GOT TIRED OF THAT HALLWAY.
Uh.
ISMIRI.
YOU LOOK... GOOD.
ISMIRI DVI-ZARALKH...

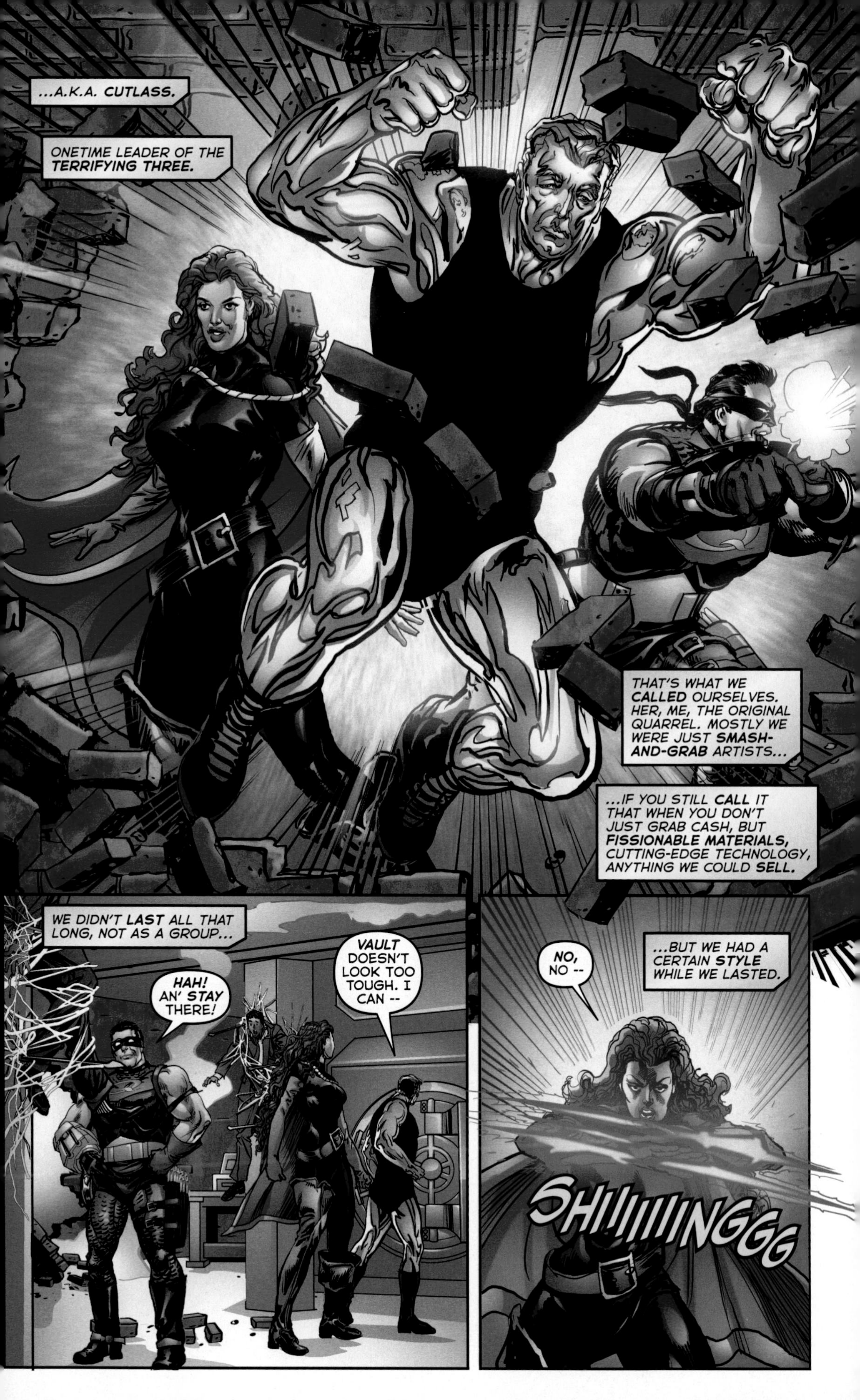
...A.K.A. CUTLASS.
ONETIME LEADER OF THE TERRIFYING THREE.
THAT'S WHAT WE CALLED OURSELVES. HER, ME, THE ORIGINAL QUARREL. MOSTLY WE WERE JUST SMASH-AND-GRAB ARTISTS...
...IF YOU STILL CALL IT THAT WHEN YOU DON'T JUST GRAB CASH, BUT FISSIONABLE MATERIALS, CUTTING-EDGE TECHNOLOGY, ANYTHING WE COULD SELL.
WE DIDN'T LAST ALL THAT LONG, NOT AS A GROUP...
HAH! AN' STAY THERE!
VAULT DOESN'T LOOK TOO TOUGH. I CAN --
NO, NO --
...BUT WE HAD A CERTAIN STYLE WHILE WE LASTED.
SHIIIIIINGGG

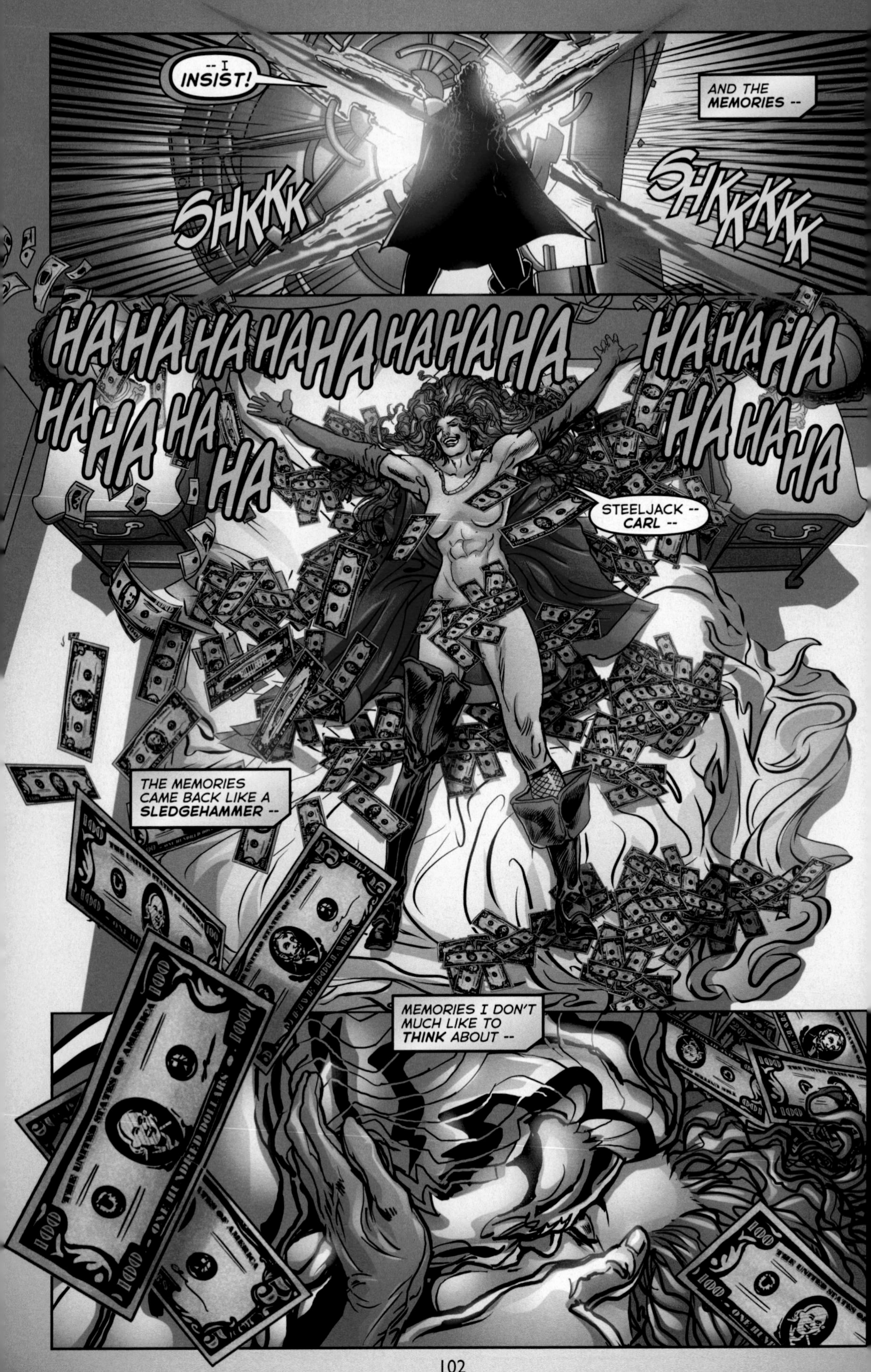
-- I INSIST!
AND THE MEMORIES --
SHKKK
SHKKKKKK
HA HA HA HA HA HA HA HA HA HA HA
HA HA HA HA
HA HA HA HA
HA HA HA HA
STEELJACK -- CARL --
THE MEMORIES CAME BACK LIKE A SLEDGEHAMMER --
MEMORIES I DON'T MUCH LIKE TO THINK ABOUT --

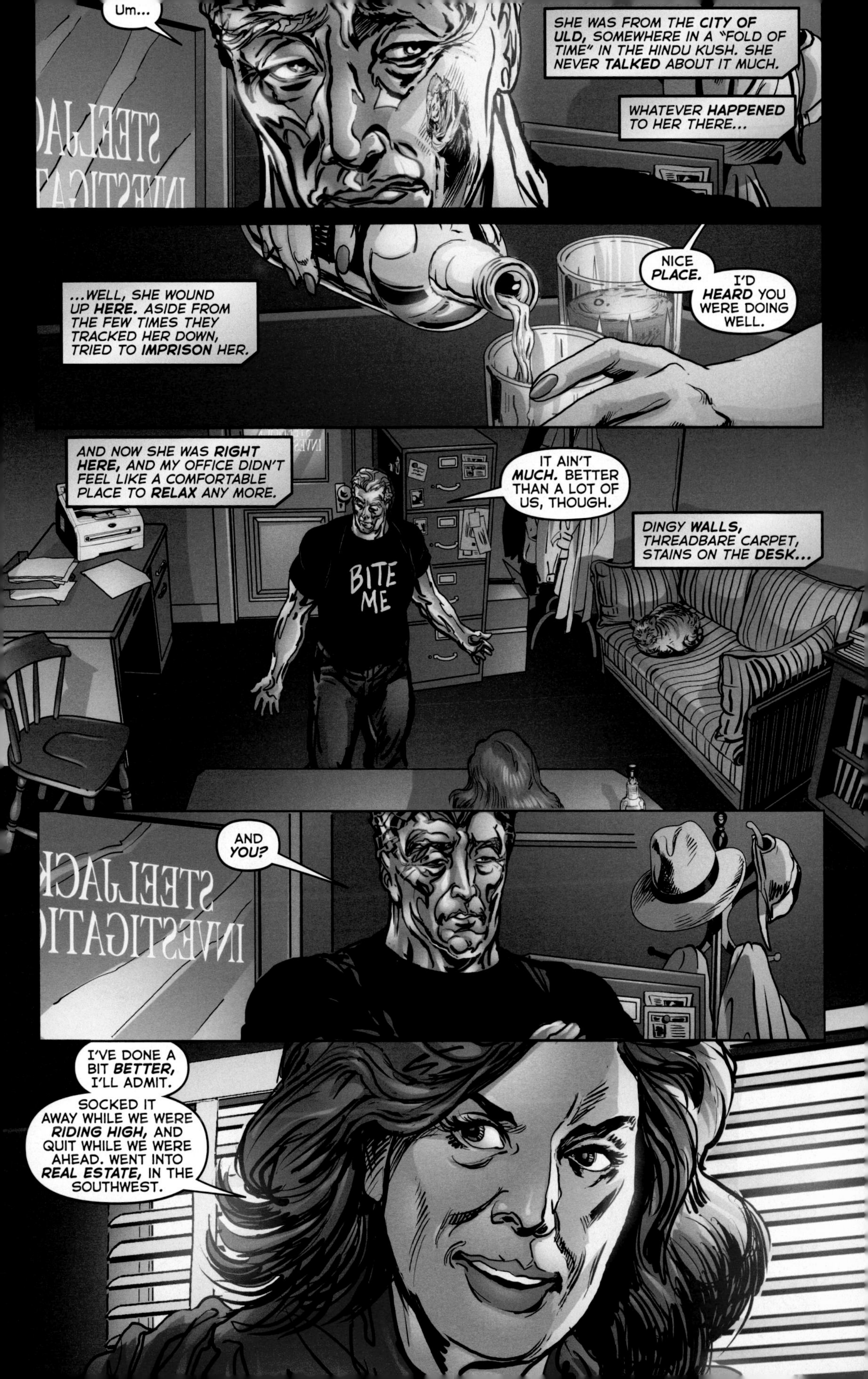
Um...
SHE WAS FROM THE CITY OF ULD, SOMEWHERE IN A "FOLD OF TIME" IN THE HINDU KUSH. SHE NEVER TALKED ABOUT IT MUCH.
WHATEVER HAPPENED TO HER THERE...
...WELL, SHE WOUND UP HERE. ASIDE FROM THE FEW TIMES THEY TRACKED HER DOWN, TRIED TO IMPRISON HER.
NICE PLACE.
I'D HEARD YOU WERE DOING WELL.
AND NOW SHE WAS RIGHT HERE, AND MY OFFICE DIDN'T FEEL LIKE A COMFORTABLE PLACE TO RELAX ANY MORE.
IT AIN'T MUCH. BETTER THAN A LOT OF US, THOUGH.
DINGY WALLS, THREADBARE CARPET, STAINS ON THE DESK...
BITE ME
AND YOU?
I'VE DONE A BIT BETTER, I'LL ADMIT.
SOCKED IT AWAY WHILE WE WERE RIDING HIGH, AND QUIT WHILE WE WERE AHEAD. WENT INTO REAL ESTATE, IN THE SOUTHWEST.

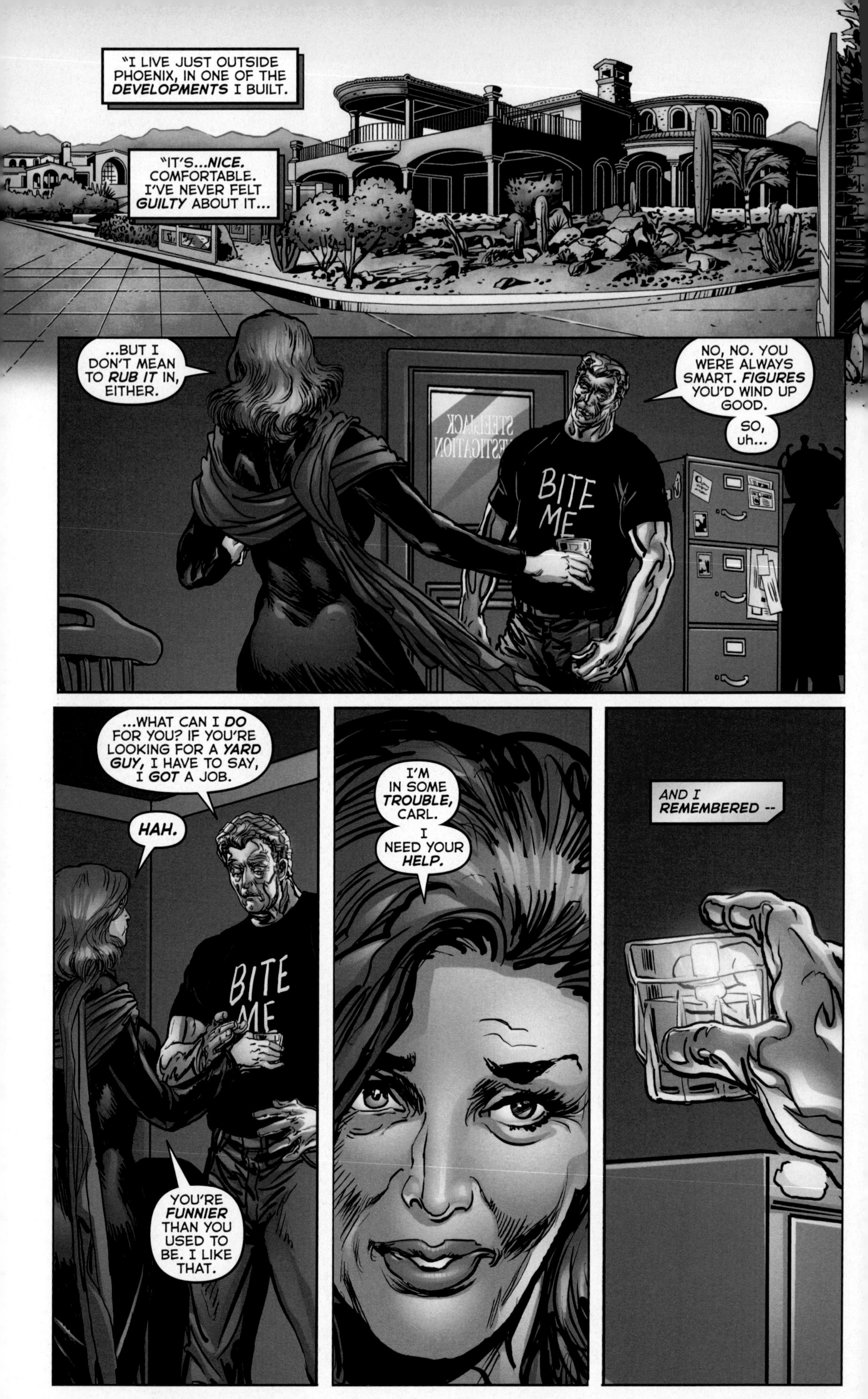
"I LIVE JUST OUTSIDE PHOENIX, IN ONE OF THE DEVELOPMENTS I BUILT.
"IT'S...NICE. COMFORTABLE. I'VE NEVER FELT GUILTY ABOUT IT...
...BUT I DON'T MEAN TO RUB IT IN, EITHER.
NO, NO. YOU WERE ALWAYS SMART. FIGURES YOU'D WIND UP GOOD.
SO, uh...
BITE ME
...WHAT CAN I DO FOR YOU? IF YOU'RE LOOKING FOR A YARD GUY, I HAVE TO SAY, I GOT A JOB.
HAH.
BITE ME
YOU'RE FUNNIER THAN YOU USED TO BE. I LIKE THAT.
I'M IN SOME TROUBLE, CARL.
I NEED YOUR HELP.
AND I REMEMBERED --

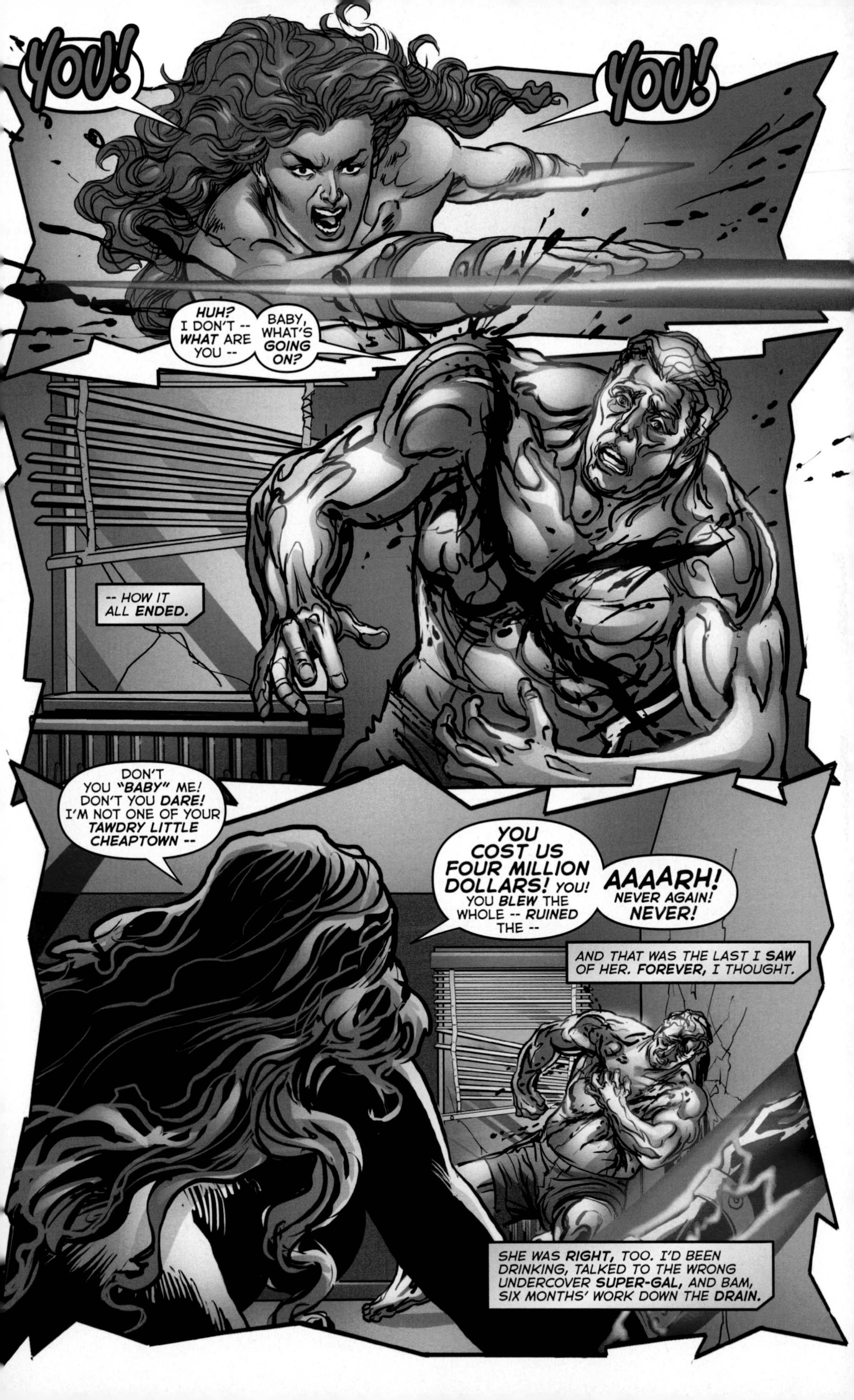
YOU!
YOU!
HUH? I DON'T -- WHAT ARE YOU --
BABY, WHAT'S GOING ON?
-- HOW IT ALL ENDED.
DON'T YOU "BABY" ME! DON'T YOU DARE! I'M NOT ONE OF YOUR TAWDRY LITTLE CHEAPTOWN --
YOU COST US FOUR MILLION DOLLARS! YOU! YOU BLEW THE WHOLE -- RUINED THE --
AAAARH! NEVER AGAIN! NEVER!
AND THAT WAS THE LAST I SAW OF HER. FOREVER, I THOUGHT.
SHE WAS RIGHT, TOO. I'D BEEN DRINKING, TALKED TO THE WRONG UNDERCOVER SUPER-GAL, AND BAM, SIX MONTHS' WORK DOWN THE DRAIN.

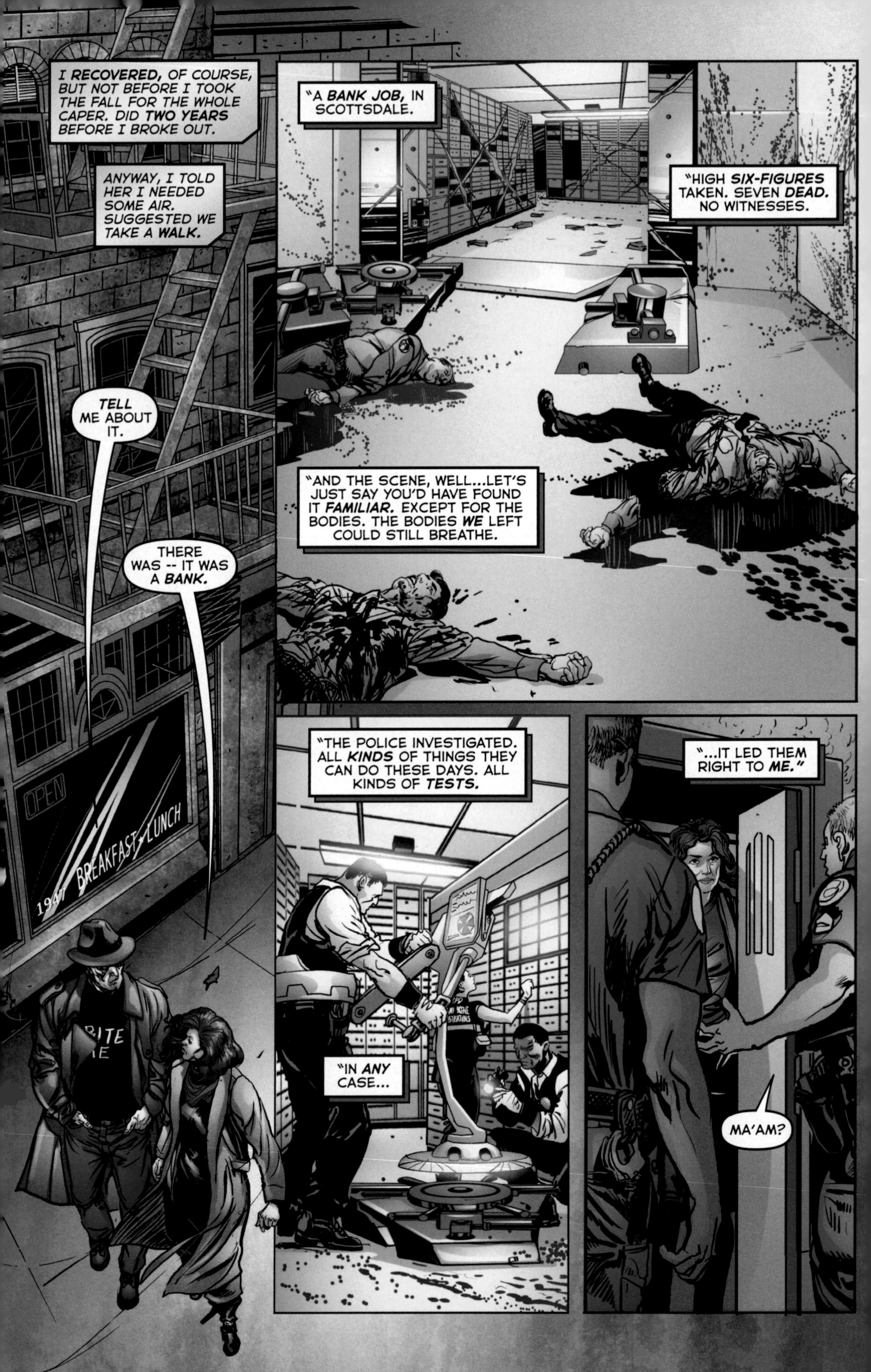
I RECOVERED, OF COURSE, BUT NOT BEFORE I TOOK THE FALL FOR THE WHOLE CAPER. DID TWO YEARS BEFORE I BROKE OUT.
ANYWAY, I TOLD HER I NEEDED SOME AIR. SUGGESTED WE TAKE A WALK.
TELL ME ABOUT IT.
THERE WAS -- IT WAS A BANK.
OPEN
1947 BREAKFAST LUNCH
"A BANK JOB, IN SCOTTSDALE.
"HIGH SIX-FIGURES TAKEN. SEVEN DEAD. NO WITNESSES.
"AND THE SCENE, WELL...LET'S JUST SAY YOU'D HAVE FOUND IT FAMILIAR. EXCEPT FOR THE BODIES. THE BODIES WE LEFT COULD STILL BREATHE.
"THE POLICE INVESTIGATED. ALL KINDS OF THINGS THEY CAN DO THESE DAYS. ALL KINDS OF TESTS.
"IN ANY CASE...
"...IT LED THEM RIGHT TO ME."
MA'AM?

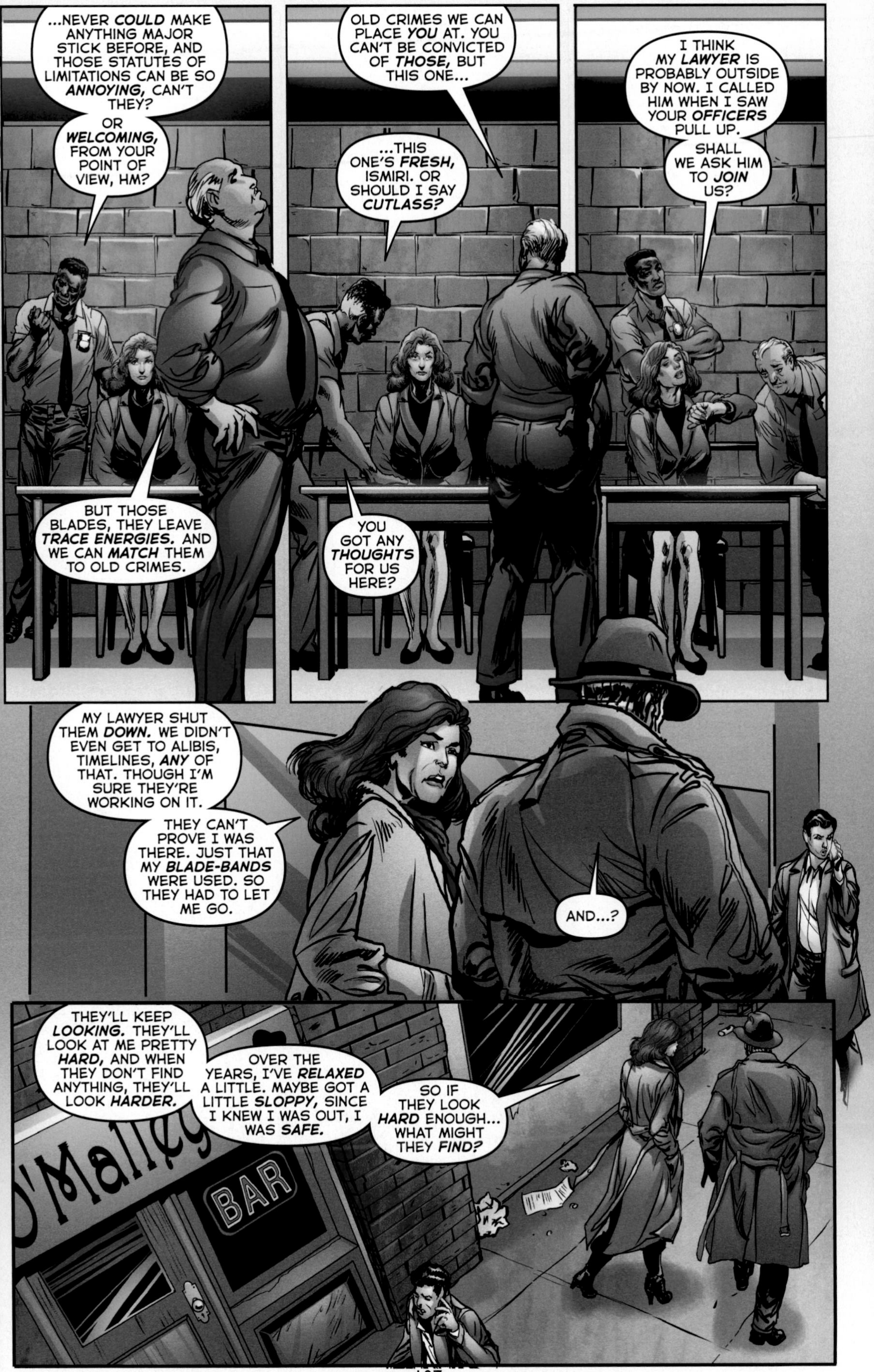
...NEVER COULD MAKE ANYTHING MAJOR STICK BEFORE, AND THOSE STATUTES OF LIMITATIONS CAN BE SO ANNOYING, CAN'T THEY?
OR WELCOMING, FROM YOUR POINT OF VIEW, HM?
BUT THOSE BLADES, THEY LEAVE TRACE ENERGIES. AND WE CAN MATCH THEM TO OLD CRIMES.
OLD CRIMES WE CAN PLACE YOU AT. YOU CAN'T BE CONVICTED OF THOSE, BUT THIS ONE...
...THIS ONE'S FRESH, ISMIRI. OR SHOULD I SAY CUTLASS?
YOU GOT ANY THOUGHTS FOR US HERE?
I THINK MY LAWYER IS PROBABLY OUTSIDE BY NOW. I CALLED HIM WHEN I SAW YOUR OFFICERS PULL UP.
SHALL WE ASK HIM TO JOIN US?
MY LAWYER SHUT THEM DOWN. WE DIDN'T EVEN GET TO ALIBIS, TIMELINES, ANY OF THAT. THOUGH I'M SURE THEY'RE WORKING ON IT.
THEY CAN'T PROVE I WAS THERE. JUST THAT MY BLADE-BANDS WERE USED. SO THEY HAD TO LET ME GO.
AND...?
THEY'LL KEEP LOOKING. THEY'LL LOOK AT ME PRETTY HARD, AND WHEN THEY DON'T FIND ANYTHING, THEY'LL LOOK HARDER.
OVER THE YEARS, I'VE RELAXED A LITTLE. MAYBE GOT A LITTLE SLOPPY, SINCE I KNEW I WAS OUT, I WAS SAFE.
SO IF THEY LOOK HARD ENOUGH... WHAT MIGHT THEY FIND?
O'Malley
BAR

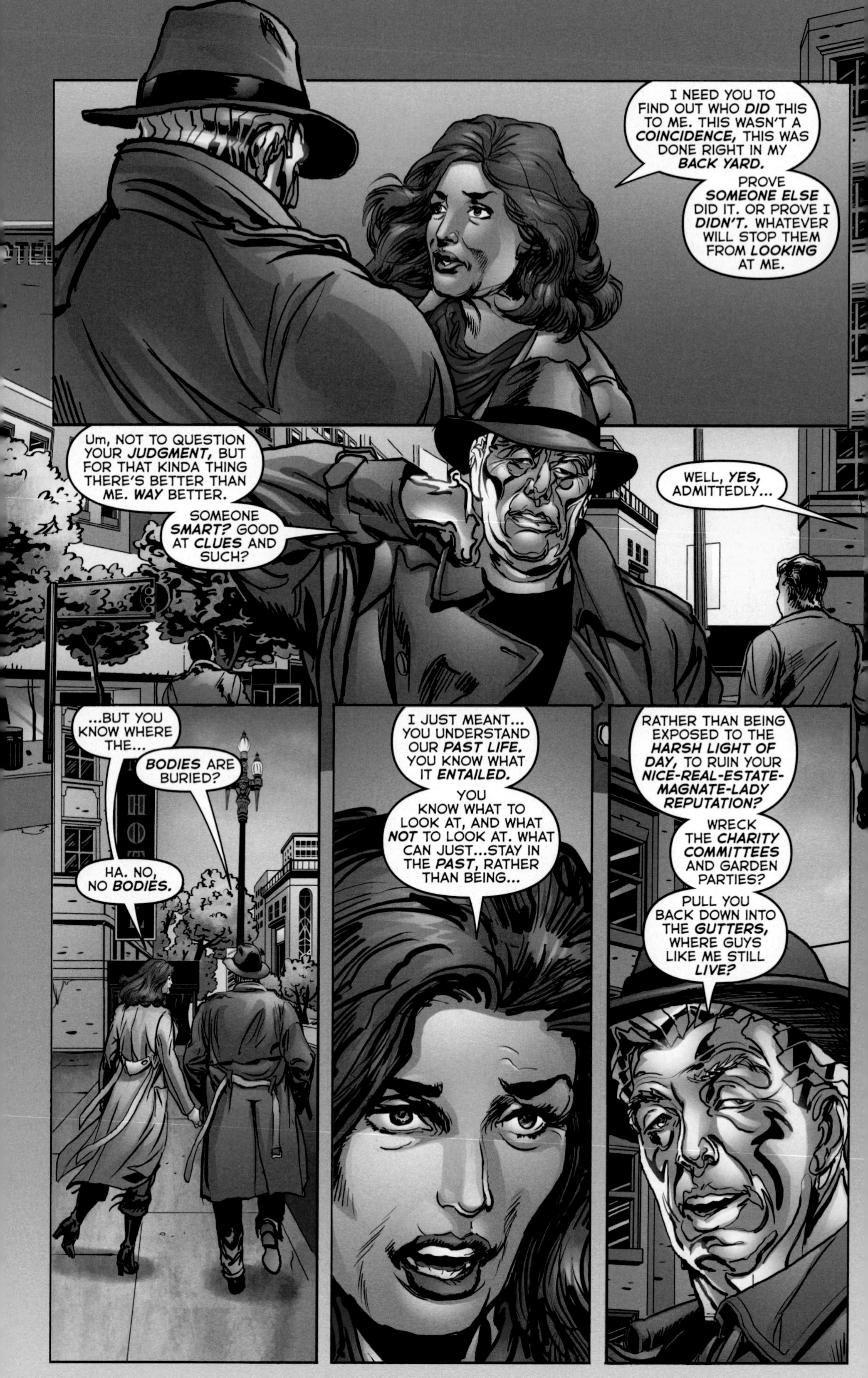
I NEED YOU TO FIND OUT WHO *DID* THIS TO ME. THIS WASN'T A *COINCIDENCE,* THIS WAS DONE RIGHT IN MY *BACK YARD.*
PROVE *SOMEONE ELSE* DID IT. OR PROVE I *DIDN'T.* WHATEVER WILL STOP THEM FROM *LOOKING* AT ME.
Um, NOT TO QUESTION YOUR *JUDGMENT,* BUT FOR THAT KINDA THING THERE'S BETTER THAN ME. *WAY* BETTER.
SOMEONE *SMART?* GOOD AT *CLUES* AND SUCH?
WELL, *YES,* ADMITTEDLY...
...BUT YOU KNOW WHERE THE...
BODIES ARE BURIED?
HA. NO, NO *BODIES.*
I JUST MEANT... YOU UNDERSTAND OUR *PAST LIFE.* YOU KNOW WHAT IT *ENTAILED.*
YOU KNOW WHAT TO LOOK AT, AND WHAT *NOT* TO LOOK AT. WHAT CAN JUST...STAY IN THE *PAST,* RATHER THAN BEING...
RATHER THAN BEING EXPOSED TO THE *HARSH LIGHT OF DAY,* TO RUIN YOUR *NICE-REAL-ESTATE-MAGNATE-LADY REPUTATION?*
WRECK THE *CHARITY COMMITTEES* AND GARDEN PARTIES?
PULL YOU BACK DOWN INTO THE *GUTTERS,* WHERE GUYS LIKE ME STILL *LIVE?*

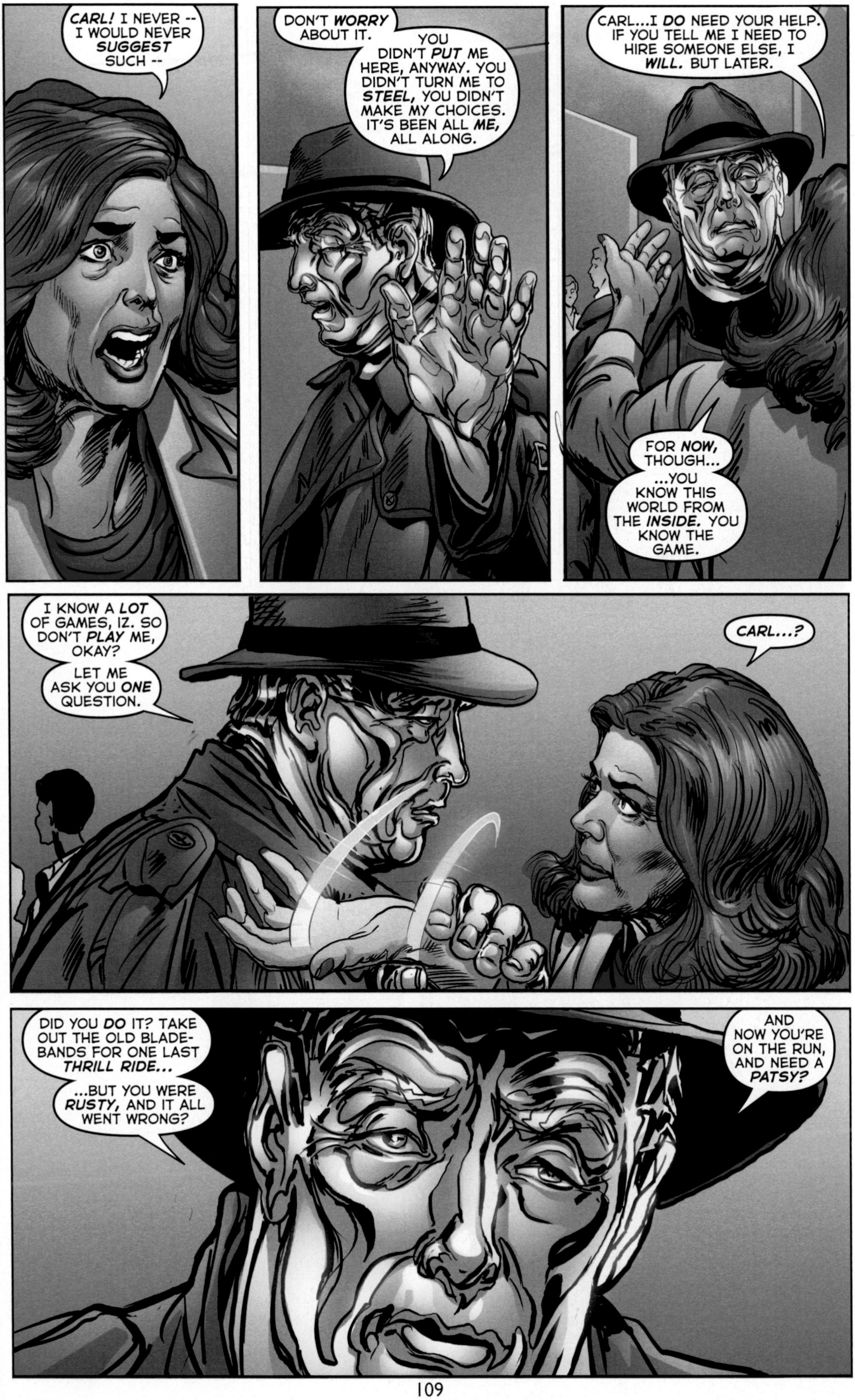
CARL! I NEVER -- I WOULD NEVER SUGGEST SUCH --
DON'T WORRY ABOUT IT.
YOU DIDN'T PUT ME HERE, ANYWAY. YOU DIDN'T TURN ME TO STEEL, YOU DIDN'T MAKE MY CHOICES. IT'S BEEN ALL ME, ALL ALONG.
CARL...I DO NEED YOUR HELP. IF YOU TELL ME I NEED TO HIRE SOMEONE ELSE, I WILL. BUT LATER.
FOR NOW, THOUGH...
...YOU KNOW THIS WORLD FROM THE INSIDE. YOU KNOW THE GAME.
I KNOW A LOT OF GAMES, IZ. SO DON'T PLAY ME, OKAY?
LET ME ASK YOU ONE QUESTION.
CARL...?
DID YOU DO IT? TAKE OUT THE OLD BLADE-BANDS FOR ONE LAST THRILL RIDE...
...BUT YOU WERE RUSTY, AND IT ALL WENT WRONG?
AND NOW YOU'RE ON THE RUN, AND NEED A PATSY?

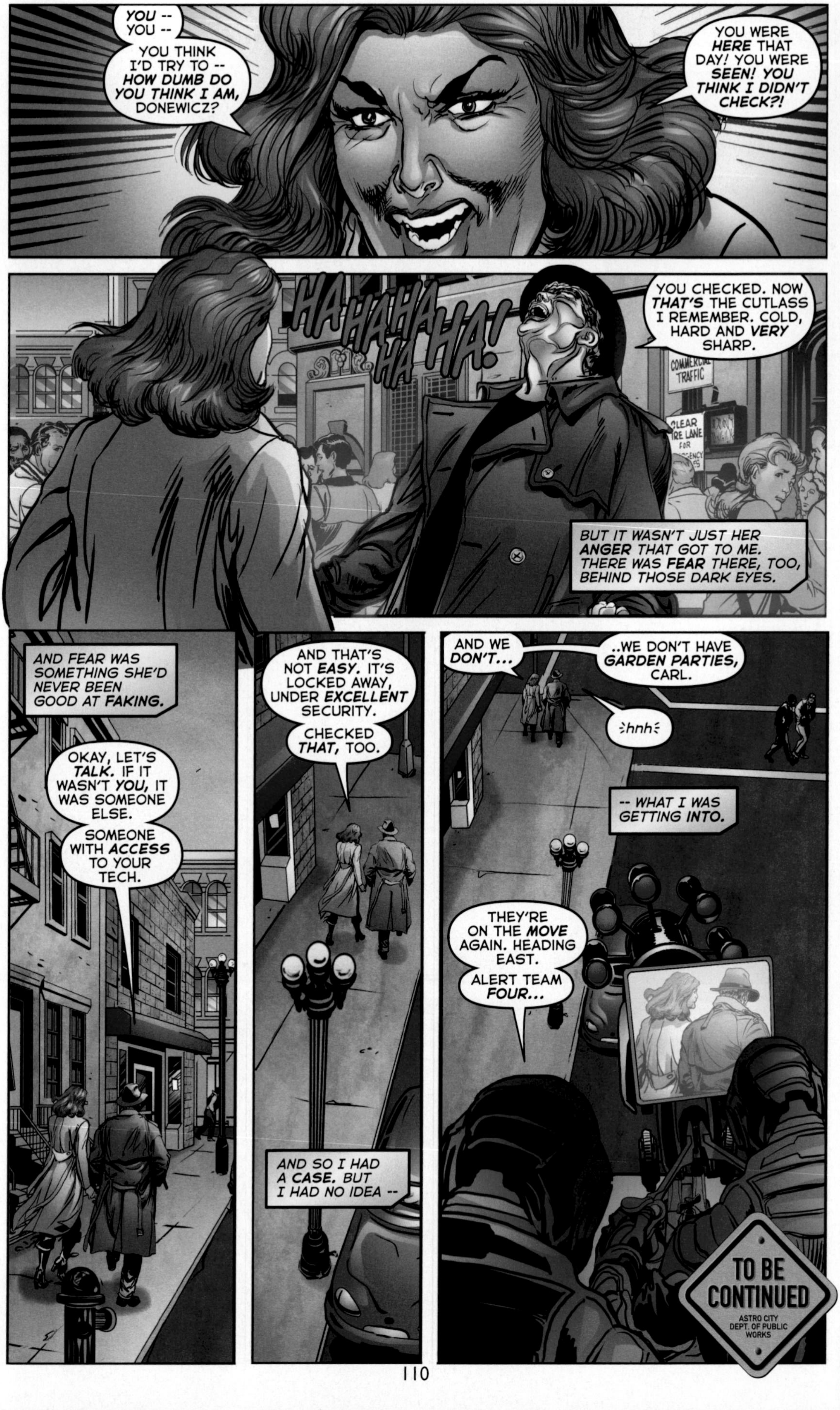
YOU -- YOU --
YOU THINK I'D TRY TO -- HOW DUMB DO YOU THINK I AM, DONEWICZ?
YOU WERE HERE THAT DAY! YOU WERE SEEN! YOU THINK I DIDN'T CHECK?!
HA HA HA HA HA HA HA!
YOU CHECKED. NOW THAT'S THE CUTLASS I REMEMBER. COLD, HARD AND VERY SHARP.
COMMERCIAL TRAFFIC
BUT IT WASN'T JUST HER ANGER THAT GOT TO ME. THERE WAS FEAR THERE, TOO, BEHIND THOSE DARK EYES.
AND FEAR WAS SOMETHING SHE'D NEVER BEEN GOOD AT FAKING.
OKAY, LET'S TALK. IF IT WASN'T YOU, IT WAS SOMEONE ELSE.
SOMEONE WITH ACCESS TO YOUR TECH.
AND THAT'S NOT EASY. IT'S LOCKED AWAY, UNDER EXCELLENT SECURITY.
CHECKED THAT, TOO.
AND SO I HAD A CASE. BUT I HAD NO IDEA --
AND WE DON'T...
..WE DON'T HAVE GARDEN PARTIES, CARL.
hnh
-- WHAT I WAS GETTING INTO.
THEY'RE ON THE MOVE AGAIN. HEADING EAST.
ALERT TEAM FOUR...
TO BE CONTINUED
ASTRO CITY DEPT. OF PUBLIC WORKS

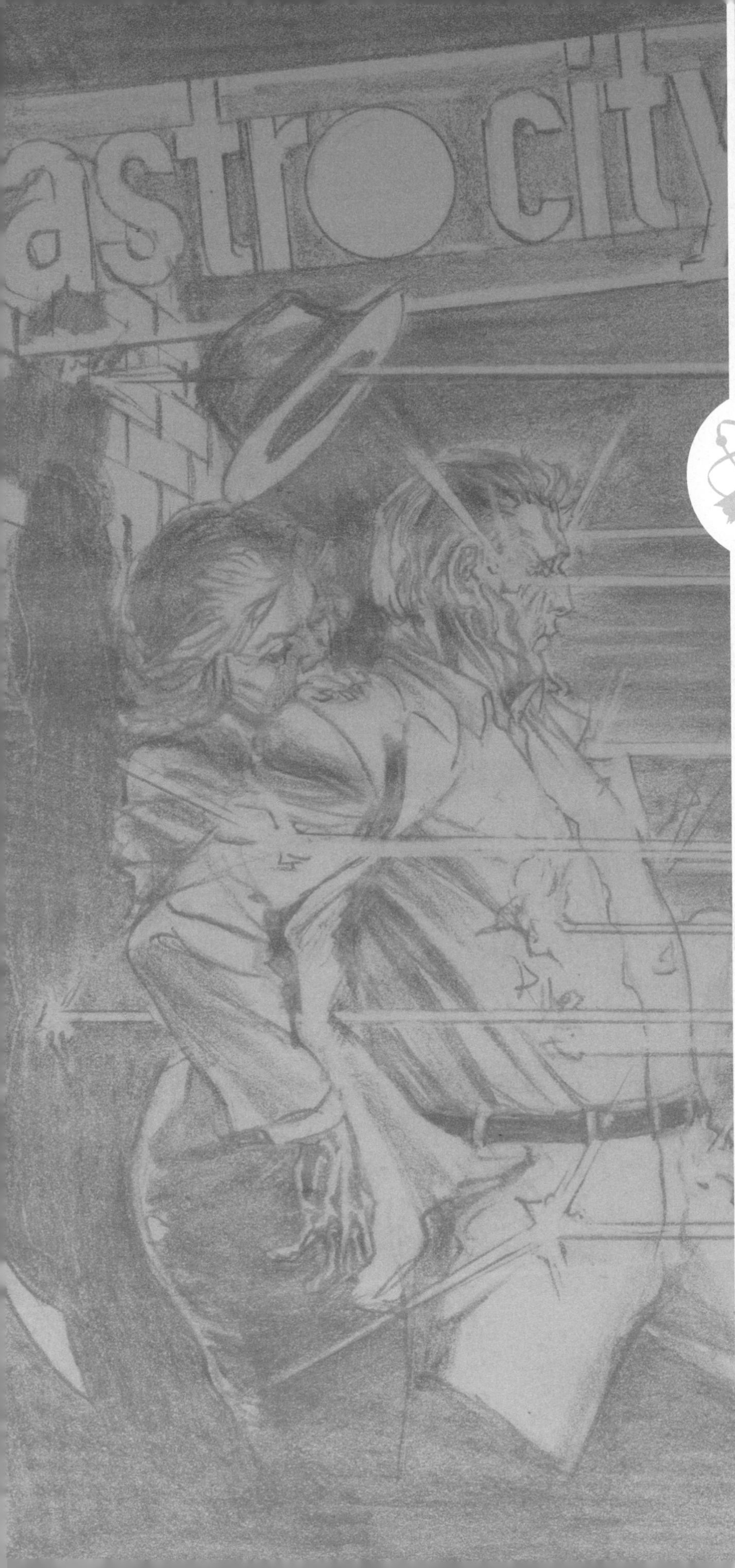
astro city

5

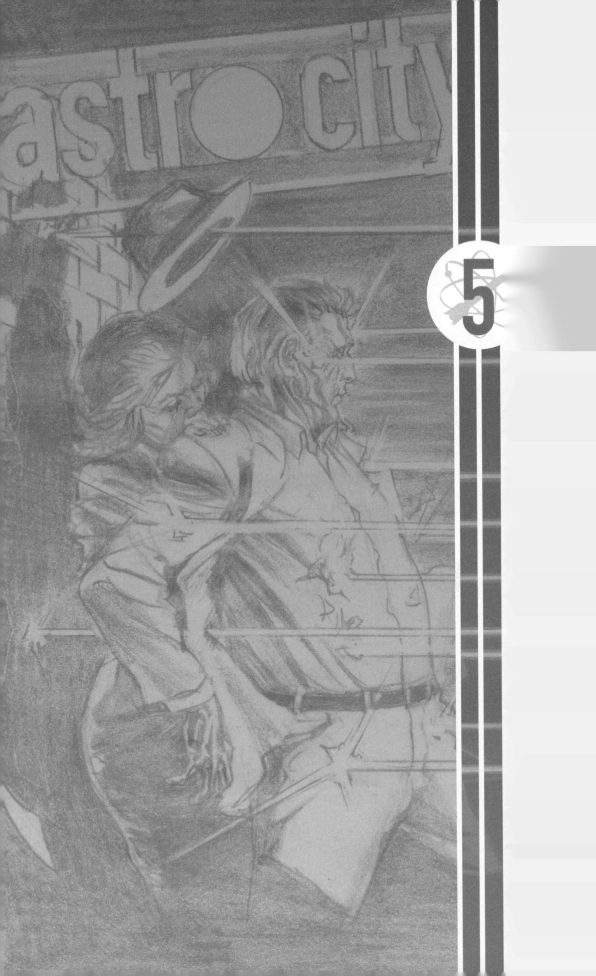

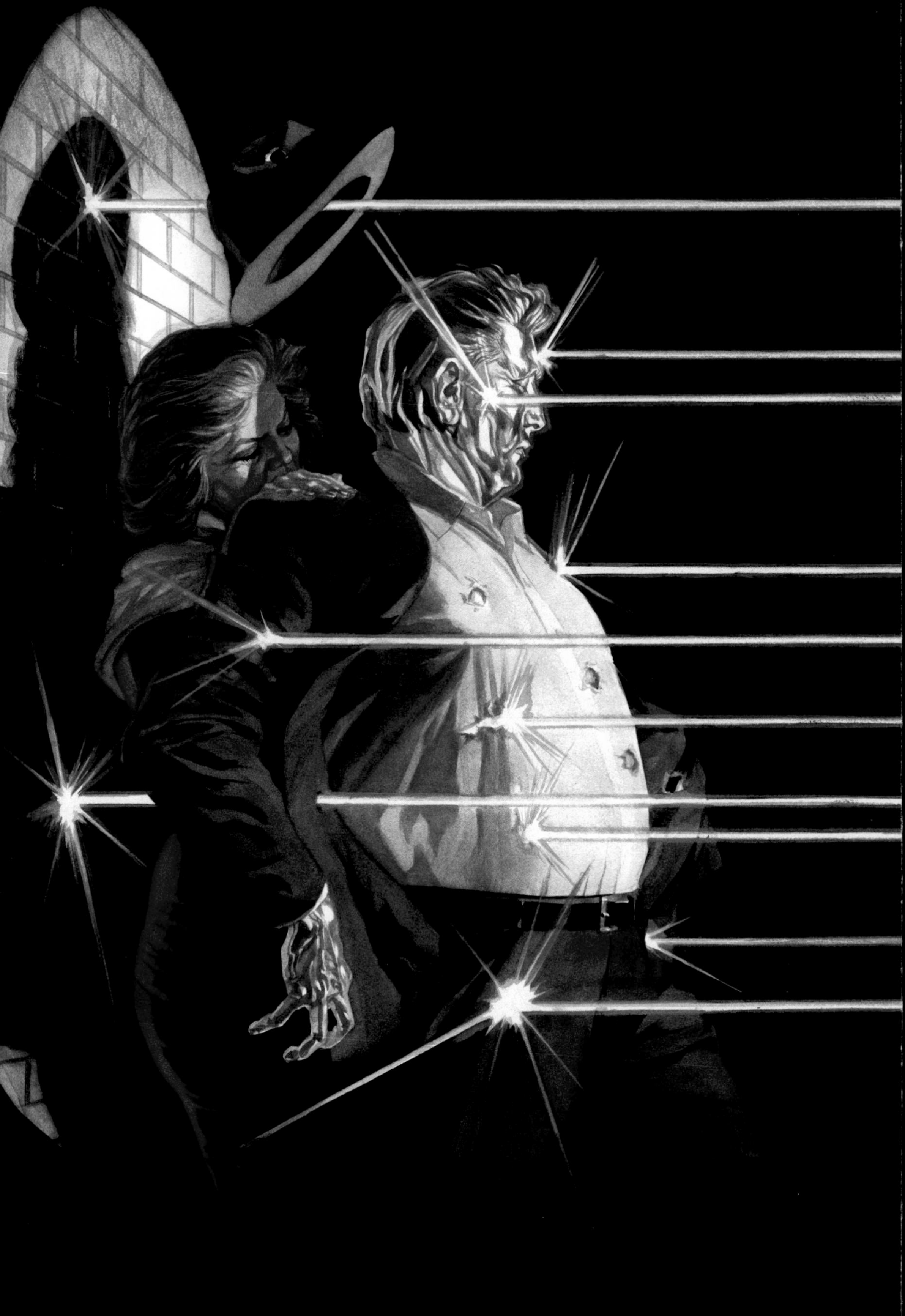

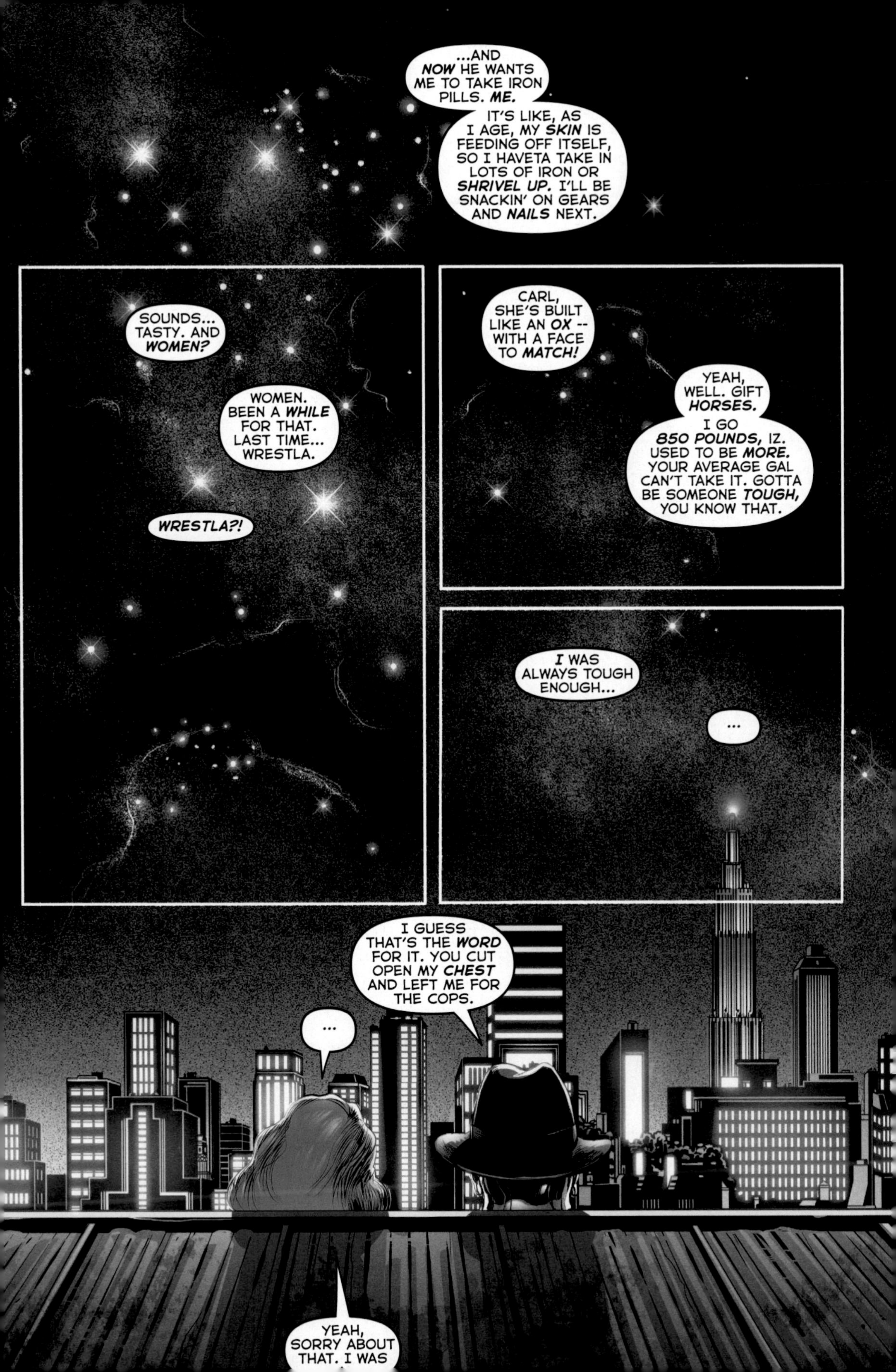
...AND NOW HE WANTS ME TO TAKE IRON PILLS. ME.
IT'S LIKE, AS I AGE, MY SKIN IS FEEDING OFF ITSELF, SO I HAVETA TAKE IN LOTS OF IRON OR SHRIVEL UP. I'LL BE SNACKIN' ON GEARS AND NAILS NEXT.
SOUNDS... TASTY. AND WOMEN?
WOMEN. BEEN A WHILE FOR THAT. LAST TIME... WRESTLA.
WRESTLA?!
CARL, SHE'S BUILT LIKE AN OX -- WITH A FACE TO MATCH!
YEAH, WELL. GIFT HORSES.
I GO 850 POUNDS, IZ. USED TO BE MORE. YOUR AVERAGE GAL CAN'T TAKE IT. GOTTA BE SOMEONE TOUGH, YOU KNOW THAT.
I WAS ALWAYS TOUGH ENOUGH...
...
I GUESS THAT'S THE WORD FOR IT. YOU CUT OPEN MY CHEST AND LEFT ME FOR THE COPS.
...
YEAH, SORRY ABOUT THAT. I WAS

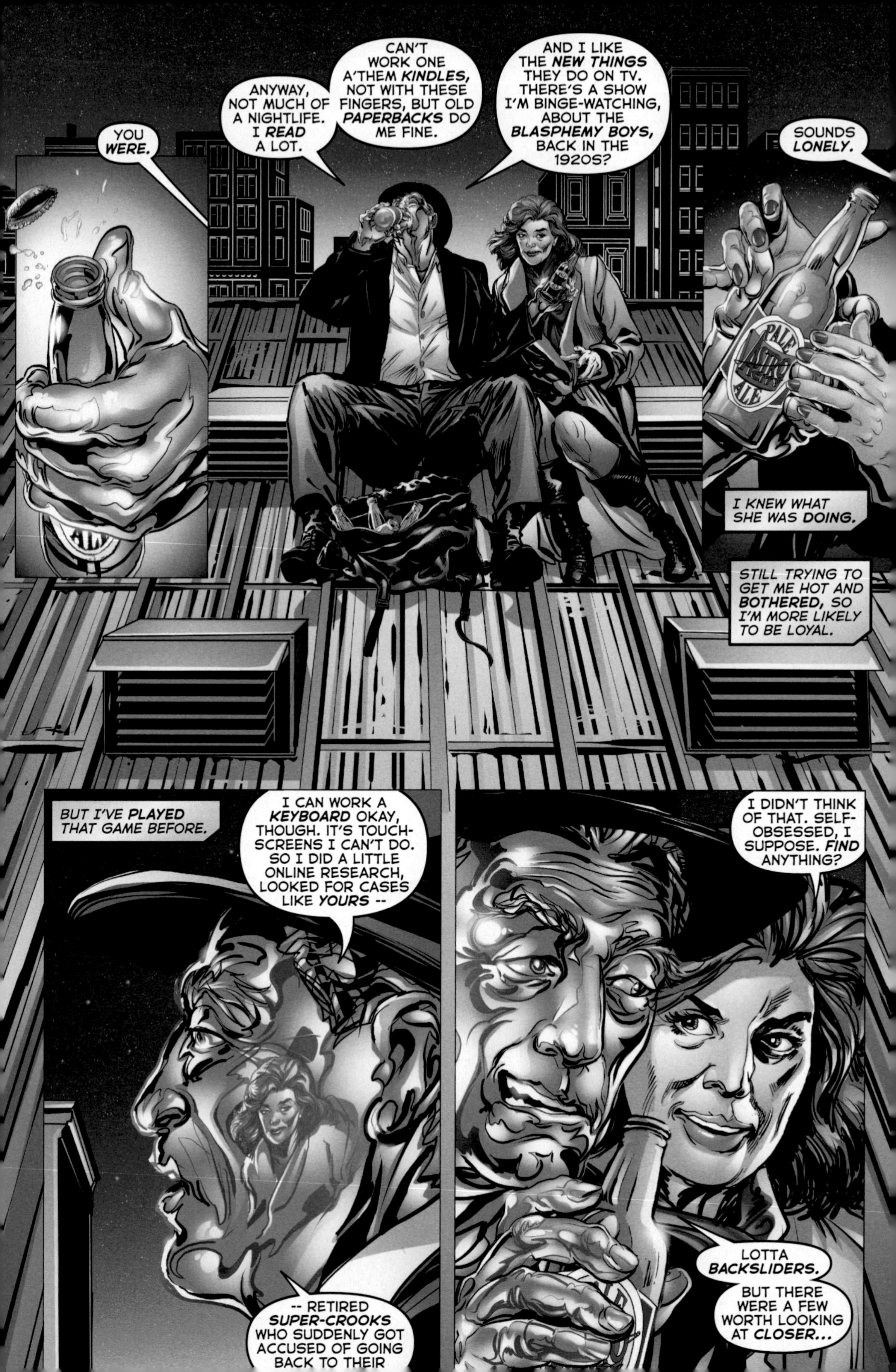

YOU WERE.
ANYWAY, NOT MUCH OF A NIGHTLIFE. I READ A LOT.
CAN'T WORK ONE A'THEM KINDLES, NOT WITH THESE FINGERS, BUT OLD PAPERBACKS DO ME FINE.
AND I LIKE THE NEW THINGS THEY DO ON TV. THERE'S A SHOW I'M BINGE-WATCHING, ABOUT THE BLASPHEMY BOYS, BACK IN THE 1920S?
SOUNDS LONELY.
PALE ALE
I KNEW WHAT SHE WAS DOING.
STILL TRYING TO GET ME HOT AND BOTHERED, SO I'M MORE LIKELY TO BE LOYAL.
BUT I'VE PLAYED THAT GAME BEFORE.
I CAN WORK A KEYBOARD OKAY, THOUGH. IT'S TOUCH-SCREENS I CAN'T DO. SO I DID A LITTLE ONLINE RESEARCH, LOOKED FOR CASES LIKE YOURS --
-- RETIRED SUPER-CROOKS WHO SUDDENLY GOT ACCUSED OF GOING BACK TO THEIR
I DIDN'T THINK OF THAT. SELF-OBSESSED, I SUPPOSE. FIND ANYTHING?
LOTTA BACKSLIDERS.
BUT THERE WERE A FEW WORTH LOOKING AT CLOSER...

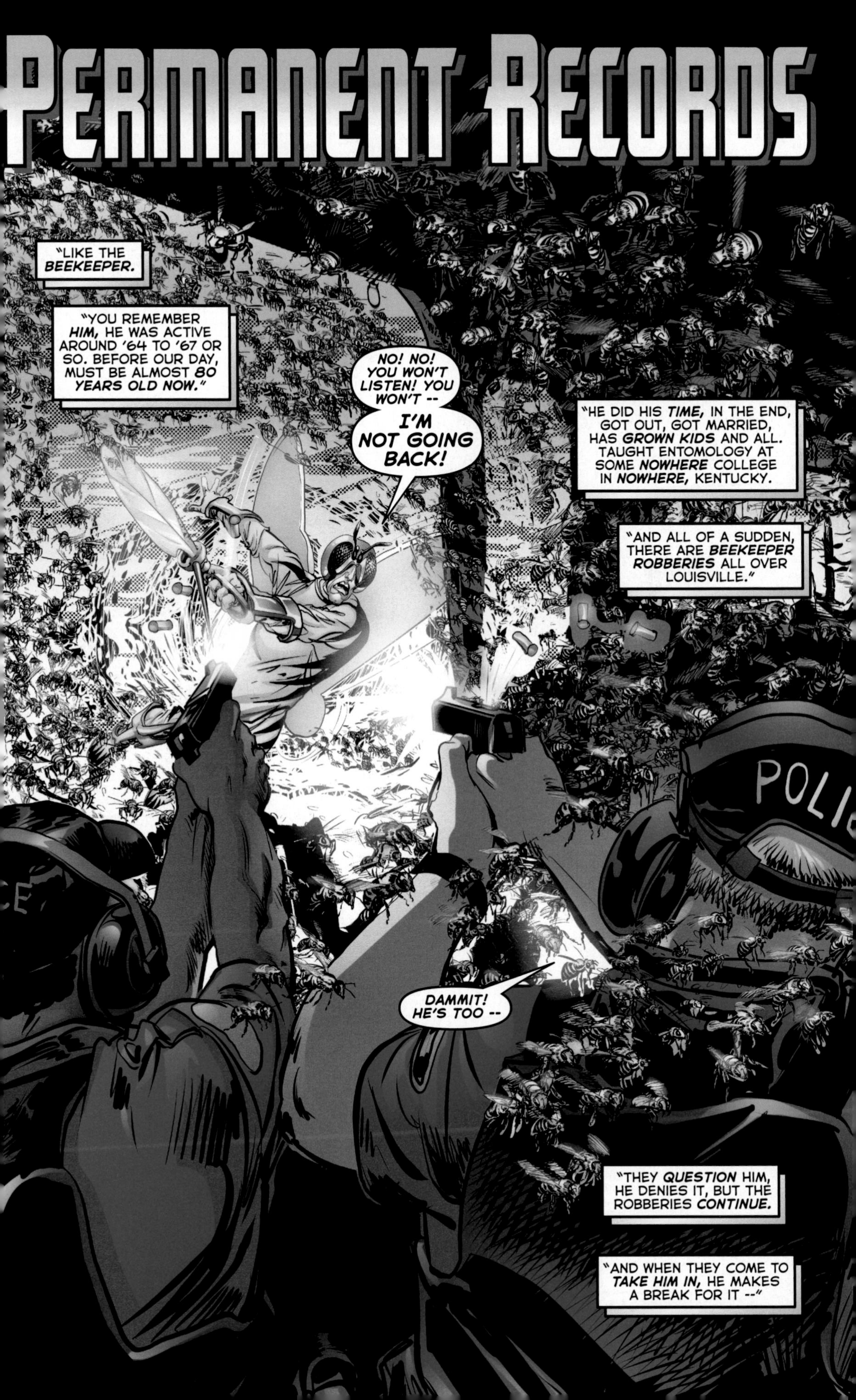
PERMANENT RECORDS
"LIKE THE BEEKEEPER.
"YOU REMEMBER HIM, HE WAS ACTIVE AROUND '64 TO '67 OR SO. BEFORE OUR DAY, MUST BE ALMOST 80 YEARS OLD NOW."
NO! NO! YOU WON'T LISTEN! YOU WON'T --
I'M NOT GOING BACK!
"HE DID HIS TIME, IN THE END, GOT OUT, GOT MARRIED, HAS GROWN KIDS AND ALL. TAUGHT ENTOMOLOGY AT SOME NOWHERE COLLEGE IN NOWHERE, KENTUCKY.
"AND ALL OF A SUDDEN, THERE ARE BEEKEEPER ROBBERIES ALL OVER LOUISVILLE."
DAMMIT! HE'S TOO --
"THEY QUESTION HIM, HE DENIES IT, BUT THE ROBBERIES CONTINUE.
"AND WHEN THEY COME TO TAKE HIM IN, HE MAKES A BREAK FOR IT --"

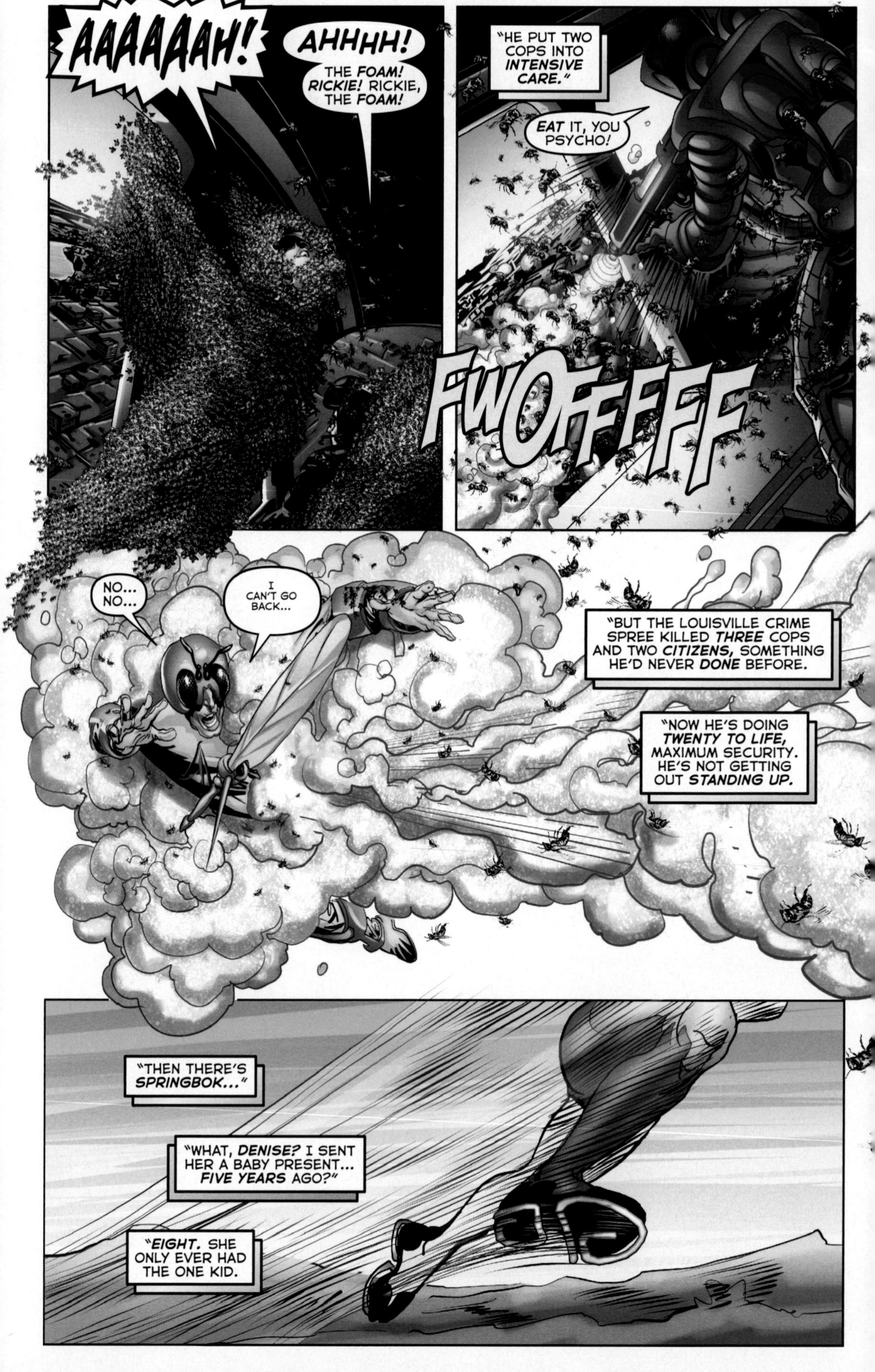
AAAAAAH!
AHHHH! THE FOAM! RICKIE! RICKIE, THE FOAM!
"HE PUT TWO COPS INTO INTENSIVE CARE."
EAT IT, YOU PSYCHO!
FWOFFFFF
NO... NO...
I CAN'T GO BACK...
"BUT THE LOUISVILLE CRIME SPREE KILLED THREE COPS AND TWO CITIZENS, SOMETHING HE'D NEVER DONE BEFORE.
"NOW HE'S DOING TWENTY TO LIFE, MAXIMUM SECURITY. HE'S NOT GETTING OUT STANDING UP.
"THEN THERE'S SPRINGBOK..."
"WHAT, DENISE? I SENT HER A BABY PRESENT... FIVE YEARS AGO?"
"EIGHT. SHE ONLY EVER HAD THE ONE KID.

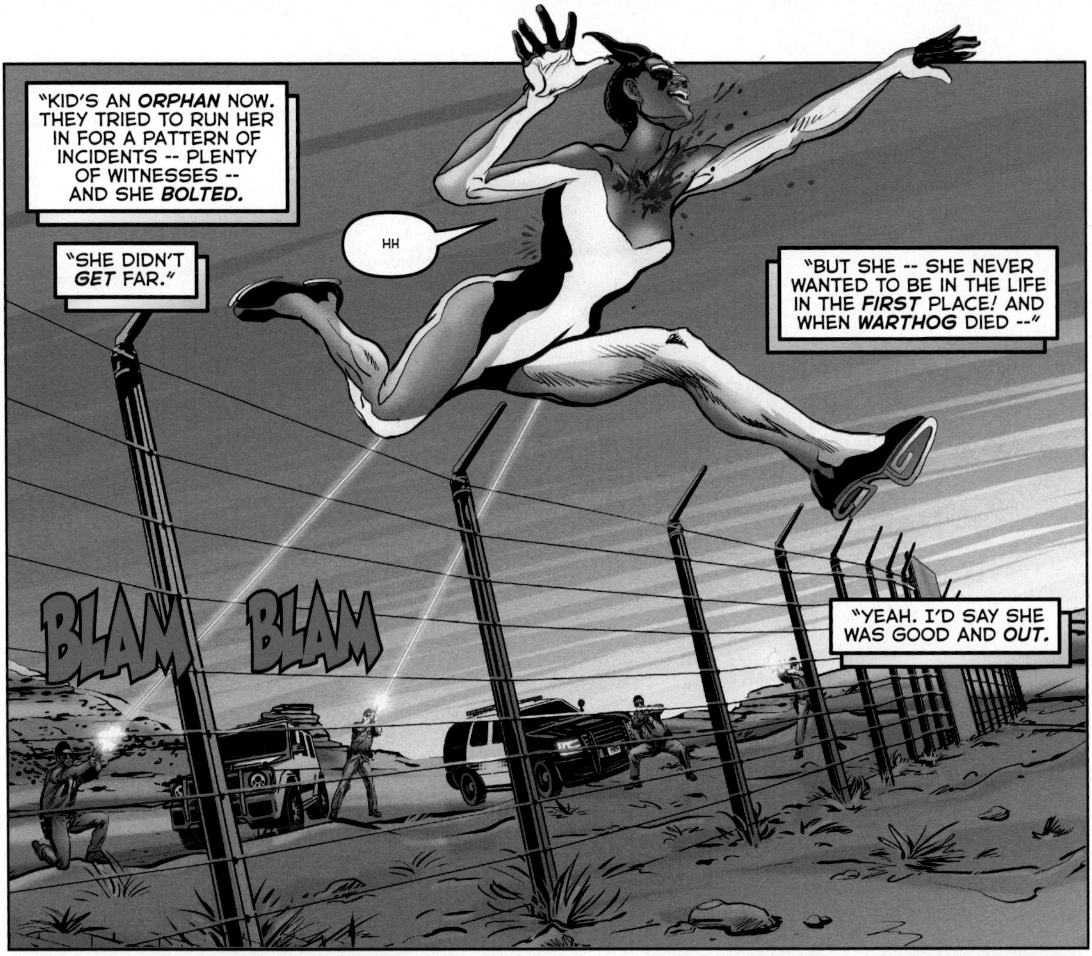
"KID'S AN ORPHAN NOW. THEY TRIED TO RUN HER IN FOR A PATTERN OF INCIDENTS -- PLENTY OF WITNESSES -- AND SHE BOLTED.
HH
"SHE DIDN'T GET FAR."
"BUT SHE -- SHE NEVER WANTED TO BE IN THE LIFE IN THE FIRST PLACE! AND WHEN WARTHOG DIED --"
BLAM BLAM
"YEAH. I'D SAY SHE WAS GOOD AND OUT.

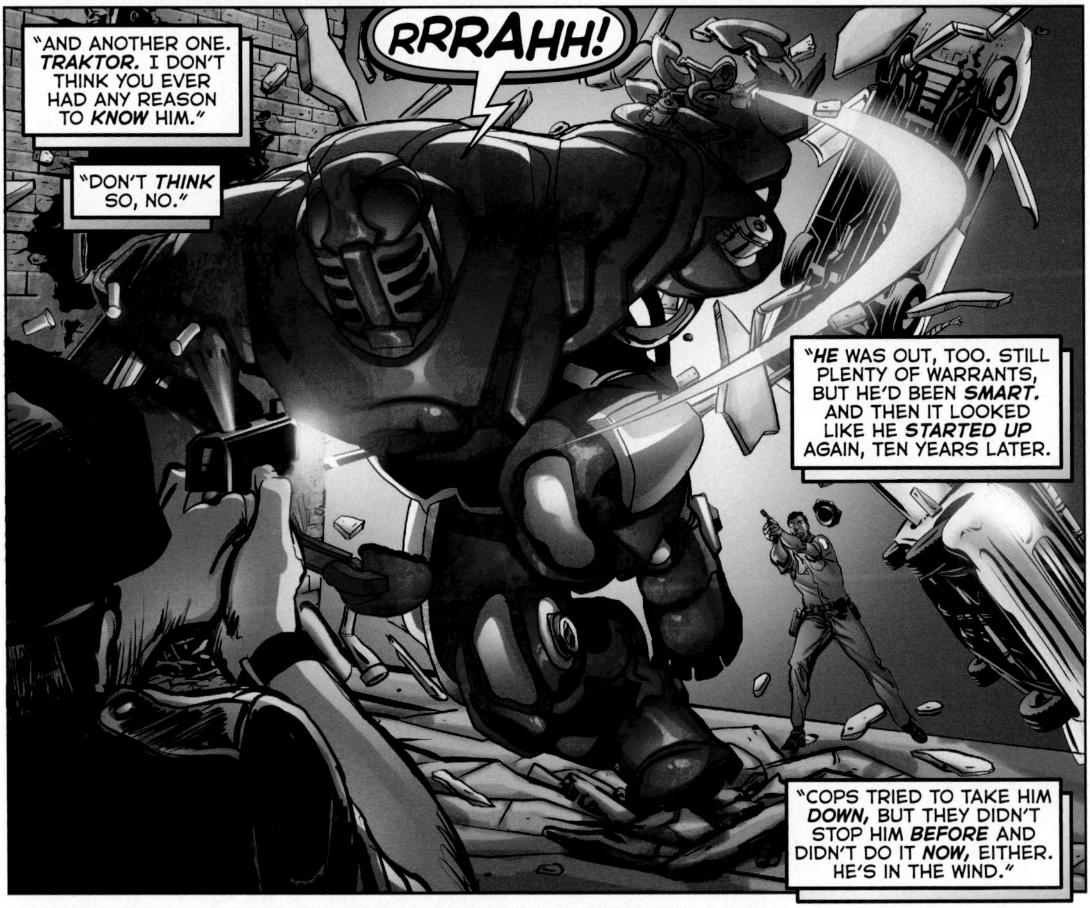
"AND ANOTHER ONE. TRAKTOR. I DON'T THINK YOU EVER HAD ANY REASON TO KNOW HIM."
RRRAHH!
"DON'T THINK SO, NO."
"HE WAS OUT, TOO. STILL PLENTY OF WARRANTS, BUT HE'D BEEN SMART. AND THEN IT LOOKED LIKE HE STARTED UP AGAIN, TEN YEARS LATER.
"COPS TRIED TO TAKE HIM DOWN, BUT THEY DIDN'T STOP HIM BEFORE AND DIDN'T DO IT NOW, EITHER. HE'S IN THE WIND."

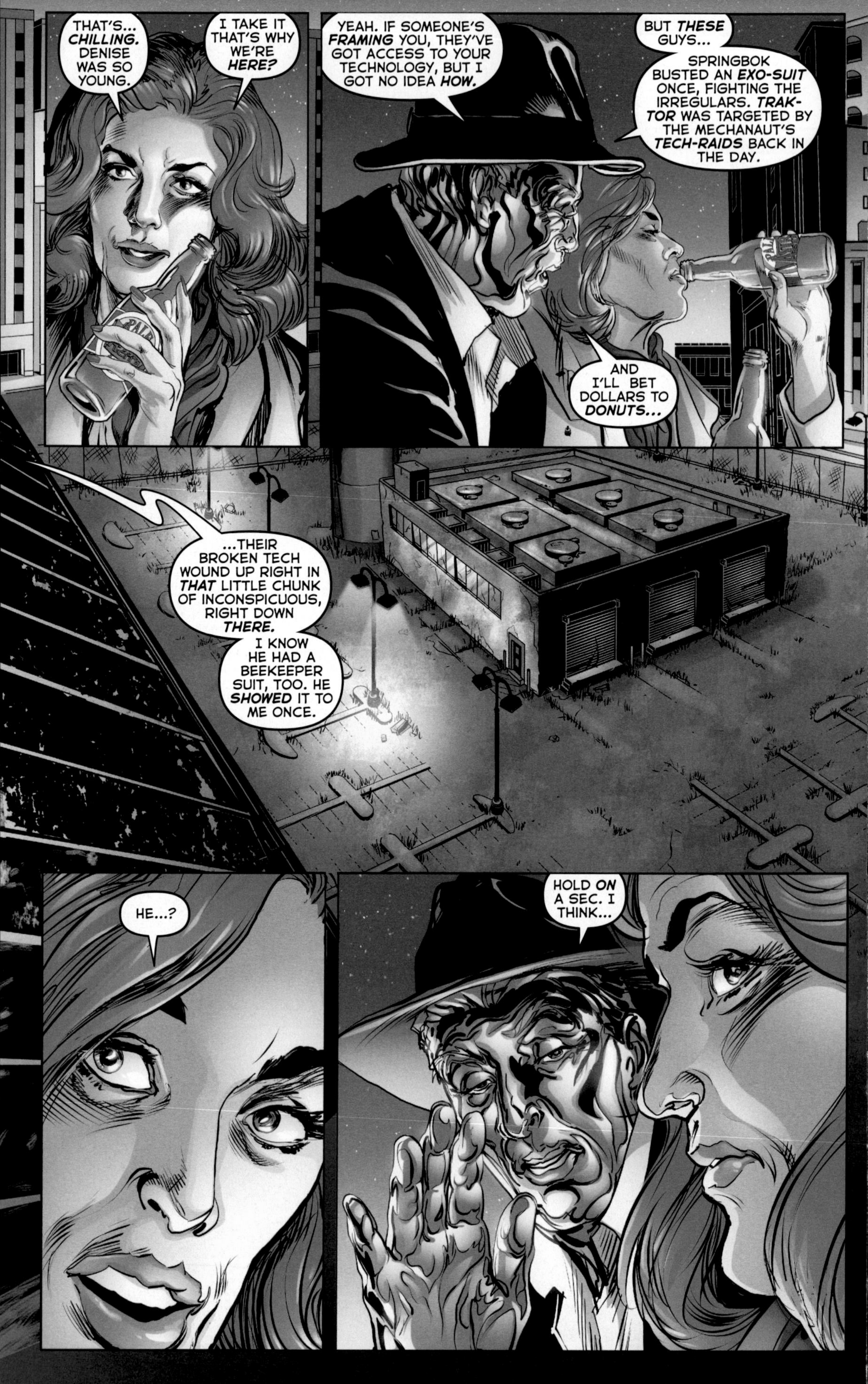
THAT'S... CHILLING. DENISE WAS SO YOUNG.
I TAKE IT THAT'S WHY WE'RE HERE?
YEAH. IF SOMEONE'S FRAMING YOU, THEY'VE GOT ACCESS TO YOUR TECHNOLOGY, BUT I GOT NO IDEA HOW.
BUT THESE GUYS...
SPRINGBOK BUSTED AN EXO-SUIT ONCE, FIGHTING THE IRREGULARS. TRAKTOR WAS TARGETED BY THE MECHANAUT'S TECH-RAIDS BACK IN THE DAY.
AND I'LL BET DOLLARS TO DONUTS...
...THEIR BROKEN TECH WOUND UP RIGHT IN THAT LITTLE CHUNK OF INCONSPICUOUS, RIGHT DOWN THERE.
I KNOW HE HAD A BEEKEEPER SUIT, TOO. HE SHOWED IT TO ME ONCE.
HE...?
HOLD ON A SEC. I THINK...

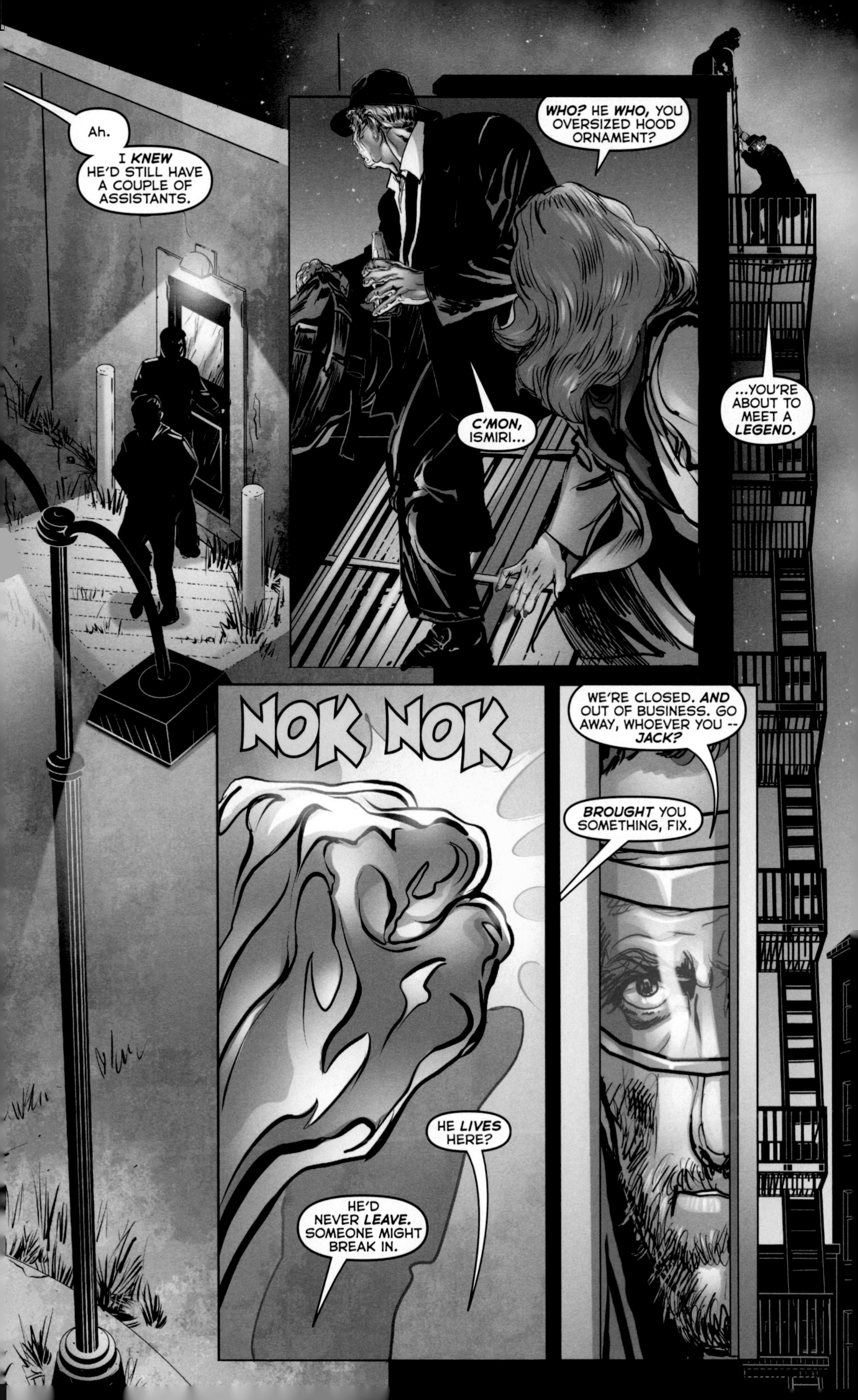

Ah.
I KNEW HE'D STILL HAVE A COUPLE OF ASSISTANTS.
WHO? HE WHO, YOU OVERSIZED HOOD ORNAMENT?
C'MON, ISMIRI...
...YOU'RE ABOUT TO MEET A LEGEND.
NOK NOK
HE LIVES HERE?
HE'D NEVER LEAVE. SOMEONE MIGHT BREAK IN.
WE'RE CLOSED. AND OUT OF BUSINESS. GO AWAY, WHOEVER YOU -- JACK?
BROUGHT YOU SOMETHING, FIX.

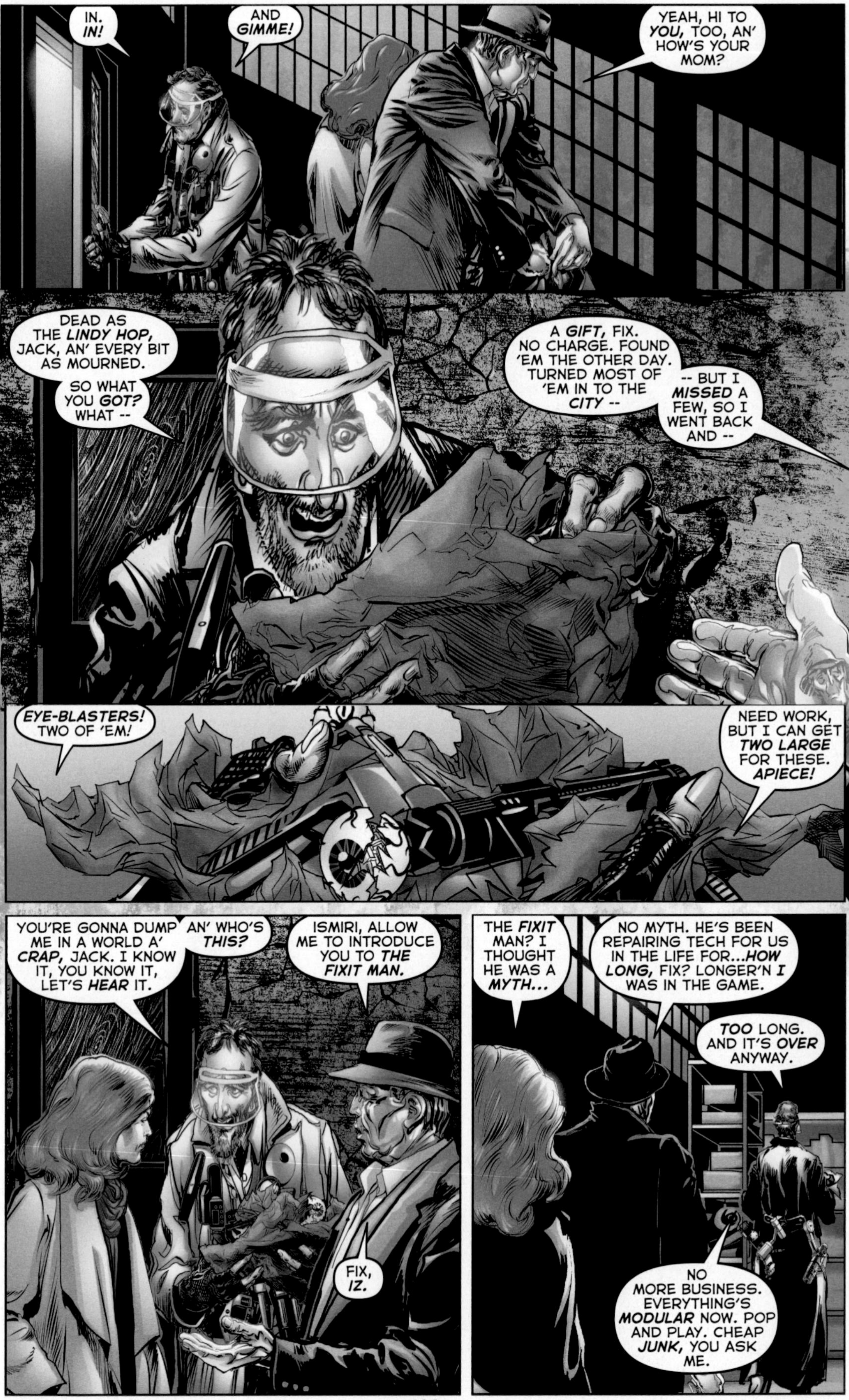

IN. IN!
AND GIMME!
YEAH, HI TO YOU, TOO, AN' HOW'S YOUR MOM?
DEAD AS THE LINDY HOP, JACK, AN' EVERY BIT AS MOURNED.
SO WHAT YOU GOT? WHAT --
A GIFT, FIX. NO CHARGE. FOUND 'EM THE OTHER DAY. TURNED MOST OF 'EM IN TO THE CITY --
-- BUT I MISSED A FEW, SO I WENT BACK AND --
EYE-BLASTERS! TWO OF 'EM!
NEED WORK, BUT I CAN GET TWO LARGE FOR THESE. APIECE!
YOU'RE GONNA DUMP ME IN A WORLD A' CRAP, JACK. I KNOW IT, YOU KNOW IT, LET'S HEAR IT.
AN' WHO'S THIS?
ISMIRI, ALLOW ME TO INTRODUCE YOU TO THE FIXIT MAN.
FIX, IZ.
THE FIXIT MAN? I THOUGHT HE WAS A MYTH...
NO MYTH. HE'S BEEN REPAIRING TECH FOR US IN THE LIFE FOR...HOW LONG, FIX? LONGER'N I WAS IN THE GAME.
TOO LONG. AND IT'S OVER ANYWAY.
NO MORE BUSINESS. EVERYTHING'S MODULAR NOW. POP AND PLAY. CHEAP JUNK, YOU ASK ME.

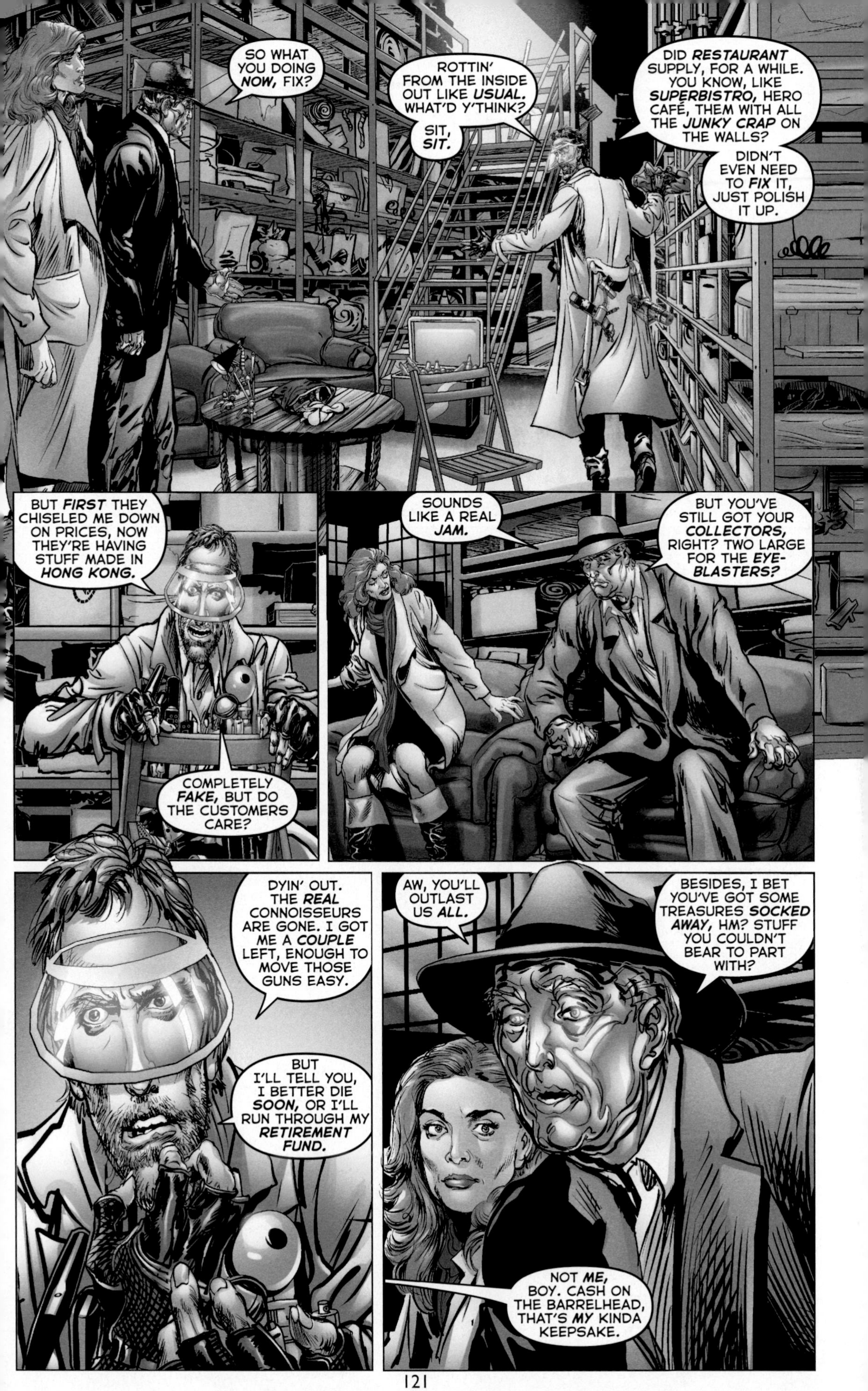
SO WHAT YOU DOING NOW, FIX?
ROTTIN' FROM THE INSIDE OUT LIKE USUAL. WHAT'D Y'THINK?
SIT, SIT.
DID RESTAURANT SUPPLY, FOR A WHILE. YOU KNOW, LIKE SUPERBISTRO, HERO CAFÉ, THEM WITH ALL THE JUNKY CRAP ON THE WALLS?
DIDN'T EVEN NEED TO FIX IT, JUST POLISH IT UP.
BUT FIRST THEY CHISELED ME DOWN ON PRICES, NOW THEY'RE HAVING STUFF MADE IN HONG KONG.
COMPLETELY FAKE, BUT DO THE CUSTOMERS CARE?
SOUNDS LIKE A REAL JAM.
BUT YOU'VE STILL GOT YOUR COLLECTORS, RIGHT? TWO LARGE FOR THE EYE-BLASTERS?
DYIN' OUT. THE REAL CONNOISSEURS ARE GONE. I GOT ME A COUPLE LEFT, ENOUGH TO MOVE THOSE GUNS EASY.
BUT I'LL TELL YOU, I BETTER DIE SOON, OR I'LL RUN THROUGH MY RETIREMENT FUND.
AW, YOU'LL OUTLAST US ALL.
BESIDES, I BET YOU'VE GOT SOME TREASURES SOCKED AWAY, HM? STUFF YOU COULDN'T BEAR TO PART WITH?
NOT ME, BOY. CASH ON THE BARRELHEAD, THAT'S MY KINDA KEEPSAKE.

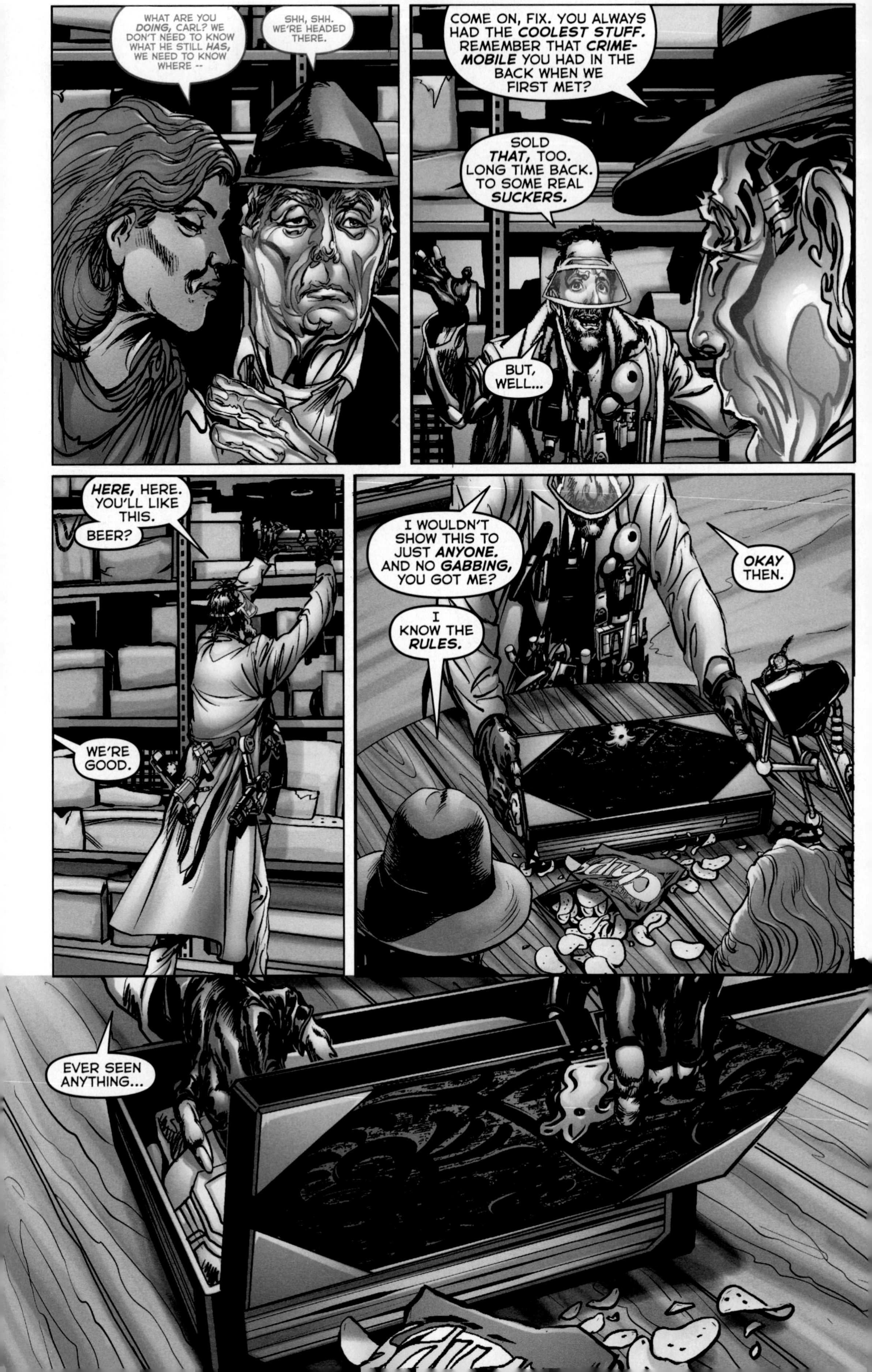

WHAT ARE YOU DOING, CARL? WE DON'T NEED TO KNOW WHAT HE STILL HAS, WE NEED TO KNOW WHERE --
SHH, SHH. WE'RE HEADED THERE.
COME ON, FIX. YOU ALWAYS HAD THE COOLEST STUFF. REMEMBER THAT CRIME-MOBILE YOU HAD IN THE BACK WHEN WE FIRST MET?
SOLD THAT, TOO. LONG TIME BACK. TO SOME REAL SUCKERS.
BUT, WELL...
HERE, HERE. YOU'LL LIKE THIS.
BEER?
WE'RE GOOD.
I WOULDN'T SHOW THIS TO JUST ANYONE. AND NO GABBING, YOU GOT ME?
OKAY THEN.
I KNOW THE RULES.
EVER SEEN ANYTHING...

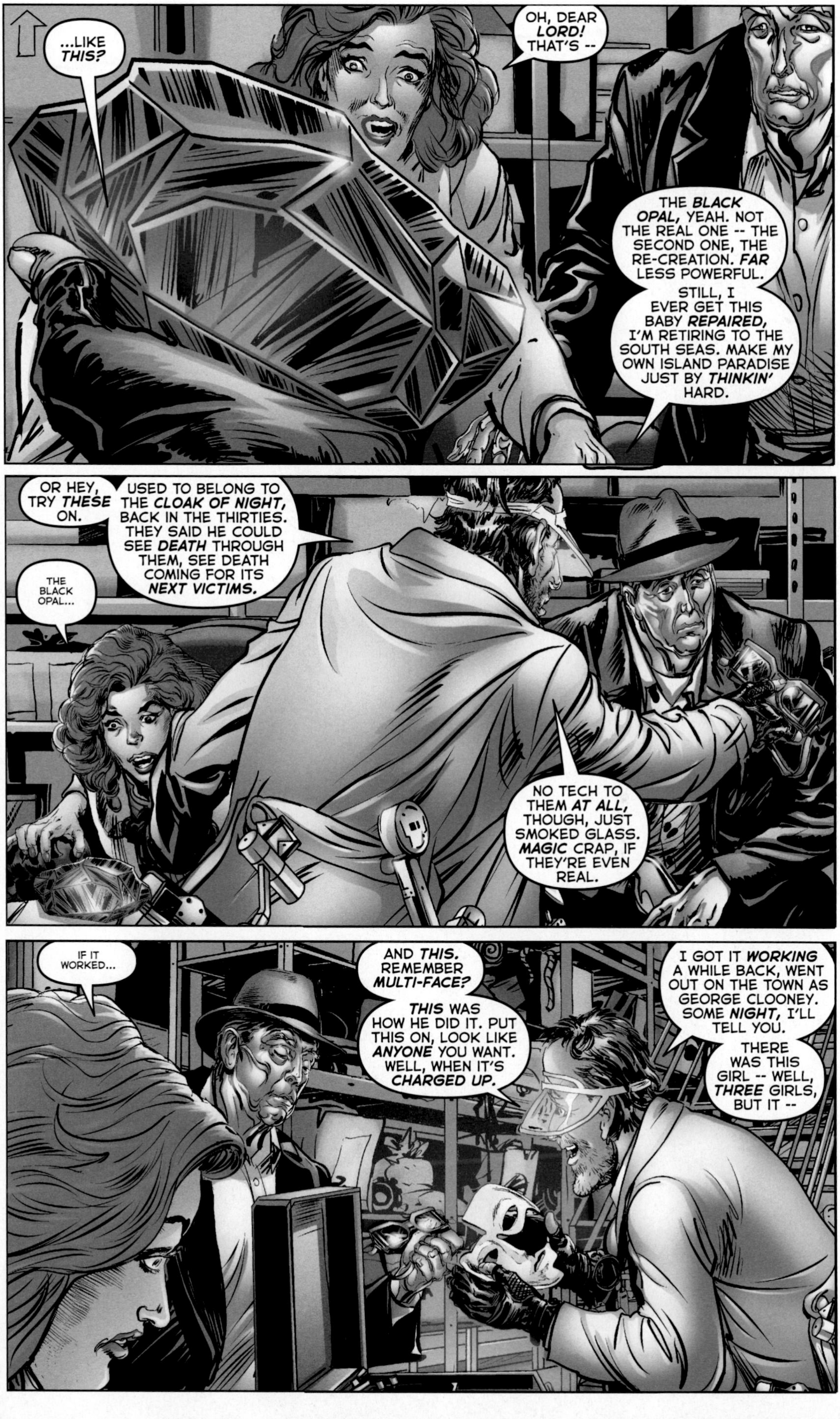

...LIKE THIS?
OH, DEAR LORD! THAT'S --
THE BLACK OPAL, YEAH. NOT THE REAL ONE -- THE SECOND ONE, THE RE-CREATION. FAR LESS POWERFUL.
STILL, I EVER GET THIS BABY REPAIRED, I'M RETIRING TO THE SOUTH SEAS. MAKE MY OWN ISLAND PARADISE JUST BY THINKIN' HARD.
OR HEY, TRY THESE ON.
USED TO BELONG TO THE CLOAK OF NIGHT, BACK IN THE THIRTIES. THEY SAID HE COULD SEE DEATH THROUGH THEM, SEE DEATH COMING FOR ITS NEXT VICTIMS.
THE BLACK OPAL...
NO TECH TO THEM AT ALL, THOUGH, JUST SMOKED GLASS. MAGIC CRAP, IF THEY'RE EVEN REAL.
IF IT WORKED...
AND THIS. REMEMBER MULTI-FACE?
THIS WAS HOW HE DID IT. PUT THIS ON, LOOK LIKE ANYONE YOU WANT. WELL, WHEN IT'S CHARGED UP.
I GOT IT WORKING A WHILE BACK, WENT OUT ON THE TOWN AS GEORGE CLOONEY. SOME NIGHT, I'LL TELL YOU.
THERE WAS THIS GIRL -- WELL, THREE GIRLS, BUT IT --

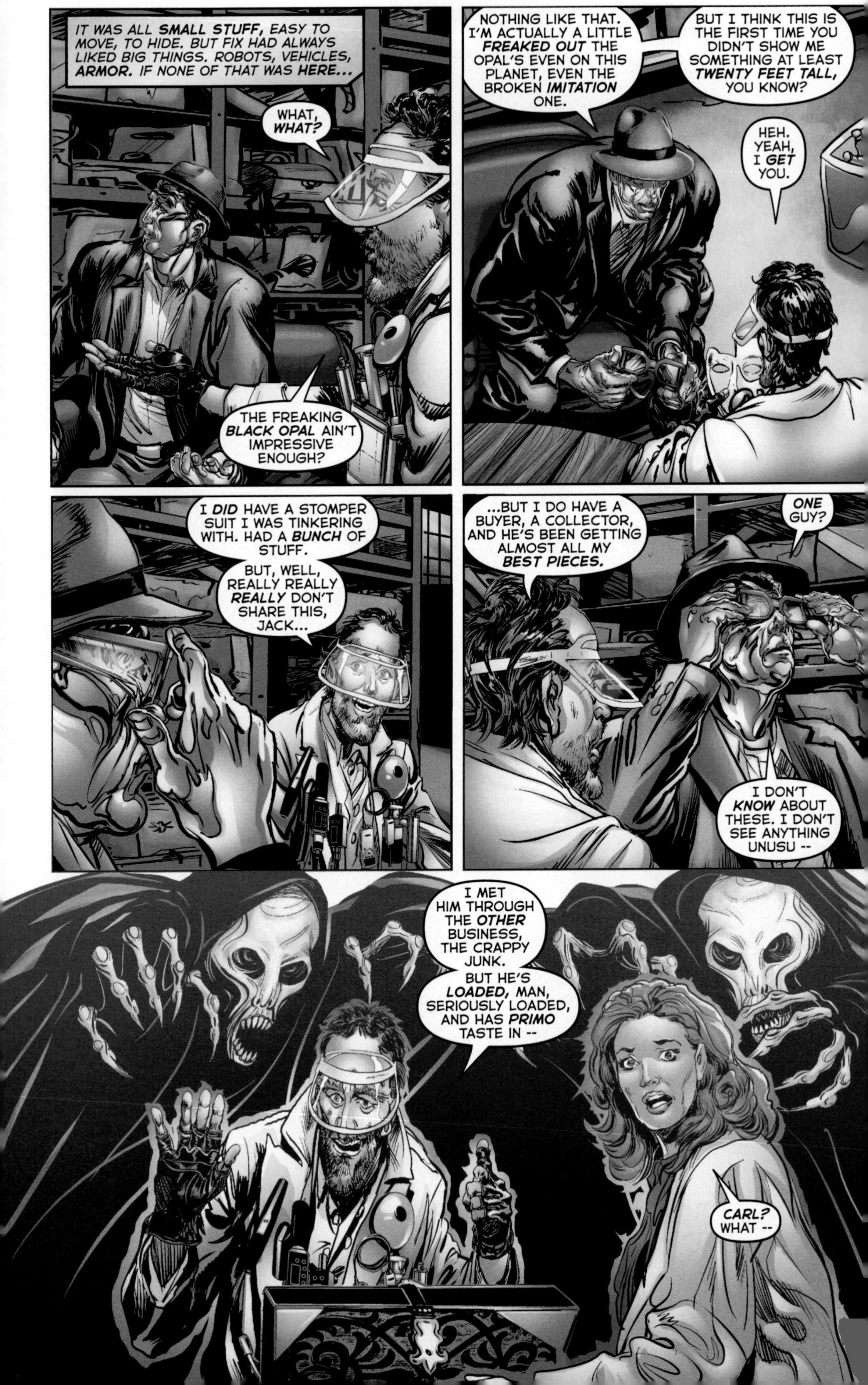
IT WAS ALL SMALL STUFF, EASY TO MOVE, TO HIDE. BUT FIX HAD ALWAYS LIKED BIG THINGS. ROBOTS, VEHICLES, ARMOR. IF NONE OF THAT WAS HERE...
WHAT, WHAT?
THE FREAKING BLACK OPAL AIN'T IMPRESSIVE ENOUGH?
NOTHING LIKE THAT. I'M ACTUALLY A LITTLE FREAKED OUT THE OPAL'S EVEN ON THIS PLANET, EVEN THE BROKEN IMITATION ONE.
BUT I THINK THIS IS THE FIRST TIME YOU DIDN'T SHOW ME SOMETHING AT LEAST TWENTY FEET TALL, YOU KNOW?
HEH. YEAH, I GET YOU.
I DID HAVE A STOMPER SUIT I WAS TINKERING WITH. HAD A BUNCH OF STUFF.
BUT, WELL, REALLY REALLY REALLY DON'T SHARE THIS, JACK...
...BUT I DO HAVE A BUYER, A COLLECTOR, AND HE'S BEEN GETTING ALMOST ALL MY BEST PIECES.
ONE GUY?
I DON'T KNOW ABOUT THESE. I DON'T SEE ANYTHING UNUSU --
I MET HIM THROUGH THE OTHER BUSINESS, THE CRAPPY JUNK.
BUT HE'S LOADED, MAN, SERIOUSLY LOADED, AND HAS PRIMO TASTE IN --
CARL? WHAT --

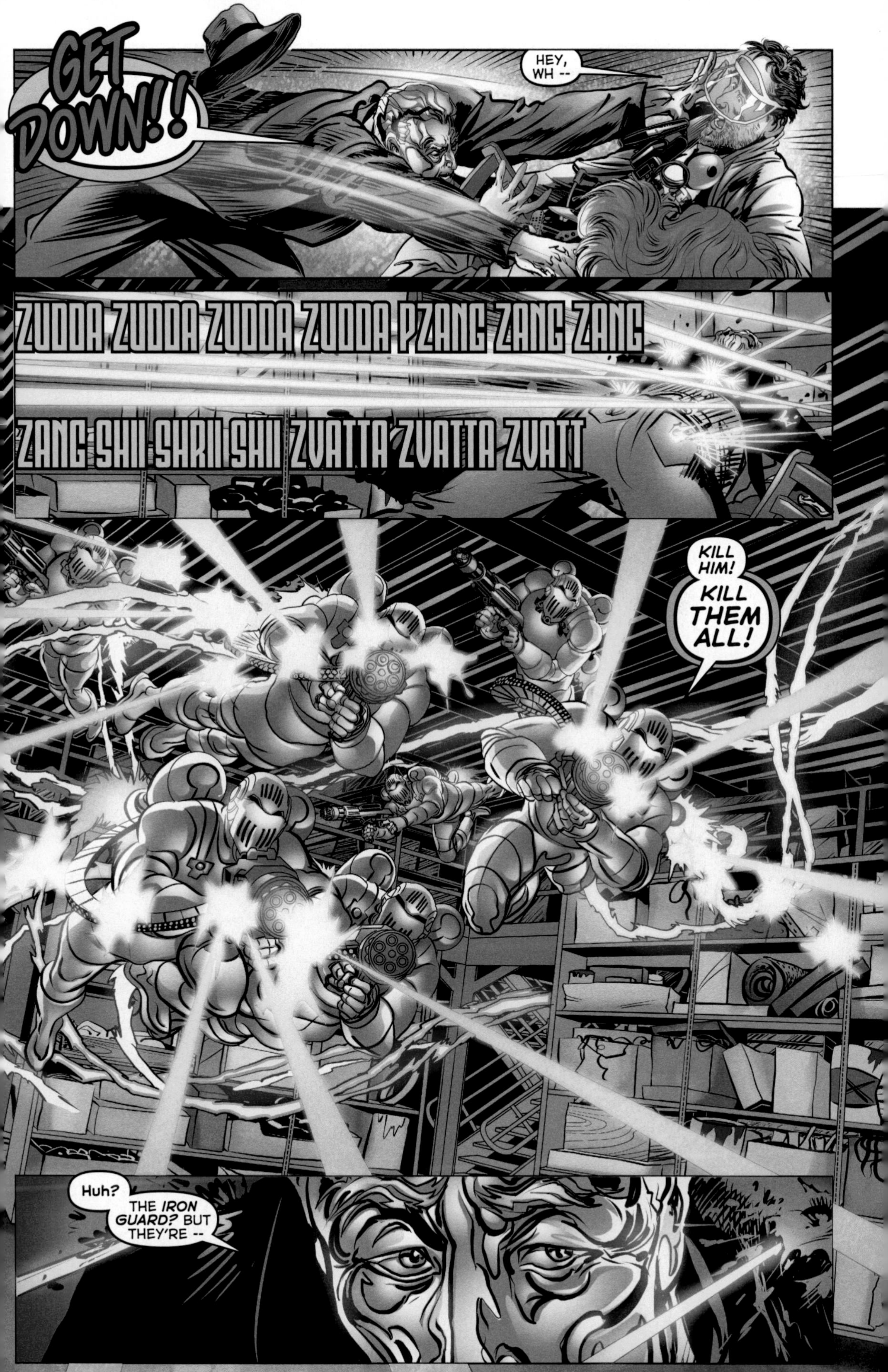
GET DOWN!!
HEY, WH --
ZUDDA ZUDDA ZUDDA ZUDDA PZANG ZANG ZANG
ZANG SHII SHRII SHII ZVATTA ZVATTA ZVATT
KILL HIM! KILL THEM ALL!
Huh?
THE IRON GUARD? BUT THEY'RE --

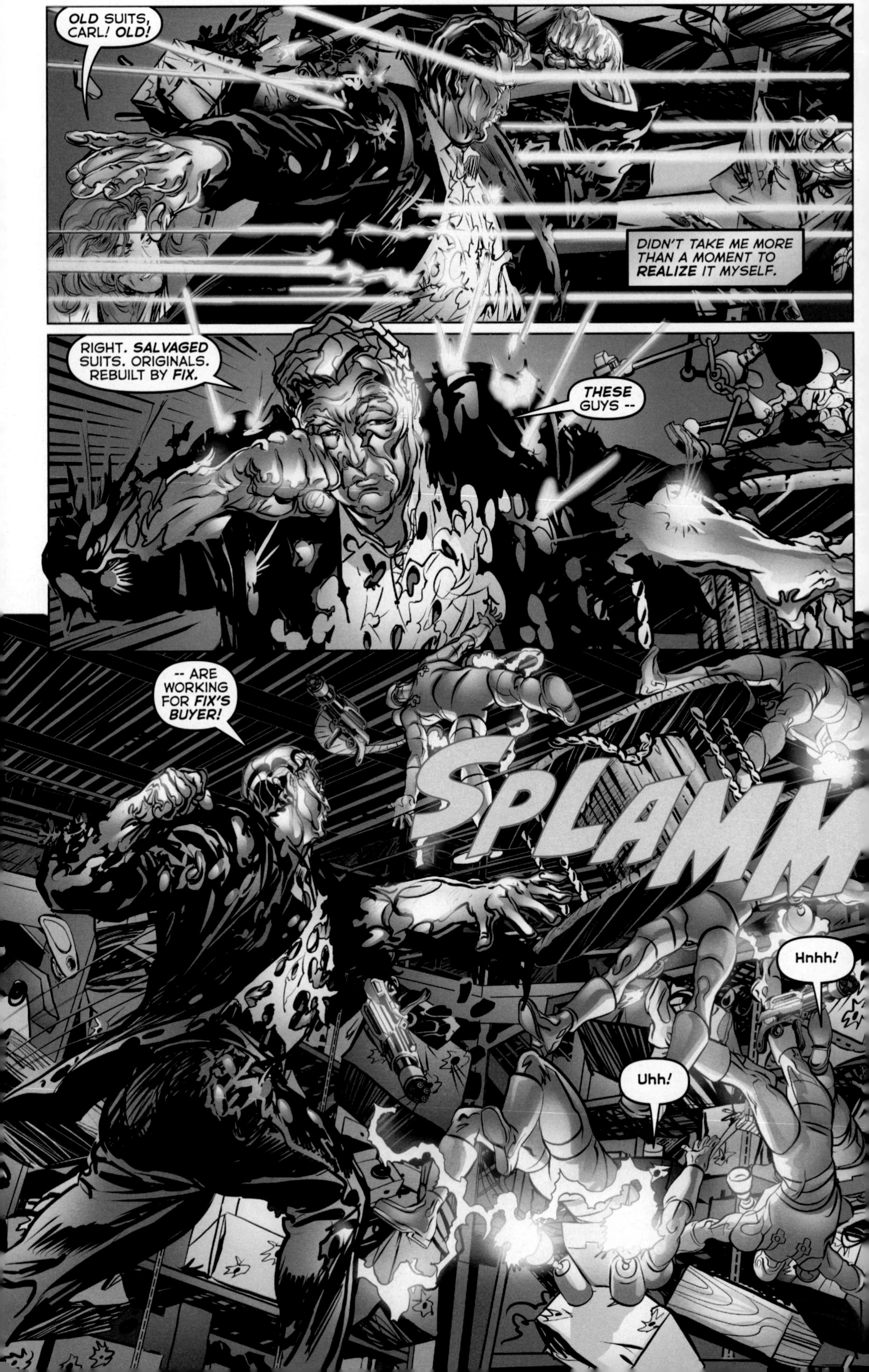
OLD SUITS, CARL! OLD!
DIDN'T TAKE ME MORE THAN A MOMENT TO REALIZE IT MYSELF.
RIGHT. SALVAGED SUITS. ORIGINALS. REBUILT BY FIX.
THESE GUYS --
-- ARE WORKING FOR FIX'S BUYER!
SPLAMM
Hnhh!
Uhh!

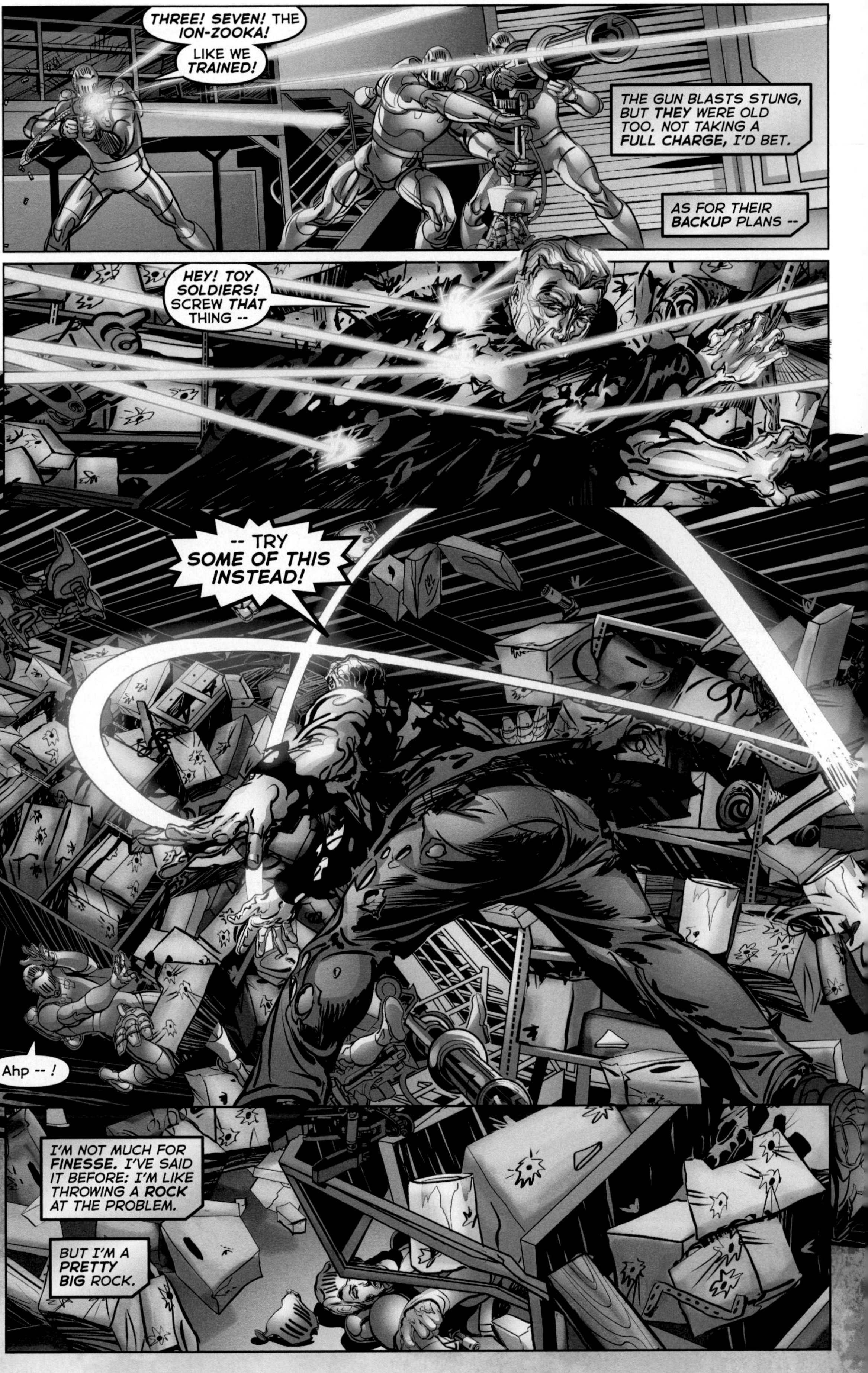
THREE! SEVEN! THE ION-ZOOKA!
LIKE WE TRAINED!
THE GUN BLASTS STUNG, BUT THEY WERE OLD TOO. NOT TAKING A FULL CHARGE, I'D BET.
AS FOR THEIR BACKUP PLANS --
HEY! TOY SOLDIERS! SCREW THAT THING --
-- TRY SOME OF THIS INSTEAD!
Ahp -- !
I'M NOT MUCH FOR FINESSE. I'VE SAID IT BEFORE: I'M LIKE THROWING A ROCK AT THE PROBLEM.
BUT I'M A PRETTY BIG ROCK.

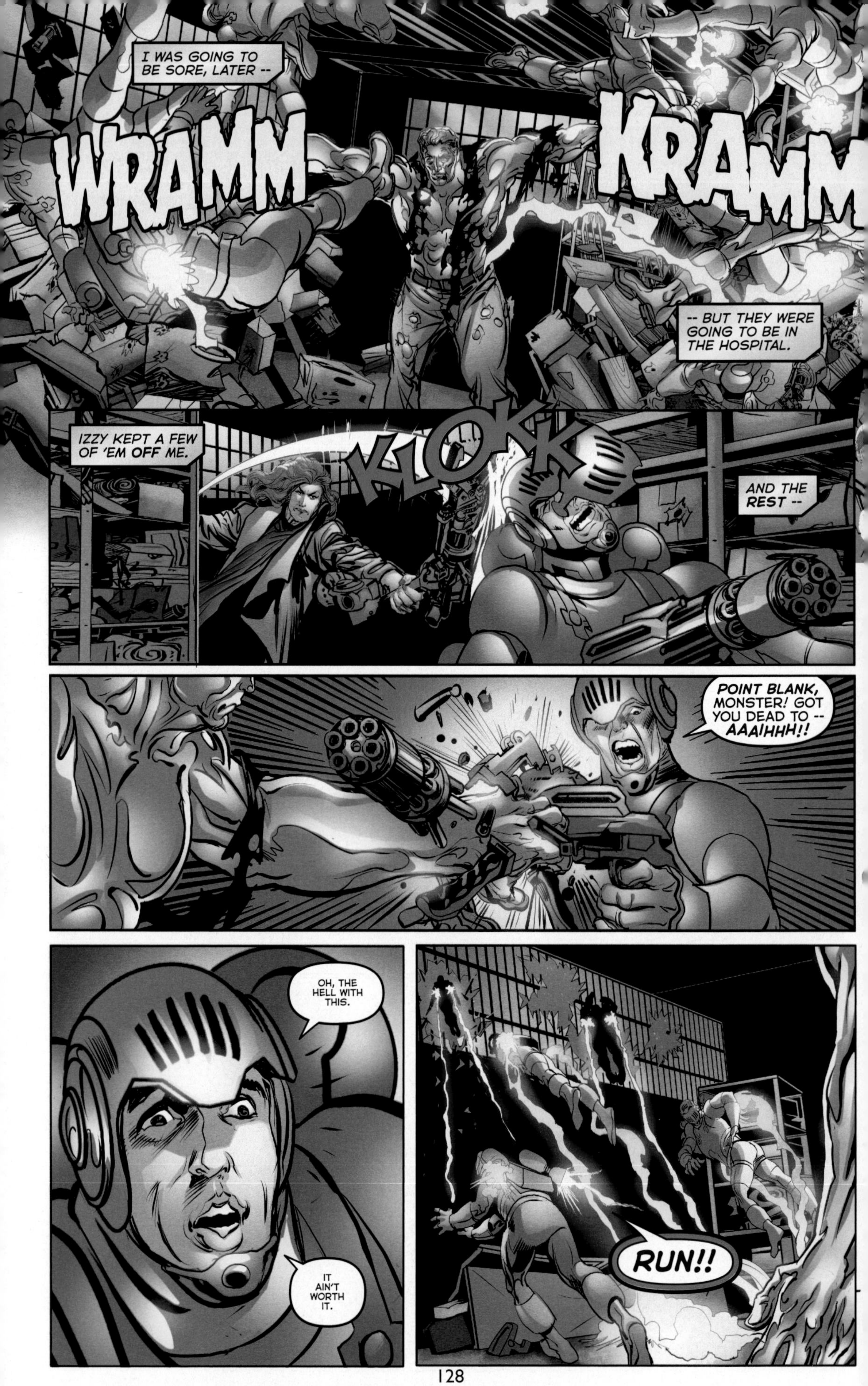

I WAS GOING TO BE SORE, LATER --
WRAMM
KRAMM
-- BUT THEY WERE GOING TO BE IN THE HOSPITAL.
IZZY KEPT A FEW OF 'EM OFF ME.
KLOKK
AND THE REST --
POINT BLANK, MONSTER! GOT YOU DEAD TO -- AAAIHHH!!
OH, THE HELL WITH THIS.
IT AIN'T WORTH IT.
RUN!!

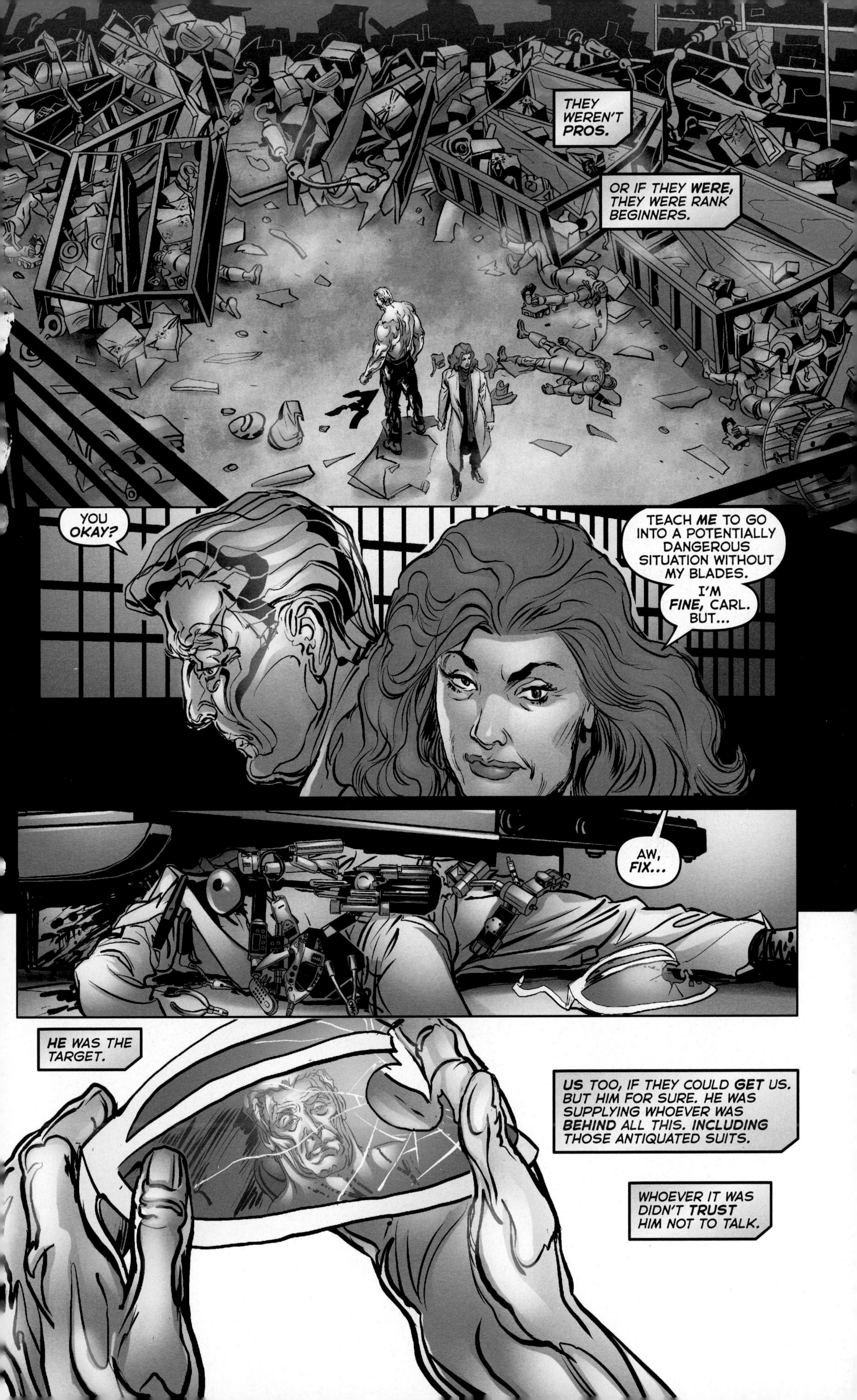
THEY WEREN'T PROS.
OR IF THEY WERE, THEY WERE RANK BEGINNERS.
YOU OKAY?
TEACH ME TO GO INTO A POTENTIALLY DANGEROUS SITUATION WITHOUT MY BLADES.
I'M FINE, CARL. BUT...
AW, FIX...
HE WAS THE TARGET.
US TOO, IF THEY COULD GET US. BUT HIM FOR SURE. HE WAS SUPPLYING WHOEVER WAS BEHIND ALL THIS. INCLUDING THOSE ANTIQUATED SUITS.
WHOEVER IT WAS DIDN'T TRUST HIM NOT TO TALK.

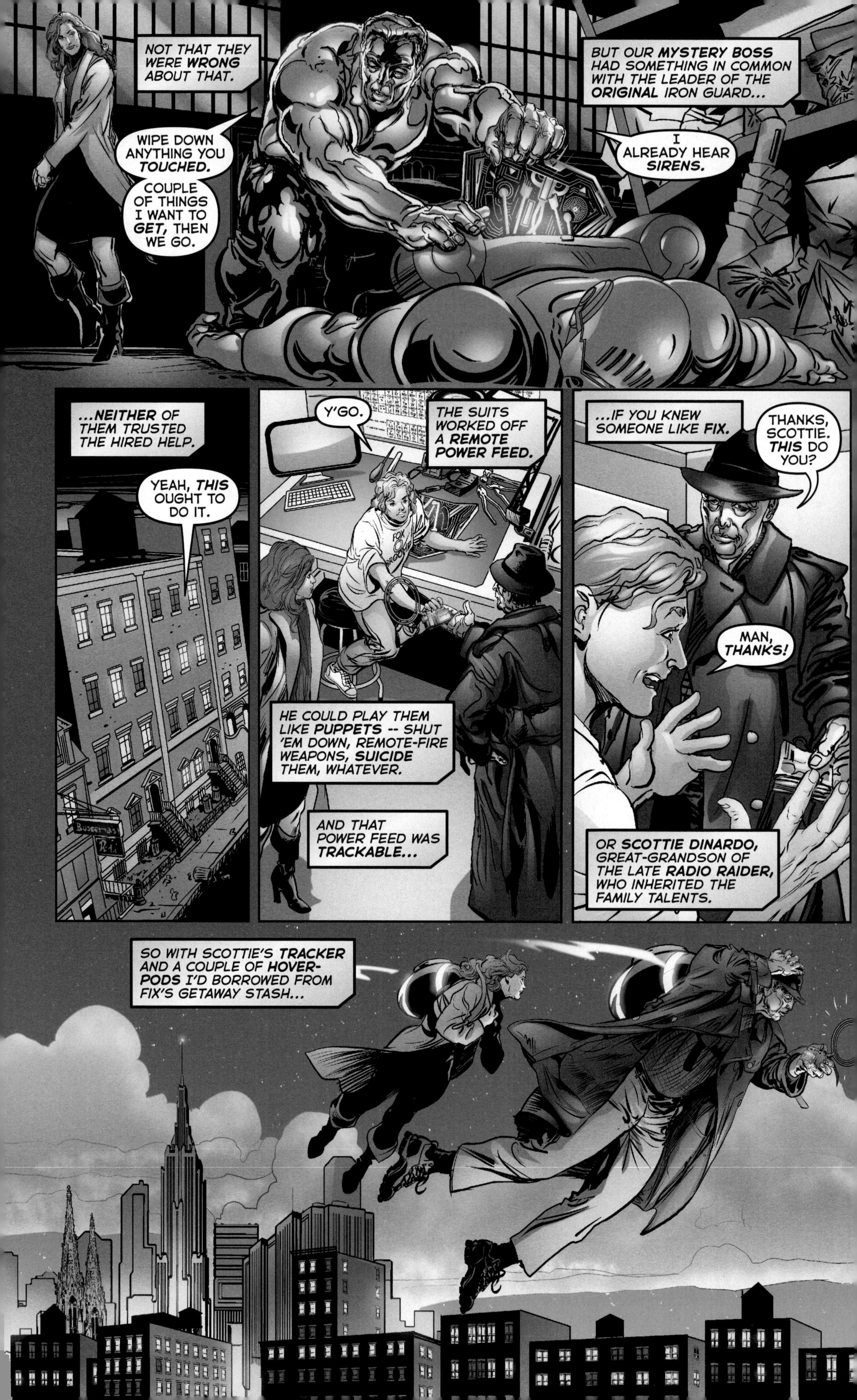
NOT THAT THEY WERE WRONG ABOUT THAT.
WIPE DOWN ANYTHING YOU TOUCHED.
COUPLE OF THINGS I WANT TO GET, THEN WE GO.
BUT OUR MYSTERY BOSS HAD SOMETHING IN COMMON WITH THE LEADER OF THE ORIGINAL IRON GUARD...
I ALREADY HEAR SIRENS.
...NEITHER OF THEM TRUSTED THE HIRED HELP.
YEAH, THIS OUGHT TO DO IT.
Y'GO.
THE SUITS WORKED OFF A REMOTE POWER FEED.
HE COULD PLAY THEM LIKE PUPPETS -- SHUT 'EM DOWN, REMOTE-FIRE WEAPONS, SUICIDE THEM, WHATEVER.
AND THAT POWER FEED WAS TRACKABLE...
...IF YOU KNEW SOMEONE LIKE FIX.
THANKS, SCOTTIE. THIS DO YOU?
MAN, THANKS!
OR SCOTTIE DINARDO, GREAT-GRANDSON OF THE LATE RADIO RAIDER, WHO INHERITED THE FAMILY TALENTS.
SO WITH SCOTTIE'S TRACKER AND A COUPLE OF HOVER-PODS I'D BORROWED FROM FIX'S GETAWAY STASH...

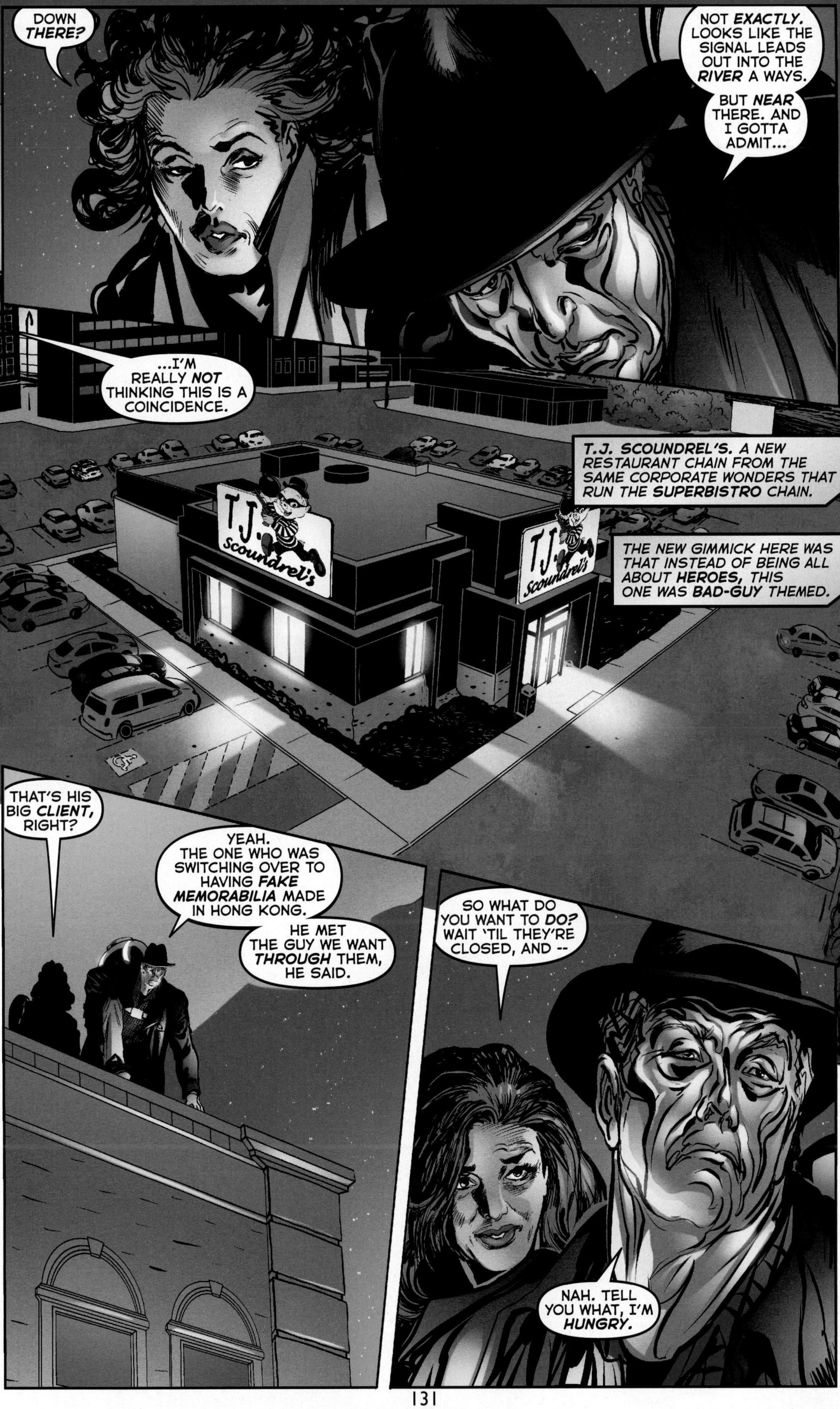
DOWN THERE?
NOT EXACTLY. LOOKS LIKE THE SIGNAL LEADS OUT INTO THE RIVER A WAYS.
BUT NEAR THERE. AND I GOTTA ADMIT...
...I'M REALLY NOT THINKING THIS IS A COINCIDENCE.
T.J. SCOUNDREL'S. A NEW RESTAURANT CHAIN FROM THE SAME CORPORATE WONDERS THAT RUN THE SUPERBISTRO CHAIN.
THE NEW GIMMICK HERE WAS THAT INSTEAD OF BEING ALL ABOUT HEROES, THIS ONE WAS BAD-GUY THEMED.
T.J. Scoundrel's
T.J. Scoundrel's
THAT'S HIS BIG CLIENT, RIGHT?
YEAH. THE ONE WHO WAS SWITCHING OVER TO HAVING FAKE MEMORABILIA MADE IN HONG KONG.
HE MET THE GUY WE WANT THROUGH THEM, HE SAID.
SO WHAT DO YOU WANT TO DO? WAIT 'TIL THEY'RE CLOSED, AND --
NAH. TELL YOU WHAT, I'M HUNGRY.

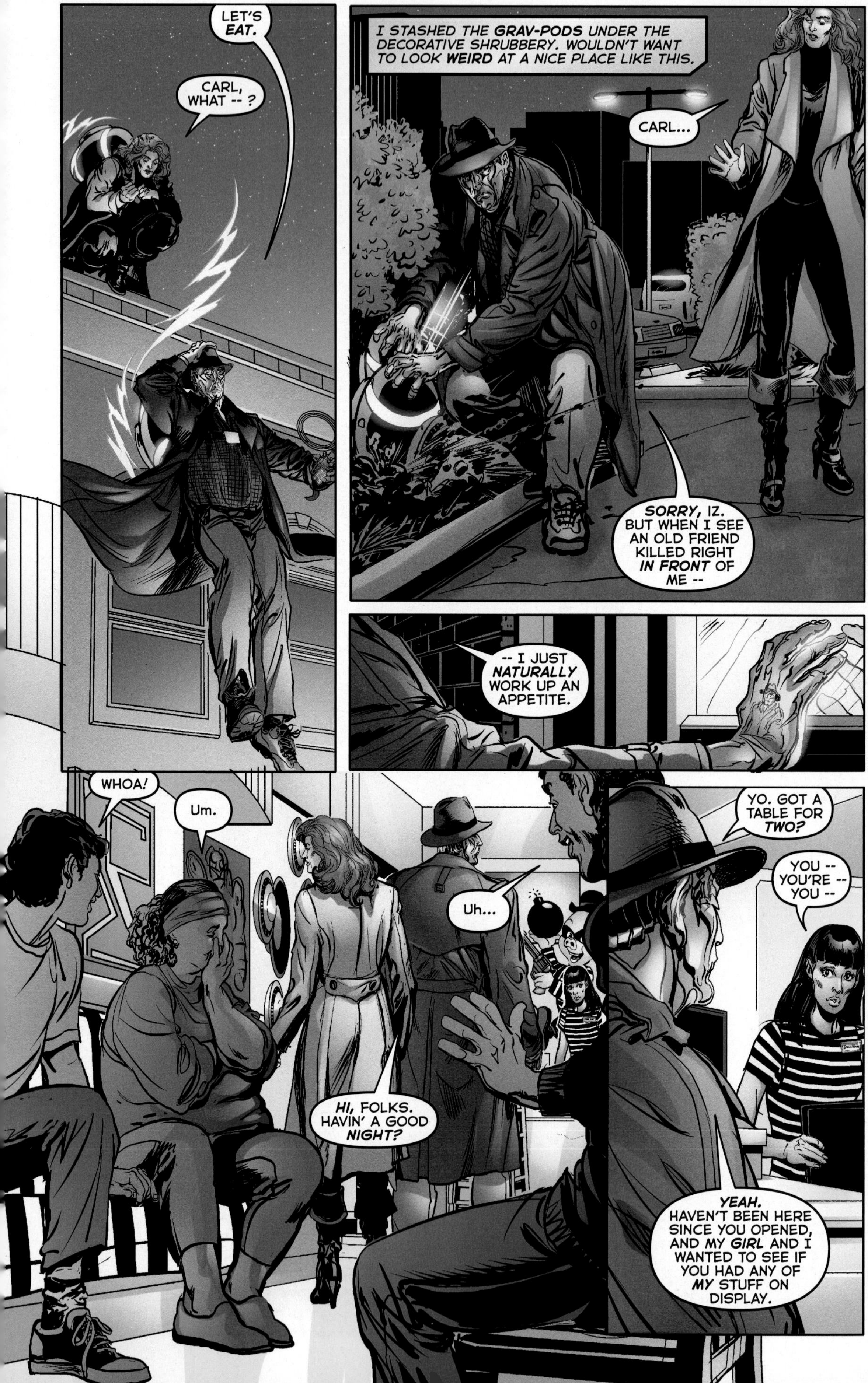
LET'S EAT.
CARL, WHAT -- ?
I STASHED THE GRAV-PODS UNDER THE DECORATIVE SHRUBBERY. WOULDN'T WANT TO LOOK WEIRD AT A NICE PLACE LIKE THIS.
CARL...
SORRY, IZ. BUT WHEN I SEE AN OLD FRIEND KILLED RIGHT IN FRONT OF ME --
-- I JUST NATURALLY WORK UP AN APPETITE.
WHOA!
Um.
Uh...
HI, FOLKS. HAVIN' A GOOD NIGHT?
YO. GOT A TABLE FOR TWO?
YOU -- YOU'RE -- YOU --
YEAH. HAVEN'T BEEN HERE SINCE YOU OPENED, AND MY GIRL AND I WANTED TO SEE IF YOU HAD ANY OF MY STUFF ON DISPLAY.

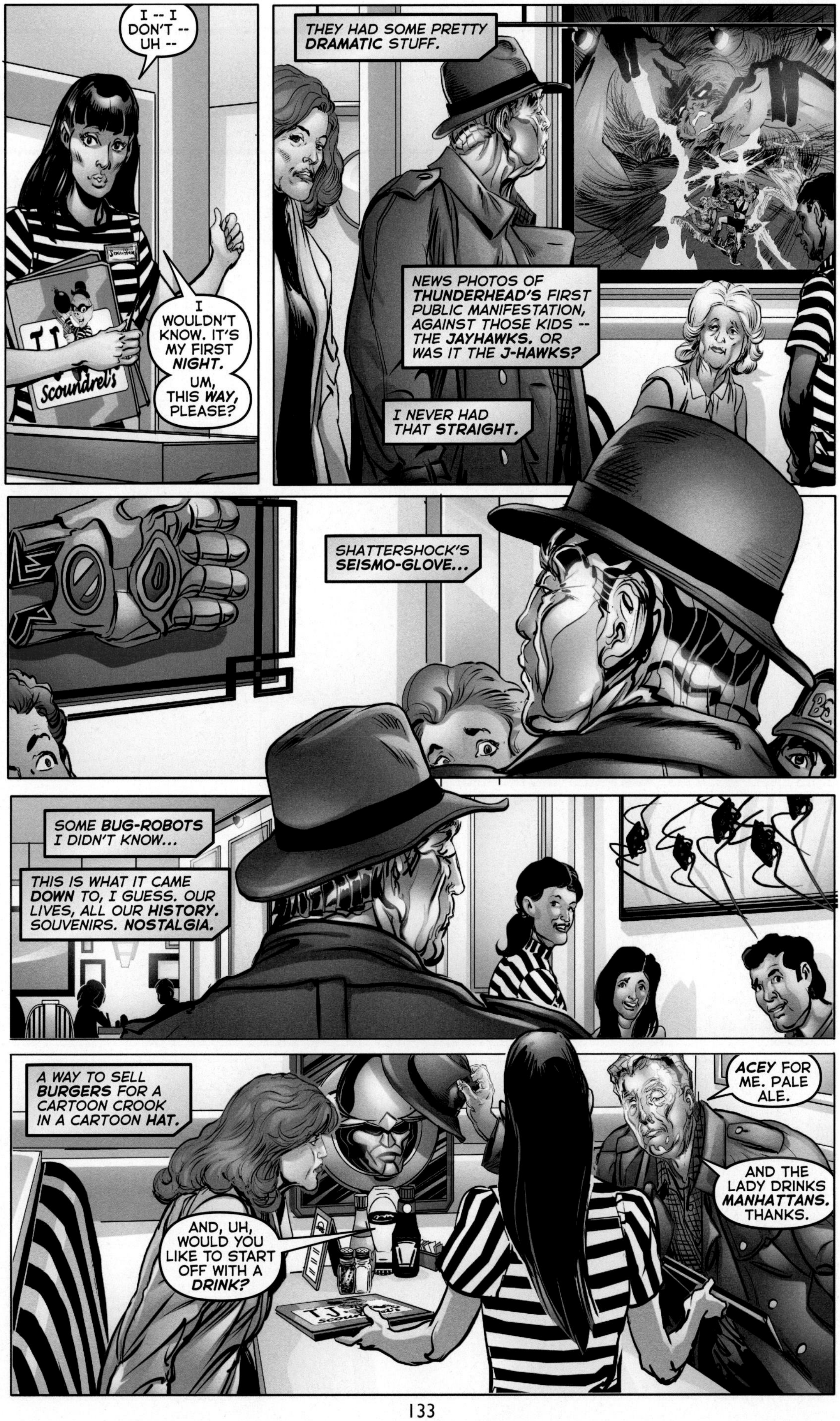
I -- I DON'T -- UH --
I WOULDN'T KNOW. IT'S MY FIRST NIGHT.
UM, THIS WAY, PLEASE?
Scoundrel's
THEY HAD SOME PRETTY DRAMATIC STUFF.
NEWS PHOTOS OF THUNDERHEAD'S FIRST PUBLIC MANIFESTATION, AGAINST THOSE KIDS -- THE JAYHAWKS. OR WAS IT THE J-HAWKS?
I NEVER HAD THAT STRAIGHT.
SHATTERSHOCK'S SEISMO-GLOVE...
SOME BUG-ROBOTS I DIDN'T KNOW...
THIS IS WHAT IT CAME DOWN TO, I GUESS. OUR LIVES, ALL OUR HISTORY. SOUVENIRS. NOSTALGIA.
A WAY TO SELL BURGERS FOR A CARTOON CROOK IN A CARTOON HAT.
AND, UH, WOULD YOU LIKE TO START OFF WITH A DRINK?
ACEY FOR ME. PALE ALE.
AND THE LADY DRINKS MANHATTANS. THANKS.

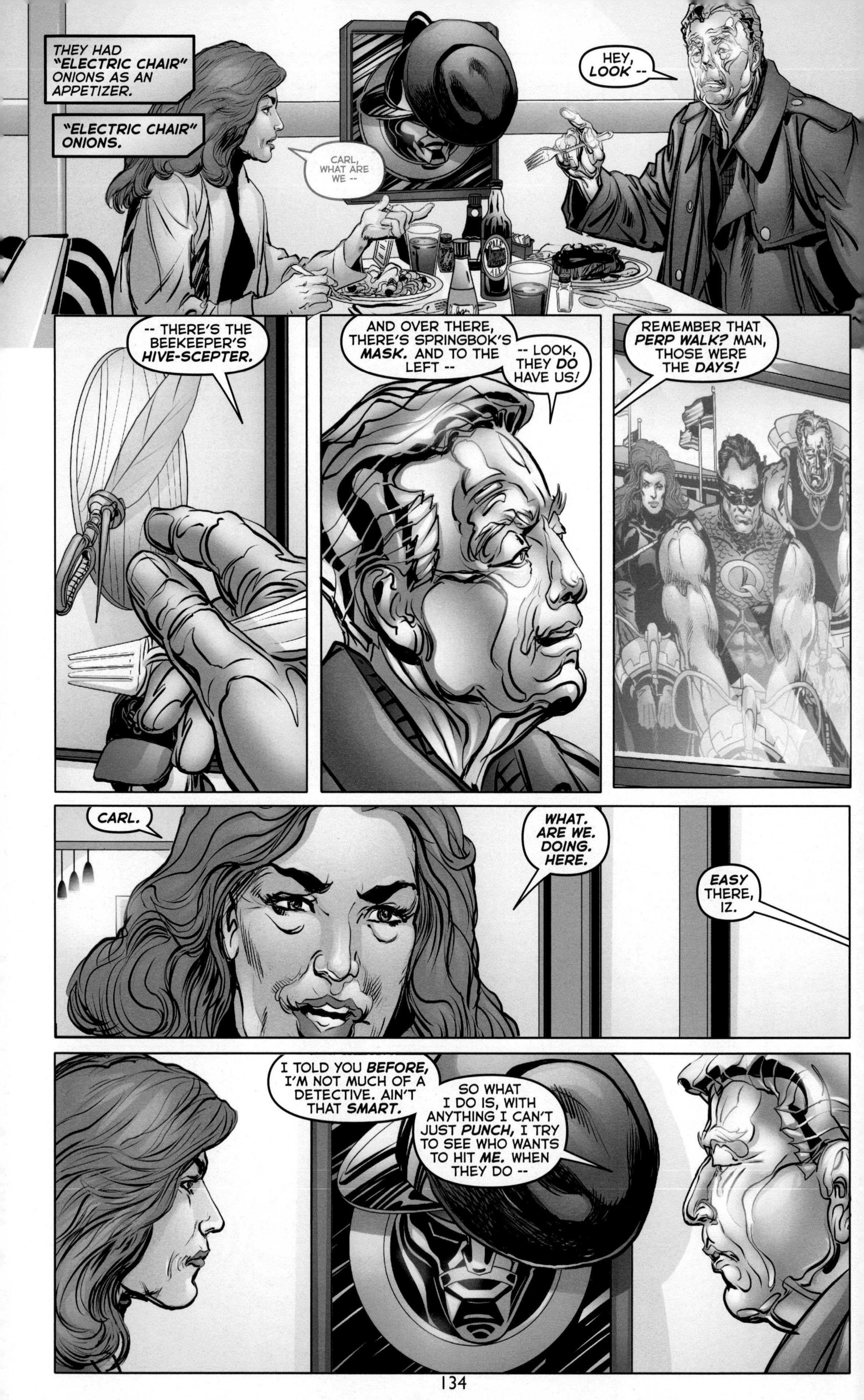
THEY HAD "ELECTRIC CHAIR" ONIONS AS AN APPETIZER.
"ELECTRIC CHAIR" ONIONS.
CARL, WHAT ARE WE --
HEY, LOOK --
-- THERE'S THE BEEKEEPER'S HIVE-SCEPTER.
AND OVER THERE, THERE'S SPRINGBOK'S MASK. AND TO THE LEFT --
-- LOOK, THEY DO HAVE US!
REMEMBER THAT PERP WALK? MAN, THOSE WERE THE DAYS!
CARL.
WHAT. ARE WE. DOING. HERE.
EASY THERE, IZ.
I TOLD YOU BEFORE, I'M NOT MUCH OF A DETECTIVE. AIN'T THAT SMART.
SO WHAT I DO IS, WITH ANYTHING I CAN'T JUST PUNCH, I TRY TO SEE WHO WANTS TO HIT ME. WHEN THEY DO --

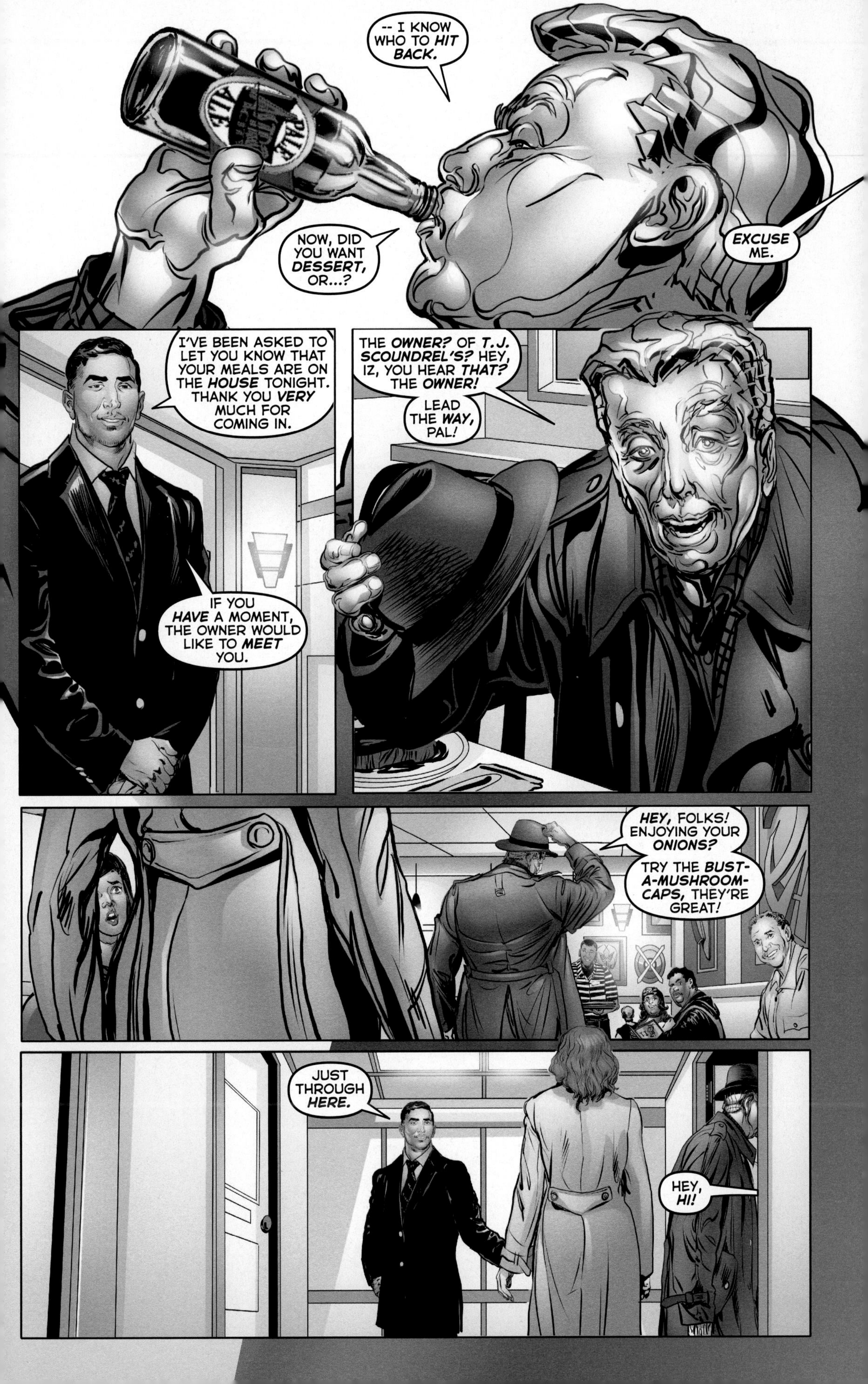
-- I KNOW WHO TO HIT BACK.
NOW, DID YOU WANT DESSERT, OR...?
EXCUSE ME.
I'VE BEEN ASKED TO LET YOU KNOW THAT YOUR MEALS ARE ON THE HOUSE TONIGHT. THANK YOU VERY MUCH FOR COMING IN.
IF YOU HAVE A MOMENT, THE OWNER WOULD LIKE TO MEET YOU.
THE OWNER? OF T.J. SCOUNDREL'S? HEY, IZ, YOU HEAR THAT? THE OWNER!
LEAD THE WAY, PAL!
HEY, FOLKS! ENJOYING YOUR ONIONS?
TRY THE BUST-A-MUSHROOM-CAPS, THEY'RE GREAT!
JUST THROUGH HERE.
HEY, HI!

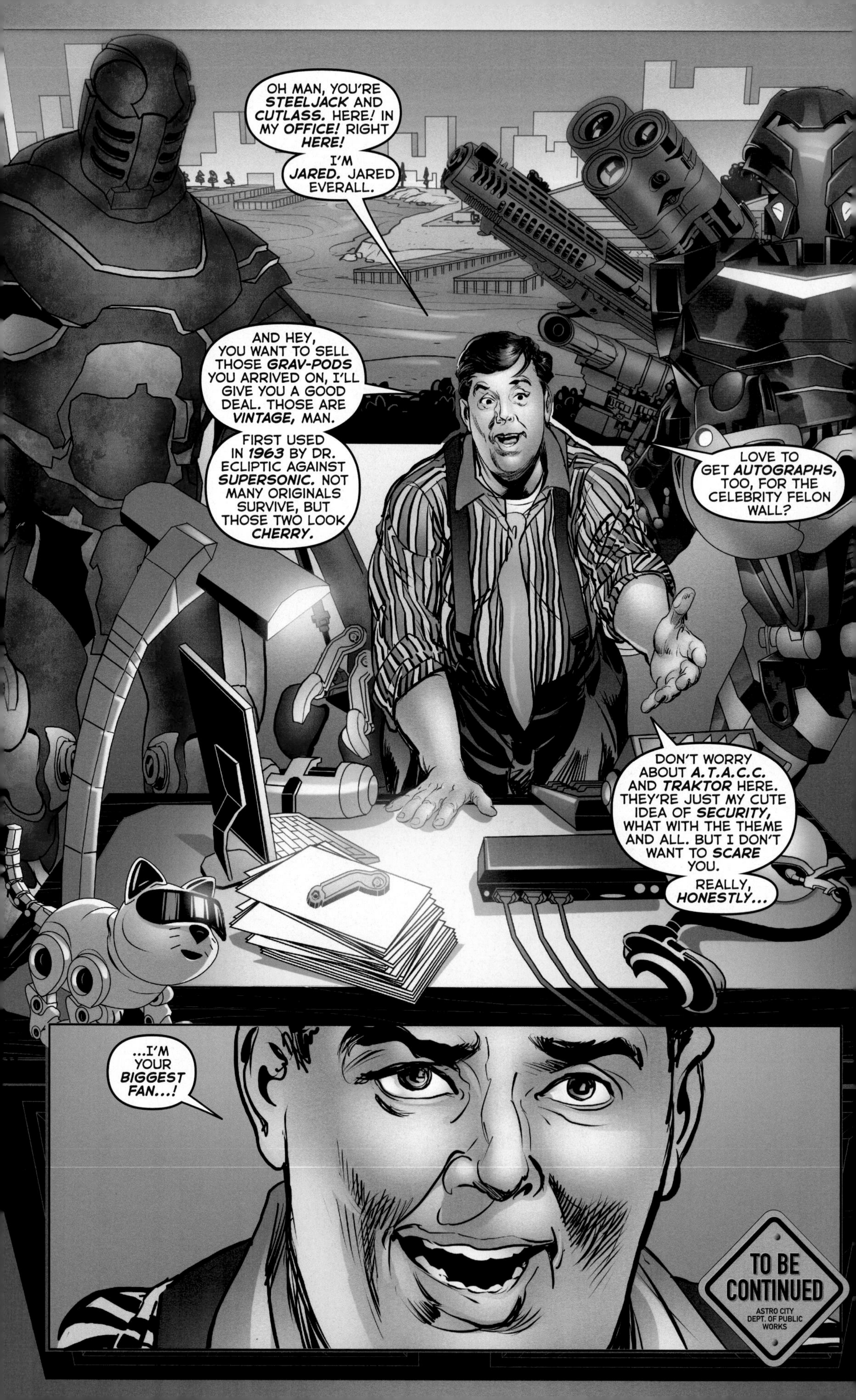
OH MAN, YOU'RE *STEELJACK* AND *CUTLASS.* HERE! IN MY *OFFICE!* RIGHT *HERE!*
I'M *JARED.* JARED EVERALL.
AND HEY, YOU WANT TO SELL THOSE *GRAV-PODS* YOU ARRIVED ON, I'LL GIVE YOU A GOOD DEAL. THOSE ARE *VINTAGE,* MAN.
FIRST USED IN *1963* BY DR. ECLIPTIC AGAINST *SUPERSONIC.* NOT MANY ORIGINALS SURVIVE, BUT THOSE TWO LOOK *CHERRY.*
LOVE TO GET *AUTOGRAPHS,* TOO, FOR THE CELEBRITY FELON WALL?
DON'T WORRY ABOUT *A.T.A.C.C.* AND *TRAKTOR* HERE. THEY'RE JUST MY CUTE IDEA OF *SECURITY,* WHAT WITH THE THEME AND ALL. BUT I DON'T WANT TO *SCARE* YOU.
REALLY, *HONESTLY...*
...I'M YOUR *BIGGEST FAN...!*
TO BE CONTINUED
ASTRO CITY DEPT. OF PUBLIC WORKS

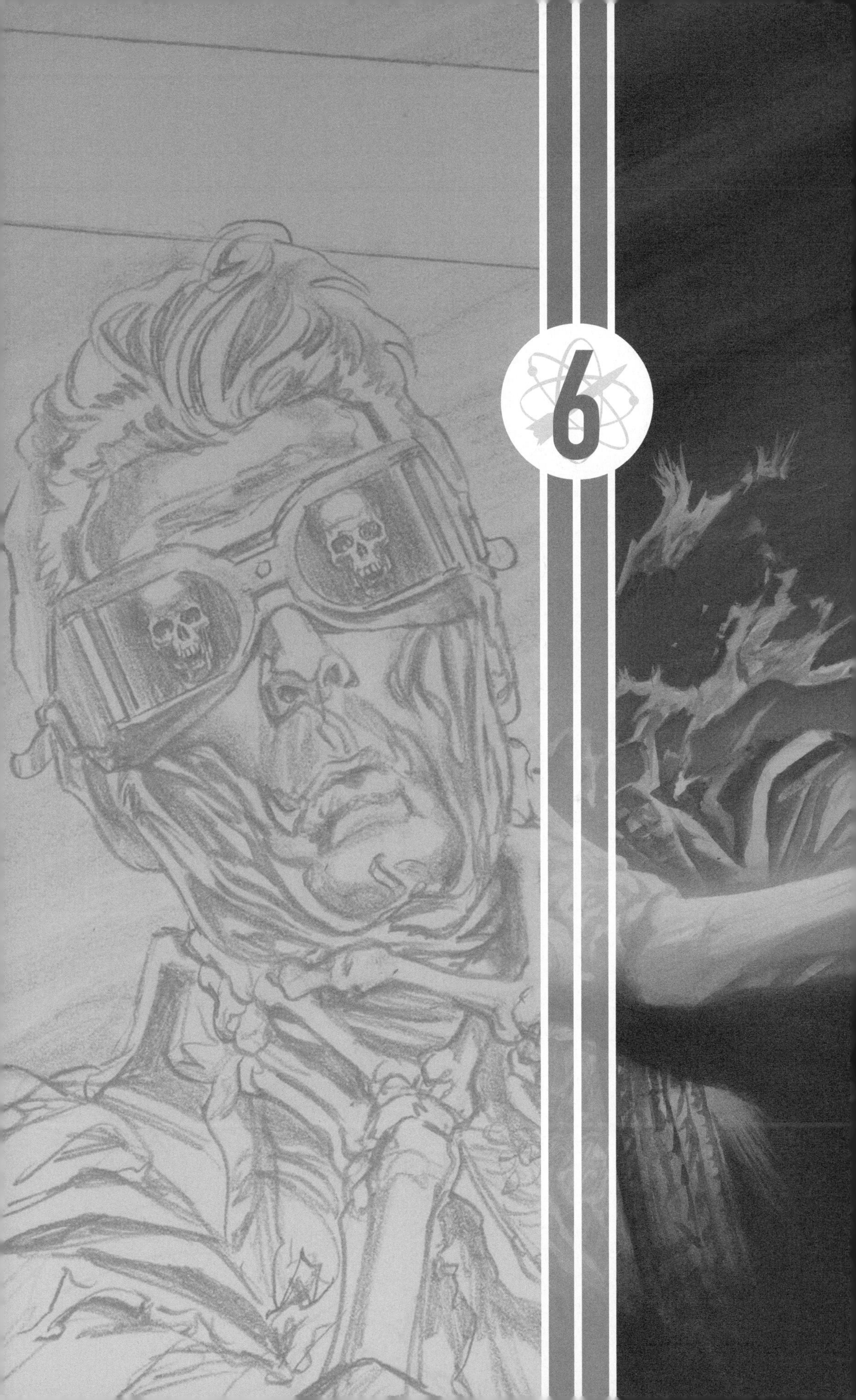
6

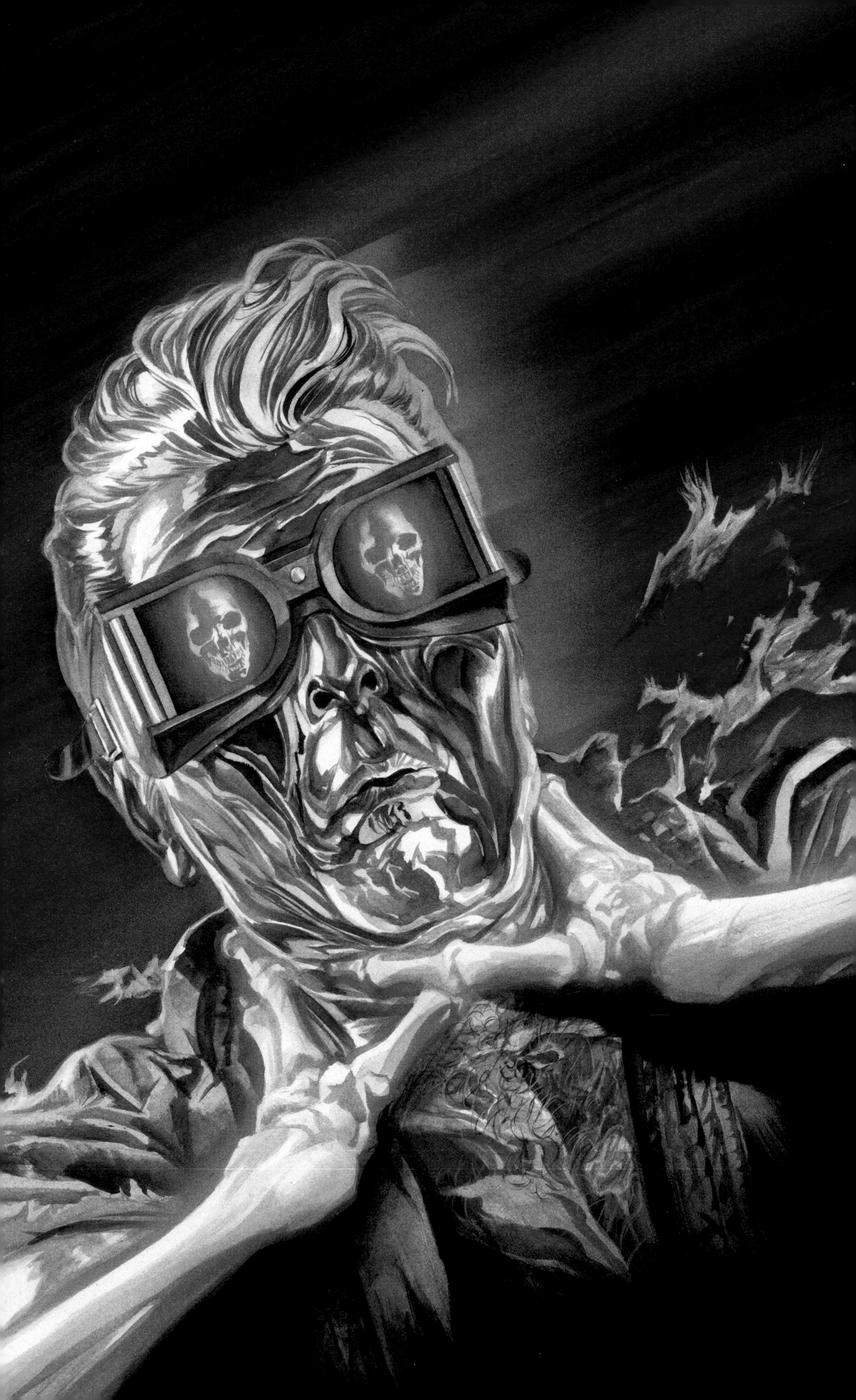

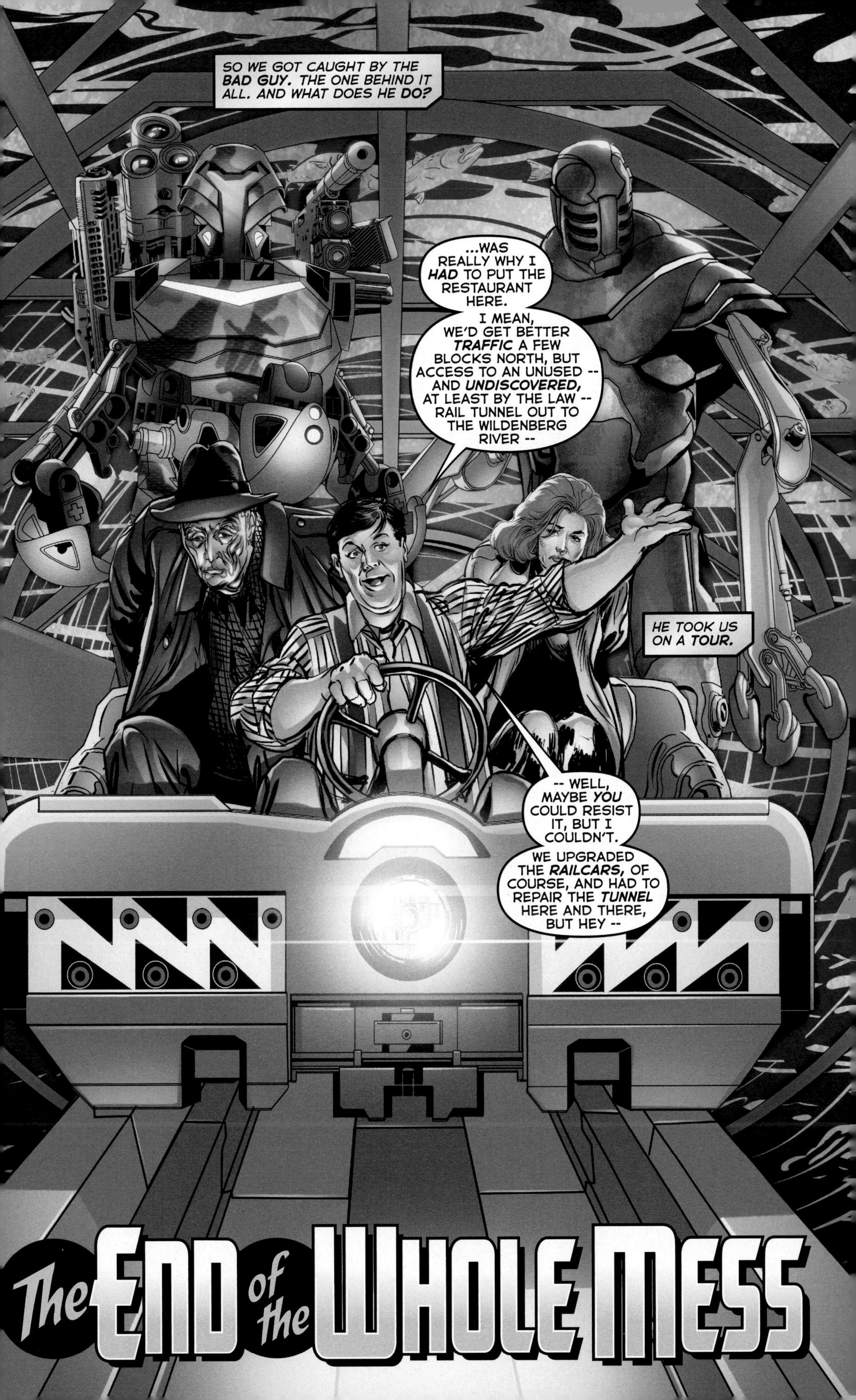
SO WE GOT CAUGHT BY THE BAD GUY. THE ONE BEHIND IT ALL. AND WHAT DOES HE DO?
...WAS REALLY WHY I HAD TO PUT THE RESTAURANT HERE.
I MEAN, WE'D GET BETTER TRAFFIC A FEW BLOCKS NORTH, BUT ACCESS TO AN UNUSED -- AND UNDISCOVERED, AT LEAST BY THE LAW -- RAIL TUNNEL OUT TO THE WILDENBERG RIVER --
HE TOOK US ON A TOUR.
-- WELL, MAYBE YOU COULD RESIST IT, BUT I COULDN'T.
WE UPGRADED THE RAILCARS, OF COURSE, AND HAD TO REPAIR THE TUNNEL HERE AND THERE, BUT HEY --
The END of the WHOLE MESS

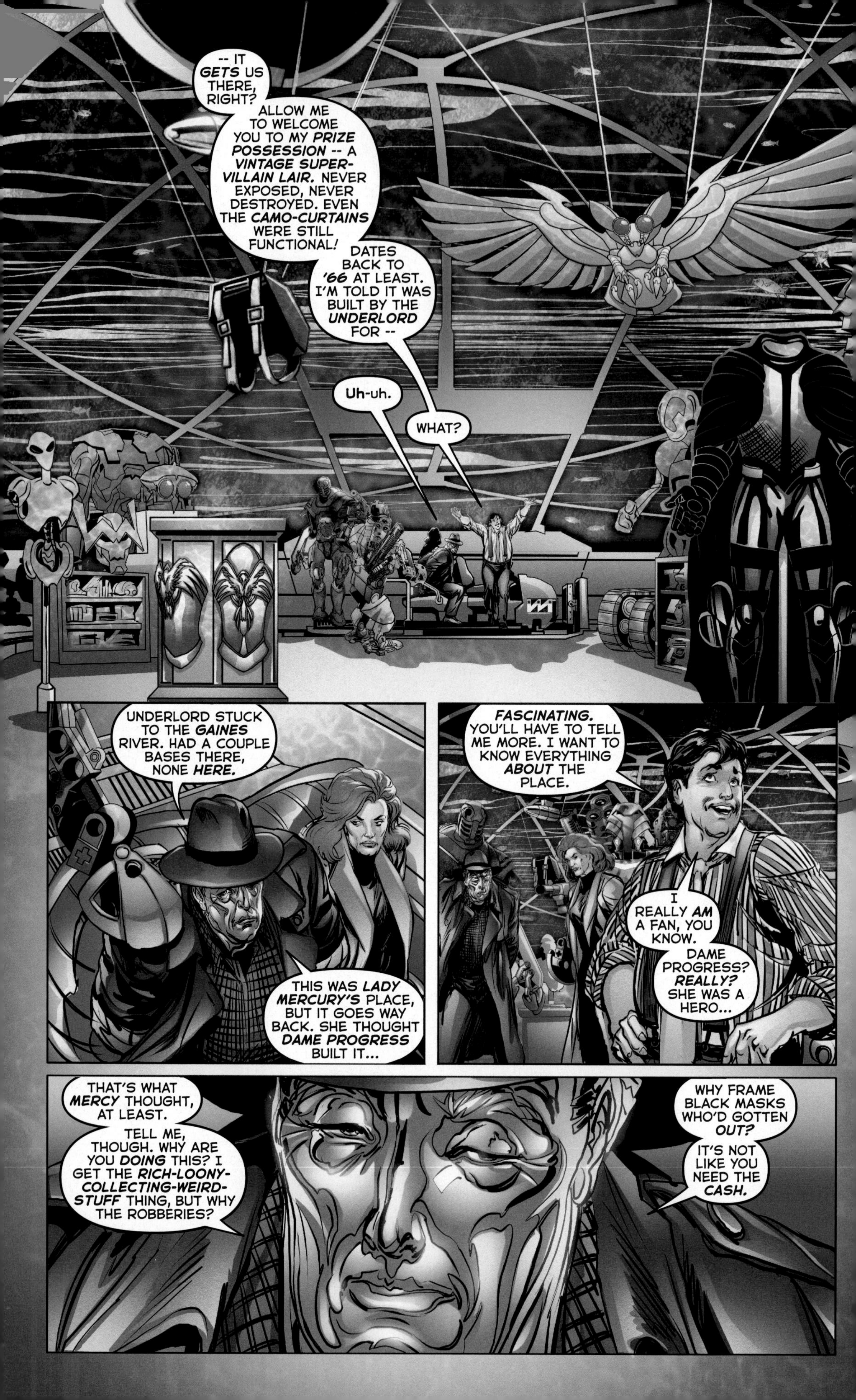
-- IT GETS US THERE, RIGHT?
ALLOW ME TO WELCOME YOU TO MY PRIZE POSSESSION -- A VINTAGE SUPER-VILLAIN LAIR. NEVER EXPOSED, NEVER DESTROYED. EVEN THE CAMO-CURTAINS WERE STILL FUNCTIONAL!
DATES BACK TO '66 AT LEAST. I'M TOLD IT WAS BUILT BY THE UNDERLORD FOR --
Uh-uh.
WHAT?
UNDERLORD STUCK TO THE GAINES RIVER. HAD A COUPLE BASES THERE, NONE HERE.
THIS WAS LADY MERCURY'S PLACE, BUT IT GOES WAY BACK. SHE THOUGHT DAME PROGRESS BUILT IT...
FASCINATING. YOU'LL HAVE TO TELL ME MORE. I WANT TO KNOW EVERYTHING ABOUT THE PLACE.
I REALLY AM A FAN, YOU KNOW.
DAME PROGRESS? REALLY? SHE WAS A HERO...
THAT'S WHAT MERCY THOUGHT, AT LEAST.
TELL ME, THOUGH. WHY ARE YOU DOING THIS? I GET THE RICH-LOONY-COLLECTING-WEIRD-STUFF THING, BUT WHY THE ROBBERIES?
WHY FRAME BLACK MASKS WHO'D GOTTEN OUT?
IT'S NOT LIKE YOU NEED THE CASH.

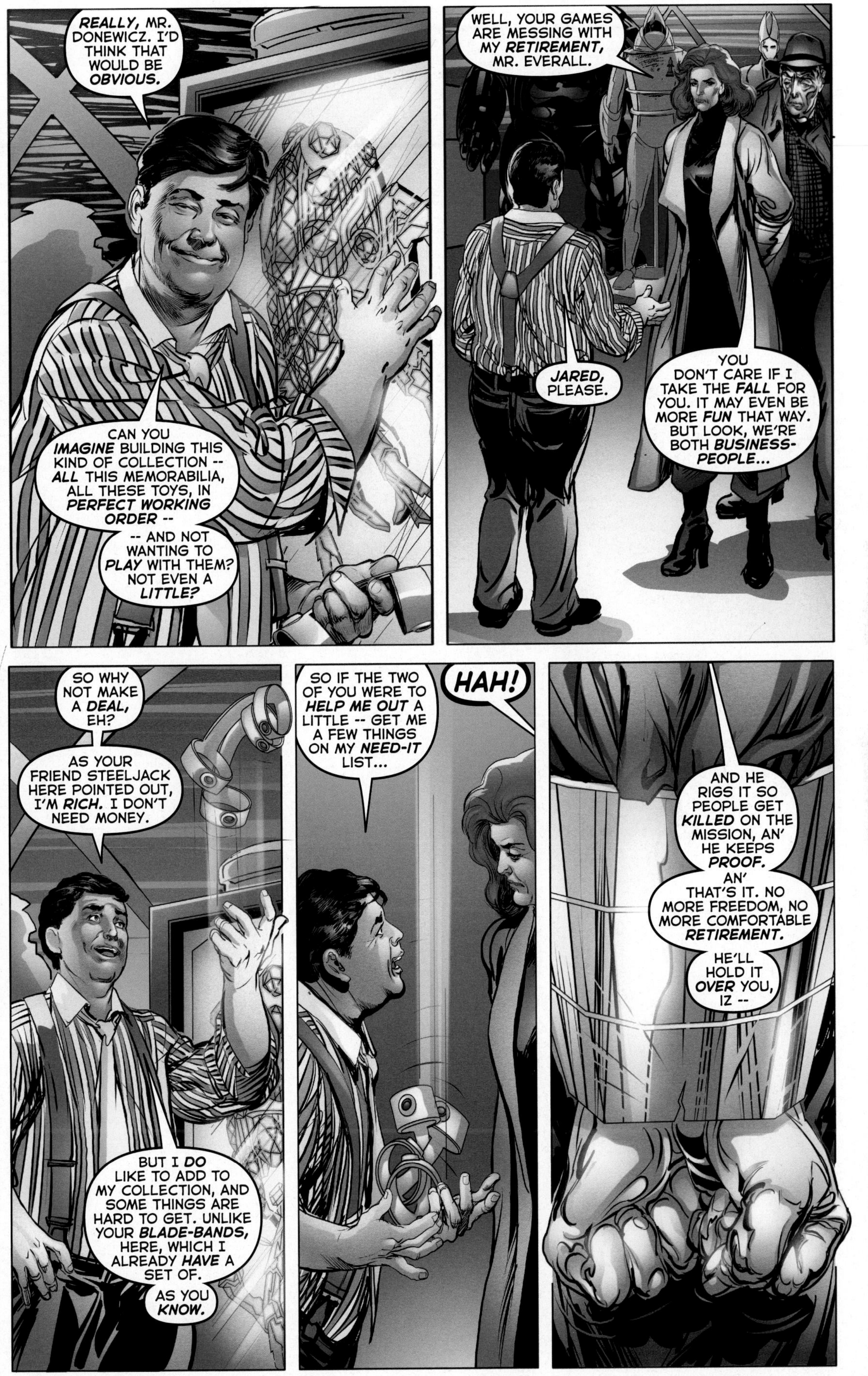
REALLY, MR. DONEWICZ. I'D THINK THAT WOULD BE OBVIOUS.
CAN YOU IMAGINE BUILDING THIS KIND OF COLLECTION -- ALL THIS MEMORABILIA, ALL THESE TOYS, IN PERFECT WORKING ORDER --
-- AND NOT WANTING TO PLAY WITH THEM? NOT EVEN A LITTLE?
WELL, YOUR GAMES ARE MESSING WITH MY RETIREMENT, MR. EVERALL.
JARED, PLEASE.
YOU DON'T CARE IF I TAKE THE FALL FOR YOU. IT MAY EVEN BE MORE FUN THAT WAY. BUT LOOK, WE'RE BOTH BUSINESS-PEOPLE...
SO WHY NOT MAKE A DEAL, EH?
AS YOUR FRIEND STEELJACK HERE POINTED OUT, I'M RICH. I DON'T NEED MONEY.
BUT I DO LIKE TO ADD TO MY COLLECTION, AND SOME THINGS ARE HARD TO GET. UNLIKE YOUR BLADE-BANDS, HERE, WHICH I ALREADY HAVE A SET OF.
AS YOU KNOW.
SO IF THE TWO OF YOU WERE TO HELP ME OUT A LITTLE -- GET ME A FEW THINGS ON MY NEED-IT LIST...
HAH!
AND HE RIGS IT SO PEOPLE GET KILLED ON THE MISSION, AN' HE KEEPS PROOF.
AN' THAT'S IT. NO MORE FREEDOM, NO MORE COMFORTABLE RETIREMENT.
HE'LL HOLD IT OVER YOU, IZ --

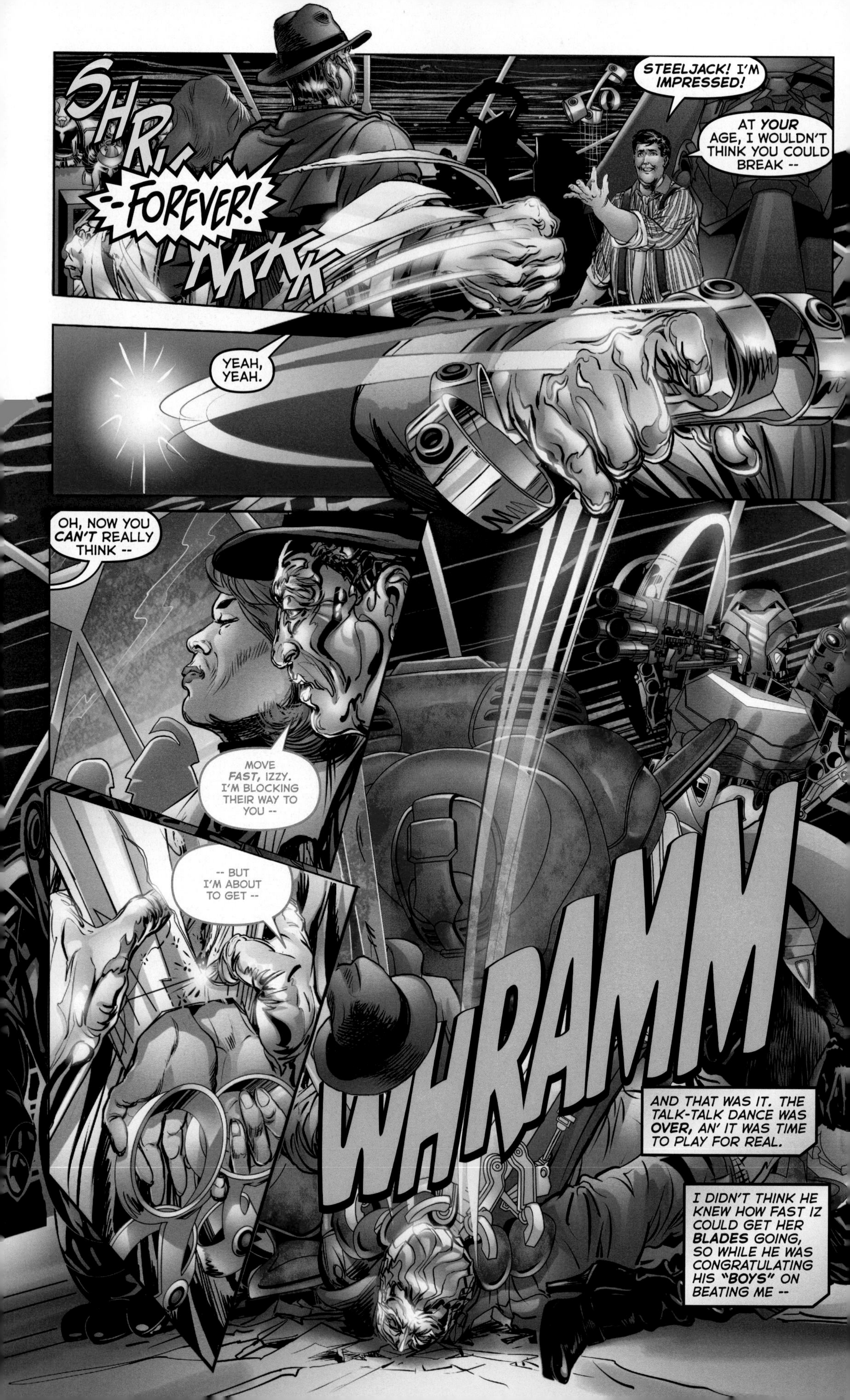
SHR
-- FOREVER!
YNKKK
STEELJACK! I'M IMPRESSED!
AT YOUR AGE, I WOULDN'T THINK YOU COULD BREAK --
YEAH, YEAH.
OH, NOW YOU CAN'T REALLY THINK --
MOVE FAST, IZZY. I'M BLOCKING THEIR WAY TO YOU --
-- BUT I'M ABOUT TO GET --
WHRAMM
AND THAT WAS IT. THE TALK-TALK DANCE WAS OVER, AN' IT WAS TIME TO PLAY FOR REAL.
I DIDN'T THINK HE KNEW HOW FAST IZ COULD GET HER BLADES GOING, SO WHILE HE WAS CONGRATULATING HIS "BOYS" ON BEATING ME --

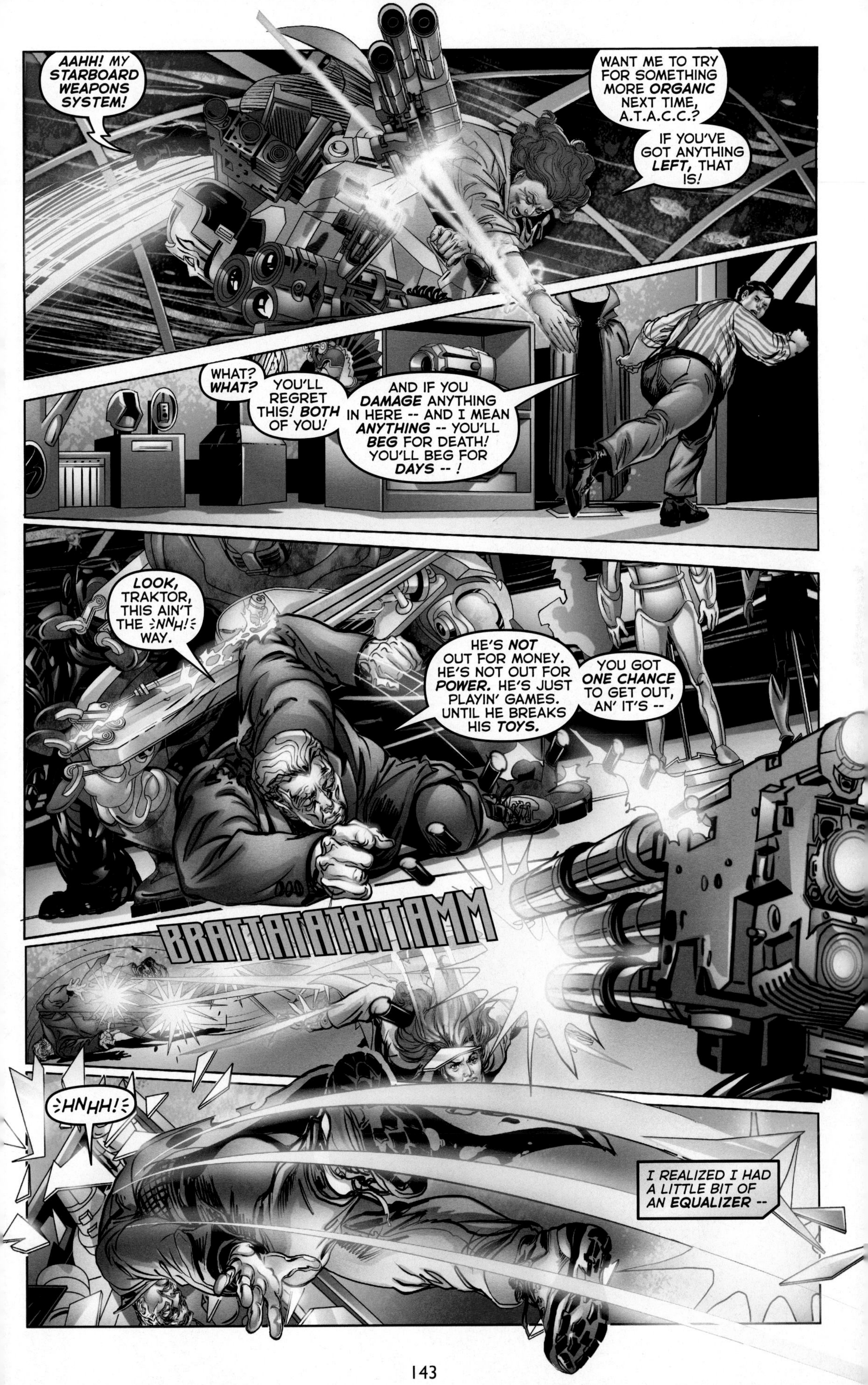
AAHH! MY STARBOARD WEAPONS SYSTEM!
WANT ME TO TRY FOR SOMETHING MORE ORGANIC NEXT TIME, A.T.A.C.C.?
IF YOU'VE GOT ANYTHING LEFT, THAT IS!
WHAT? WHAT?
YOU'LL REGRET THIS! BOTH OF YOU!
AND IF YOU DAMAGE ANYTHING IN HERE -- AND I MEAN ANYTHING -- YOU'LL BEG FOR DEATH! YOU'LL BEG FOR DAYS -- !
LOOK, TRAKTOR, THIS AIN'T THE NNH! WAY.
HE'S NOT OUT FOR MONEY. HE'S NOT OUT FOR POWER. HE'S JUST PLAYIN' GAMES. UNTIL HE BREAKS HIS TOYS.
YOU GOT ONE CHANCE TO GET OUT, AN' IT'S --
BRATTATATATTAMM
HNHH!
I REALIZED I HAD A LITTLE BIT OF AN EQUALIZER --

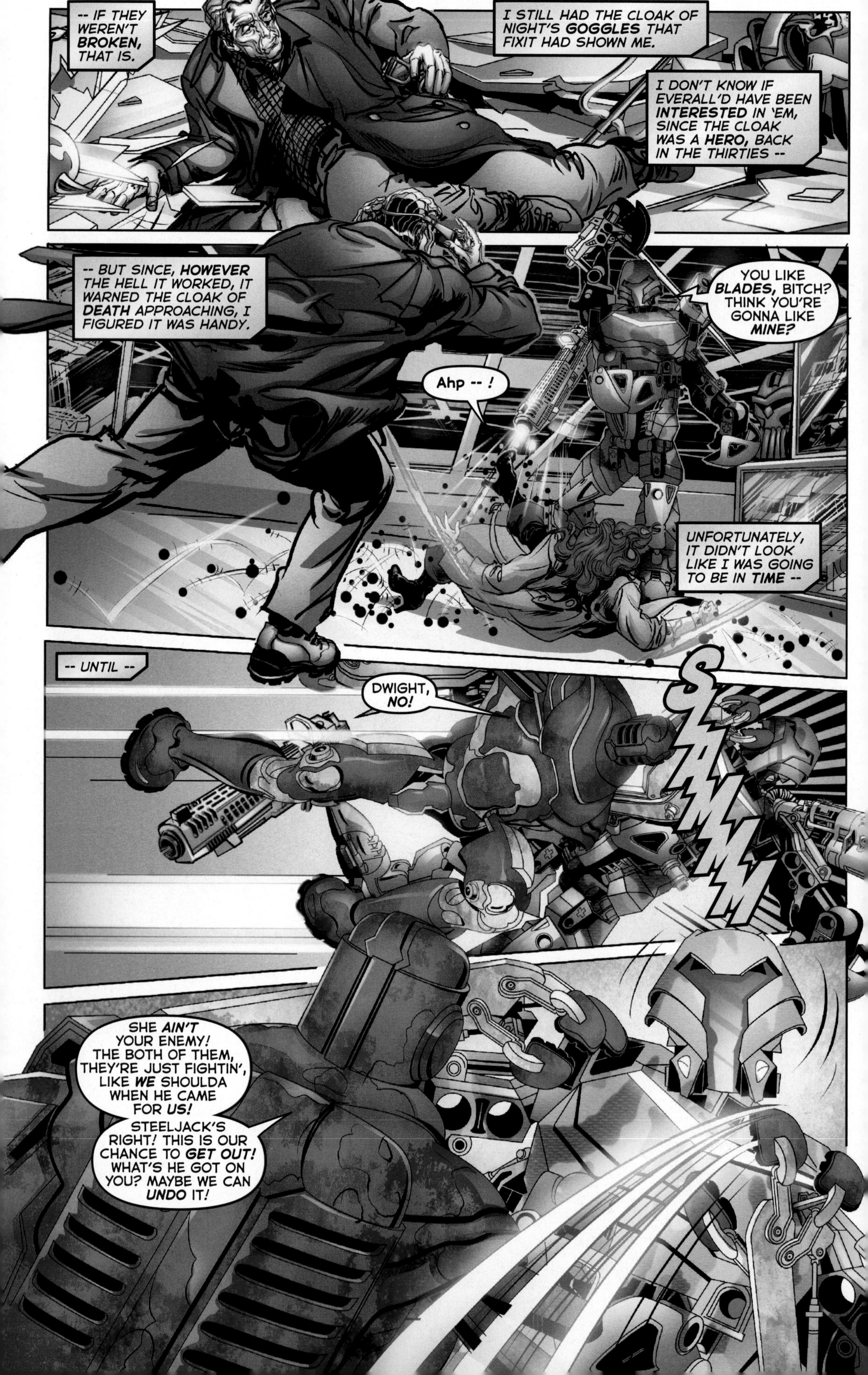
-- IF THEY WEREN'T BROKEN, THAT IS.
I STILL HAD THE CLOAK OF NIGHT'S GOGGLES THAT FIXIT HAD SHOWN ME.
I DON'T KNOW IF EVERALL'D HAVE BEEN INTERESTED IN 'EM, SINCE THE CLOAK WAS A HERO, BACK IN THE THIRTIES --
-- BUT SINCE, HOWEVER THE HELL IT WORKED, IT WARNED THE CLOAK OF DEATH APPROACHING, I FIGURED IT WAS HANDY.
YOU LIKE BLADES, BITCH? THINK YOU'RE GONNA LIKE MINE?
Ahp -- !
UNFORTUNATELY, IT DIDN'T LOOK LIKE I WAS GOING TO BE IN TIME --
-- UNTIL --
DWIGHT, NO!
SLAMMM
SHE AIN'T YOUR ENEMY! THE BOTH OF THEM, THEY'RE JUST FIGHTIN', LIKE WE SHOULDA WHEN HE CAME FOR US!
STEELJACK'S RIGHT! THIS IS OUR CHANCE TO GET OUT! WHAT'S HE GOT ON YOU? MAYBE WE CAN UNDO IT!

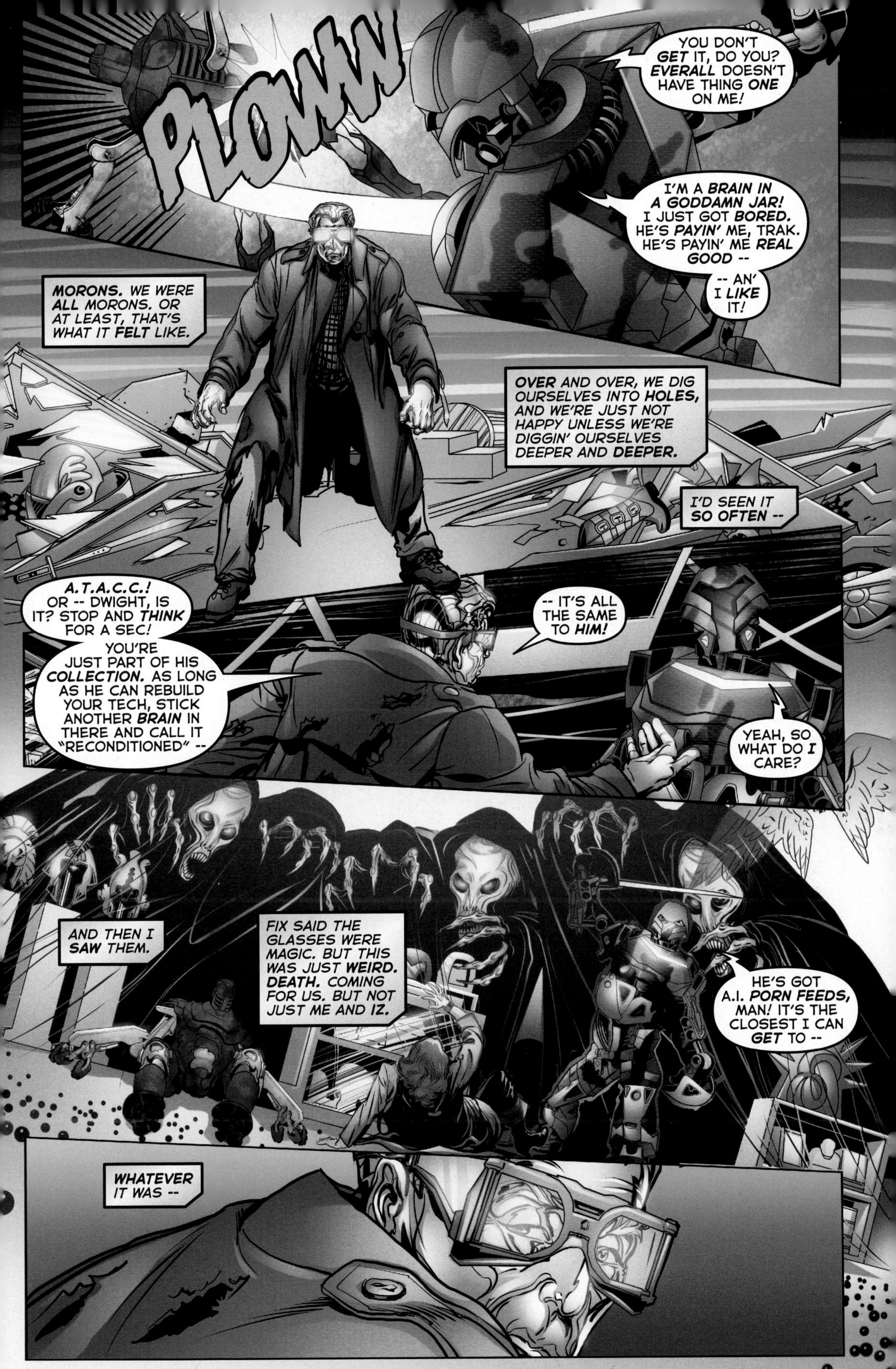
PLOWW
YOU DON'T GET IT, DO YOU? EVERALL DOESN'T HAVE THING ONE ON ME!
I'M A BRAIN IN A GODDAMN JAR! I JUST GOT BORED. HE'S PAYIN' ME, TRAK. HE'S PAYIN' ME REAL GOOD --
-- AN' I LIKE IT!
MORONS. WE WERE ALL MORONS. OR AT LEAST, THAT'S WHAT IT FELT LIKE.
OVER AND OVER, WE DIG OURSELVES INTO HOLES, AND WE'RE JUST NOT HAPPY UNLESS WE'RE DIGGIN' OURSELVES DEEPER AND DEEPER.
I'D SEEN IT SO OFTEN --
A.T.A.C.C.! OR -- DWIGHT, IS IT? STOP AND THINK FOR A SEC!
YOU'RE JUST PART OF HIS COLLECTION. AS LONG AS HE CAN REBUILD YOUR TECH, STICK ANOTHER BRAIN IN THERE AND CALL IT "RECONDITIONED" --
-- IT'S ALL THE SAME TO HIM!
YEAH, SO WHAT DO I CARE?
AND THEN I SAW THEM.
FIX SAID THE GLASSES WERE MAGIC. BUT THIS WAS JUST WEIRD. DEATH. COMING FOR US. BUT NOT JUST ME AND IZ.
HE'S GOT A.I. PORN FEEDS, MAN! IT'S THE CLOSEST I CAN GET TO --
WHATEVER IT WAS --

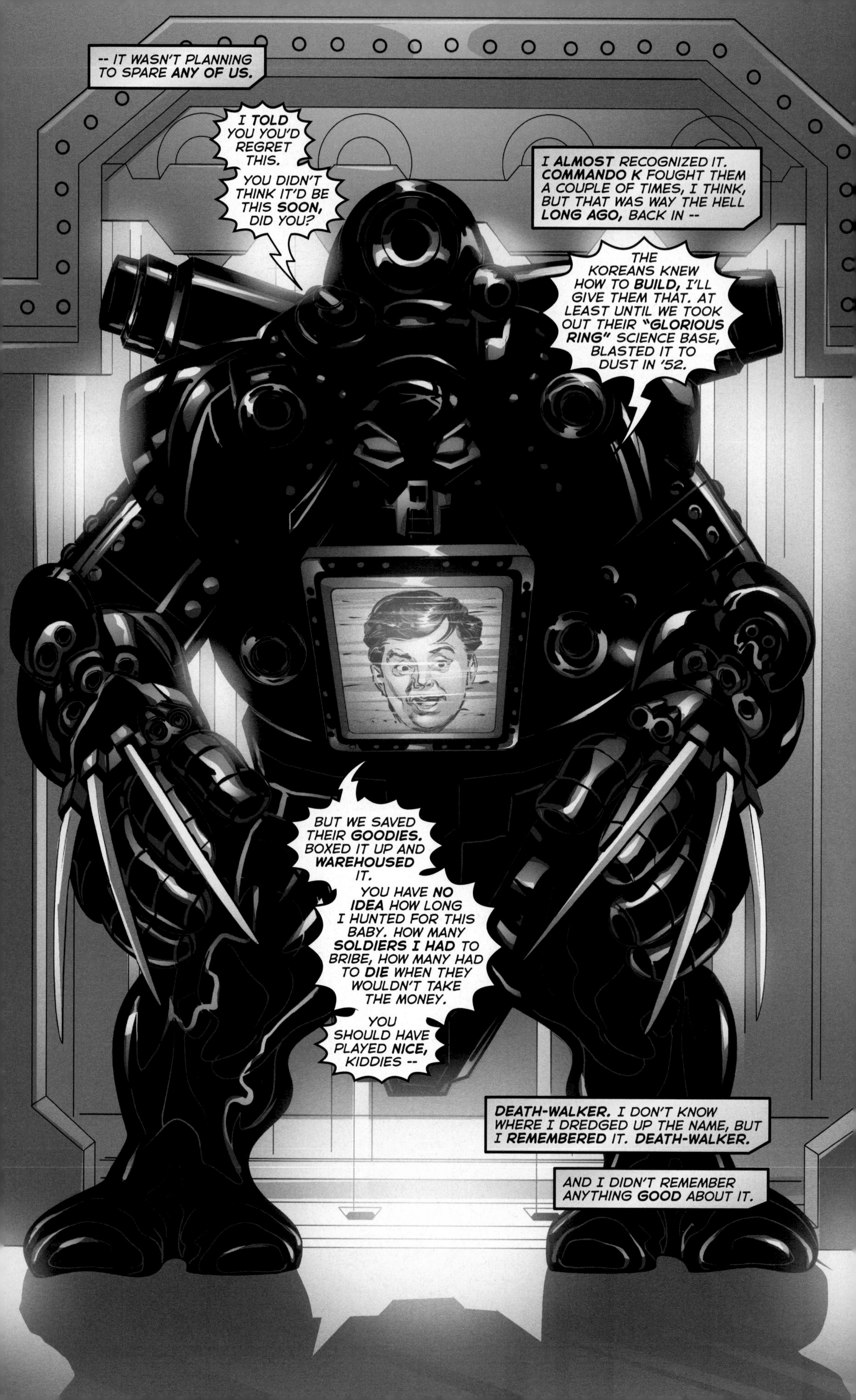
-- IT WASN'T PLANNING TO SPARE ANY OF US.
I TOLD YOU YOU'D REGRET THIS.
YOU DIDN'T THINK IT'D BE THIS SOON, DID YOU?
I ALMOST RECOGNIZED IT. COMMANDO K FOUGHT THEM A COUPLE OF TIMES, I THINK, BUT THAT WAS WAY THE HELL LONG AGO, BACK IN --
THE KOREANS KNEW HOW TO BUILD, I'LL GIVE THEM THAT. AT LEAST UNTIL WE TOOK OUT THEIR "GLORIOUS RING" SCIENCE BASE, BLASTED IT TO DUST IN '52.
BUT WE SAVED THEIR GOODIES. BOXED IT UP AND WAREHOUSED IT.
YOU HAVE NO IDEA HOW LONG I HUNTED FOR THIS BABY. HOW MANY SOLDIERS I HAD TO BRIBE, HOW MANY HAD TO DIE WHEN THEY WOULDN'T TAKE THE MONEY.
YOU SHOULD HAVE PLAYED NICE, KIDDIES --
DEATH-WALKER. I DON'T KNOW WHERE I DREDGED UP THE NAME, BUT I REMEMBERED IT. DEATH-WALKER.
AND I DIDN'T REMEMBER ANYTHING GOOD ABOUT IT.

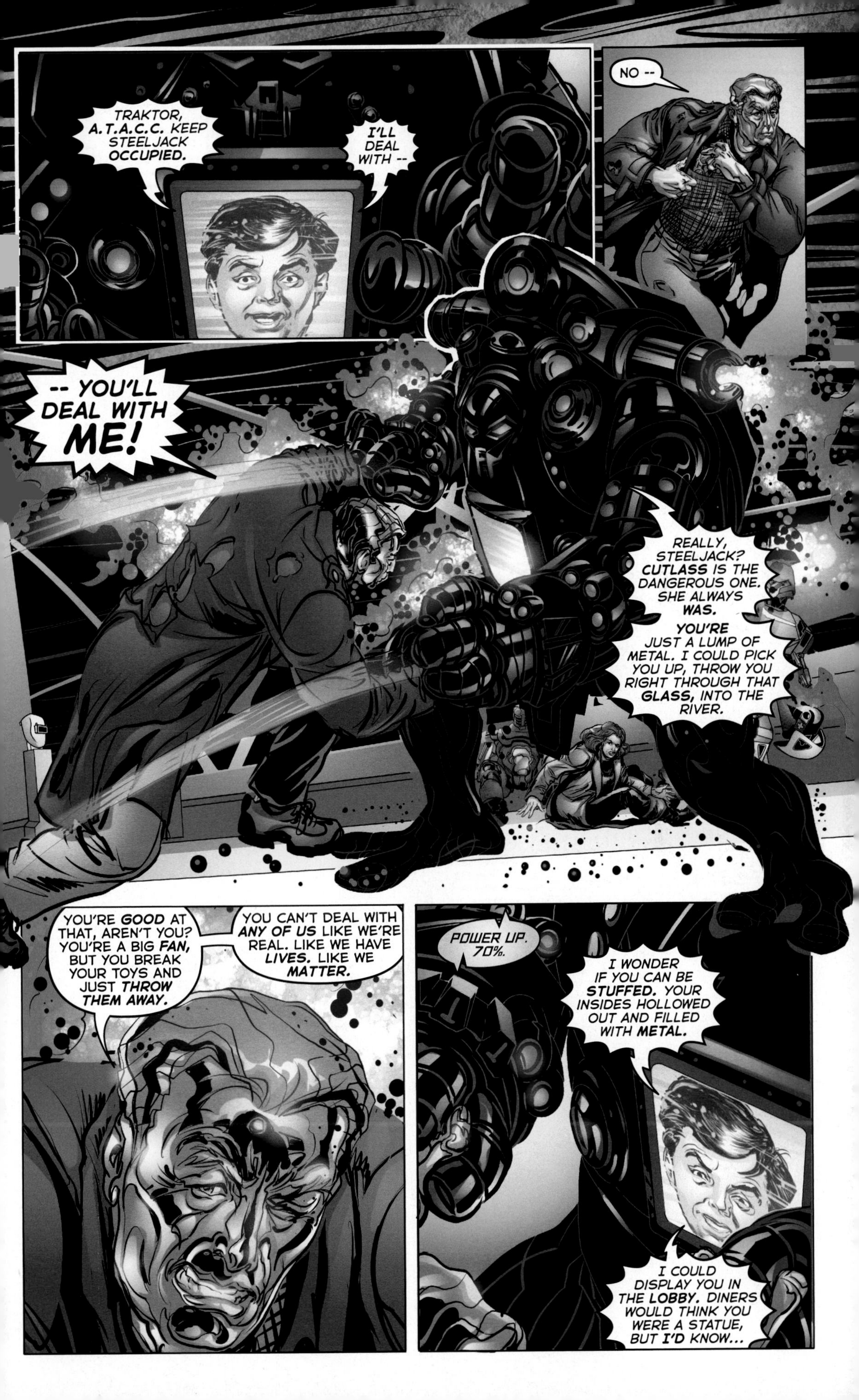
TRAKTOR, A.T.A.C.C. KEEP STEELJACK OCCUPIED.
I'LL DEAL WITH --
NO --
-- YOU'LL DEAL WITH ME!
REALLY, STEELJACK? CUTLASS IS THE DANGEROUS ONE. SHE ALWAYS WAS.
YOU'RE JUST A LUMP OF METAL. I COULD PICK YOU UP, THROW YOU RIGHT THROUGH THAT GLASS, INTO THE RIVER.
YOU'RE GOOD AT THAT, AREN'T YOU? YOU'RE A BIG FAN, BUT YOU BREAK YOUR TOYS AND JUST THROW THEM AWAY.
YOU CAN'T DEAL WITH ANY OF US LIKE WE'RE REAL. LIKE WE HAVE LIVES. LIKE WE MATTER.
POWER UP. 70%.
I WONDER IF YOU CAN BE STUFFED. YOUR INSIDES HOLLOWED OUT AND FILLED WITH METAL.
I COULD DISPLAY YOU IN THE LOBBY. DINERS WOULD THINK YOU WERE A STATUE, BUT I'D KNOW...

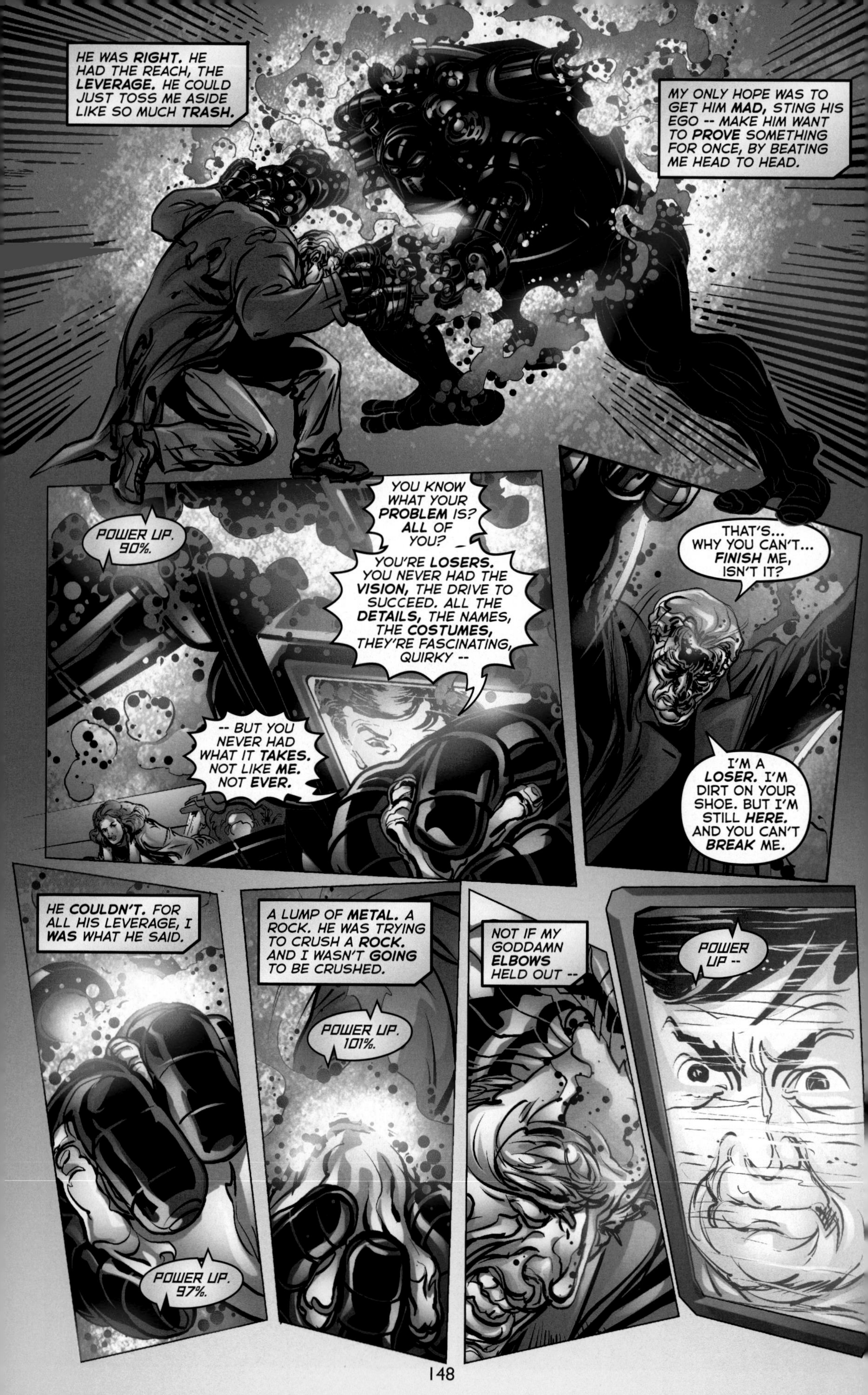
HE WAS RIGHT. HE HAD THE REACH, THE LEVERAGE. HE COULD JUST TOSS ME ASIDE LIKE SO MUCH TRASH.
MY ONLY HOPE WAS TO GET HIM MAD, STING HIS EGO -- MAKE HIM WANT TO PROVE SOMETHING FOR ONCE, BY BEATING ME HEAD TO HEAD.
POWER UP. 90%.
YOU KNOW WHAT YOUR PROBLEM IS? ALL OF YOU?
YOU'RE LOSERS. YOU NEVER HAD THE VISION, THE DRIVE TO SUCCEED. ALL THE DETAILS, THE NAMES, THE COSTUMES, THEY'RE FASCINATING, QUIRKY --
-- BUT YOU NEVER HAD WHAT IT TAKES. NOT LIKE ME. NOT EVER.
THAT'S... WHY YOU CAN'T... FINISH ME, ISN'T IT?
I'M A LOSER. I'M DIRT ON YOUR SHOE. BUT I'M STILL HERE. AND YOU CAN'T BREAK ME.
HE COULDN'T. FOR ALL HIS LEVERAGE, I WAS WHAT HE SAID.
POWER UP. 97%.
A LUMP OF METAL. A ROCK. HE WAS TRYING TO CRUSH A ROCK. AND I WASN'T GOING TO BE CRUSHED.
POWER UP. 101%.
NOT IF MY GODDAMN ELBOWS HELD OUT --
POWER UP --

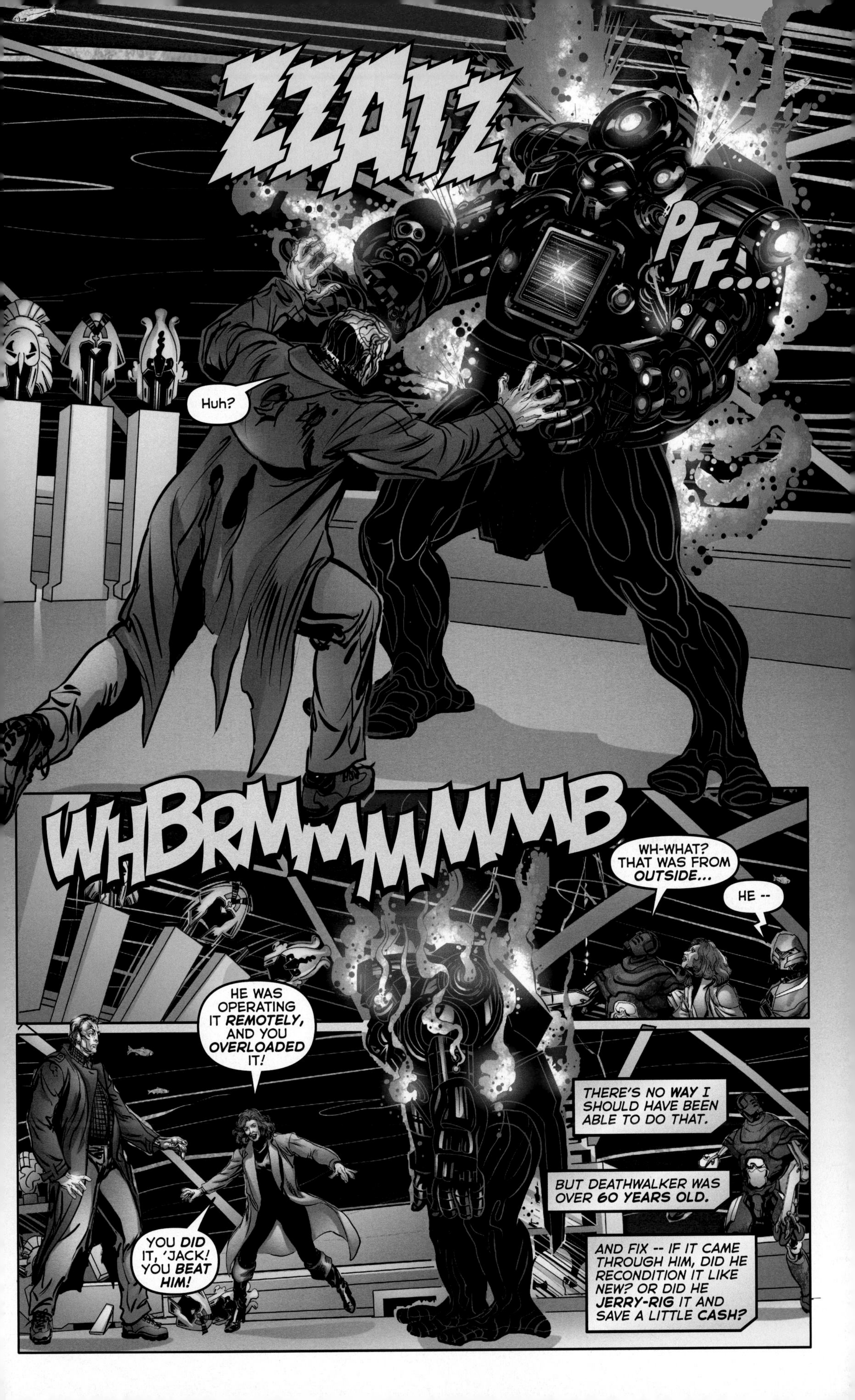
ZZATZ
PFF...
Huh?
WHBRMMMMMB
WH-WHAT? THAT WAS FROM OUTSIDE...
HE --
HE WAS OPERATING IT REMOTELY, AND YOU OVERLOADED IT!
THERE'S NO WAY I SHOULD HAVE BEEN ABLE TO DO THAT.
BUT DEATHWALKER WAS OVER 60 YEARS OLD.
YOU DID IT, 'JACK! YOU BEAT HIM!
AND FIX -- IF IT CAME THROUGH HIM, DID HE RECONDITION IT LIKE NEW? OR DID HE JERRY-RIG IT AND SAVE A LITTLE CASH?

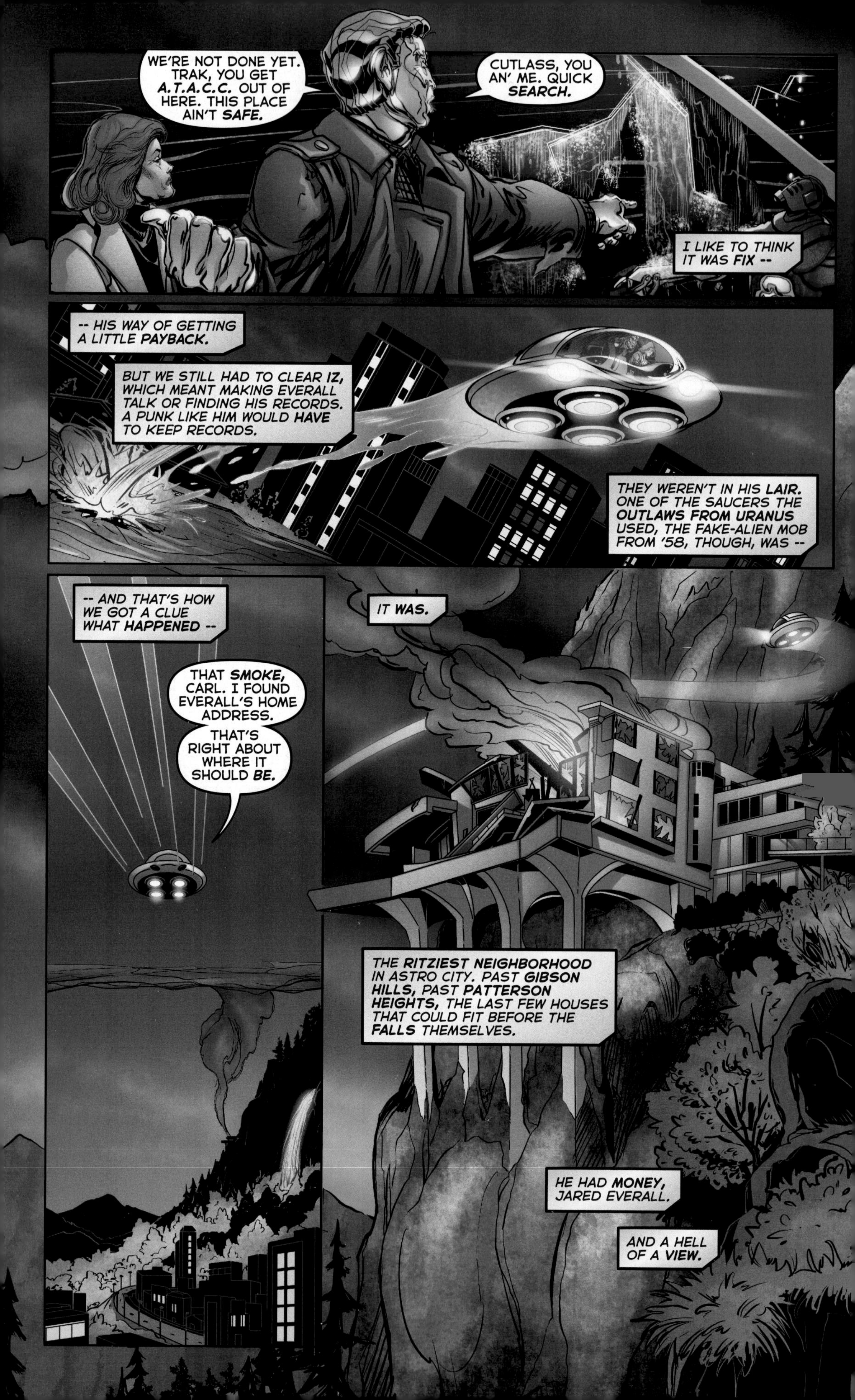

WE'RE NOT DONE YET. TRAK, YOU GET A.T.A.C.C. OUT OF HERE. THIS PLACE AIN'T SAFE.
CUTLASS, YOU AN' ME. QUICK SEARCH.
I LIKE TO THINK IT WAS FIX --
-- HIS WAY OF GETTING A LITTLE PAYBACK.
BUT WE STILL HAD TO CLEAR IZ, WHICH MEANT MAKING EVERALL TALK OR FINDING HIS RECORDS. A PUNK LIKE HIM WOULD HAVE TO KEEP RECORDS.
THEY WEREN'T IN HIS LAIR. ONE OF THE SAUCERS THE OUTLAWS FROM URANUS USED, THE FAKE-ALIEN MOB FROM '58, THOUGH, WAS --
-- AND THAT'S HOW WE GOT A CLUE WHAT HAPPENED --
THAT SMOKE, CARL. I FOUND EVERALL'S HOME ADDRESS.
THAT'S RIGHT ABOUT WHERE IT SHOULD BE.
IT WAS.
THE RITZIEST NEIGHBORHOOD IN ASTRO CITY. PAST GIBSON HILLS, PAST PATTERSON HEIGHTS, THE LAST FEW HOUSES THAT COULD FIT BEFORE THE FALLS THEMSELVES.
HE HAD MONEY, JARED EVERALL.
AND A HELL OF A VIEW.

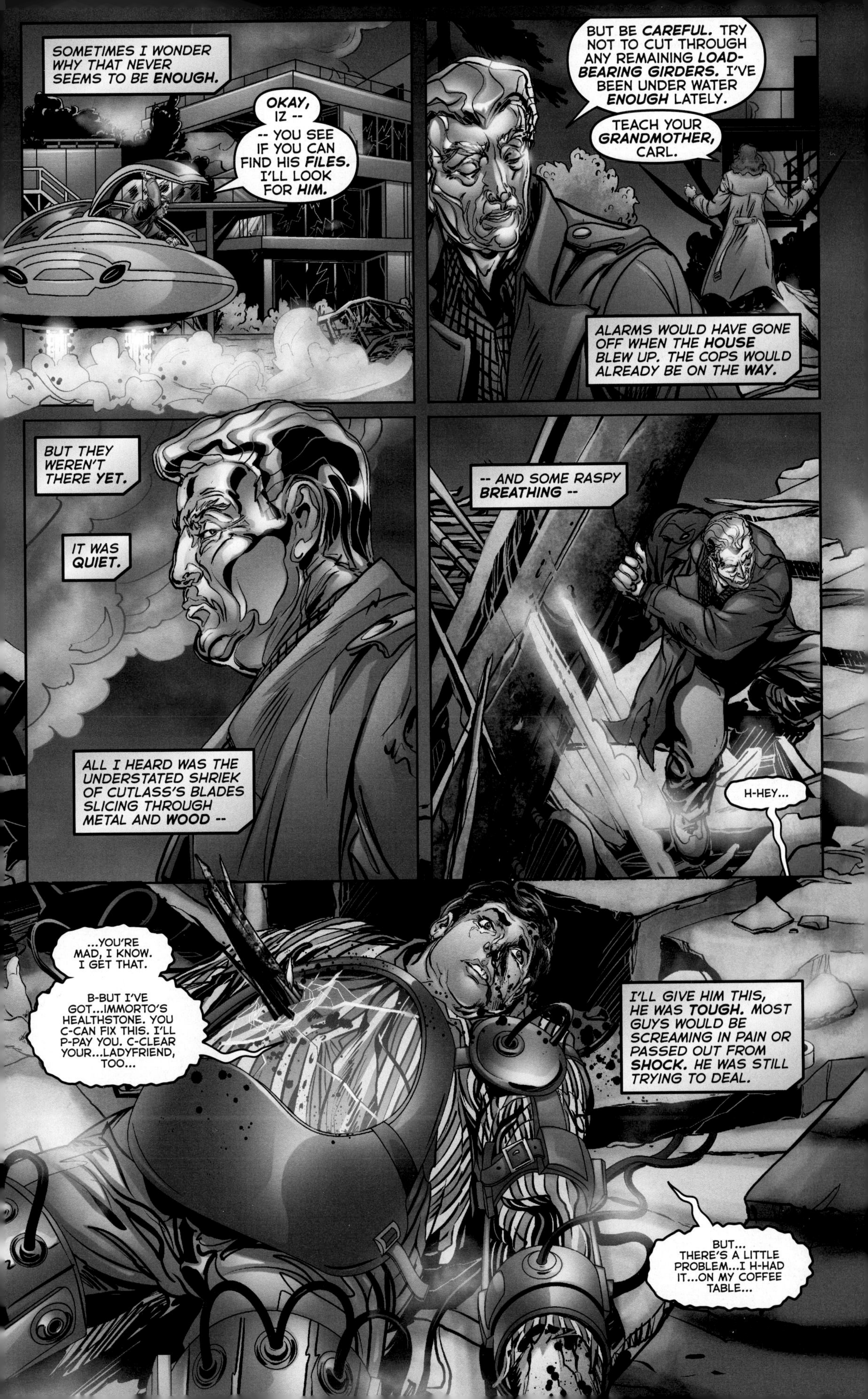
SOMETIMES I WONDER WHY THAT NEVER SEEMS TO BE ENOUGH.
OKAY, IZ --
-- YOU SEE IF YOU CAN FIND HIS FILES. I'LL LOOK FOR HIM.
BUT BE CAREFUL. TRY NOT TO CUT THROUGH ANY REMAINING LOAD-BEARING GIRDERS. I'VE BEEN UNDER WATER ENOUGH LATELY.
TEACH YOUR GRANDMOTHER, CARL.
ALARMS WOULD HAVE GONE OFF WHEN THE HOUSE BLEW UP. THE COPS WOULD ALREADY BE ON THE WAY.
BUT THEY WEREN'T THERE YET.
IT WAS QUIET.
ALL I HEARD WAS THE UNDERSTATED SHRIEK OF CUTLASS'S BLADES SLICING THROUGH METAL AND WOOD --
-- AND SOME RASPY BREATHING --
H-HEY...
...YOU'RE MAD, I KNOW. I GET THAT.
B-BUT I'VE GOT...IMMORTO'S HEALTHSTONE. YOU C-CAN FIX THIS. I'LL P-PAY YOU. C-CLEAR YOUR...LADYFRIEND, TOO...
I'LL GIVE HIM THIS, HE WAS TOUGH. MOST GUYS WOULD BE SCREAMING IN PAIN OR PASSED OUT FROM SHOCK. HE WAS STILL TRYING TO DEAL.
BUT... THERE'S A LITTLE PROBLEM...I H-HAD IT...ON MY COFFEE TABLE...

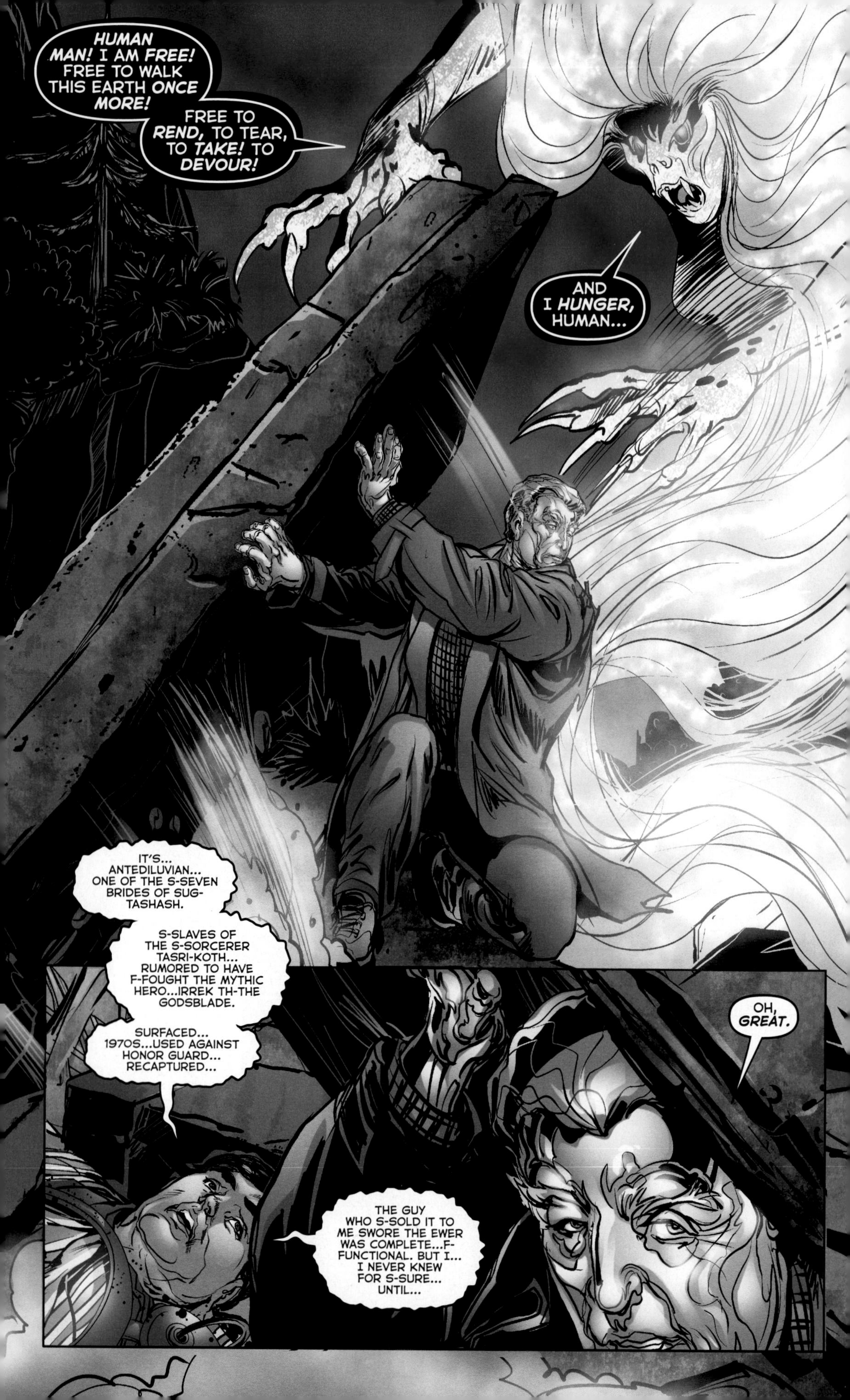
HUMAN MAN! I AM FREE! FREE TO WALK THIS EARTH ONCE MORE!
FREE TO REND, TO TEAR, TO TAKE! TO DEVOUR!
AND I HUNGER, HUMAN...
IT'S... ANTEDILUVIAN... ONE OF THE S-SEVEN BRIDES OF SUG-TASHASH.
S-SLAVES OF THE S-SORCERER TASRI-KOTH... RUMORED TO HAVE F-FOUGHT THE MYTHIC HERO...IRREK TH-THE GODSBLADE.
SURFACED... 1970S...USED AGAINST HONOR GUARD... RECAPTURED...
OH, GREAT.
THE GUY WHO S-SOLD IT TO ME SWORE THE EWER WAS COMPLETE...F-FUNCTIONAL. BUT I... I NEVER KNEW FOR S-SURE... UNTIL...

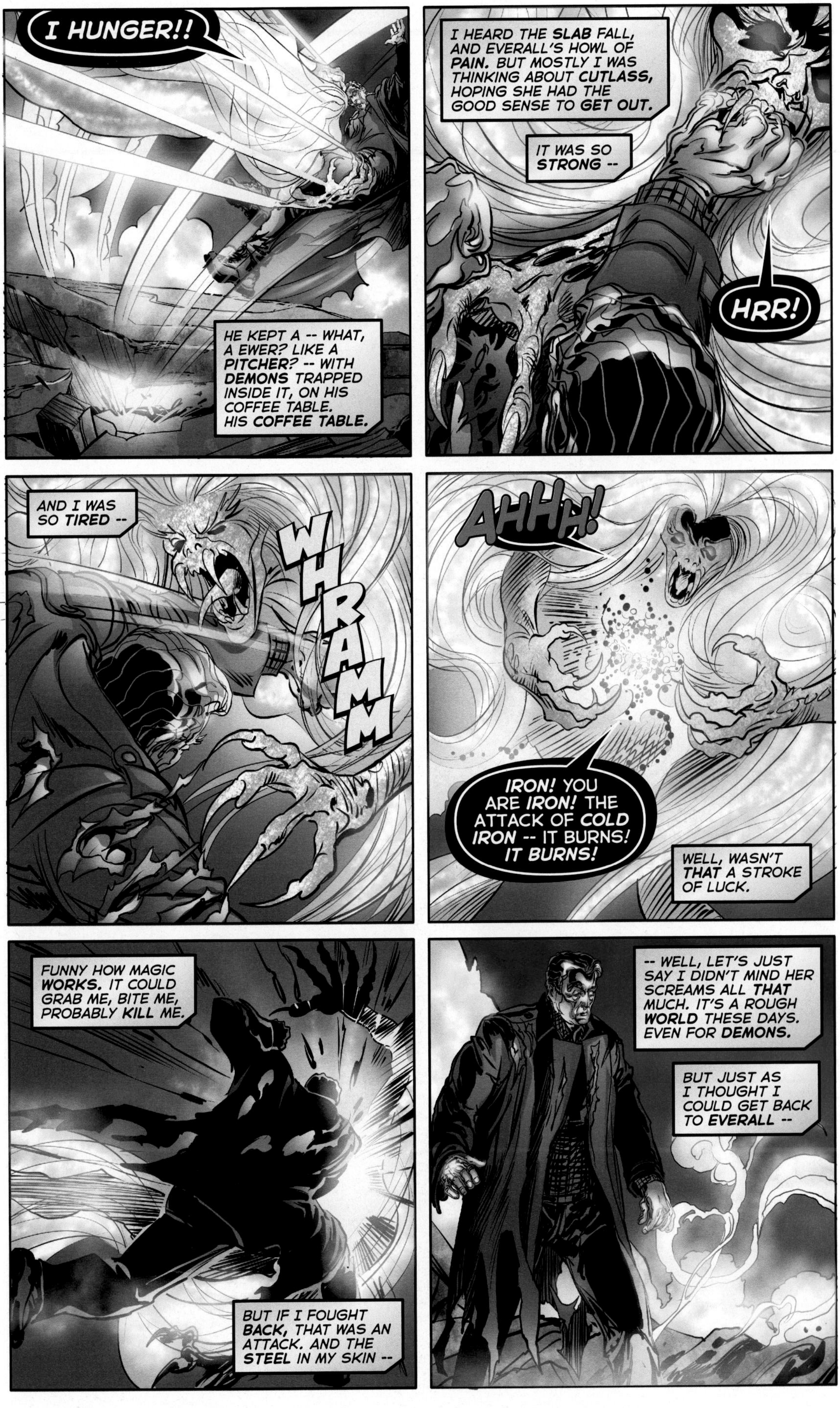

I HUNGER!!
HE KEPT A -- WHAT, A EWER? LIKE A PITCHER? -- WITH DEMONS TRAPPED INSIDE IT, ON HIS COFFEE TABLE. HIS COFFEE TABLE.
I HEARD THE SLAB FALL, AND EVERALL'S HOWL OF PAIN. BUT MOSTLY I WAS THINKING ABOUT CUTLASS, HOPING SHE HAD THE GOOD SENSE TO GET OUT.
IT WAS SO STRONG --
HRR!
AND I WAS SO TIRED --
WHRAMM
AHHH!
IRON! YOU ARE IRON! THE ATTACK OF COLD IRON -- IT BURNS! IT BURNS!
WELL, WASN'T THAT A STROKE OF LUCK.
FUNNY HOW MAGIC WORKS. IT COULD GRAB ME, BITE ME, PROBABLY KILL ME.
BUT IF I FOUGHT BACK, THAT WAS AN ATTACK. AND THE STEEL IN MY SKIN --
-- WELL, LET'S JUST SAY I DIDN'T MIND HER SCREAMS ALL THAT MUCH. IT'S A ROUGH WORLD THESE DAYS. EVEN FOR DEMONS.
BUT JUST AS I THOUGHT I COULD GET BACK TO EVERALL --

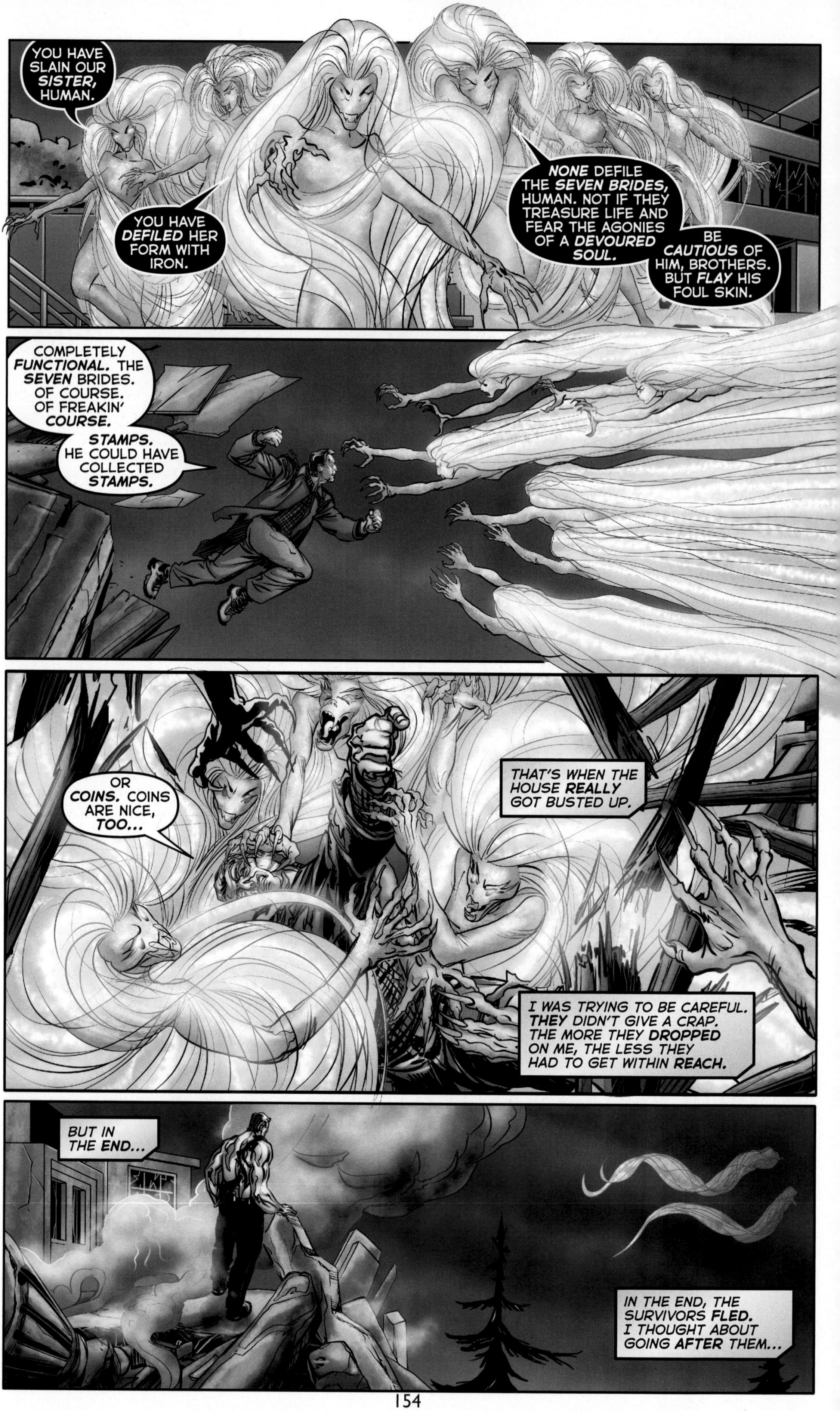
YOU HAVE SLAIN OUR SISTER, HUMAN.
YOU HAVE DEFILED HER FORM WITH IRON.
NONE DEFILE THE SEVEN BRIDES, HUMAN. NOT IF THEY TREASURE LIFE AND FEAR THE AGONIES OF A DEVOURED SOUL.
BE CAUTIOUS OF HIM, BROTHERS. BUT FLAY HIS FOUL SKIN.
COMPLETELY FUNCTIONAL. THE SEVEN BRIDES. OF COURSE. OF FREAKIN' COURSE.
STAMPS. HE COULD HAVE COLLECTED STAMPS.
OR COINS. COINS ARE NICE, TOO...
THAT'S WHEN THE HOUSE REALLY GOT BUSTED UP.
I WAS TRYING TO BE CAREFUL. THEY DIDN'T GIVE A CRAP. THE MORE THEY DROPPED ON ME, THE LESS THEY HAD TO GET WITHIN REACH.
BUT IN THE END...
IN THE END, THE SURVIVORS FLED. I THOUGHT ABOUT GOING AFTER THEM...

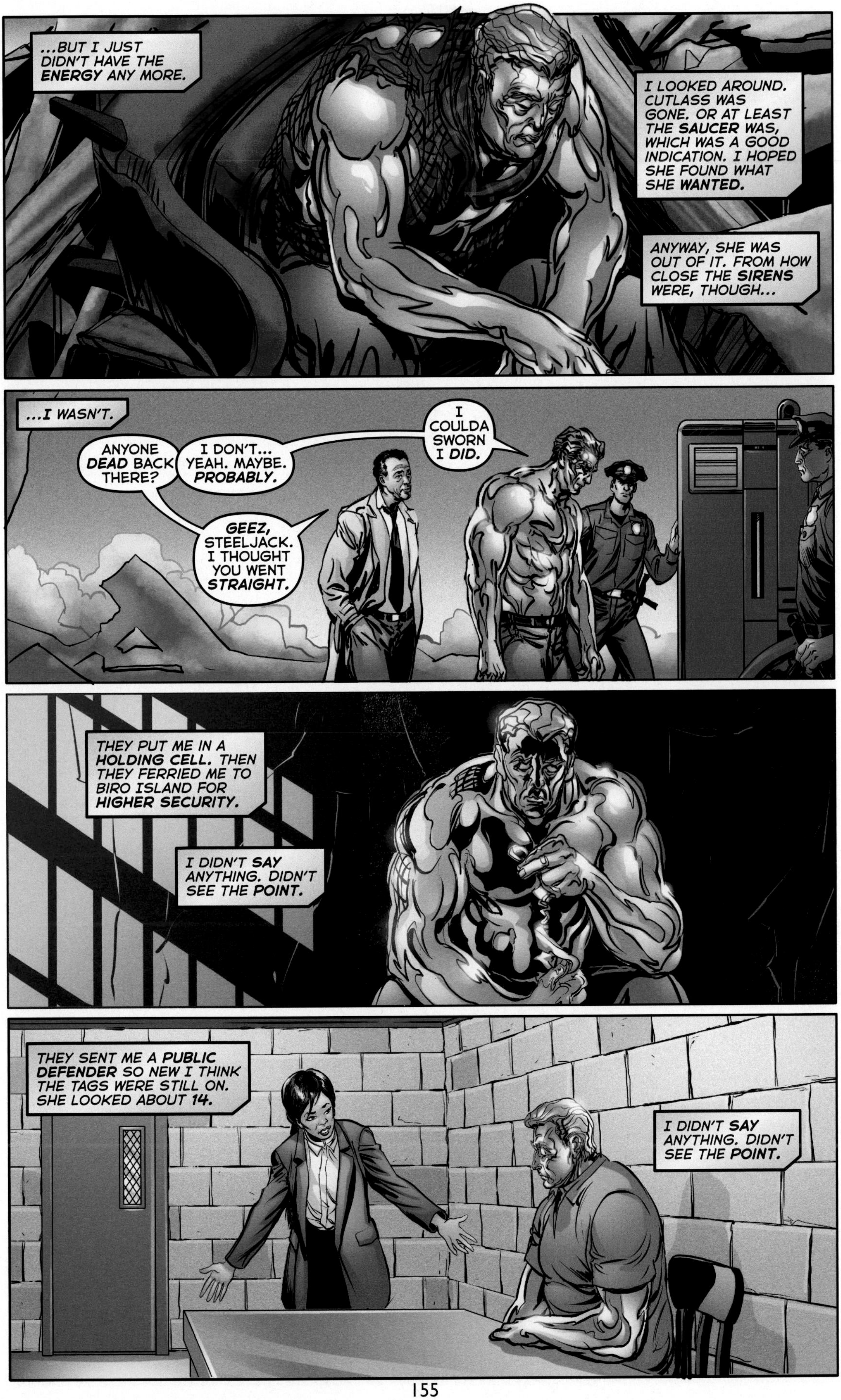
...BUT I JUST DIDN'T HAVE THE ENERGY ANY MORE.
I LOOKED AROUND. CUTLASS WAS GONE. OR AT LEAST THE SAUCER WAS, WHICH WAS A GOOD INDICATION. I HOPED SHE FOUND WHAT SHE WANTED.
ANYWAY, SHE WAS OUT OF IT. FROM HOW CLOSE THE SIRENS WERE, THOUGH...
...I WASN'T.
ANYONE DEAD BACK THERE?
I DON'T... YEAH. MAYBE. PROBABLY.
I COULDA SWORN I DID.
GEEZ, STEELJACK. I THOUGHT YOU WENT STRAIGHT.
THEY PUT ME IN A HOLDING CELL. THEN THEY FERRIED ME TO BIRO ISLAND FOR HIGHER SECURITY.
I DIDN'T SAY ANYTHING. DIDN'T SEE THE POINT.
THEY SENT ME A PUBLIC DEFENDER SO NEW I THINK THE TAGS WERE STILL ON. SHE LOOKED ABOUT 14.
I DIDN'T SAY ANYTHING. DIDN'T SEE THE POINT.

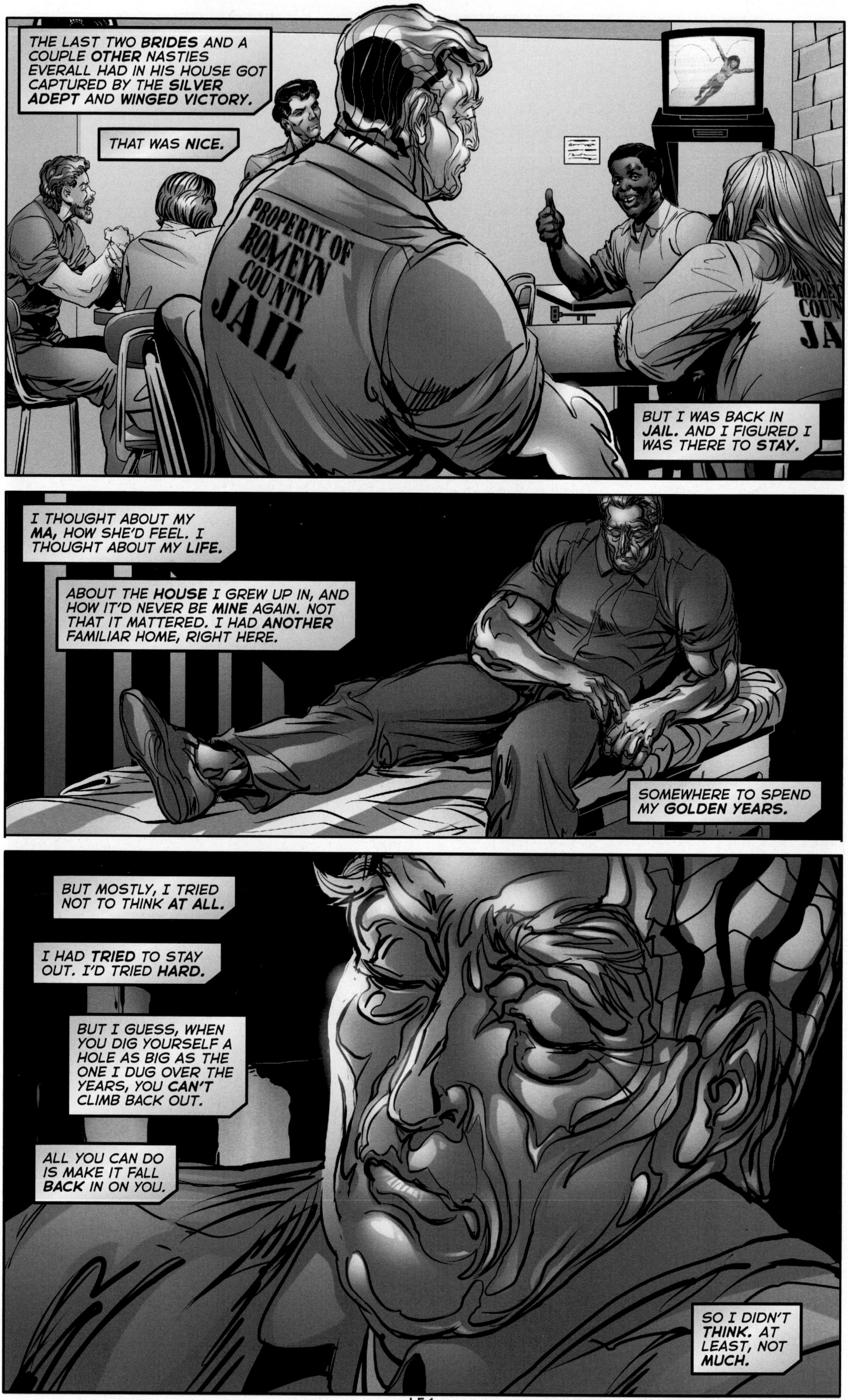
THE LAST TWO BRIDES AND A COUPLE OTHER NASTIES EVERALL HAD IN HIS HOUSE GOT CAPTURED BY THE SILVER ADEPT AND WINGED VICTORY.
THAT WAS NICE.
PROPERTY OF ROMEYN COUNTY JAIL
BUT I WAS BACK IN JAIL. AND I FIGURED I WAS THERE TO STAY.
I THOUGHT ABOUT MY MA, HOW SHE'D FEEL. I THOUGHT ABOUT MY LIFE.
ABOUT THE HOUSE I GREW UP IN, AND HOW IT'D NEVER BE MINE AGAIN. NOT THAT IT MATTERED. I HAD ANOTHER FAMILIAR HOME, RIGHT HERE.
SOMEWHERE TO SPEND MY GOLDEN YEARS.
BUT MOSTLY, I TRIED NOT TO THINK AT ALL.
I HAD TRIED TO STAY OUT. I'D TRIED HARD.
BUT I GUESS, WHEN YOU DIG YOURSELF A HOLE AS BIG AS THE ONE I DUG OVER THE YEARS, YOU CAN'T CLIMB BACK OUT.
ALL YOU CAN DO IS MAKE IT FALL BACK IN ON YOU.
SO I DIDN'T THINK. AT LEAST, NOT MUCH.

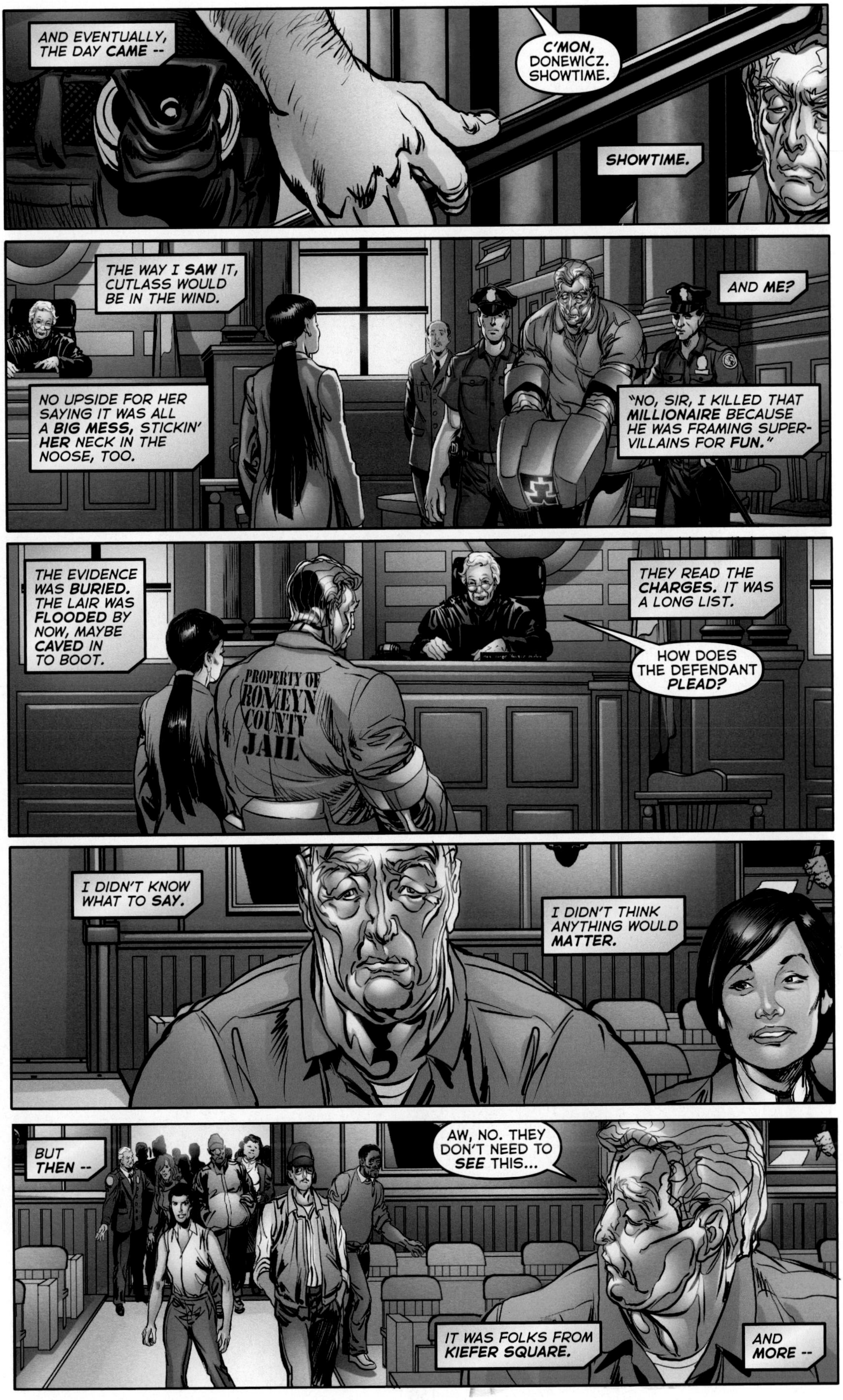
AND EVENTUALLY, THE DAY CAME --
C'MON, DONEWICZ. SHOWTIME.
SHOWTIME.
THE WAY I SAW IT, CUTLASS WOULD BE IN THE WIND.
NO UPSIDE FOR HER SAYING IT WAS ALL A BIG MESS, STICKIN' HER NECK IN THE NOOSE, TOO.
AND ME?
"NO, SIR, I KILLED THAT MILLIONAIRE BECAUSE HE WAS FRAMING SUPER-VILLAINS FOR FUN."
THE EVIDENCE WAS BURIED. THE LAIR WAS FLOODED BY NOW, MAYBE CAVED IN TO BOOT.
PROPERTY OF ROMEYN COUNTY JAIL
THEY READ THE CHARGES. IT WAS A LONG LIST.
HOW DOES THE DEFENDANT PLEAD?
I DIDN'T KNOW WHAT TO SAY.
I DIDN'T THINK ANYTHING WOULD MATTER.
BUT THEN --
AW, NO. THEY DON'T NEED TO SEE THIS...
IT WAS FOLKS FROM KIEFER SQUARE.
AND MORE --

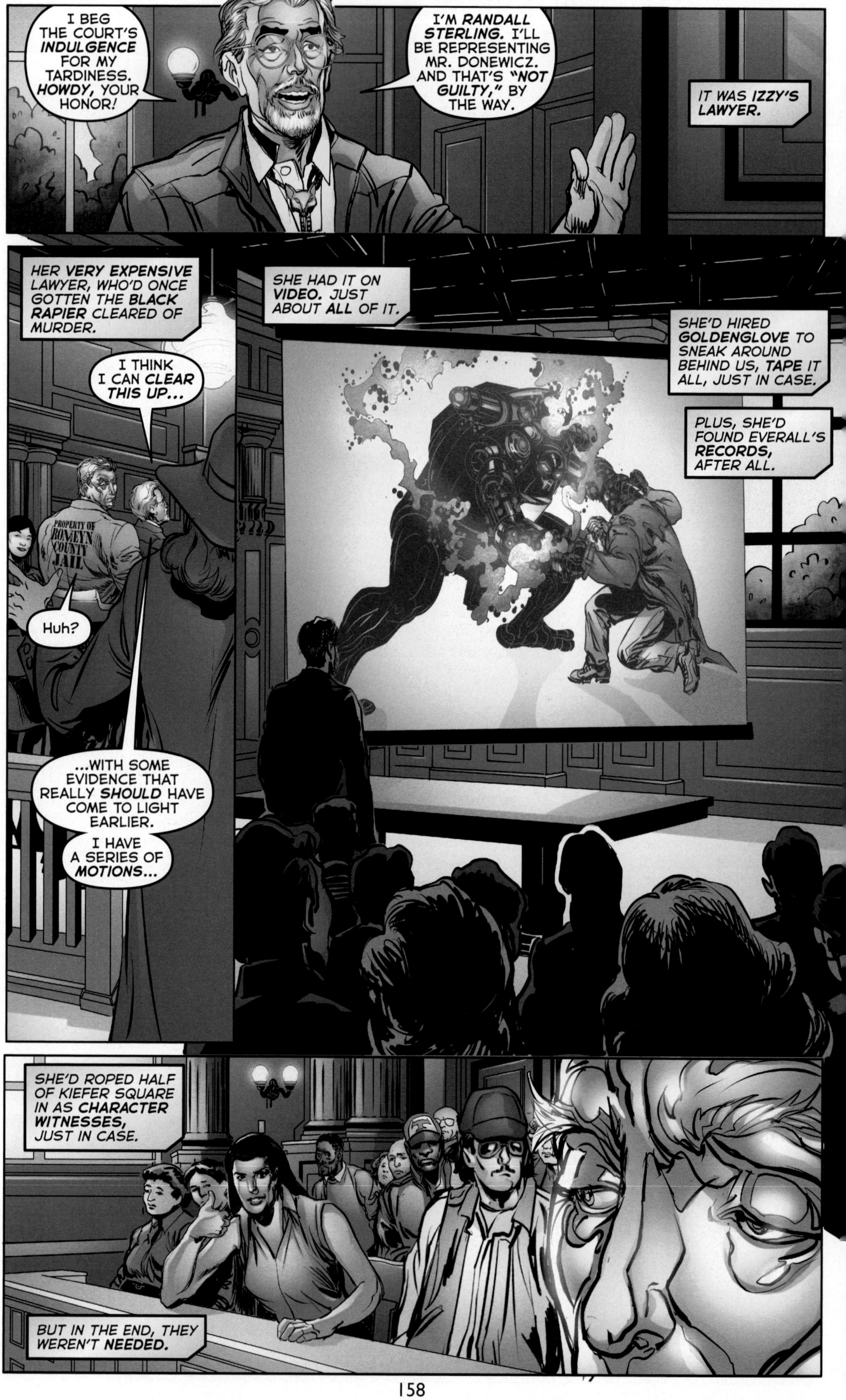
I BEG THE COURT'S INDULGENCE FOR MY TARDINESS. HOWDY, YOUR HONOR!
I'M RANDALL STERLING. I'LL BE REPRESENTING MR. DONEWICZ. AND THAT'S "NOT GUILTY," BY THE WAY.
IT WAS IZZY'S LAWYER.
HER VERY EXPENSIVE LAWYER, WHO'D ONCE GOTTEN THE BLACK RAPIER CLEARED OF MURDER.
I THINK I CAN CLEAR THIS UP...
PROPERTY OF ROMEYN COUNTY JAIL
Huh?
...WITH SOME EVIDENCE THAT REALLY SHOULD HAVE COME TO LIGHT EARLIER.
I HAVE A SERIES OF MOTIONS...
SHE HAD IT ON VIDEO. JUST ABOUT ALL OF IT.
SHE'D HIRED GOLDENGLOVE TO SNEAK AROUND BEHIND US, TAPE IT ALL, JUST IN CASE.
PLUS, SHE'D FOUND EVERALL'S RECORDS, AFTER ALL.
SHE'D ROPED HALF OF KIEFER SQUARE IN AS CHARACTER WITNESSES, JUST IN CASE.
BUT IN THE END, THEY WEREN'T NEEDED.

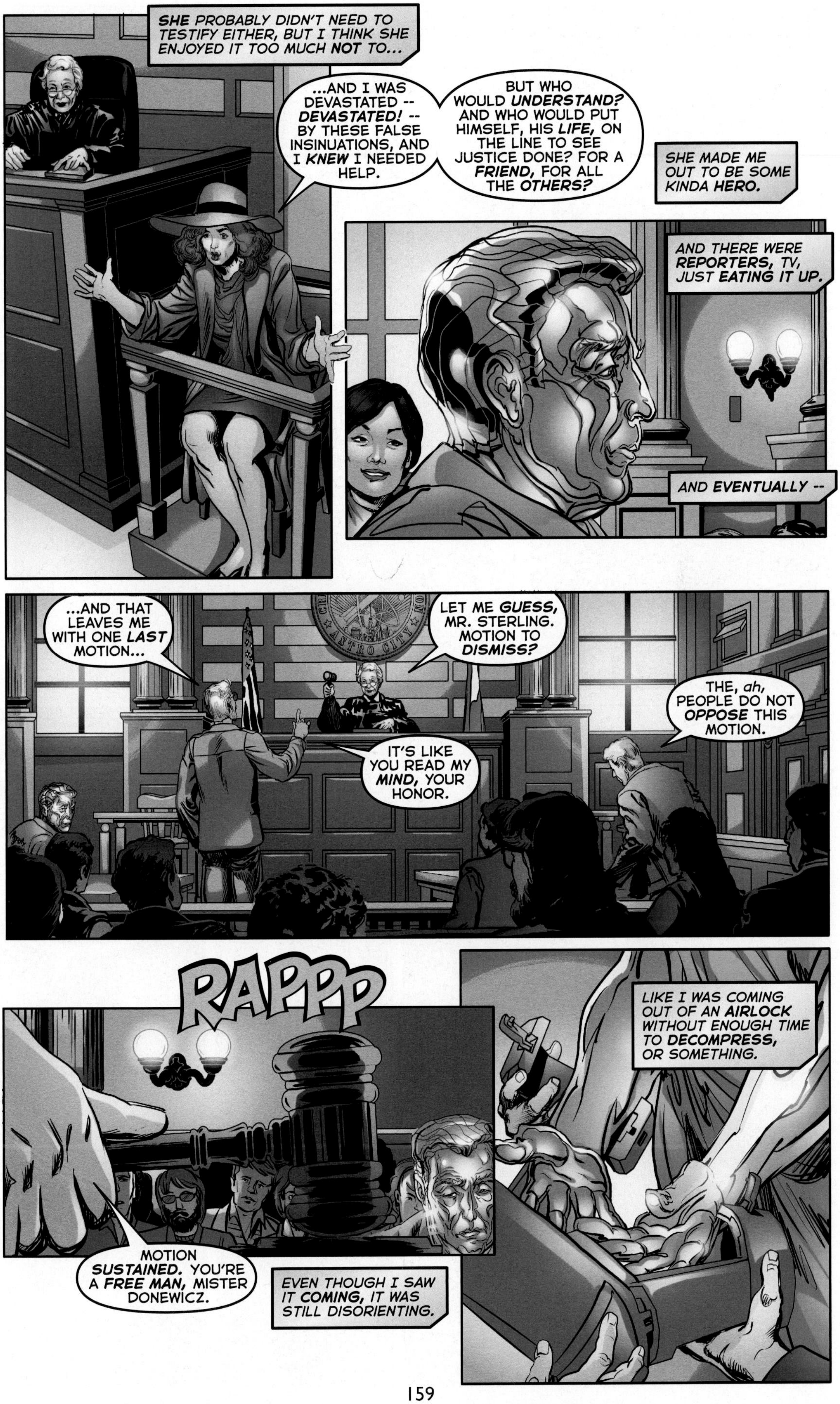
SHE PROBABLY DIDN'T NEED TO TESTIFY EITHER, BUT I THINK SHE ENJOYED IT TOO MUCH NOT TO...
...AND I WAS DEVASTATED -- DEVASTATED! -- BY THESE FALSE INSINUATIONS, AND I KNEW I NEEDED HELP.
BUT WHO WOULD UNDERSTAND? AND WHO WOULD PUT HIMSELF, HIS LIFE, ON THE LINE TO SEE JUSTICE DONE? FOR A FRIEND, FOR ALL THE OTHERS?
SHE MADE ME OUT TO BE SOME KINDA HERO.
AND THERE WERE REPORTERS, TV, JUST EATING IT UP.
AND EVENTUALLY --
...AND THAT LEAVES ME WITH ONE LAST MOTION...
LET ME GUESS, MR. STERLING. MOTION TO DISMISS?
IT'S LIKE YOU READ MY MIND, YOUR HONOR.
THE, ah, PEOPLE DO NOT OPPOSE THIS MOTION.
RAPPP
MOTION SUSTAINED. YOU'RE A FREE MAN, MISTER DONEWICZ.
EVEN THOUGH I SAW IT COMING, IT WAS STILL DISORIENTING.
LIKE I WAS COMING OUT OF AN AIRLOCK WITHOUT ENOUGH TIME TO DECOMPRESS, OR SOMETHING.

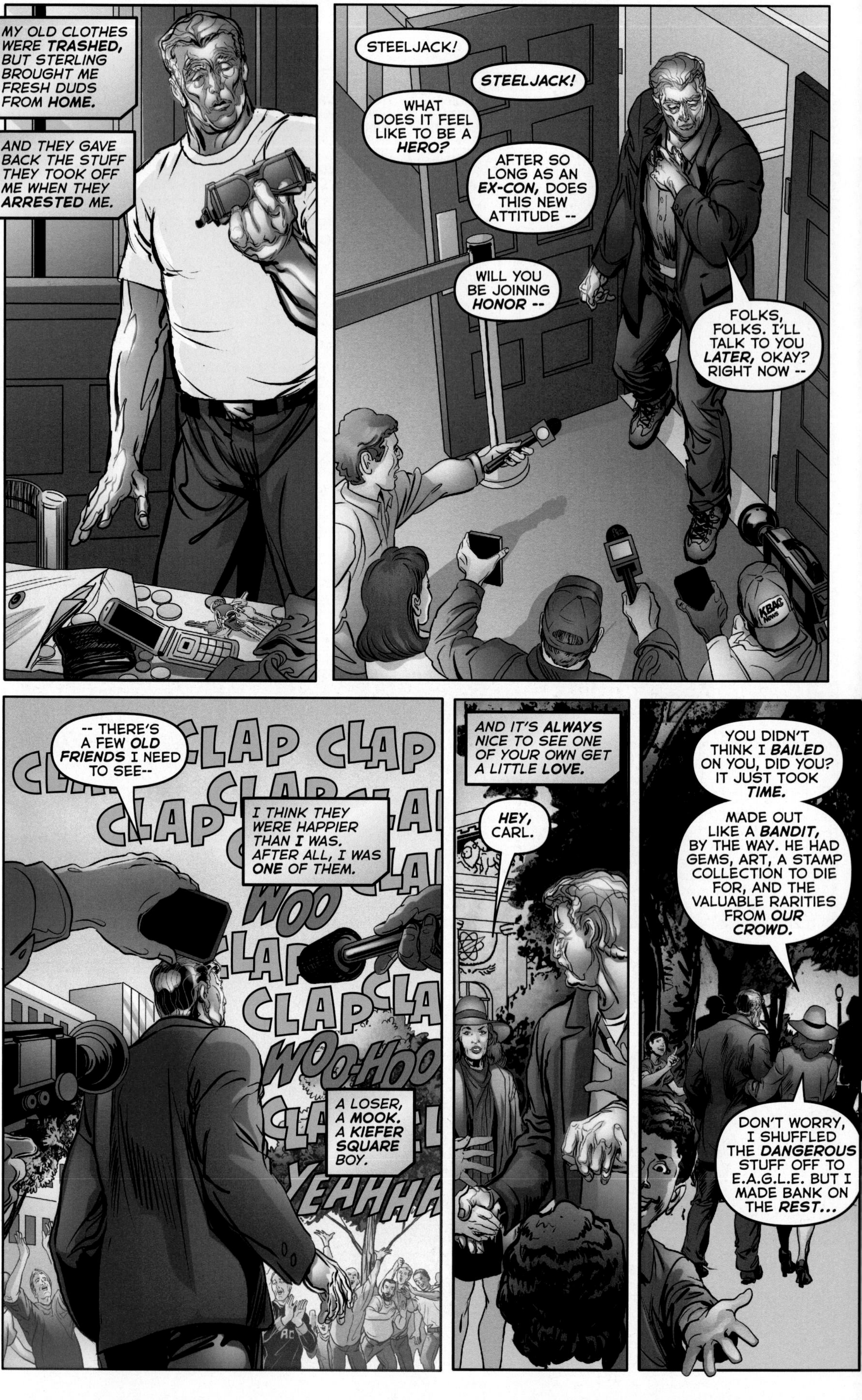
MY OLD CLOTHES WERE TRASHED, BUT STERLING BROUGHT ME FRESH DUDS FROM HOME.
AND THEY GAVE BACK THE STUFF THEY TOOK OFF ME WHEN THEY ARRESTED ME.
STEELJACK!
STEELJACK!
WHAT DOES IT FEEL LIKE TO BE A HERO?
AFTER SO LONG AS AN EX-CON, DOES THIS NEW ATTITUDE --
WILL YOU BE JOINING HONOR --
FOLKS, FOLKS. I'LL TALK TO YOU LATER, OKAY? RIGHT NOW --
KBAG News
-- THERE'S A FEW OLD FRIENDS I NEED TO SEE--
CLAP CLAP
CLAP CLAP
I THINK THEY WERE HAPPIER THAN I WAS. AFTER ALL, I WAS ONE OF THEM.
WOO
CLAP
CLAP
WOO-HOO
A LOSER, A MOOK. A KIEFER SQUARE BOY.
YEHHHH
AND IT'S ALWAYS NICE TO SEE ONE OF YOUR OWN GET A LITTLE LOVE.
HEY, CARL.
YOU DIDN'T THINK I BAILED ON YOU, DID YOU? IT JUST TOOK TIME.
MADE OUT LIKE A BANDIT, BY THE WAY. HE HAD GEMS, ART, A STAMP COLLECTION TO DIE FOR, AND THE VALUABLE RARITIES FROM OUR CROWD.
DON'T WORRY, I SHUFFLED THE DANGEROUS STUFF OFF TO E.A.G.L.E. BUT I MADE BANK ON THE REST...

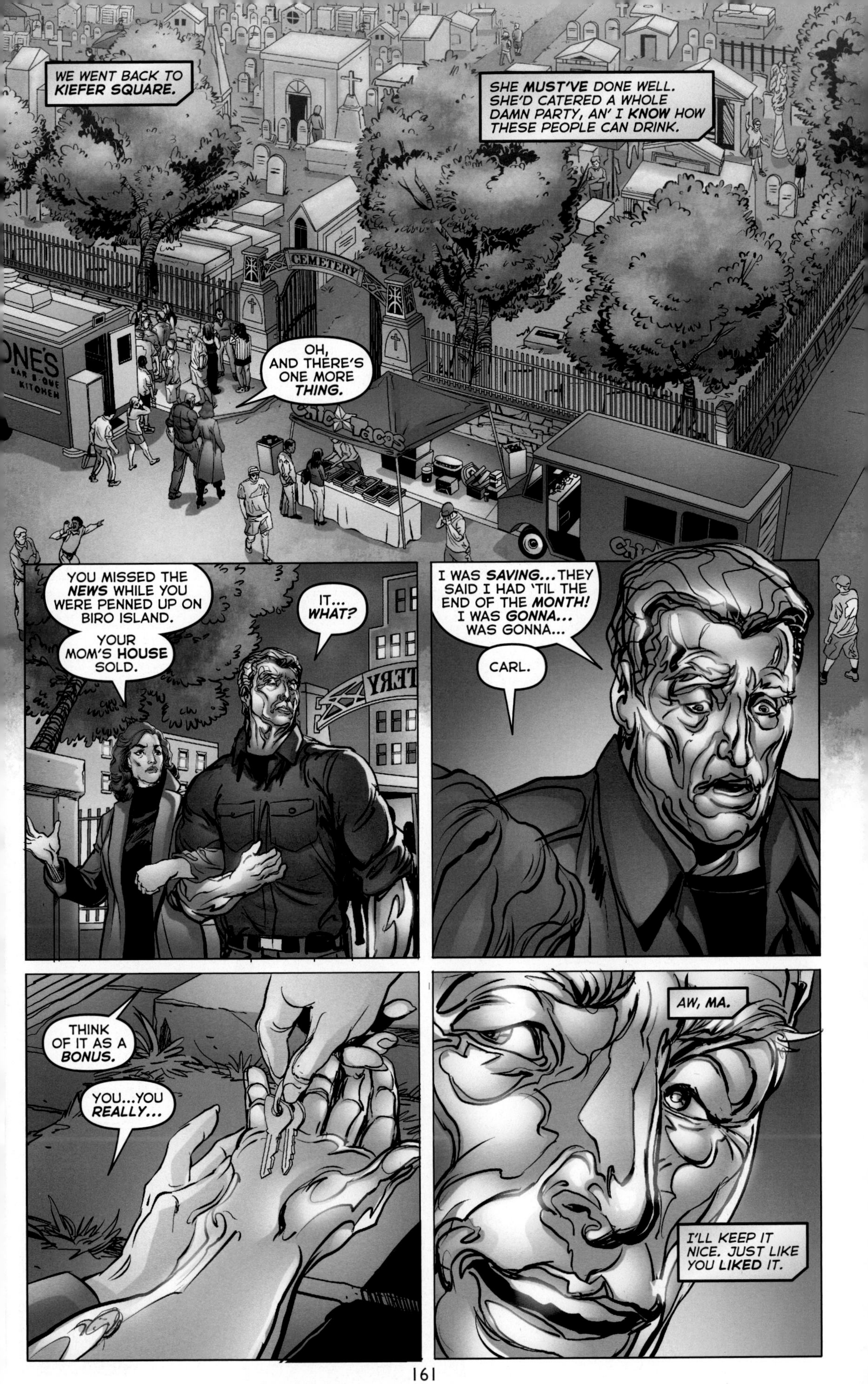
WE WENT BACK TO KIEFER SQUARE.
SHE MUST'VE DONE WELL. SHE'D CATERED A WHOLE DAMN PARTY, AN' I KNOW HOW THESE PEOPLE CAN DRINK.
CEMETERY
OH, AND THERE'S ONE MORE THING.
YOU MISSED THE NEWS WHILE YOU WERE PENNED UP ON BIRO ISLAND.
YOUR MOM'S HOUSE SOLD.
IT... WHAT?
I WAS SAVING... THEY SAID I HAD 'TIL THE END OF THE MONTH! I WAS GONNA... WAS GONNA...
CARL.
THINK OF IT AS A BONUS.
YOU...YOU REALLY...
AW, MA.
I'LL KEEP IT NICE. JUST LIKE YOU LIKED IT.

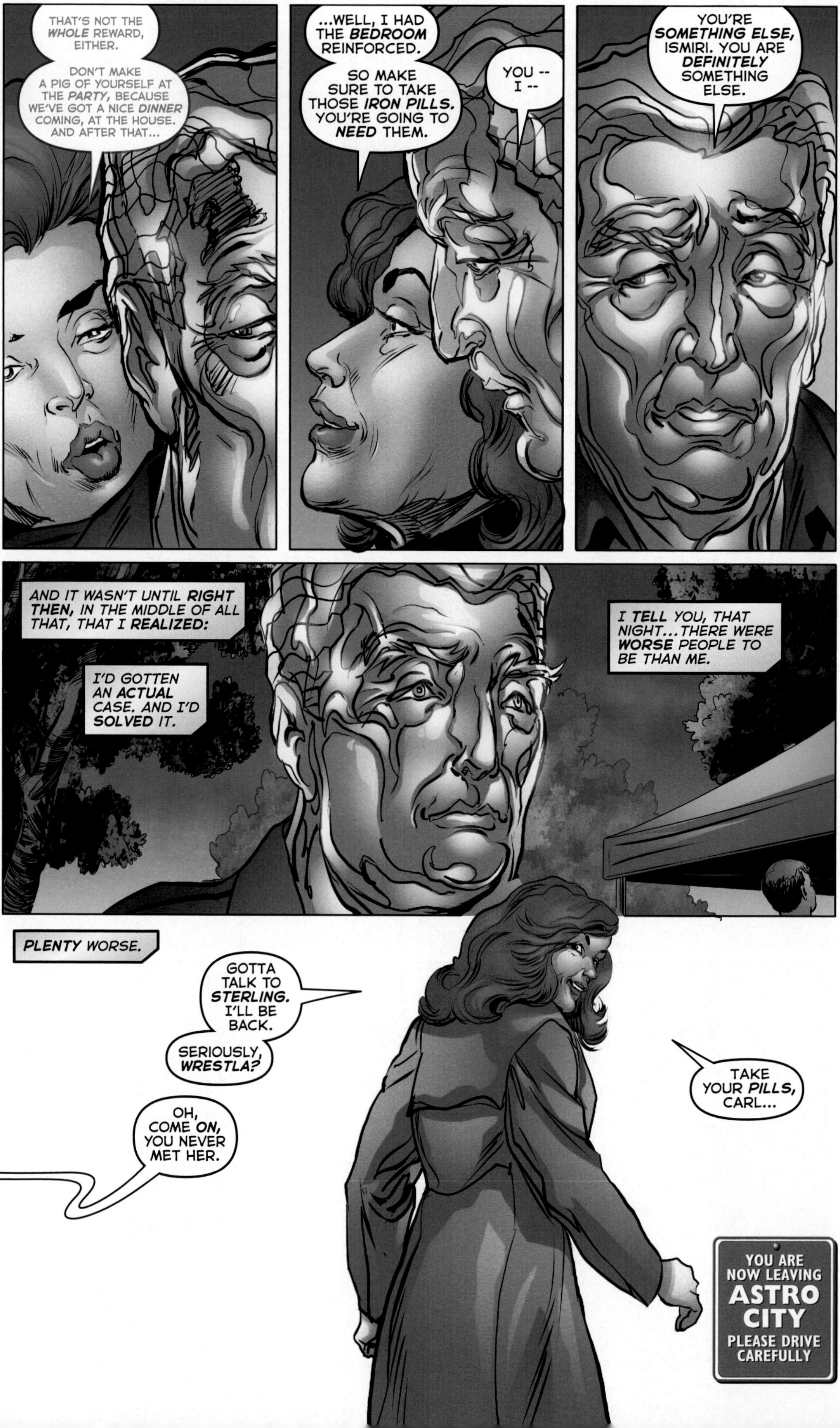
THAT'S NOT THE WHOLE REWARD, EITHER.
DON'T MAKE A PIG OF YOURSELF AT THE PARTY, BECAUSE WE'VE GOT A NICE DINNER COMING, AT THE HOUSE. AND AFTER THAT...
...WELL, I HAD THE BEDROOM REINFORCED.
SO MAKE SURE TO TAKE THOSE IRON PILLS. YOU'RE GOING TO NEED THEM.
YOU -- I --
YOU'RE SOMETHING ELSE, ISMIRI. YOU ARE DEFINITELY SOMETHING ELSE.
AND IT WASN'T UNTIL RIGHT THEN, IN THE MIDDLE OF ALL THAT, THAT I REALIZED:
I'D GOTTEN AN ACTUAL CASE. AND I'D SOLVED IT.
I TELL YOU, THAT NIGHT...THERE WERE WORSE PEOPLE TO BE THAN ME.
PLENTY WORSE.
GOTTA TALK TO STERLING. I'LL BE BACK.
SERIOUSLY, WRESTLA?
OH, COME ON, YOU NEVER MET HER.
TAKE YOUR PILLS, CARL...
YOU ARE NOW LEAVING ASTRO CITY PLEASE DRIVE CAREFULLY

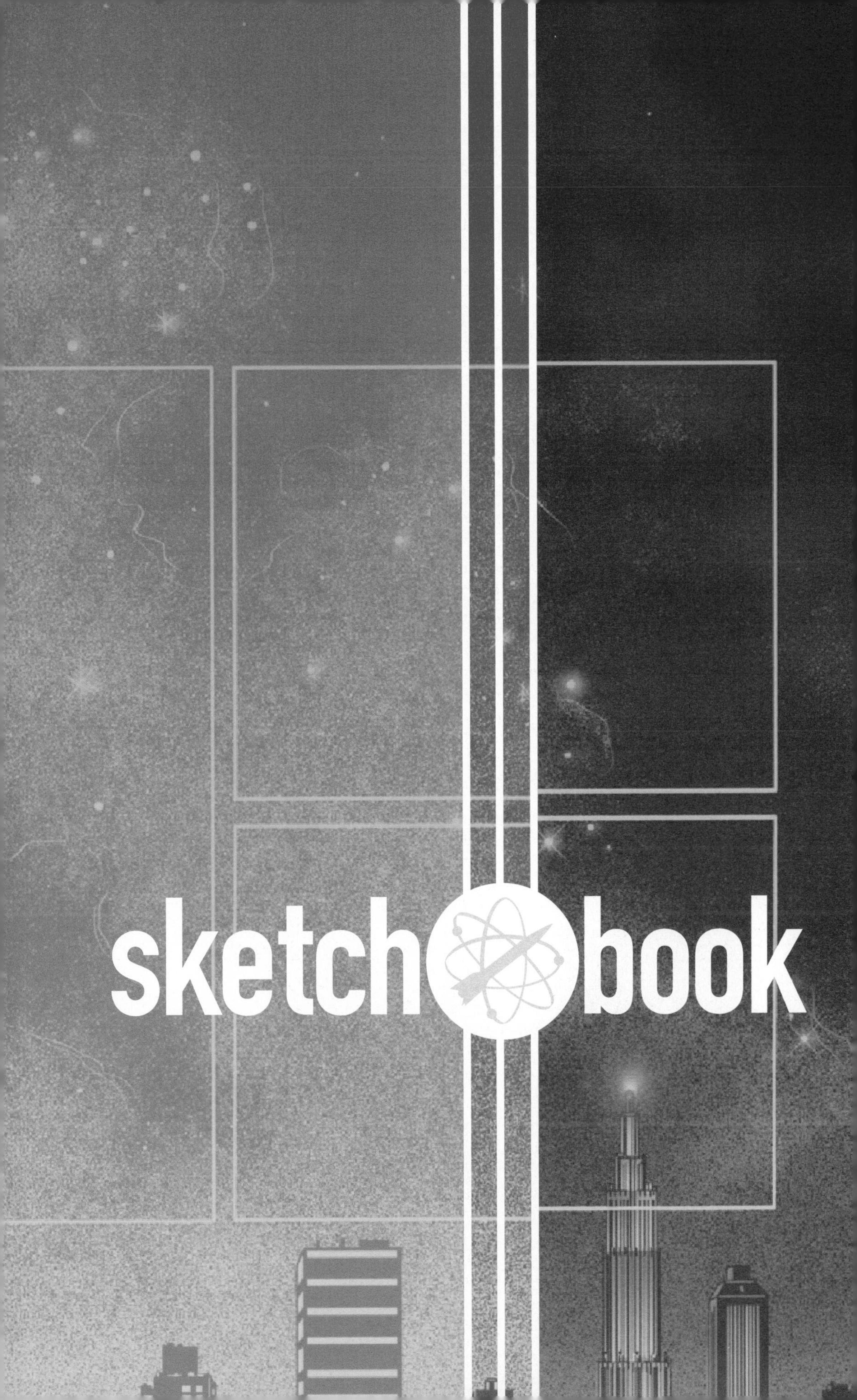
sketchbook

in dreams 2015

Issue 26 was our 20th anniversary issue, so we wanted to harken back to our very first issue, in 1995, in both the story and the cover.

For the cover, Alex Ross did a sketch homaging the very first splash...

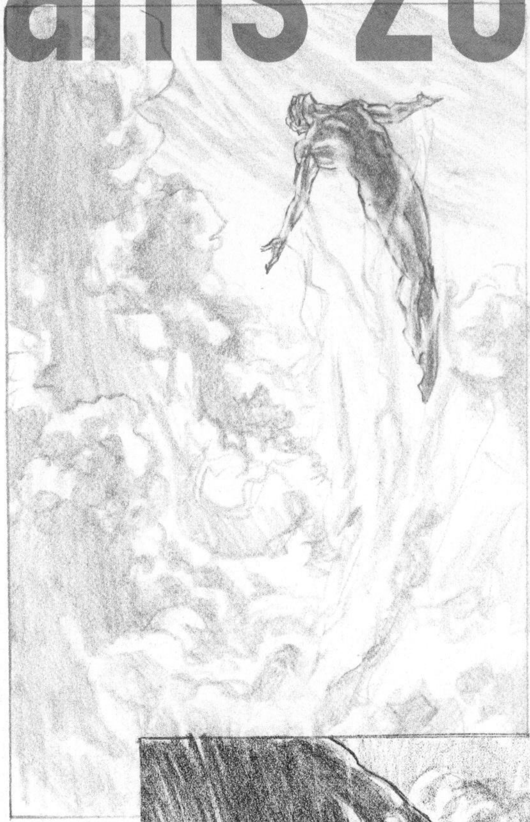

...but there were concerns about having a naked guy on the cover, so he varied it up a little...

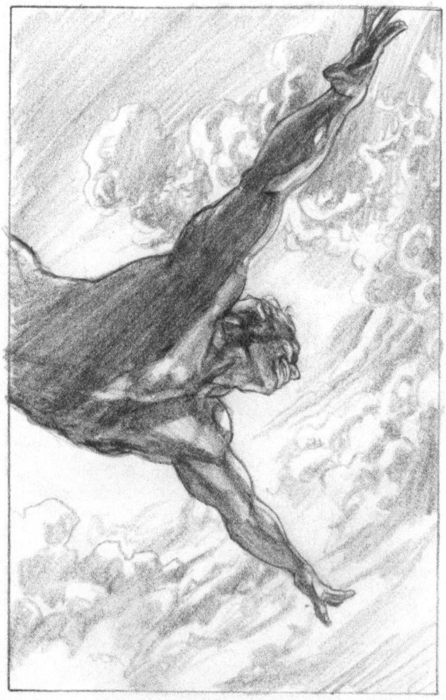

...and ultimately, we settled on a gorgeous design.

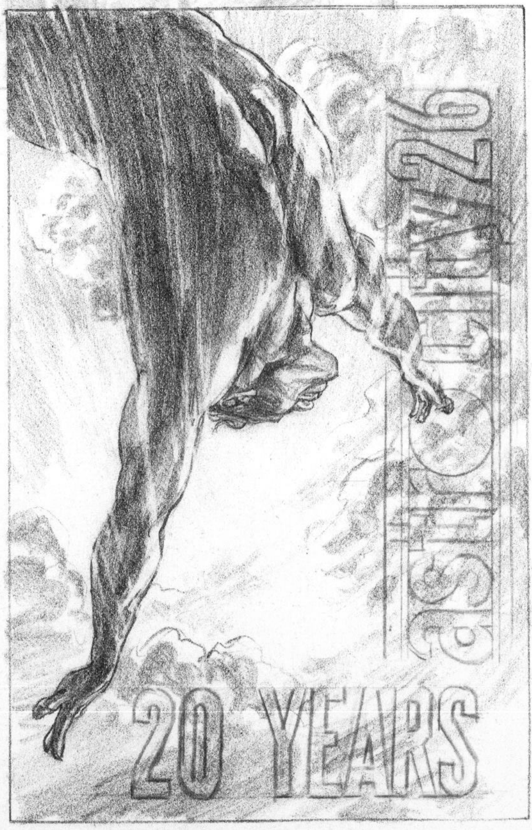
20 YEARS

We moved the text around from Alex's original suggestion, and it all came out striking and memorable.

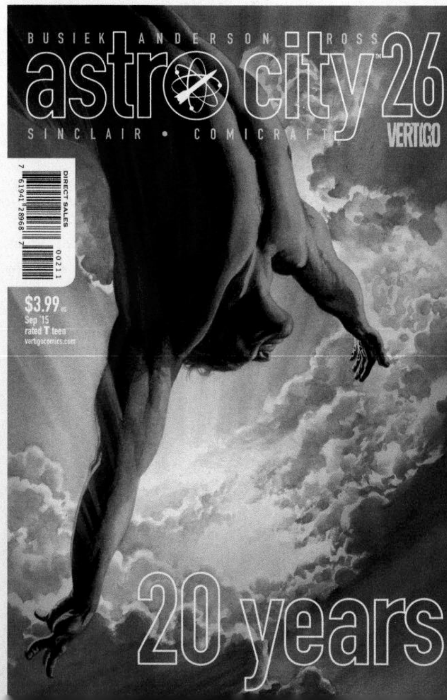
BUSIEK ANDERSON ROSS
astro city 26
SINCLAIR • COMICRAFT
VERTIGO
DIRECT SALES
$3.99
Sep '15
rated T teen
vertigocomics.com
20 years

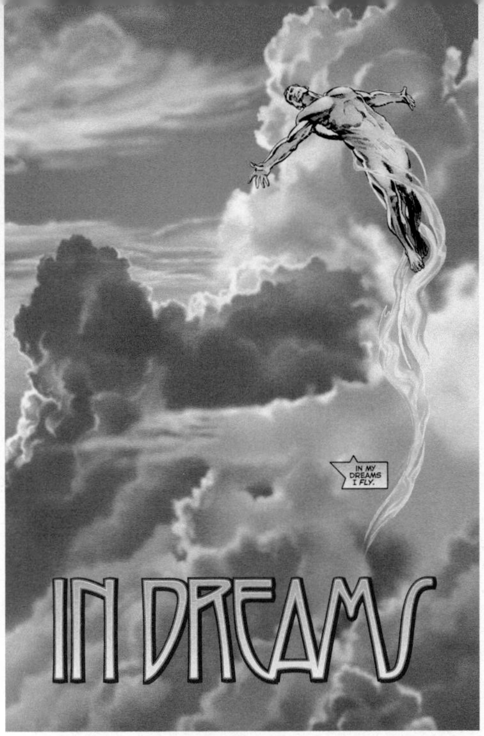
IN MY DREAMS I FLY.
IN DREAMS

For the interior, of course, we had no problems homaging that first splash page—naked guy worked in 1995, naked guy would work fine in 2015.

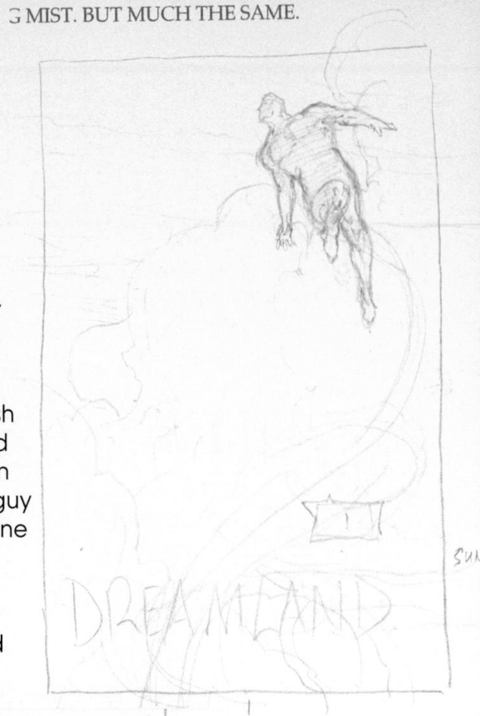
G MIST. BUT MUCH THE SAME.
DREAMLAND

So Brent recapitulated that image...

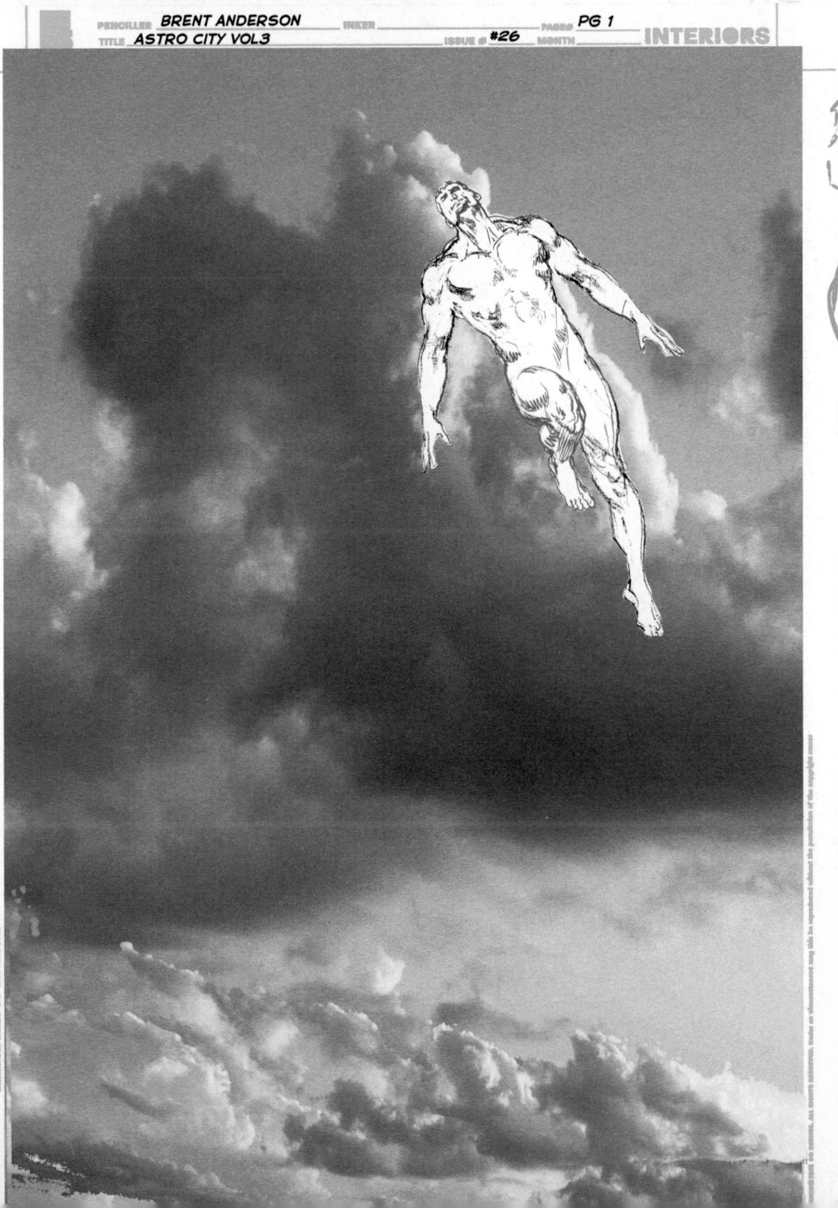
PENCILLER BRENT ANDERSON
INKER
PAGE# PG 1
TITLE ASTRO CITY VOL3
ISSUE # #26
MONTH
INTERIORS

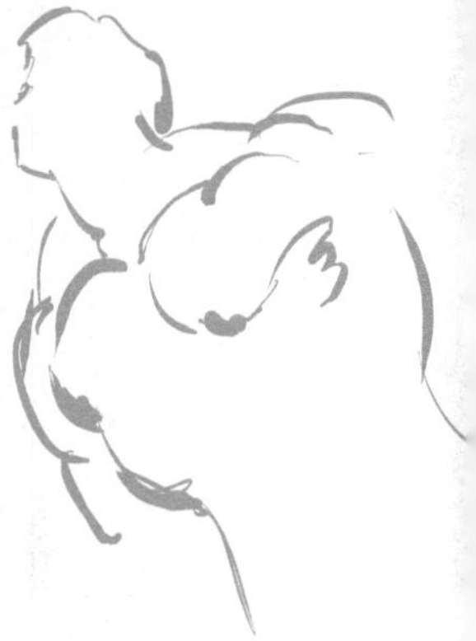

...and refined it, along with some color reference to guide Alex Sinclair in realizing the background.

Sinc used a different palette in the actual printed page—we wanted to set a different mood, a more ominous quality to the dream—and there we were. Same dream, twenty years later.

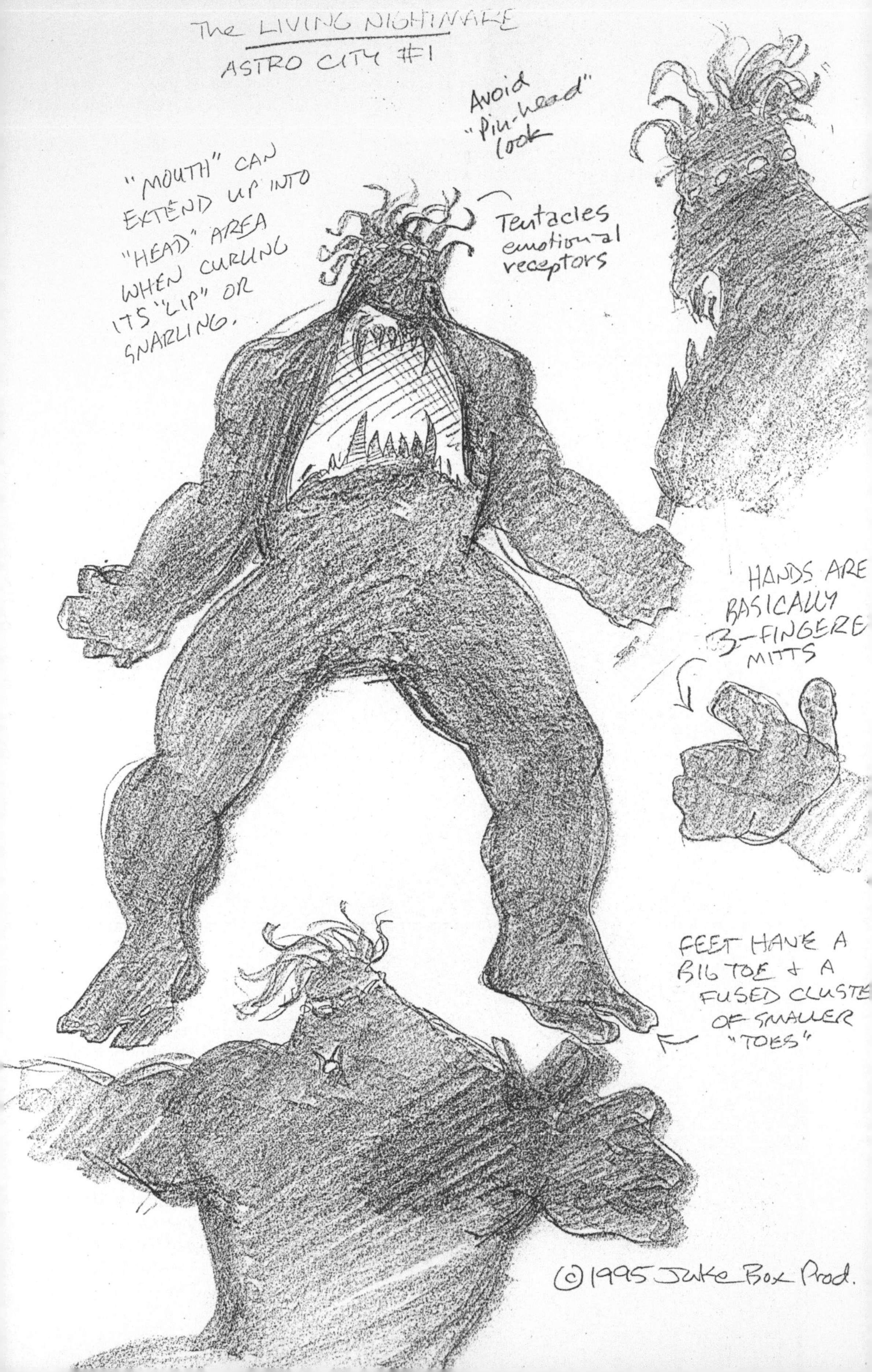
The LIVING NIGHTMARE
ASTRO CITY #1
Avoid "Pin-head" look
"MOUTH" CAN EXTEND UP INTO "HEAD" AREA WHEN CURLING ITS "LIP" OR SNARLING.
Tentacles emotional receptors
HANDS ARE BASICALLY 3-FINGERE MITTS
FEET HAVE A BIG TOE + A FUSED CLUSTE OF SMALLER "TOES"
©1995 Juke Box Prod.

the living nightmare

Here's a blast from the past: Brent's design sketches for the Living Nightmare, from way back in 1995, when we were working on that first issue.

For some reason, we didn't include these in the first ASTRO CITY collection. Maybe we just couldn't find them. Or got hit on the head that day.

In any case, enjoy!

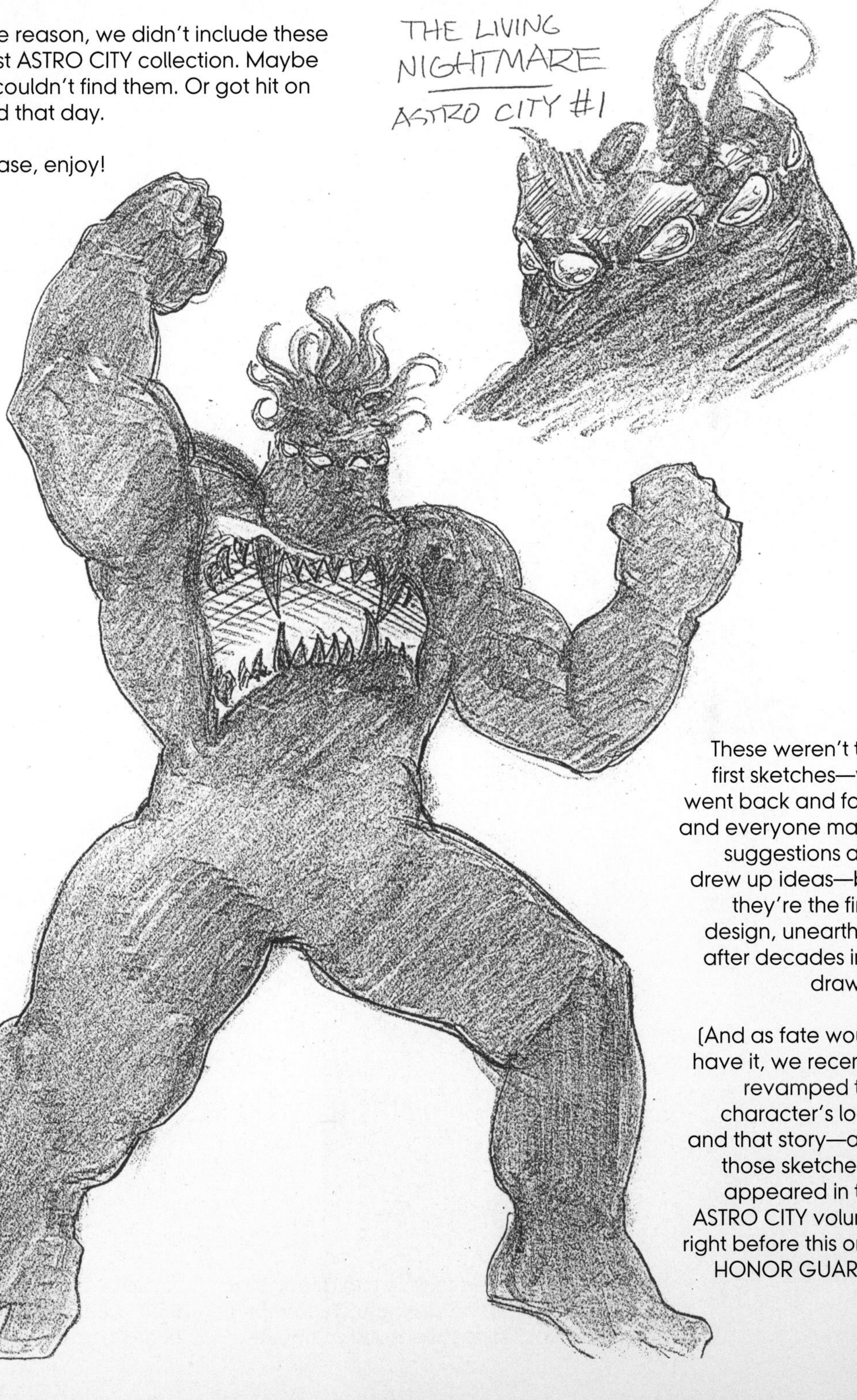
THE LIVING
NIGHTMARE
ASTRO CITY #1

These weren't the first sketches—we went back and forth and everyone made suggestions and drew up ideas—but they're the final design, unearthed after decades in a drawer.

[And as fate would have it, we recently revamped the character's look, and that story—and those sketches—appeared in the ASTRO CITY volume right before this one, HONOR GUARD.]

When Karl and Sasha Furst were introduced, as minor characters in the ASTRA two-parter, we were in something of a hurry, and didn't have a lot of time to think his power through. So we kind of evolved him on the fly, figuring that as he grew older his powers matured with him.

In his first appearance, he blew up like a beachball and bounced around. In his second, he inflated his upper body into a hyper-muscled strongman look. But we weren't fully satisfied, so when we started in on a story spotlighting him, Alex started digging into the character and making visual suggestions.

One idea was to take the "inflating muscles" look and combine it with the First Family's distinctively Kirby-esque energy...

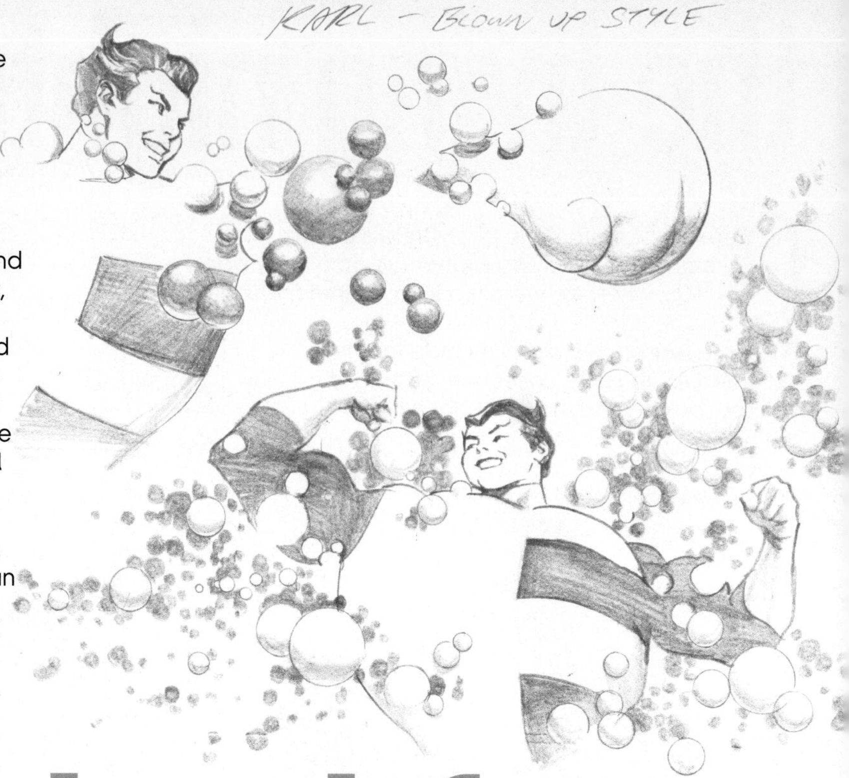
KARL - BLOWN UP STYLE

karl furst

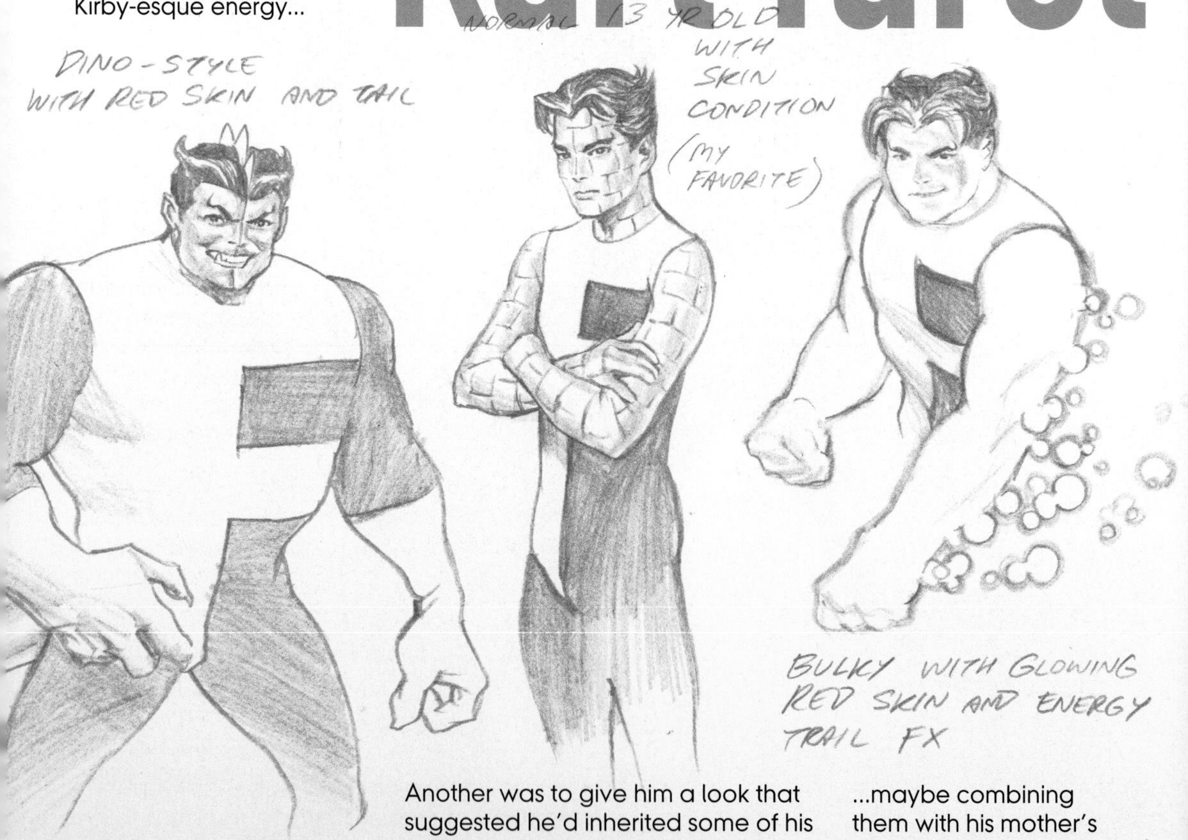
DINO-STYLE
WITH RED SKIN AND TAIL
NORMAL 13 YR OLD
WITH
SKIN
CONDITION
(MY
FAVORITE)
BULKY WITH GLOWING
RED SKIN AND ENERGY
TRAIL FX

Another was to give him a look that suggested he'd inherited some of his father's dinosaur-esque attributes...

...maybe combining them with his mother's energy-crackle.

In the end, we tried to keep it simple. He can shift and reshape his body, using the "sphericality" energy, as we named it, making himself more powerful and versatile, but in a look that suited a young teenager who wasn't a child anymore.

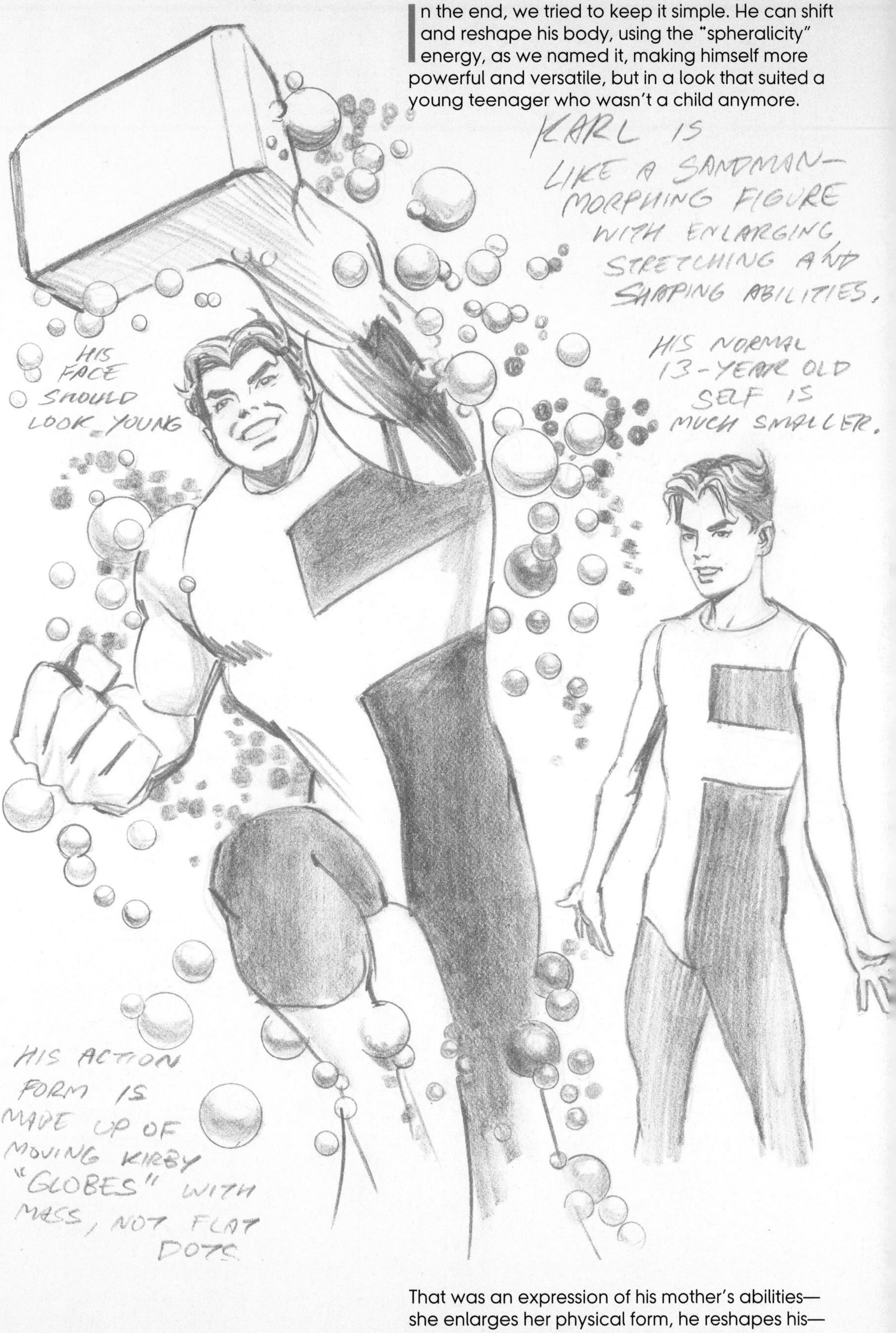

KARL IS LIKE A SANDMAN— MORPHING FIGURE WITH ENLARGING STRETCHING AND SHAPING ABILITIES.
HIS FACE SHOULD LOOK YOUNG
HIS NORMAL 13-YEAR OLD SELF IS MUCH SMALLER.
HIS ACTION FORM IS MADE UP OF MOVING KIRBY "GLOBES" WITH MASS, NOT FLAT DOTS.

That was an expression of his mother's abilities—she enlarges her physical form, he reshapes his—in a way that gave him a look and specialty that was still different from anyone else on the team.

sasha furst

For Sasha, we knew right from the start that she'd inherited powers from her grandfather on her mother's side, Kaspian of the Beast-Men. But Alex got a chance to tweak her look, giving her teen look a sleek, feral elegance.

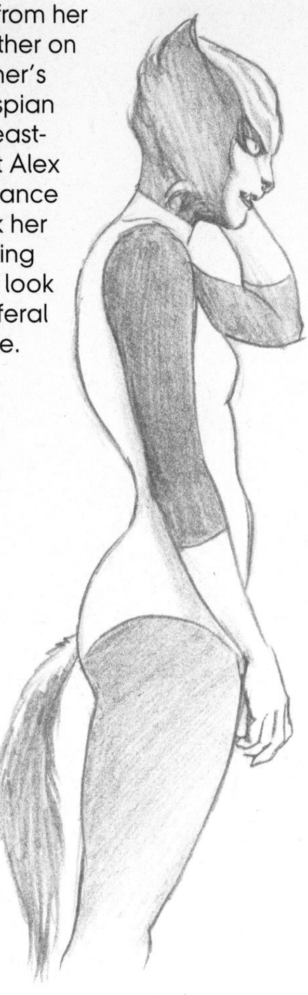

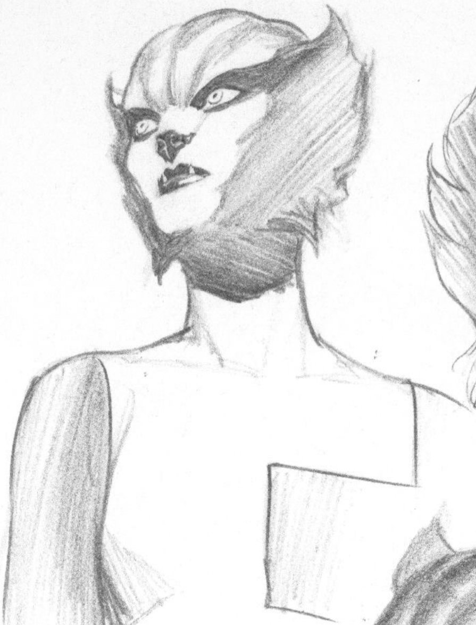

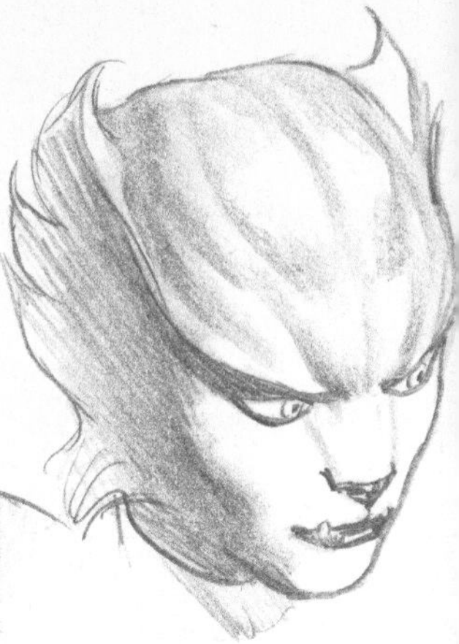

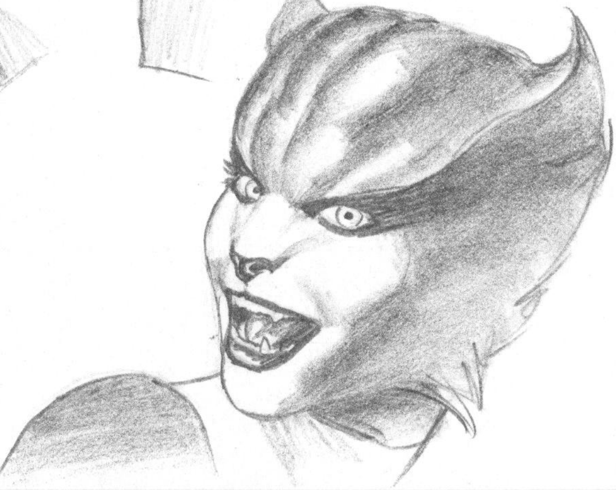

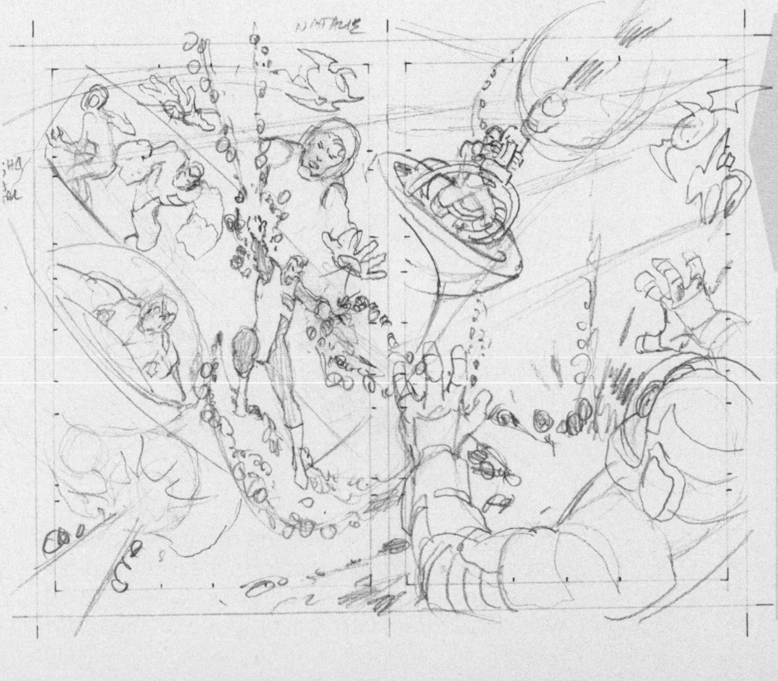

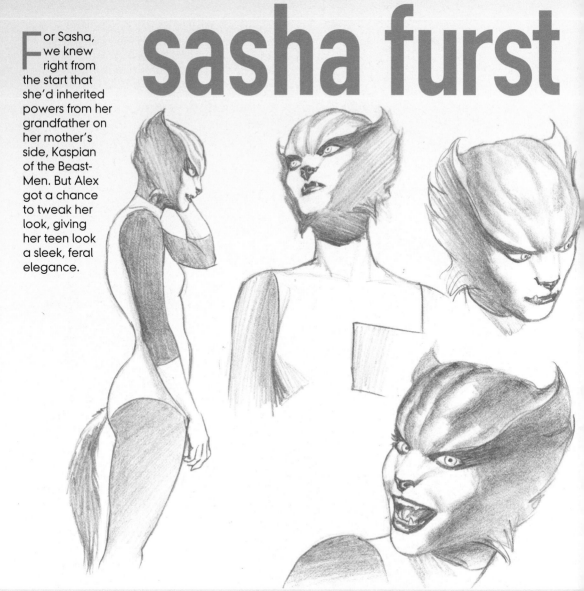

At the time Brent was laying out issue 29, either the cover hadn't been done yet or Brent hadn't seen it, so he roughed in his own concept of the First Family's flying car...

...and Alex did more detailed design sketches to expand on the shot he'd put on the cover, so we could keep the car consistent throughout, and giving the vehicle a kind of late-Fifties station wagon aesthetic, suitable to the Fursts' family dynamic.

Sasha and Karl, folks!
Ain't they sweet?

(This was another of the developmental designs for Karl, before we'd settled on his final look. But it's a great drawing, isn't it?)

KARL

the family rambler

STRO CITY BATTLE CAR 1

WHAT SHOULD THE AREA CONNECTING THEM LOOK LIKE?

FRONT CAR, TWO SEATS OR SINGLE SEATER?

W MANY URSTS SHOULD T CARRY? S OR 8? GHT NOW ITS A TIGHT FIT FOR 5.

IF THESE SEATS COULD FIT TWO, THEY WOULD HAVE TO BE DEEPER.

THESE SEATS LOOK A LITTLE SHALLOW, TOO.

ASTRO CITY BATTLE CAR 2

MY ROUGH EXPANSION TAKE WITH ALL POD STATIONS HAVING ROOM FOR TWO

REX COULD PROBABLY NOT FIT ANYONE NEXT TO HIM

NOW IT'S WAR WAGON WIDE

DEEPER STRUCTURE

the ubersaurus

Doomsday monster! Gotta have a good doomsday monster! Here's Alex's initial design...

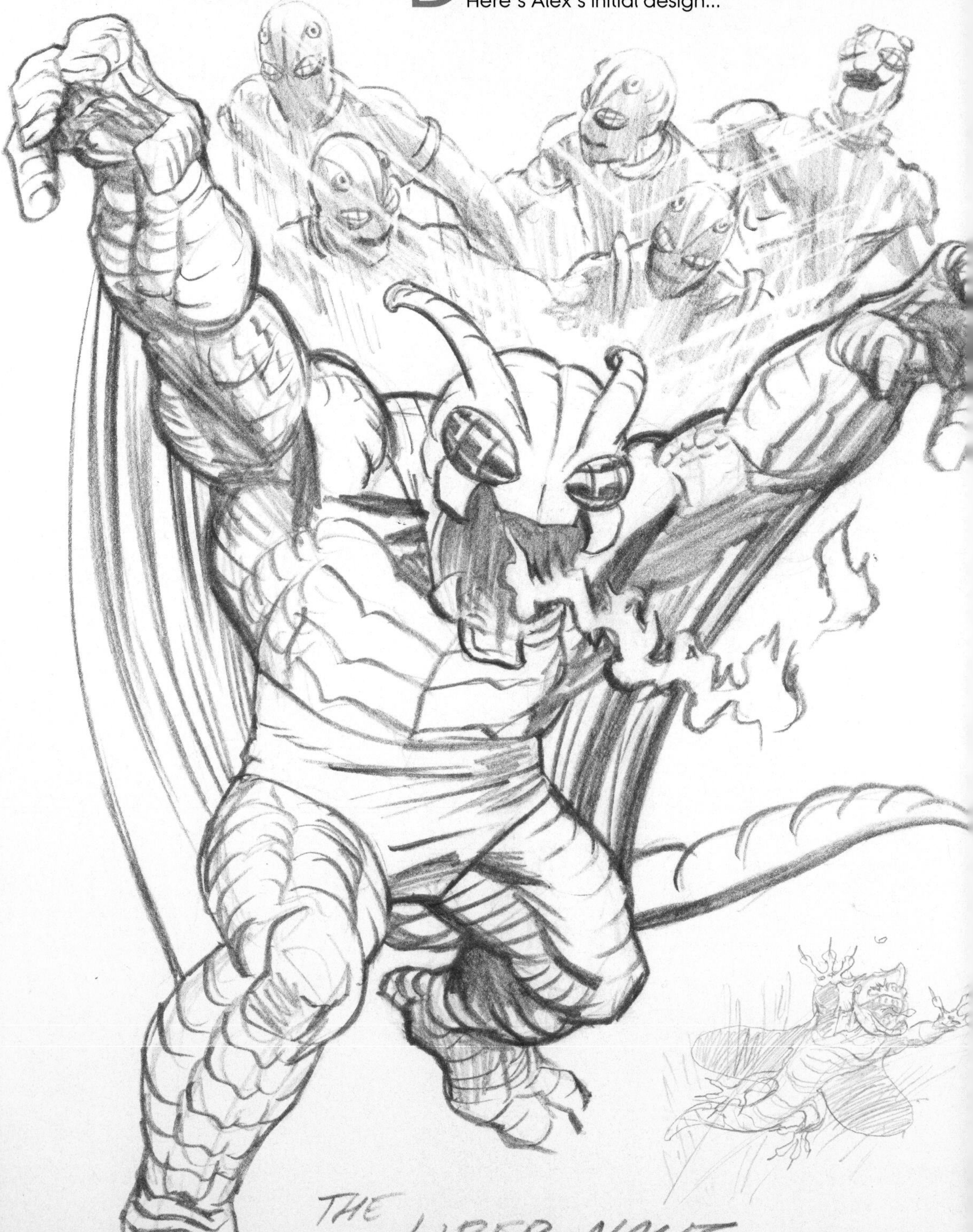
THE UBER-NAUT

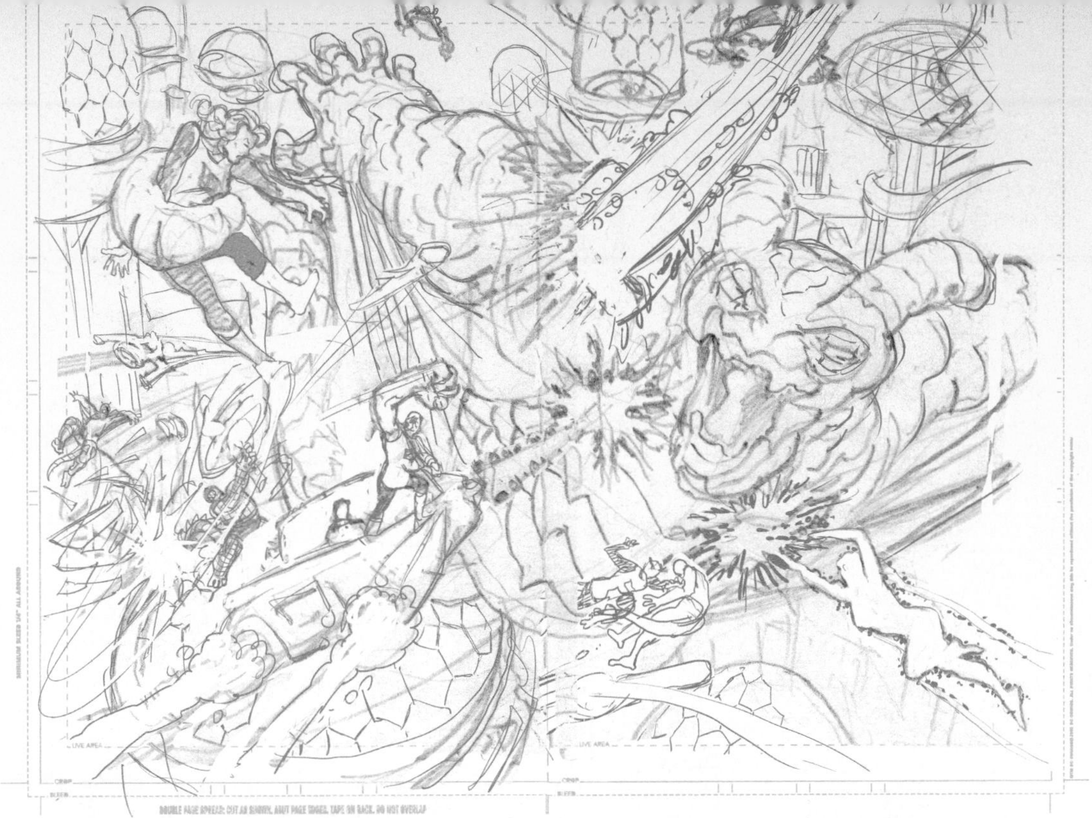

...and Brent's page rough for his debut!

the zirrst family

Alex designed the general look of Zozat and his family, as well.

We modified them a little, to make Zo's parents feel less like idealized specimens and more relaxed and lived-in, but these sketches also set the tone for the whole Zirr species.

Left: Zozat's faithful pet Grum.

Below: Zozat's school project.

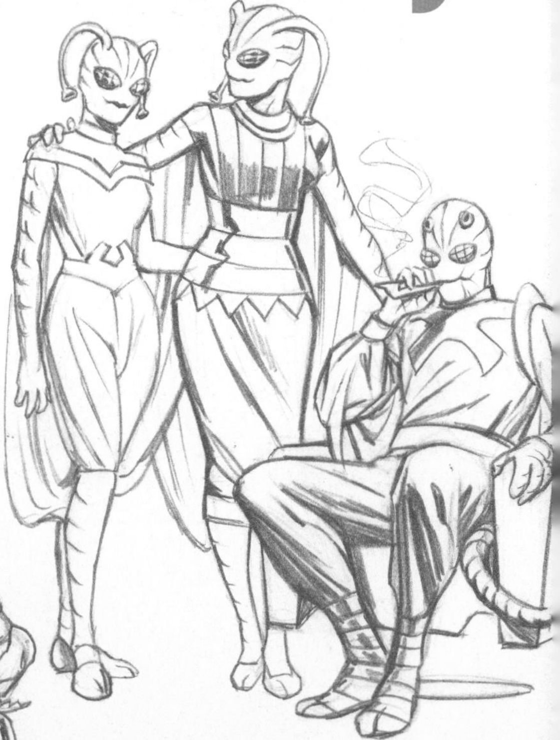

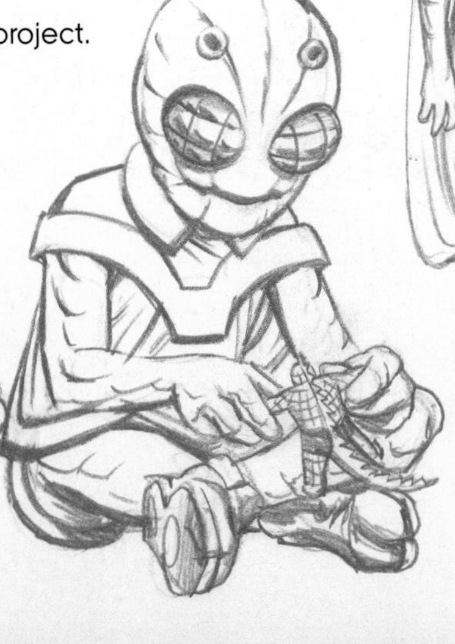

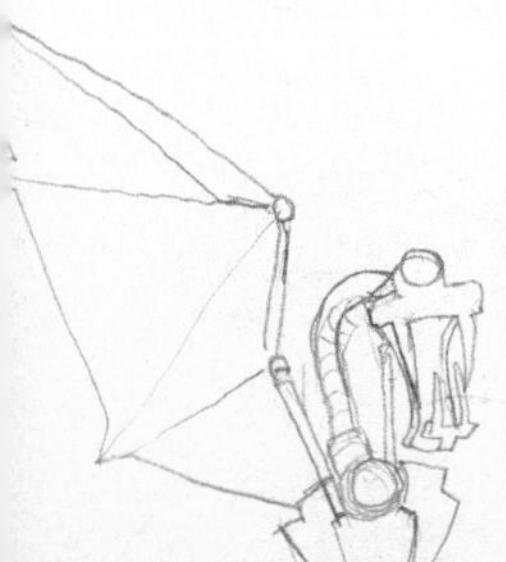

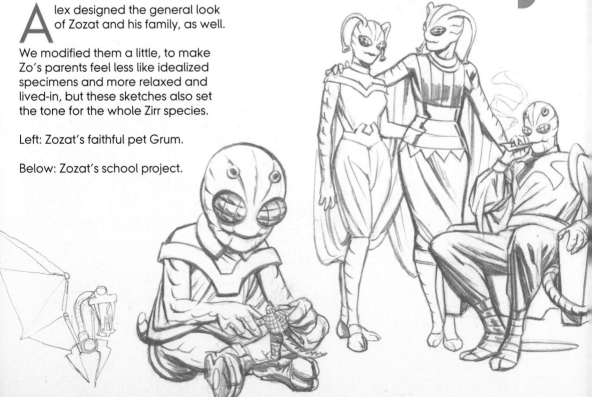

the goggles of night

The Cloak of Night had been mentioned before, but we'd never gotten a good look at him. So to design his goggles for Steeljack to use, we needed to know more about how he looked.

Alex had some ideas on that, which allowed us to make the goggles look appropriate in the story...

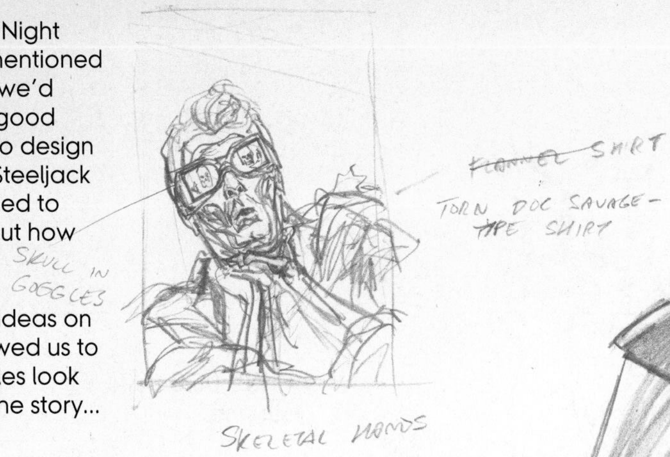

SKULL IN GOGGLES
~~FLANNEL~~ SHIRT?
TORN DOC SAVAGE-TYPE SHIRT
SKELETAL HANDS

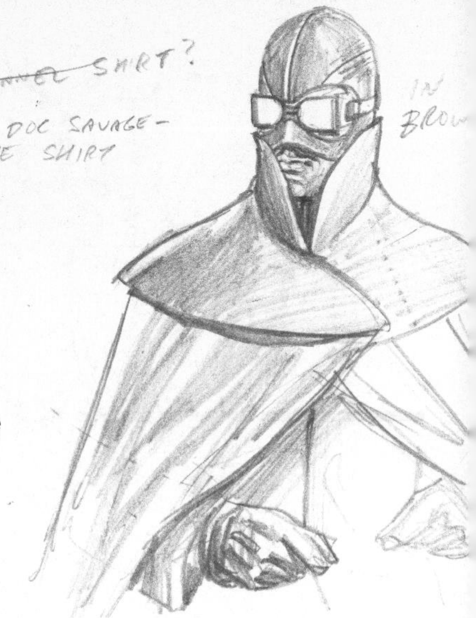

...and then the Cloak himself turned up a few issues later anyway, so it was nice to have him designed!

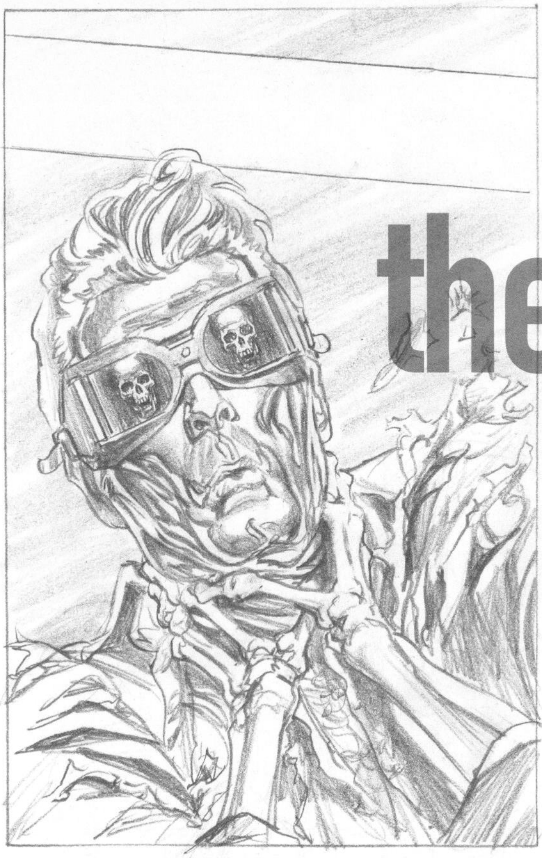

ASTRO CITY #34

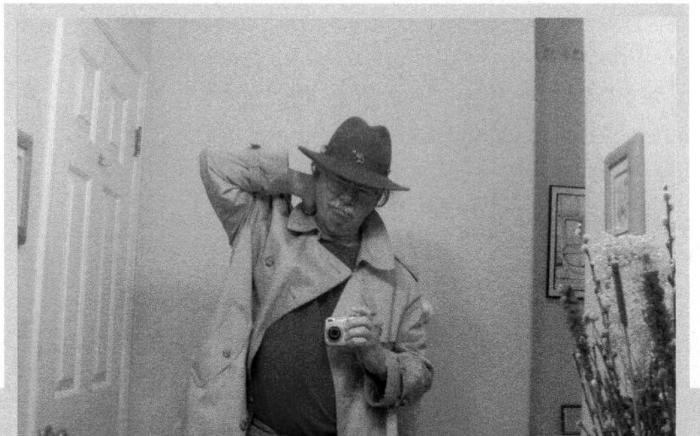

Even when you're a big steel guy, you gotta get your fabric folds right. Here's Brent's photo-reference of himself as Steeljack, trenchcoating confusion...

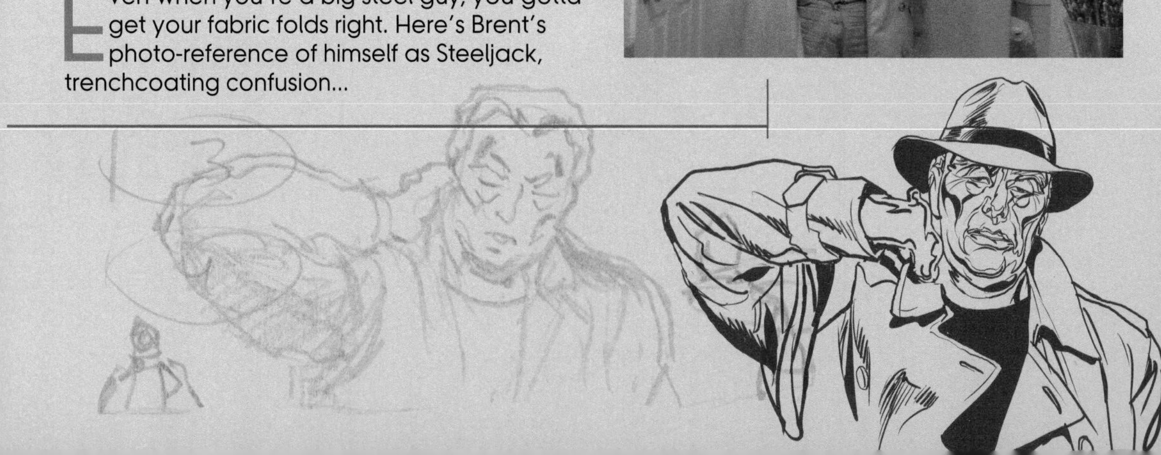

cutlass

Here's an example of parallel development: Brent's layout for Cutlass's first appearance in the story...

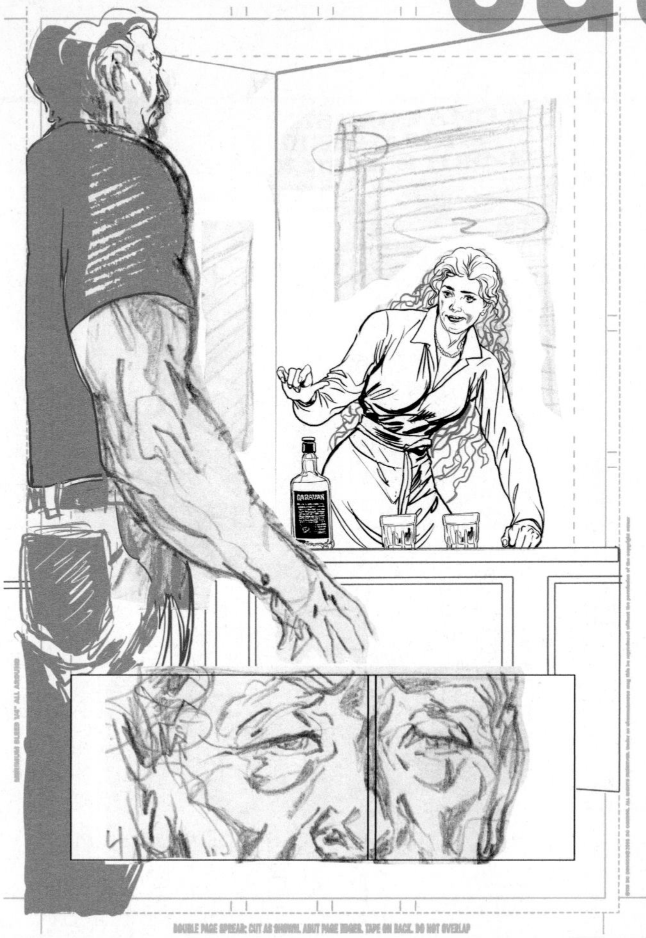
DOUBLE PAGE SPREAD: CUT AS SHOWN. ABUT PAGE EDGES. TAPE ON BACK. DO NOT OVERLAP

...and Alex's design for her appearance on the cover.

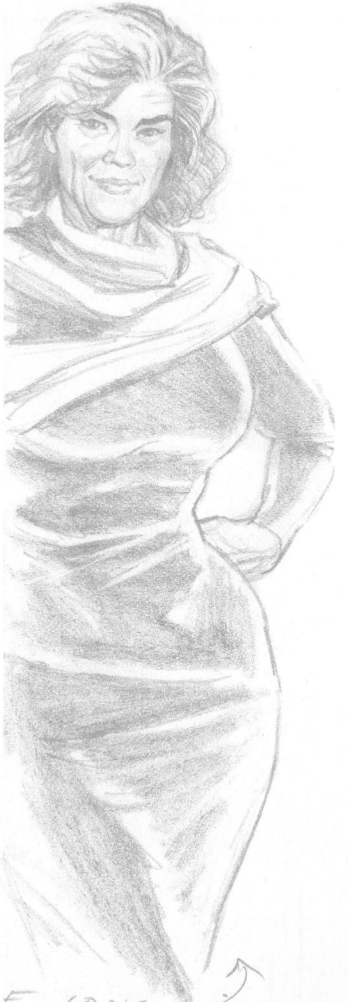
POSSIBLE LOOK
FOR THE OLDER
70-SOMETHING CUTLASS.
SHE'S NOT WEARING A COSTUME

trenchcoating

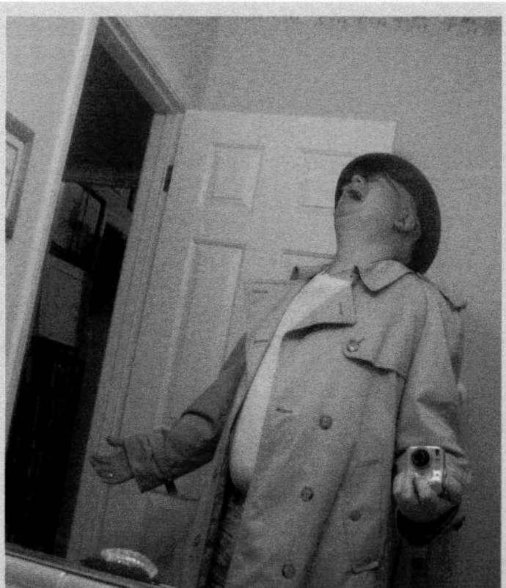

...and mirth!

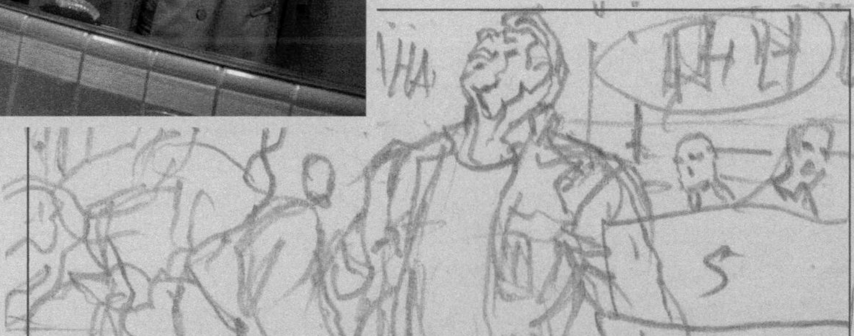

And so we end...on literal reflections. That's ASTRO CITY for you. From alien races to thematic grace notes, we do it all! And not by coincidence, either, no way! Seriously, would we even *do* that?

—Kurt Busiek

don't miss the rest of the astro city series:

astro city
life in the big city
KURT BUSIEK • BRENT ANDERSON • ALEX ROSS

astro city
confession
KURT BUSIEK • BRENT ANDERSON • ALEX ROSS

astro city
family album
KURT BUSIEK • BRENT ANDERSON • ALEX ROSS

HOMAGE COMICS
KURT BUSIEK'S
Astro City
The TARNISHED ANGEL
BUSIEK
ANDERSON
BLYBERG
SINCLAIR
ROSS &
COMICRAFT
Introduction by
FRANK MILLER
COMPLETE AND UNABRIDGED

ASTRO CITY
LOCAL HEROES

ASTRO CITY
BROTHERS & OTHER STRANGERS
BUSIEK
ANDERSON
ROSS
SINCLAIR
COMICRAFT

ASTRO CITY
BROTHERS IN ARMS
BUSIEK
ANDERSON
ROSS
SINCLAIR
COMICRAFT

astro city
SHINING STARS
BUSIEK • ANDERSON • ROSS • SINCLAIR • COMICRAFT

astro city
through open doors
KURT BUSIEK • BRENT ANDERSON • ALEX ROSS
VERTIGO

astro city
victory
KURT BUSIEK • BRENT ANDERSON • ALEX ROSS
VERTIGO

astro city
private lives
KURT BUSIEK • BRENT ANDERSON • ALEX ROSS
VERTIGO

astro city
VERTIGO
lovers quarrel
KURT BUSIEK • BRENT ANDERSON • ALEX ROSS

astro city
honor guard
VERTIGO

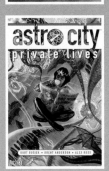

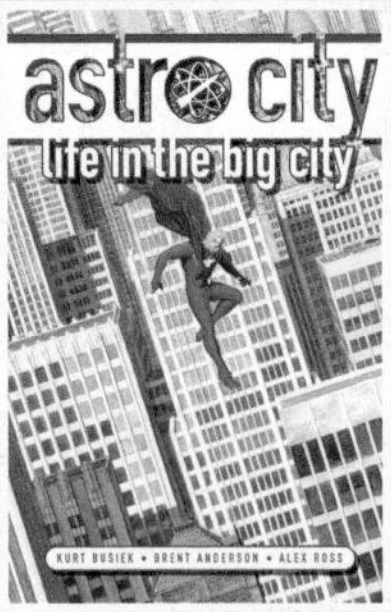

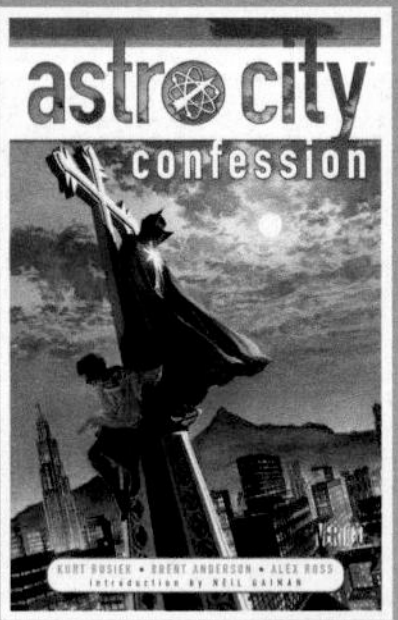

about the creators

KURT BUSIEK broke into comics after graduating college in 1982, with scripts at both DC and Marvel. Since then, he's been an editor, a literary agent, a sales manager and more, but is best known as the multiple-award-winning writer of *Astro City, Marvels, Superman, Conan, Arrowsmith, Superstar, The Autumnlands* and many others. He lives in the Pacific Northwest.

PETER PANTAZIS was "discovered" while working at an art gallery across the street from Wildstorm Studios, and became a valued member of the Wildstorm FX team, coloring books such as *Voodoo, WildCATs* and *Gen13*. Since then, his work has graced such series as *Aquaman: Sword of Atlantis, Trinity, Powers, Justice League, Superman, Blue Beetle, Earth 2* and more.

BRENT ANDERSON began making his own comics in junior high school, and graduated to professional work less than a decade later. He's drawn such projects as *Ka-Zar the Savage, X-Men: God Loves Man Kills, Strikeforce: Morituri, Somerset Holmes, Rising Stars* and, of course, *Astro City*, for which he's won multiple Eisner and Harvey Awards. He makes his home in Northern California.

ALEX SINCLAIR has colored virtually every character DC Comics has, and more besides. Best known for his award-winning work with Jim Lee and Scott Williams, he's graced such books as *Batman: Hush, Superman: For Tomorrow, Blackest Night, Batman & Robin, Wonder Woman, Arrowsmith* and *Kingdom Come: Superman.*

ALEX ROSS worked on *Terminator: The Burning Earth* and *Clive Barker's Hellraiser* before *Marvels* made him an overnight superstar. Since then, he's painted, plotted and/or written such series as *Kingdom Come, Superman: Peace on Earth, Justice, Earth X* and *Project Superpowers*, won over two dozen industry awards and painted 1.2 gazillion covers.

JOHN ROSHELL joined Comicraft in 1992, helping propel the lettering/design studio to prominence in the industry. As Senior Design Wizard, he's lettered thousands of comics pages, along with creating logos and fonts, designing book editions and more.